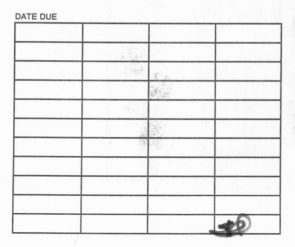

WOODSTOCK
THE ORAL HISTORY

WOODSTOCK
THE ORAL HISTORY

by Joel Makower

A TILDEN PRESS BOOK

Doubleday

NEW YORK   LONDON   TORONTO   SYDNEY   AUCKLAND

A Doubleday Book
Published by Doubleday, a division of
Bantam Doubleday Dell Publishing Group, Inc.
666 Fifth Avenue, New York, NY 10103

Doubleday and the portrayal of
an anchor with a dolphin are trademarks of
Doubleday, a division of Bantam Doubleday Dell Publishing Group, Inc.

WOODSTOCK and the DOVE & GUITAR LOGO are registered trademarks of
Woodstock Ventures, and are used with license permission.

Library of Congress Cataloging-in-Publication Data

Makower, Joel, 1952–
    Woodstock : the oral history / by Joel Makower. — 1st ed.
    p.   cm.
    ISBN 0-385-24716-8 — ISBN 0-385-24717-6 (pbk.)
    1. Woodstock Festival, Woodstock, N.Y., 1969.   2. Rock music–
History and criticism.   I. Title.
    ML38.W66M34   1989
    784.5'4'007974734 — dc19   89-1593
                                                              CIP
                                                              MN

August 1989
First Edition

CONTENTS

PREFACE

There are a thousand stories behind the Woodstock Music and Art Fair of August 1969—five hundred thousand stories, perhaps. The essential story, two decades later, is legend: a half-million or so ebullient children of the sixties descending on a quiet community in upstate New York, an unprecedented—and unequaled—gathering of bodies, minds, spirits, and talent.

The other stories are no less fascinating: tales of art and politics, life and death, generosity and greed, Utopian visions and broken dreams, enlightenment and disenchantment. From the sacred to the profane, the ridiculous to the sublime.

What unfolds in the pages that follow is an in-depth telling of that story, culled from face-to-face interviews conducted during 1988 with the people who made Woodstock happen: producers, performers, doctors, cops, neighbors, shopkeepers, carpenters, electricians, lawyers, journalists, filmmakers, and an assemblage of just plain folks who, by design or circumstance, became part of the event. Their collective story is told as a sort of conversation, as if all of them had been metaphysically transported to one gigantic living room, each individual contributing his or her own piece of the story at appropriate moments.

What emerges is the story of a music festival, to be sure, but it is far more than that. Indeed, if there are any sweeping conclusions to be drawn from having interviewed these myriad souls, there are two: that despite the all-star line-up of talent that performed at Woodstock, hardly anyone—from the onstage producers to the audience—remembers the music; and that in some way, large or small, nearly everyone involved seems to date their life around the festival.

By all measures, Woodstock should have been a disaster. Legally barred from its planned location just a month before its scheduled date, the promoters had to quickly regroup and relocate. In their haste, there was little time for planning certain facilities and amenities, some of which fell by the wayside. One key ingredient were the fences and gates, which never materialized satisfactorily, and the overflow crowds that showed up were admitted for free. The crowds caused traffic jams that paralzyed miles of highways, rendering them useless and requiring alternative measures to bring in food and medicine and supplies, and to evacuate the ill, among others. The National Guard and the U.S. Army got involved, as did a wide range of community, business, and religious organizations. It began as an exercise in hip capitalism; it turned into a multimillion-dollar financial nightmare for its producers.

And then it rained. The grounds, already muddy from weeks of summer showers, turned to muck as the skies opened repeatedly—often violently—during the festival weekend. Few who came were adequately prepared to camp out for three days even in comfortable climes, let alone in soggy, intensely overcrowded conditions. The fierce storms also threatened to bring down the structures, and to put the infrastructure—electricity, water, sewerage—in jeopardy. Needless to say, none of this aided the well-being of the countless individuals who had drunk, smoked, or ingested ungodly amounts of licit and illicit substances, many of whom had to be ministered to, one of whom died.

And yet Woodstock was not a disaster. Far from it. There was much joy and humanity, and heroics galore. Starting with a rag-tag crew of idealistic and energetic youth—Woodstock essentially was financed and produced by those in their mid twenties to early thirties—the festival's staff mushroomed into hundreds of hippies, hucksters, handymen, and hangers-on. As the plans became reality, these people met the troubles they encountered—the weather, drugs, radical politicos, and on and on—with high levels of ingenuity and integrity. It is ironic, albeit not surprising, that many of those involved liken being at Woodstock to having been through a war.

• • • •

There was considerable frustration and satisfaction in the oral history approach to this subject. The satisfaction came with the opportunity to sit—often in multiple sessions, sometimes for six hours or more—in individuals' living rooms and offices, hearing their still-passionate accounts, even after all these years. The frustration came in having to draw limits on the number of interviews, and to the amount of each person's account, that could be included.

It also should be pointed out that there were a great many people who could not be interviewed. As one person so poignantly put it: "Death robbed you of a lot of good stories." Indeed, many of those who could have provided a key point of view of the Woodstock story have passed on, several rather prematurely. Others have managed to vanish into the landscape, having lost touch with their former neighbors, friends, or colleagues, or could not otherwise be located. Still others declined to be interviewed on the subject of Woodstock, including some of the festival's neighbors in Sullivan County, New York, for whom the festival has left scars. Also reticent were several of the musicians who performed. As one explained, "We made so little money from Woodstock, yet others have made millions of dollars exploiting an event at which we performed. I'm tired of contributing to others' fortunes." Several other musicians regarded Woodstock as an old story, an event whose reputation has long outlived its contribution to society.

Not likely. Woodstock continues to live on in the hearts and minds of many, including many of a younger generation scarcely born in 1969, some of whom have since made the pilgrimage to the festival site, which only recently has been memorialized with a modest monument to the three days of peace and music. Some are drawn by the ghost of Jimi Hendrix or Janis Joplin. Others seek to recapture the can-do innocence of a time in which young Americans were fighting a system they felt was unjust, and demonstrating, often with startling success, that there was a better way. If Woodstock demonstrated anything, it was that people, coming together for whatever purpose, can collectively find a better way, under even the most unpleasant of circumstances. Musically, Woodstock may be but a footnote to the rich history of rock 'n' roll, but culturally, it helped to define a generation.

Some of those interviewed for this book are truly worthy of a book themselves. The life of Wesley Pomeroy, for example, the enlightened Justice Department official (who later toured with Led Zeppelin, providing security), hired by the producers to head the security detail at the festival, could have filled chapters. So, too, the life of Wavy Gravy, nee Hugh Romney, cofounder and life spirit of the Hog Farm, a two-decades-old commune, whose efforts and good humor, by many estimations, saved Woodstock from the disaster it could have been. Others—among them, Chip Monck, John Morris, Chris Langhart, Mel Lawrence, Stan Goldstein, and Bill Hanley—are part and parcel of the history of rock music performance, having booked, produced, and toured with the top musical acts of the era.

Together, it's a wonderful bunch of humanity—and a wonderful story.

PROLOGUE

**"It's nothing like you're probably hearing about.
It's just a rock festival."**
—Alan Green

DIANA WARSHAWSKY: I was living in San Francisco in the Haight-Ashbury area, sort of across the panhandle from the Haight proper, and I heard that there was going to be some kind of gathering of music and it was supposed to be in New York in a place called Woodstock and had something to do with a ranch owned by Bob Dylan. That's what I heard, that's what the rumor had it. And some of the people from the area were thinking of going. I really had no idea what it was going to be; I didn't read newspapers or watch TV at the time. If it was publicized, I didn't have any inkling. It was just something that sounded pretty interesting. And so I made arrangements to go. It just worked out that people from the area were going and I arranged to go with them.

JOSEPH COAKLEY: I was reading a copy of *Ramparts* magazine, flying back from Denver to Cleveland, Ohio, after spending the summer working on a ranch in Wyoming. It's kind of irrelevant, but I was lamenting the fact that I'd just paid forty dollars for a standby ticket, which reflected a week's worth of wages on my ranch that I'd been working on. I saw this little ad in the back of the magazine that had this rather interesting looking music festival that was going to be happening. And what caught my eye was some of the musicians that I recognized, and I decided that this could be a lot of fun. I ended up calling up my cousin Jim and he knew a few people that were going and we ended up going together. Actually, there were six of us that all went together, but somehow, within a half hour, we'd lost three of the people.

RICK GAVRAS: I was living in Montreal, Quebec. I was nineteen years old and had moved to Montreal with my family in '67. I was fairly conservative. I grew up in south Florida in the mid- and latter fifties and I was very kind of collegiate. And when I got to Montreal, I was quite shocked at everything that was going on, because it was a big cosmopolitan East Coast city and there were people with real long hair and I was still wearing Weejuns. And I had a real frame of reference to look at people like that as being very, very weird, very odd. And it was scary for me. I didn't know quite what was going on. But I learned quickly, and I became involved in it. I suppose it was a combination of just what was going on at the time—acceptance from peers, getting involved with LSD and smoking marijuana, getting involved in kind of Eastern approaches to life. I don't remember exactly how I heard about Woodstock, except it was being, I'm sure, broadcast on the radio and stuff like that. And since Montreal was only a three- or four-hour drive from Woodstock, it just seemed to fall into place to drive to Woodstock, which I planned to do with three or four friends.

ALAN GREEN: It was right after my freshman year of college. I was working at the Department of Public Works in Teaneck as a maintenance man, painting fences. I painted bus shelters all summer. They'd drop me off at a bus shelter with a ladder and a roller and all day long I'd paint bus shelters. And they'd pick me up and drive me to another one. I had this girlfriend, Eve, who lived out in Long Island in Hicksville. And every night I'd drive out to Hicksville. I'd stay there till about midnight and I'd line up five cigarettes in my car and I'd drive home to Jersey and I would be fighting sleep. So this went on the whole summer and towards the end of the summer, I remember Woodstock sort of slipping in and out of my consciousness. There were some posters up at record stores and it sounded like something that would be fun but I didn't remember any kind of great electricity. I don't remember a lot of my friends even talking about it; there were sort of casual mentions. But as it got closer to the day, there started to be a little more excitement and I remember saying to Eve—she was in high school—and I said, "Well, we should go to Woodstock," which really thrilled her parents. So I remember going to a record store to buy tickets and spending eighteen dollars a ticket and thinking that was a pretty good deal, although I still didn't quite grasp the whole enormity of it. So her parents let her go and I quit my job. My last day of painting fences was the day before we were going to go to Woodstock, and I was going to buy a car—a Volkswagen—from my brother that day to take to Woodstock. I went to the bank to pay off his note and planned to take possession of the car, but I had never driven a stick before and I figured I would learn on my way to Woodstock. That was the plan.

JOE TINKELMAN: I had dropped out of college, but all my college friends were home for the summer in Poughkeepsie, New York, which was at most twenty miles from White Lake. And I had been spending a lot of time with my friend Larry Woodside, who had had a kidney transplant the year before. I grew up with Larry. Both his kidneys were removed and one of his grandmother's was implanted and at the time I think there weren't a lot of kidney transplants going on. And so they were doing a lot of experimenting with him with experimental drugs to combat rejection. I was just spending a lot of time with him. We happened to see ads in the *Times* that there was going to be a concert and that originally it was scheduled for Woodstock and that now it was going to be near Monticello.

DIANA WARSHAWSKY: There was a guy in the area that had a Volkswagen that was just like a cargo van, and it had two seats in the front and just a cargo area in the back. So although it wasn't very hospitable, you know, he took a few people, not too many—maybe four or five people, something like that, all together. But much to my good fortune, the van broke down in Elko, Nevada, in the middle of the heat. It was summer and it was hot and the van broke down and there was a Volkswagen dealer in Elko, Nevada. So we went to this Elko dealer and it sounded like the repairs were going to take a couple days to do. I wasn't friendly with or didn't really know any of the people I was riding with, including the guy whose van it was. And it turned out that parked at the same Volkswagen dealer were two young men from New York who were on their way back to New York, also to go to Woodstock. They had been traveling all over the country and their Volkswagen was nice and new and had just been fully repaired, and they were ready to start off and were amenable to having me come with them and help defray expenses—you know, split gas and all of that. So I ended up for the rest of the journey going in a really nice brand-new van with curtains and ice boxes, and it was really nice. It was really a comfortable trip and they were very nice people, good company. They were from Scarsdale, so they were quite affluent and I guess that's how they had this nice new van. All the people I knew had just real scroungy stuff.

JOSEPH COAKLEY: It's kind of interesting. I look at this festival as a very definite—not to sound trite—but it had significant meaning to my life in the sense that I had been busted by my parents the night before for smoking pot and my mom had flushed all of my stuff down the toilet. It made me feel like I was a reject to society and all these other things. Anyways, it was really funny because I remember going up in the car and this one guy had some hash with him and I wouldn't have anything to do with it. I'd vowed to myself that I'd never have anything to do with this stuff again, and I made it as far as somewhere between the general store of White Lake and the festival site before I decided to break down and buy something.

RICK GAVRAS: We all jumped in the car. At the time, I had just turned nineteen and I was supposed to meet my girlfriend. I had my first significant relationship or girlfriend at that time. I was a rather shy person at those times. I was supposed to meet her at Woodstock and, of course, little did we know that there was going to be a few hundred thousand people there. So I never did meet her. I suppose we thought there was some sort of front gate or something of that sort. Apparently, we didn't have it too well planned—"I'll meet you at Woodstock." I don't know what exactly we were expecting. When I got there it was just, well, there was a lot of land. I don't know how many acres it was, but there was no front entrance at that point. I think everybody was pretty much being allowed just to go in. It was just kind of like a long field and just people sort of en masse kind of converging on the spot, and I realized right away I wasn't going to meet Mimi.

ALAN GREEN: I remember a lot of my friends were planning to go and one of my friends saying the day before, "Well, I'll see you at Woodstock." And it almost sounded logical because there was no idea of how big the thing could possibly be, and it was sort of "I'll see you there." And I figured, "Well, maybe he will." So we packed up a little bit of food, some dope, a jacket—once again, there was no planning at all, unlike a lot of people who seemed to arrive with all sorts of provisions. We had absolutely no idea of how to do this stuff and figured that we'll find hot-dog stands or there'd be plenty of food. I picked her up on Friday morning and I think we started out around noon and picked up someone hitchhiking, and as we started getting closer, there was this almost—it was like things were switching to different gears. Because as you got closer, all of a sudden from around

New York City there was no one hitchhiking, but as you started to get up the Thruway and up the Quickway, there were people all of a sudden appearing with signs: WOODSTOCK. And as it got closer, it was really obvious that something was happening and there was this—it was sort of weird.

JOE TINKELMAN: A bunch of friends got together in several cars. Before we got together we all said, "Let's go over for the afternoon. There's going to be a concert." Although there had been news reports that there was a real large turnout, we, living very close by, thought we could just sort of go over for the afternoon and then leave. And nobody brought anything to camp with or to stay over with—I mean, that wasn't the plan at all. Just to sort of catch the first afternoon of the program. In any case, Larry and I were going to travel together and weren't going to be prepared to even stay that long because Larry didn't have a lot of strength and I don't even think he brought that much medication. So we took off in separate cars and that was the last we saw of our other friends. It was just Larry and I.

DIANA WARSHAWSKY: We arrived in Scarsdale at about four in the morning and took a shower, and I was met there and found myself in a convertible with my friend and his friends heading to upstate New York. It was very strange. I remember the weather was that smoggy, real kind of hazy weather they have on the East Coast. I'd never experienced it before. It was humid, the sky looked like it was going to rain, but it was hot. It was very confusing and it seemed real strange. I remember going across probably the Verrazano Bridge and, you know, being tired and sort of weirded out. But the strangest part was when we got close to Woodstock itself. The traffic became very thick and it was bumper-to-bumper traffic all going to Woodstock, and I had no idea this was going to be such a big thing. I thought it was really going to be basically a small gathering and I had just happened to meet up with other people that were going and it was all coincidental. It was sort of scary and frustrating. The roads narrowed to a two-lane road, the road that actually led into where we were supposed to go, and there was bumper-to-bumper traffic in that one lane going in the proper direction, but people pretty quickly became impatient and they began to use the shoulder of the road as a second lane. Then, before long, they were using the shoulder of the opposite part of the road as another lane going there, so on a two-lane road there were three lanes of traffic all headed towards Woodstock. And eventually, I seem to recall, they may or may not have taken over the whole other side of the road. In other words, the road was packed with traffic, three to four lanes streaming into this area, and I don't think that many people knew exactly where they were going. They were just following the rest of the cars figuring they'd find it.

JOSEPH COAKLEY: We drove from Cleveland and ended up spending the night on Long Island at a friend of a friend's house, where I had bought my ticket. Then we took off very early Friday morning for the festival. We hit the exit at 9 A.M. and I remember—I don't know how the roads were up there but I want to say it was Monticello—when we hit this exit, the traffic stopped, and this was at nine o'clock in the morning. There were a lot of people coming the other way saying this thing had been canceled and I thought, "Well, I can see why. I mean if they're having traffic problems at nine o'clock and the thing doesn't start till this afternoon and we're this far away from the site, there's a major problem here." So we ended up finding some really nice farmer just off the exit there, and he let us park our car in his backyard for the weekend for nothing, which was kind of the spirit of the event in a lot of ways. A lot of the local people were just super helpful and kind of made the whole thing work.

I remember getting to White Lake. We were hungry and I remember the little general store there. There was a little grocery store on the way out to the festival and the owner of the store was meeting people there and locking the door—he'd let so many people in and so many people out. He was just controlling the flow by staying at the door, and he would lock the door if he had to go do something; lock the people in and come back and let them out. I had never seen anything like that, either. That was when I knew that we were in a potential crisis situation here.

RICK GAVRAS: It was overwhelming because there were so many people. It was like something kind of colossal. There was a stage. And the stage from where I was for the first couple of days was real far away because I was way, way in back. I was busy kind of strolling all over the place. And I never really got up close to the stage until the third day, the very last day.

I pretty much stayed with my friends most of the time, or at least a couple of them. And, of course, we were all taking LSD twenty-four hours a day and smoking twenty-four hours a day, which I guess most people were doing. And so everything was very surreal.

ALAN GREEN: We figured, "We're here a few hours early so there are probably a couple of hundred people or maybe a thousand people"— who knows what—and I figured that we were just going to park and walk for a few hundred yards. So as we came over a hill, it became obvious that I was wrong. There were long, long lines of cars—I guess miles already at that point—but when you got onto Yasgur's farm there was still no idea to sort of understand what was going on because there were people milling around; there was no sort of semblance of who was going to be doing what and where it was all going to happen even. We looked around and thought, "Well, this should be fun. We'll camp out here for two days or three days and there will probably be a lot of people around." So we found a spot in the woods and we decided maybe we should smoke a joint and we were very paranoid that someone would know that we were getting high so we sort of went way back in the woods because there just weren't that many people around. There was nothing happening. There weren't mobs of people and there was no reason to expect what would ultimately happen.

So there we were in the woods and I think it was drizzling, and we sort of strung a coat up or something and we were under the coat getting high, still looking all around thinking, "Uh-oh, let's be very discreet here because you never know who's going to be walking by and we'll get busted." We had left all the food in the car because we figured we'd just walk to the car if we needed to get our groceries. I left my jacket in the car. It never occurred to us that we would never get back there.

We figured it must be time for the music to start and we walked down to the hill and, once again, it did not seem like there were that many people. But the amazing thing, as we were sitting off in the woods before we went in to see the music, there was this parade of people that just seemed to never stop and it kept getting deeper and wider, and the flow of people seemed to be picking up. But it still didn't seem like a big deal. It was another concert—that's what it really seemed like—although it was sort of exciting to see those giant towers with the speakers and this big stage. And then all the rumors started. "Dylan's coming," was the first great rumor. And I thought, "Well, great. Dylan's coming."

JOE TINKELMAN: We drove past Monticello Raceway and within a very few miles the road just became filled with cars stopped on both sides. The state highway became a parking lot. I would say we were five or six miles short of Yasgur's farm. We were really sort of puzzled by it all. It wasn't expected to be a big thing at all. We were saying, "What it this? Is it an accident ahead?" And we were beginning to understand as we saw young people piling out of cars all around us and behind us that this was the concert. This was parking for the concert. And these cars were just going to stay right here. And we got out of the car and started walking in the direction of White Lake. Then, as we walked five to ten car lengths in front of our car, we started to see people setting up lawn chairs on their front lawns—the houses that fronted on the highway—to watch this spectacle. And the feeling sort of changed over to a sense of exhilaration that all these people had gotten together— I think people at that age, if the normal course of life is disrupted, that makes it a big thing. I mean, and it looked like this whole part of New York State, in the minds of us at that time, was just being turned upside down.

DIANA WARSHAWSKY: We had to park pretty far away and we had sleeping bags and duffel bags and walked for a long time to get there, you know, following streams of other people all walking with their sleeping bags and duffel bags, and hot, humid. We finally arrived at the area and it was a very strange scene. It was muddy and there was some grass. It was all in browns and grays, you know, from the sky and the overcast and the humidity, and there was a huge—like a big mud puddle is all I can call it—that was as big as a small swimming pool. And all these people had their clothes off and thought they were swimming or something, I don't know. They were all bathing in this muddy water and I remember—I'll never forget this—all these muddy brown bodies, you know, bathing and sort of frolicking in this water hole. It didn't look appealing at all to me. I thought, "Boy, who knows, some people will jump at the chance to do anything." The field was huge and it was surrounded, they had it all surrounded by barbed wire, this area that the concert was taking place in. And we eventually found, with our stuff with us, you know, found a spot in this field. I guess it was sort of like a dry, grassy field. We just walked in, I guess. I don't know what the story was. Were they selling tickets? Were there supposed to be tickets?

JOSEPH COAKLEY: I can remember having my ticket, looking for someplace to give my ticket as we walked to the gate, which turns out had been busted, I guess, wide open. And there was a rumor going around that there was this very left-wing political group from New York called Up Against the Wall that had apparently threatened to have some sort of political event and had stormed the gate, and I don't know if they collected tickets early or what, but the place was wide open when we got there in the early afternoon.

RICK GAVRAS: There was just so much stuff going on that looking back on it now it seems as though it was some sort of episode out of maybe a Fellini movie or something. Just so bizarre and so weird and yet there I was, experiencing a lot of personal conflict too. Having discussions and arguments about the war. And being that I was with Canadian friends, there was a lot of stuff going on for me personally that was kind of conflictive, like, "What was I doing living in Canada when there was this going on in the U.S.?" There were talks about the nature of the war and why America was there and how they had a sense that if they were American they would be probably contributing to the war effort or whatever. That kind of triggered feelings in me of not being a part of it, guilt and stuff like that. So it was real kind of conflictive stuff between us. We were friends and we were there together, but it was very tense a lot of the time. This was all kind of like just regular everyday stuff, and yet here I was in the midst of this experience that was so overwhelming. And all the visual stuff—just adding large doses of hallucinogens. I mean, it was a very powerful experience.

ALAN GREEN: We found a spot in the woods where we originally had been when we came in Friday afternoon to sleep and it was sort of well behind the hill and kind of off the main road leading into the festival. And when I woke up in the morning, this stream of people was still moving through the road and I realized that maybe this had never stopped. We walked from where we were in the woods to the stage and looked out and all of a sudden what had been what seemed to me a few thousand people had become this half million people and it all seemed to have happened on Friday night in the middle of the night. At that moment, when I was standing and thinking, "Oh my God, this is unbelievable," my friend Andy, who had said, "I'll see you at Woodstock," walked up to me and said, "Hey, how are you doing? We're over there back in the woods." And I looked at him and he said, "Well, what's the matter?" And I said, "There's about a million people here and I'd bump into you." He said, "Well, yeah. I told you I'd see you at Woodstock." So he had bumped into everyone and everyone had gotten together. These were all my Teaneck friends and they had taken this giant tarp and strung it together between trees and had set up this little kind of camp back in the woods, sort of between where the Hog Farm was and the top of the hill.

JOE TINKELMAN: Larry had a lot of energy at first because he was in reasonable physical shape at the time. And we just plunged ahead and walked with a bunch of other people, some of whom had camping equipment. Others were there just like we were, going for the afternoon. And the mood really became festive all the way. It turned out to be a very big risk, perhaps too vigorous a day for Larry. But we just plunged ahead and we were having a great time. We started walking along and people started singing. A couple of people became troubadours and played guitars as we were walking along. And we walked for many, many miles. By the time we got within maybe the last mile, Larry was starting to flag and we had to take fairly frequent breaks. My sense of exhilaration was starting to evaporate and I was starting to really worry, "What have we done here to this guy?"

DIANA WARSHAWSKY: It wasn't ever an out-of-control situation. I know they had emergency stands, you know, in case somebody was flipping out or sick or hurt or anything, and it was a very peaceful group of people. People were just happy, you know, getting stoned and just being happy to be there. But I found it very unnerving to be with this many people inside a barbed wire. And there was a helicopter flying over. I got very paranoid and I didn't like it at all. The whole situation of just being—I felt like I was trapped because I knew I couldn't get out on the road, all the traffic was swarming in one direction. I was sort of encircled by barbed wire, a helicopter flying overhead, and I didn't like the feeling. I was having a good time because of, you know, being with my friends, the person I was with, and I remember, in terms of music, I have almost no recollection of the music except that the only performer that I remember is Richie Havens. I remember him and I remember really liking that and that's it. I don't know who else performed that night. Actually, I'd be curious to know.

I do remember that when the music was over for that evening, we sort of trudged down a road and found a relatively hospitable place to unroll sleeping bags off the side of the road, and slept that night. And there was no question about the fact that I wanted to leave the next morning. And so we ended up hitchhiking out of the area back into New York City. I guess I felt the potential of danger either from within or from without. They had us all caged in the barbed wire, especially with the helicopter flying overhead, and it seemed more like a war zone that happened to be peaceful at the moment. It was real strange and I didn't care for it.

JOSEPH COAKLEY: I remember how incredibly crowded it was. I can remember putting my hand somewhere and then not being able to move it for two hours. Then someone would move their leg and you'd quickly get your leg in there; you'd go to that spot so your circulation would work for another two hours. It was just incredibly cramped. I guess it kind of mellowed out a little bit in terms of space. I remember going to sleep, right on the spot where I'd sat all day.

I remember it rained that night. I can remember we were hungry and there were some concession stands at the top of the bowl that for all intents and purposes were the only places I knew of to eat, and these political people, you know, that were wandering around the area— you didn't see them or whatever, but I understand that some of the concessions got torched that night due to their high prices or whatever, which further burdened the whole problem of what to eat. But as I remember waking up the next morning, it was a sea of mud. That bowl was just incredible. Everybody was cold and wet. Just a very unpleasant camping experience out there in the bowl. But as I remember, the music stopped Friday night; I don't think they played all night Friday night. I don't remember if they did or not.

Rick Gavras: As far as the music goes, what I remember mostly was they had two stages set up on the sides of the main stage. I remember one night at the main stage real vividly, but most of my memories of music were on the side stages. And there was where you could kind of lay in the grass and it wasn't real crowded. The Grateful Dead played there a lot. That was good. They were really into relating with the people. I remember seeing them a lot and sitting on the stage and how wonderful they were at that time. And the music I remember the most out of everything was on one night and that was basically the people that stand out mostly in my mind: Santana and Sly and the Family Stone. I think they all played on one night. Janis Joplin. That was kind of the most connected night I had. I was just totally enveloped in the music. A lot of times I think it was difficult to really—the music was real important but there was just so much stuff going on. And if you weren't—I wasn't right close to it so sometimes it was hard to have a connection with the music.

There was so much other stuff going on. I think maybe a lot of it had to do with kind of maintaining a sense of sanity for me, especially when you're tripping twenty-four hours a day. A lot of stuff sure appeared weird. Maybe a lot of that had to do with how people looked and everybody just being together and kind of walking through that ocean of people and just seeing so many strange, strangely adorned people and all the costumes and just the intensity of how the people were relating to each other in a lot of ways. Not so much through speaking and everything, but just through the experience and the being there and people kind of smiling and dancing. People were giving away drugs, LSD and stuff like that. There certainly wasn't a lack of it.

Alan Green: It was almost like being in an Army unit and going out to do reconnaissance to hear someone play music. I remember we were laying on the tarp and someone would say, "Hey, Canned Heat is playing," and people would go out. I remember someone went from where we were down to the stage. It took them about half a day, and then came back to report on what was going on. I remember going back to the Hog Farm because we figured that's where we would get our food. They had this just horrible rice with raisins or something and it was just the most disgusting thing. But I don't even remember hearing a lot of music after that. We could hear the music from where we were and every now and then we'd sort of head out to the crowd and stand up and look out from the top of the hill on everything and then go back to the tarp.

Then it started with people climbing on the light towers and all the announcements. When they first started they were mostly the

15

things you would hear at an airport: "Meet your friend at so-and-so." And then they seemed to take on sort of odder proportions almost, and they gravitated from, "Meet your friend," to "Your friend is ill," to "Your friend took bad acid," to—anything imaginable. And it almost got to be kind of exciting to hear announcements. I remember walking into our tarp and one of my friends was doing acid and I said to him, "Hey, you got a phone call." I was just sort of kidding around. And he said, "What?" and I said, "Yeah, you got a phone call. Didn't you hear the announcement? They just announced you had a phone call." He said, "What are you talking about?" I said, "Well, they just announced you got a phone call." And he said, "You're telling me they stopped the concert to announce that I got a phone call?" I said, "Yeah." Then he knew I was kidding and I remember him saying, "You're nuts!" and he ran off into the woods.

JOE TINKELMAN: Larry and I had a long talk and we decided that we'd get a little closer, as close as we could to see what this was all about, and not stay. He was just running out of gas. And he was really very pissed. He was very patient with his illness all those months, but he was very impatient with his illness that day. This was too good a time for his body to be failing him now. But it was. I was trying to face it for him and convince him to go back. I don't even really feel like I was disappointed. I don't remember feeling disappointed. I was just really concerned about him, especially since I was having such a hard job convincing him that we had to go back. We had walked miles and I wanted to turn back right then and there as a matter of fact, and not even see what was going on. We got to a point where we got to the edge of the farm and we saw—I don't know whether it was anything near the full turnout; I doubt it. But we just saw this kind of bowl of people. And at that moment there wasn't real music. There was sort of sporadic announcements that we could still just barely hear because we were not into the crowd at all. And we just stood there for a few minutes watching.

I didn't have a hard time convincing Larry to turn back at that point; the decision had been made about a mile before. And we thought, "Well this was really something to see," but I think we both knew we had to turn around and start walking back. And we did. It got a little scary on the way back because he was totally out of gas and riding on my back for part of the time. He wasn't a heavyweight any more anyway, so it wasn't that bad.

Larry died December 10, 1969. He was twenty-one, the same age as I was.

JOSEPH COAKLEY: I can remember having to go to the bathroom really badly, and I was afraid of losing my cousin Jim. I remember finally I had to do something about it and I had to leave this little sanctuary that I'd been guarding or calling home for the last eight to ten hours or whatever, and Creedence Clearwater was playing and I decided to venture out into the unknown—the black of "out there"—and try to find a toilet. This was Saturday night and I remember going out there and finding a bathroom and wandering around. Coming back, I looked out there and I was lost. I mean, I had no idea. I kind of had a general idea of where I'd been sitting, but I was just looking at this huge mass and there were no ushers, no seats, nobody there with a flashlight to help you out, and miraculously, after I wandered around for, I don't know—it seemed like a long time—I remember tripping over this body and it ended up being my cousin Jim. I woke him up. That's how I found him.

RICK GAVRAS: Seeing the emphasis on people being concerned with helping other people in a sense of like doing it for free—that's one of the things that stood out in my mind, even today—the emphasis on people doing for other people. I think that was important to me because in those days I kind of considered myself a hippie, but in retrospect, I wasn't. I mean, I was involved in a lot of drug dealing and I always had a significant chunk of money, so it was easy to call myself a hippie and all that. Especially when you have money in your pockets. A lot of the principles and everything, although they sounded good to me, I don't know how fond of them I would have been if I really had to live them. I mean, you talk about being able to live in a way that didn't place an emphasis on everything you had and not needing to have everything in order to survive and having more concern about deeper human interaction and what was going on with people. I think that would have been pretty scary for me in those younger years to be in that kind of condition, to be on the streets, or to be living a life like that. My life was very drug-oriented. And I'm one of the ones who continued down that path for many years in going further and deeper into the drug experience and eventually ending up a heroin addict. That's another story, although it's part of it; it's progression—or regression.

It was a very, very moving and powerful time because I think it was that night when I was so connected with the music and with everything that was going on around me, the people that were in my immediate area, that it was—that's when I seemed to have a sense that it was all kind of a oneness of experience, that everybody was there together and enjoying themselves and celebrating in that sense of togetherness. Sometimes it's difficult for me to express that kind of stuff because sometimes it sounds vague. I think it's some of my skepticism and cynicism that I've developed over the years, and I'm trying to kind of let go of it. What was it that was so meaningful about that whole experience? What was it that we were trying to say to each other and express? I think it's simply that there is a desire for people to just want to accept other people and be at some sort of peace with them. The way I see it, those were the days when that whole thing was flowering and opening up. Because it was so dependent on drugs, it had a lot of illusory qualities to it.

ALAN GREEN: The most bizarre kinds of people started floating through the woods. I wish I could remember who they were, but I remember we were just sitting around while people were cutting down limbs or something, pulling branches off trees and some guy coming through and standing and talking about how we should all stare up at the sun— I mean, just all kinds of odd people began filtering through this little enclave that we had back in the woods. And, for a while it was almost

17

like there was no festival because you couldn't see anything. You could hear the music and people would be filtering through the woods on their way to the Hog Farm or somewhere, but for hours I remember not moving, just laying there in the woods. And it was kind of nice because every hour or two hours or whatever it was, a new band would come along.

I was not a nerd who happened to end up at Woodstock because his friends dragged him along, but I think it was pretty clear that there were all these people who were really far out there. I don't know, it was sort of a great shock to see that many freaky people in one place and people who seemed to have been doing this kind of stuff—that was the impression I got—for years, because it looked like their hair had been growing for years. It was like running into people who have been in the military for twenty years and have a uniform full of ribbons and medals. That's what these people were like. They had years' worth of counterculture apparatus and stories and weirdness, and I think there were a lot of people who were on the fringes of that that maybe got catapulted towards that after that summer, and that three days in particular. But for me, a lot of it just didn't register.

I was one of those people who had to call home to assure my parents that everything was O.K. because that was in my normal upbringing. It never would have occurred to me to not do that. I remember standing in line at the phone and I remember someone in line commenting about, you know, "Here are the people who have to call home," but we all knew that was true. I think Eve didn't call. I did. Her parents—I don't think they didn't care, but they didn't expect it. She was really pretty crazy and her parents didn't like me because they thought that I was giving her drugs when, in fact, it was the other way around. And I remember talking to my mother, who kept saying, "Well, what is it like there? What is it like?" And I was saying, "It's nothing like you're probably hearing about. It's just a rock festival."

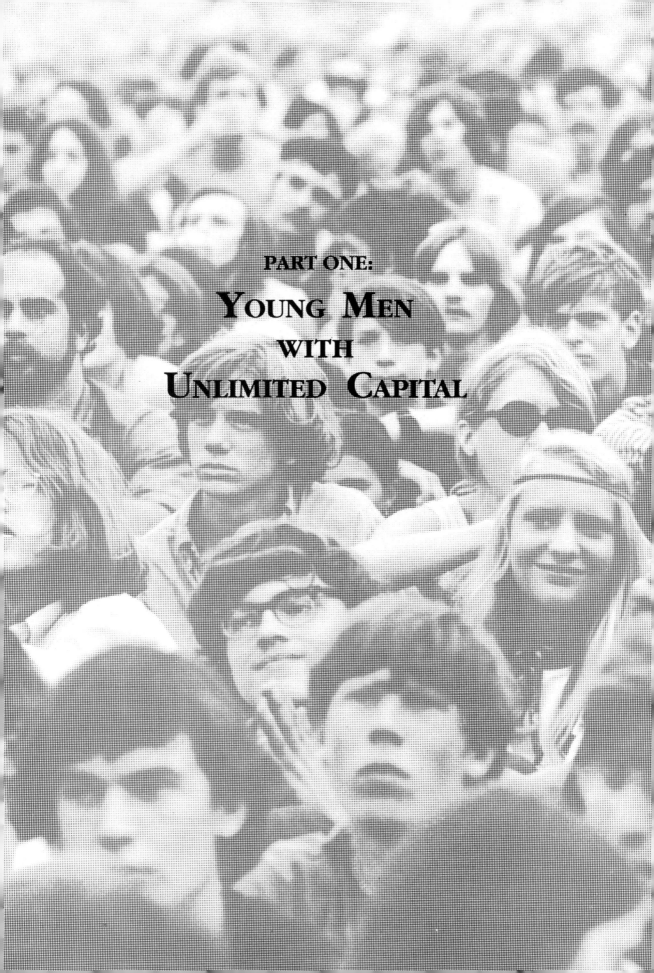

PART ONE:

YOUNG MEN
WITH
UNLIMITED CAPITAL

"I always thought if you could dream it up
you could pull it together."
—*Michael Lang*

JOHN ROBERTS: I went to the University of Pennsylvania with Joel's brother, Douglas. And in the summer of 1966, Doug invited me out to his home in Huntington, Long Island, for a weekend of golf. We were joined on the golf course by Joel, and that was the way we met. That summer I was sort of up in the air about my plans. I was doing some graduate work at the Annenberg School of Communications in Philadelphia and I had a job down on Wall Street doing research for a small brokerage firm. I was pretty much up in the air about the Army. I was a reservist and I didn't know when or if I would be called up. So I didn't know what long-range plans I could make and I had no idea where I should live; Annenberg is in Philadelphia and Wall Street is in New York. I decided to take an apartment in New York and commute to Philadelphia and bunk in with a friend down in Philadelphia for the two or three nights I had to be there. By coincidence, Joel had just graduated from law school and was starting work as a lawyer in New York and was looking for an apartment. So we talked about sharing an apartment.

JOEL ROSENMAN: It was instantly a good relationship because he was able to give me so much help in my golf game. He was able to show me how to stand and correct my grip and realign my shots—generally offer a lot of sarcastic encouragement when I duck-hooked into the woods. He had a terrific sense of humor, which was initially the basis on which we had a relationship. We both liked to kid a lot and he is the master of that sort of thing. He is legendary for it.

I was a little uneasy about taking a place in New York City and moving there. It had always seemed bigger than I was. Not so much anymore, but in those days it was intimidating. And John seemed to know the city very well; he had been here for a good part of his life before I met him and I was grateful to have somebody who knew the ropes to share an apartment with. So we traipsed into the city a couple of times and we stayed at John's dad's place at U.N. Plaza. We were taken about by rental apartment agents and finally found a spot that seemed like the perfect setting for two young guys with not-so-unlimited capital who were interested in setting up in New York City: 85th and Third Avenue. It was a high-rise and we took an apartment on a very high floor. When you stood on the balcony, you could see east, south, and north a little bit. It was an intriguing beginning.

Half of the week John was gone, down in Philadelphia. My schedule was fairly nutty. I had a job at night with a band. We played all over New York—down at the Village at the Bitter End and at the clubs on Second and Third Avenue in the Seventies, which were pretty popular at the time. Live entertainment was much in demand at that time and we had a pretty good act. It was a lot of fun. I was a singer and I played a variety of instruments, none of them very well.

JOHN ROBERTS: That's not true, he played a very good guitar.

JOEL ROSENMAN: It was very exciting. At that time I was twenty-four, twenty-five years old, and it was just the greatest way to start out in New York City. You seemed to get to know everybody very quickly that way. The problem with that was that at the end of our last set it was frequently two, three in the morning and by the time you got home and got to bed it was three-thirty, four o'clock. And then I would have to be at this law firm at nine or ten in the morning. I was starting to get a little frayed at the edges after a while.

We used to talk about what we wanted to do with our lives. He would come up from Philadelphia after that sort of weekly commute, wondering why he was doing what he was doing at Annenberg. Neither one of us was really on a career path that we knew for sure, or even reasonably sure, was the right one. I used to think of entertainment as a fun thing to do, and so exciting, but something tipped me off—maybe it was those threadbare tuxedos on the backs of those forty-five-year-old guys that we were alternating sets with up in the mountains when we played in the mountains or out in Las Vegas when we played out there. And I remember thinking to myself, "These guys haven't made it and some of them were excellent musicians and better singers than I was." And I remember thinking to myself, "This may not be the right thing to do with your life. It's fun for now but you should be doing something else." And I would go to the office during the day and I remember thinking, "This can't be what you want to do with your life." And yet those were such exhausting activities when combined that there was little room for anything else.

JOHN ROBERTS: As far as the Army was concerned, it was mostly trepidation. That was the fly in the ointment, as far as my life was concerned. I was in the Signal Corps in Fort Monmouth. And the build-up in Vietnam was going on and I didn't know if my unit would be called up and I'd be sent away. So it was very difficult for me to think of long-range planning. I kind of knew from working down on Wall Street that I didn't like that kind of environment much. And I knew from the courses I was taking at the Annenberg School that I liked that a lot. I liked writing and I liked entertainment and I thought if I had a real predilection it was going to be towards that field in some sort of way. There wasn't quite the urgency in the sixties to plug yourself into something every minute of the day. In other words, today as I see it, you go from educational achievement to educational achievement to job to advancement, and so on, and there is no breathing space. In the mid- sixties, you could take some time out and figure out a rational plan. No one succeeded in doing that, but we all succeeded in trying to do it anyway. I came from that school of thought—that I didn't want to rush into my life.

I came from a wealthy family. My mother had been the daughter of the founder of a proprietary drug company. He had died shortly before she died and left her a share in that company, the Block Drug Company. And when she died, she left her interest in the company to

John Roberts

my brothers and myself. It was in a trust fund. And I inherited when I was twenty-one about a quarter of a million dollars. For a bachelor in 1966, that was very nice.

Joel and I decided that we would really like to do some writing together. As we lived with each other more, we were drawn to each other as friends and found that the most enjoyable part of either of our day was in interacting together. Joel has always been a fine writer with a fine sense of style and loved to write, and we thought we would like to do some TV writing—sitcoms. I had identified this as a field that was right for exploitation by two people who didn't have the patience or discipline to write anything else.

This started out as a lark entirely. We came to the idea of writing a sitcom about two young men with a lot of money who get into business adventures. There had been a series on detectives and doctors and lawyers and architects, but there had never been anything on businessmen. In fact, "businessmen" was kind of a bad word in the

23

mid-sixties. But we thought this would have the makings of a very enjoyable sitcom and we were encouraged in that belief by a number of contacts in that field. The only problem was that we didn't have enough business experience to come up with episodes. So we decided to solve that problem by taking out an ad in *The Wall Street Journal*: YOUNG MEN WITH UNLIMITED CAPITAL LOOKING FOR INTERESTING AND LEGITIMATE BUSINESS IDEAS. It was a little ad in the Business Opportunities section.

We ran the ad for two weeks and we got seven thousand responses, many of which, by the way, were from writers who also thought it was a very good idea; they wanted to know what such an ad would bring. Some of the responses were marvelous. Power sources from the eighth dimension. Edible golf balls that were biodegradable. You know, if you lost it in the woods, the woodchucks would get it. And that ilk. But tucked in amongst these responses were some very intriguing business ideas.

So in the summer of 1967, Joel and I stepped out from behind the anonymity of our box number and actually contacted some of these people and began to explore these things as kind of sidelight to the rest of our lives. And through a path that is circuitous and not particularly germane, one contact led to another and another and we ended up meeting a couple of guys who wanted to build a recording studio here in New York. They came to us for capital and for partnership—essentially, to run the business end of it while they ran the musical end of if. We liked them, we liked the idea, and we liked the field, and we struck a deal. We went out and raised the money and borrowed some money from the bank and brought some other people into it, and lo and behold, Media Sound was born and it went on to all kinds of success over the years. It was a very successful operation.

Miles Lourie knew that we had been putting together this studio operation and he called us in February of '69. Miles was an attorney in New York and he had Michael Lang as a client. He said, "I have a couple of clients who are very interested in building a recording studio in Woodstock, New York. I know that you and Joel have been involved in building one in New York City. Would you meet with them?" We said, "Sure. What's on the table?" And Miles said, "Well, they are looking for some advice and maybe some capital, and I don't know what could come of it but the guys are about your age. They are a little different than you are." I remember Miles telling us, "Don't be put off by the long hair and the garb. But why don't you sit and see what comes of it?"

MICHAEL LANG: I moved to Florida to open a head shop in '66. I think a friend of mine had one in the East Village of New York. There were a couple of others opening, and Peter Max, who I'd met then, was just starting one, and it was kind of in the middle of that whole era. And I'd been to Coconut Grove before and I wanted to get out of New York for a while. The idea of the shop kind of intrigued me. And so we moved to Florida.

The shop became kind of a center for the whole little movement that was going on down there. We started a little newspaper and started having concerts in the local park and things like that, and that's how we got the idea for the Miami Pop Festival. It was kind of quick—it was like two and a half weeks from inception to production. It was at Gulfstream Racetrack and I flew up to New York and met with a guy named Hector Morales. We booked the show and put the production together, mostly through a studio called Criteria Sound. We had three stages made from flatbed trailers, and it was in the middle of a drought, I remember, the thirty-day drought. The morning before the show they went out to the Everglades and seeded the clouds. That was our first experience with rain.

I'd just moved back from Miami and the guy that I was in business with in Miami, Don Keider, who's a drummer, had moved to New York a few months before and had formed a band. And when I got to New York he asked me if I would help him out and manage the band. I had no experience but I thought, "You know, sure. Why not?" Don and I were good friends. So I did, and we were trying to get a record deal and one of the guys in the band, a guy named Abbie Rader, knew Artie Kornfeld, or knew of Artie, and suggested that I call. I did and he said, "Come on up." He was vice president of Capitol Records in New York. So I went up to his office in New York and that's how I met him.

ARTIE KORNFELD: In 1967-68, I was vice president of Capitol Records. I ran production for the East Coast—"contemporary production" was what they called it in those days. I think I was the first company freak. I didn't have long hair but I thought head-wise. I was a head. I was one of the first executives to break through and I was twenty-four. I had just finished the Cowsills. I wrote and produced all the Cowsills' stuff. I had written about twenty-five or thirty hits in the sixties and then became a producer and executive.

And anyway, my secretary said, "There's a Michael Lang here to see you." And I said, "Who's Michael Lang?" And she said, "He said he's from the neighborhood." And I said, "Well, if he's from the neighborhood, tell him to come in." Bensonhurst. It's a section of Brooklyn that's all Jewish and Italian. That's how he got in to see me; by saying he was from the neighborhood.

I think it was the days of hash, and I might have been standing on my desk at Capitol smoking hash when he walked in. I'm not sure. But he had great Colombian and we started to talk. He told me he had just gotten thrown out of his head shop by the police in Miami. He told me his story. He had a band called the Train—which was Garland Jeffries and Mickey Thomas and Ronnie Keever—which sounded not so good on tape, and he started to hang out with my late wife Linda and myself. The three of us were like Butch Cassidy and the Sundance Kid and that went on for months. I gave him a deal because I liked him, so I signed the band for like five thousand or ten thousand dollars. I took him in one night, Michael, and we got drunk and nothing really came out on the tapes or anything. So nothing became of the act, but Michael was sort of down and out at that point financially. And I had quite a bit of money because I had just had the Cowsills, and I was a writer, the producer, the publisher, and their manager. Michael started to hang out with Linda and I—every night we would sit and talk, sit and talk. As I remember it, Michael was telling me about the Miami Pop that he had worked on—this festival that didn't quite happen but had Hendrix.

25

MICHAEL LANG: I had been thinking about doing a series of concerts in Woodstock. Sort of making it a summer, like in Newport. And I had mentioned it to Artie. We used to kick it around every now and then, and then the idea of opening a recording studio up there, because it was such a good area for that. Bands liked it and there were a lot of people living there—The Band and Janis Joplin and her band and Dylan and parts of Blood, Sweat, and Tears—just lots of different producers and a lot of musicians coming in and out. So Artie and I used to get together and kick that around for a couple of months and at one point, one evening, we thought, "Well, what if we did it all at once?" because I had this experience in Miami of the festival, which was really amazing to me—it was extraordinary in the reaction of the people that came. I mean they sort of seemed transfixed and transformed in a way that evening, in Miami, so I guess that was in the back of my mind. So in discussion with Artie the idea sort of took form. And we thought, "Well, it would probably be a good idea to do this festival," I remember at the time, "and the studio also," and one sort of evolved out of the other, "and make it a yearly event." Great way to kick it off, and it was

Michael Lang

also a great way to sort of culminate all these smaller events that had been going on for the past couple of years. Just get everybody together and look at each other and see what we're here about.

ARTIE KORNFELD: And it just sort of came together. Michael talks about "How did it all happen?" He says, "Talking with Artie." And I would say that's how it happened. Talking with Michael and Linda. I always feel Linda had as much to do with it as Michael or I. She was the spiritual figure. She was a spiritual part of the three of us. I was the music business guy and Michael was the hippie and Linda was in the middle. She was the spirit.

When people say they never knew what was going to happen, if you ask Michael—this was before Joel and John—or if Linda was alive, we knew what was going to happen because we guessed. People would come. We talked about rain and what would happen. It would probably be a free concert because you never could control a crowd that big. And what the political ramifications would be. And we talked about how it would have to be nonpolitical to be political. And how we would have to deal. That was basically talked out that night, that first night, probably behind some Colombian blond, which had something to do with it. Overachieving, pseudo-intellectual Jewish kids with an idea that came from outside of us, I believe. It was the culture.

And Michael, because of his head shop and his Florida connections in that area and what he had seen, and my connections through the music business and what I had seen on the music side—you know, there was an instant connection on what had to be. I prefer to think it came from some power greater than us. And even though we get a certain amount of notoriety and fame and credit, I really don't think it—not looking to sound humble—I really don't think that we're that much different from anybody else that was there, except our job was to do it. It was our gig. It was like producing a record and promoting a record.

MICHAEL LANG: We took it to Miles Lourie. I don't remember where Miles came from other than it's possible that he must of been Artie's lawyer before that 'cause I didn't know many people in the business at all.

ARTIE KORNFELD: Miles said he knew some guys who were putting up a studio and they wanted to invest.

MICHAEL LANG: I don't remember if we went to see John and Joel about the studio or about the festival at first. John and Joel had just become involved with Media Sound. I don't know what the intent of the meeting was.

JOEL ROSENMAN: At that time, we were kind of practiced in listening to anything. We had been seduced away from our true calling as sitcom writers quite easily as you can see—one letter in seven thousand was enough to distract us. And I think from the beginning we were entrepreneurs looking for an accident to happen. We would look at anything. And although we privately agreed several times before they arrived that the last thing we wanted to do was put the other big toe in before we knew what was happening to the first big toe in New York, we were ready to listen. I was personally kind of intrigued by the warning that we had had from Miles Lourie about these guys, who I expected to be pretty exotic-looking hippies when they came in.

And, in fact, they were. When they arrived, dress-wise they were quite different from us because we were making an effort to look like businessmen at the time, in the hopes that we were becoming the same. They were making an effort to look like entertainment people on the leading edge of entertainment, meaning a lot of fringe, a lot of denim, a lot of buckskin, a lot of cowboy boots, and a great deal of hair. And so we couldn't have represented more distant ends of the spectrum.

JOHN ROBERTS: We were, in fact, the same age. Lang and I were both twenty-three and Joel and Artie were both twenty-five. So we were exact contemporaries.

JOEL ROSENMAN: Our apartment doubled as an office for us. You could tell you were in the office, thanks to a venture we elected not to get into, which was a light-box display device for use in windows in banks or whatever to illuminate the latest interest rate on your savings account. We had a sign made up by these people as a demo for us, and featured in front of this sign was our corporate name, which at that time was Challenge International Limited, which we thought was an impressive name, something that would inspire people to do business with us and sound worldwide—global. And so we would flip on this switch and the name Challenge International Limited would spring to life in kind of an ultra-violet intensity, almost a neon look. It's embarrassing to recall it now, but at the time this kind of signaled to us that we had gone from our apartment to our office. And that, with the tie and jacket, made us official.

At the same time, these guys looked as if they had just fallen backward off some rock-concert stage somewhere, or out of a recording studio, and we were not unfamiliar with this type because of the work we were doing with Media Sound. But we had never really had an intimate conversation with them about business or projects. We were curious.

JOHN ROBERTS: We were learning as we were going along—everything. A law school education or liberal arts degree were not great qualifications, as we discovered, for figuring out what to do in business or how to collect a receivable or work with an acoustical engineer, or any of the things that we had chosen to start doing in our lives. So we were very open to any kind of new experience. And meeting Lang and Kornfeld—we kind of felt this was our marketplace here. These were the people that would be using our studio. It was something we were both excited to do. I guess we figured our wit would get us by under all circumstances.

JOEL ROSENMAN: And it was clear they wanted something from us, which meant that we could sit and listen. And the tale that they unfolded was an essentially uninteresting tale about the need for a recording studio in Woodstock, New York. They impressed us with the superstars who lived in Woodstock, but they failed to make a case, we felt, for spending the money to construct a huge facility for these stars. We knew enough already, even though we hadn't yet opened our doors at Media Sound, about what it takes to make a recording studio profitable. It takes more than a few albums by a few superstars, no matter how great they are, because the fact they are going to sell a million albums does not increase your rates and does not, unfortunately, increase the amount of time they will book at the studio to produce that album. It takes a lot of little work—tape copies and advertising jingles and fill-in work in and around those superstars.

JOHN ROBERTS: My recollection was that Michael said almost nothing the entire meeting. He'd had the beatific smile. Occasionally, he would say something, but it was almost always monosyllabic and a little mysterious. Some of his comments or interjections felt like nonsequitors. It was like he was hearing a different tune.

I think one time he was talking about an experience he had—how his mind could leave his body. And he just knew things. He told me once that he had come back to an apartment that he was sharing with some friend, and I remember he said, "I couldn't go through the door." And he left it there. And I said, "What do you mean, you couldn't go through the door?" He said, "I couldn't get through that door, man." And he would just say it and smile at me. And I was thinking, "What is the purpose of this anecdote?" But Michael is an intelligent man and there was always something that he wanted to say to you that you should listen to. So I dug a little deeper and I said, "Was the door locked? Why didn't you open the door and go through it?" He said, "There was a drug bust going down inside." And the obvious question was, "How did you know that?" And he said, "It was the vibes." And he would just leave things like that—mysterious, almost Eastern in his intonations. Until this day, I don't know if Michael was putting that locution together for some effect or because that's just where his mind was. But that was sort of the way Michael would talk when he spoke at all. It was in short phrases that had a great deal of import, or you were expected to read a great deal of import beyond what he was saying.

ARTIE KORNFELD: I was the talker, Michael was the vibe. I was in my suit and still had short hair. I had just come off producing and writing a lot of hits, and they were sort of impressed by that. And Michael made a big impression because he was the only guy with long hair on the block. Michael didn't say much. He just sat there being hip. I wasn't hip yet. I could relate because I was president of my class at Adelphi, even though I did get thrown out for cheating. And Michael was the high school dropout but was in Mensa. I think he said he was in Mensa; I don't know for sure. And I liked Joel and John. I liked the fact that they had a lot of money. We didn't need a lot. We just needed the seed money to start it.

MICHAEL LANG: I liked John a lot immediately. He was a really sincere, forthright kind of guy. And Joel, I wasn't sure. I don't know, I liked Joel too; he seemed nice. I guess he was less exposed than John, but I liked

29

them. I thought they were kind of typical—I mean, you would describe them as yuppies today. They looked like that kind but they seemed, you know, curious and bright and—I mean, our values were kind of different at the time. But I liked them. Artie did, too. I think they were maybe closer to Artie's way of life anyway. I think that they thought I had just landed from the moon or something, because every once in a while you'd see sort of a look of incredulity.

ARTIE KORNFELD: I thought when I first met them that it seemed obvious that John was the power. John looked like the rich kid and Joel looked like the professional friend of the rich kid. They roomed together, they went through college together, and Joel's dad was a dentist and John obviously was the money, the big money. I liked John automatically and Joel I wanted to like and he wanted to like me but I felt a competition immediately.

JOHN ROBERTS: Kornfeld was much more a sort of caricature version of what we were used to dealing with. He was a businessman, but he was in a business that we had no experience with. He was an A&R man at Capitol Records and as a result of that there was a lot of giggling and high fives and late sixties drug rap and expressions and jiving. And he was just as charming as they come, Artie was.

JOEL ROSENMAN: He was invariably confident, up, very up—very, very, very, very up—and, in retrospect, a trained salesman, so that he was extremely alert for anything that we responded to positively. We were at a loss to determine what the purpose was of this other fellow in the room. Michael came on much more slowly and I think he had very little to say. He came in every now and then, but just muttered something and I remember that he seemed shy or diffident or both but comfortable with the little that he had to say. Artie was all over everybody all of the time. He was like a big puppy, very enthusiastic and very engaging. You wanted to be around this guy and be his friend, just to have as much fun as he was having with everything that he was doing. I enjoyed him a lot.

JOHN ROBERTS: The substance of Artie's self was quite beguiling also. What Artie said was basically that Woodstock was the center for artists and that a recording studio there would have a natural constituency and that if the four of us wonderful young men were to get together to do this, it would be a success. Because we all brought such disparate and wonderful expertises to the doing of this venture. And it was enormously illogical but strangely flattering to sit with Artie Kornfeld and hear him tell you what a great businessman you were, and what a genius your partner Joel was, and how you had just the right skills to make this into the biggest and best recording studio that the world had ever seen. You sat there thinking, "Is he noticing something that I'm not?" And yet your natural tendency was to believe this guy. Artie said, "I already bring to this the fact that I am one of the most successful A&R men at Capitol Records. That Alan Livingston, the president of Capitol Records, is a close, personal friend. And I can use those contacts to bring all of Capitol's recording artists."

FCC Seeks Ban On Cigarette Ads Over Radio, TV

Post
Washington, D.C.
February 6, 1969

30

Michael's role was different. He was a) living in Woodstock at the time and b) a man of the people. He knew all of the local people up there; they trusted him. All you'd have to do is to present Mike Lang and you could see that it was a hip business, and this was not a business where you would be ripped off. He would be responsible for creating the environment, and, in fact, would run the recording studio. He was there as the operations guy. He spoke the language, he knew the people, he knew recording, he knew music. Artie would be the business getter.

MICHAEL LANG: John and Joel seemed pretty interested when we saw them. It was pretty funny actually. I mean we were sort of from different worlds, the four of us. We expressed the ideas and I remember that John thought it was kind of cute. And I think in terms of the studio I think he was less interested at that meeting because they were so ensconced in their own studio. We left with them thinking about it, and I think we—I don't remember if we'd come to them with a budget that day or if we were going to come back with a budget the next day, or something like that happened. Probably we were going to bring one back; I don't think we would have come with a budget.

We had, in the interim, seen other people, and I think it was Larry Utall who had expressed a desire to go ahead with the project. Someone that Artie knew. And I remember that Joel in particular and John, too, I guess, was very disappointed, frustrated by the fact. I guess they were trying to get going in their own business and larger entities, that when they'd come up with a deal someone would always come up and grab it from them. So they expressed something like that. In any case, we liked them a lot. We thought it would perhaps be more interesting to do it with John and Joel. And we started to have some meetings to put the deal together.

JOEL ROSENMAN: We had this stock response when we weren't sure how the other one thought about it and I think Artie did so much of the talking and John and I did so much listening and so little back and forth with him, except asking the questions that we already knew to ask from the Media Sound project. We let him get out of the door and then we turned to each other and tried to figure it out.

JOHN ROBERTS: We had actually been a little politer than that because we had asked them if they had anything on paper, which is a fairly standard way to conclude a meeting and to gently get you from the first meeting to the second meeting. In this instance, they had nothing on paper unfortunately. If they'd had something on paper they could have left it behind and we could have called them or called Miles Lourie and said, "Really, we're not terribly interested." But they said, "No, we'll get you something." So that created the momentum for another meeting.

ARTIE KORNFELD: I had closed enough deals in the music business that I knew this was a deal. They had to go to their lawyer. And I remember Michael said, "Give me five." Michael always had the hip expressions. He was the first guy that I heard say, "Right on." Michael always had the expressions.

31

Joel Rosenman

JOHN ROBERTS: I don't know how many days later they met with us but I know Miles called that afternoon to say that his clients had had *the* most fantastic meeting of their *entire* career. And they thought that we were just the two greatest guys that they had met, and they were just so looking forward to working with us on this project. And I think Joel and I said something like, "Whoa. We weren't all that excited about their idea. They're getting us more detailed information on it. Miles, this is not a done deal." Miles said, "Well, there was a lot of good feeling created in that meeting. And I just have a feeling that you guys are going to do something together," or words to that effect. And in fairly short order, we had a proposal presented to us by Michael and Artie.

32

JOEL ROSENMAN: Within a very short period of time, we had enough written material to look at so that we knew conclusively between ourselves that this was not the kind of project that we wanted to get involved in. One of the questions that we asked them, because we were so keen on promoting the recording studio in Manhattan, was, "How are you going to let people know about the recording studio up in the woods? The locals are going to know—and we admit that these locals are not yokels—but what about the rest of the world that you need to make your studio go?" I think that tipped them off to the need for a promotional gimmick, and the promotional gimmick that they came up with was a press party to which they were going to invite recording studio execs from New York, recording studio budget people from the record companies, managers, artists—anybody they could get who had anything to do with the recording industry. They were going to ferry these people up to New York somehow—by bus, limo, whatever—and premier the studio that way. And in their written proposal they had a budget for this press party. There was nothing in there for talent because, as Michael or Artie explained to us in the second discussion, the talent was going to perform for free. They would be going to be so happy to have a recording studio in the neighborhood so they wouldn't have to hassle with New York City that they would just donate their services. Bob Dylan was going to hum a few tunes for free at the press party.

It was that little addendum to their project proposal that caught our eye. I remember saying to John, "This is really a yawn, don't you think?" And he said, "There's no way we would want to get into this project." And I said, "But you know the idea of having a concert with those stars. Why don't we just skip the studio idea and just do a big concert? We could make a fortune." And he said, "This is not what they're proposing." And I said, "These guys will go for anything." I was wrong about that. They fought tooth and nail because they had already been to a couple of concerts. They knew what a rocky road you had to travel. They knew how difficult it was to get through a rock concert with your wallet and your hide intact.

It turned out, in retrospect—and we did a lot of thinking about this—that Michael and Artie were approaching us out of a desire to make their lives a little more conservative. They were thinking about being family men; Artie had just had a daughter. These guys had been through a lot of hell-raising as entertainment creatures. And what they wanted was something a little more stable. They wanted that recording studio. They wanted it for reasons that we couldn't even conceive of. We were looking for excitement. They were looking for some stability. And they regarded that asset—a recording studio, with a lot of equipment, and a clientele, and a reputation, and a piece of property— as stable, conservative, dependable, unexciting but comforting aspects of the entertainment business. They had had their fill of excitement, I think. And when we started talking about concerts—well, the last concert that they had been involved with Michael had nearly been killed in Miami because of something to do with somebody who didn't like what he—I don't even know the story well enough to repeat it, but it wasn't attractive. And they knew that these things were risky and unpleasant, or could be. So they shied away from our suggestion that

33

we turn the project upside down, explode the press party into a big concert, and sidetrack or forget about the recording studio. They thought this was pretty dangerous talk.

As it turned out later, after considerable back and forth over the next couple of weeks, they were willing—maybe they didn't have another good project cooking or something—to go ahead with this notion of doing a concert. And we agreed that if they would do that, with the profits from the concert we would build a recording studio in Woodstock. To which Michael said, "Fine, I have just the place to put it." He had a piece of property that we could construct this studio on.

JOHN ROBERTS: That recording studio remained uppermost in their minds—in Michael's mind, certainly—all the way through. I can remember that the weekend of the festival itself, Michael and I were tooling around on his motorcycle placating landholders on Friday afternoon. And at some point he said, to me, "If we take a bath here, does that mean we won't build the recording studio?" And I said, "Well, Michael, the understanding was that we'd use the profits from this venture to build the recording studio." And I'm thinking, "How can he be thinking about that? The gates aren't up, the people are spread all over other people's land. It's not clear that the performers are going to arrive, there's fifty thousand people in the performance area, and he's thinking about that recording studio."

MICHAEL LANG: I thought that I could pull anything off. I've always thought that. I've always had that kind of confidence. I always thought if you could dream it up you could pull it together. And that was really my attitude with John and Joel in those days. I was pretty much staying in the background in the beginning of our negotiations but then, you just have a sense of how things can happen. And I knew that I would know how to make it work. I mean I had an image in my mind of what it had to be. And I knew that I could make that a reality.

Frankly, making a fortune was not an issue for me, probably to everybody's—as far as the four of us were concerned—disappointment, ultimately. But profit was not really a motive for me. I mean, sure, I thought there was an investment, we should make money, but I just wanted to see the event happen. And it wasn't even for fame at that point, either. I mean it was the notoriety, it was to have a dream come true. It was the doing of it that was, I think, my motivation.

JOHN ROBERTS: They had nothing else. These guys were open to anything. Artie was in the process of leaving Capitol Records. I don't know whether that was voluntary or involuntary—I really to this day don't know. He was casting around for other things to do.

ARTIE KORNFELD: Capitol was not thrilled with me anymore because all of a sudden these longhairs started to show up at Capitol Records in New York and that was a new experience.

JOHN ROBERTS: Michael was doing God-knows-what at that time. No, I know what he doing: He was managing a group that he had been trying to sell to Artie at Capitol Records, the Train.

34

JOEL ROSENMAN: Train was having some problems. I think they were a good group. They were sort of a heavy metal group, as I recall, and the problem was that they would get a gig and get paid for the gig and then they would have to give most of it back because of some damage that might have occurred to the plate-glass window in front of the store or the chairs or the bar or something like that. And Michael was kind of breaking even at that time.

MICHAEL LANG: I eventually made a deal with John and Joel, making our organization the manager of Train, but Train just turned into a disaster. It just sort of fell apart in some ways. There's a lot of talent in the group, but it was just very unruly and unmanageable. Garland Jeffries was in the band and a guy named Bob Lenox and Don Tyler and Abbie Rader. Don went on to have a pretty decent career on his own. And so did Bob actually. Bob went to Europe; he was always a talented, gifted keyboard player.

JOHN ROBERTS: This is Roberts and Rosenman at their most gullible, I suppose, but once we got into bed with these guys, so to speak, we— and I think it's our way—embraced them as partners. And Michael and Artie—Artie in particular—had a much broader vision of what we could do together than we did. And you can read your own motivation into this, but Artie thought that Woodstock a) was an important name and would become increasingly important as our efforts succeeded, and that we should trademark that name and b) that we should form all kinds of Woodstock companies, all of which could tie in together. There should be Woodstock Realty, that owned the land on which the recording studio was to be built. There was Woodstock Management, that would manage the artists that would be signed to our own company. There would be Woodstock Records that would record them. There would be Woodstock Publishing, Woodstock This, etc. And as our very first recording group, he said, "Look, Mike Lang is going to be the guy with the most experience in producing this festival. He's going to sign the acts. He shouldn't have to worry about this group the Train that he's managing, and for ten thousand dollars"—or some sum of money like that—"we should set up a company, take them off his hands, and we'll all own it together."

We found ourselves managing a hard-rock group. I think inside of maybe two weeks they threw one table too many through a plate-glass window and became permanently exiled from the music scene, as far as I know. I know Michael and Artie became quite evasive on the subject. But as I recall, the Train derailed very shortly after we signed them.

JOEL ROSENMAN: There was an affinity between Michael and Artie. Artie was the substantial character, at least it appeared that way. He had the home—it was a nicely furnished home—and Michael was bunking in with him and he had the job and money.

ARTIE KORNFELD: I had just come off having big money, and to me, coming from a poor family, six hundred thousand dollars earned in a year in 1967 was a lot of money. But I was using it to support Michael's

900 Students Routed From Wisconsin U.

Tribune
Chicago, Ill.
February 12, 1969

35

trips and my trips at that point. Michael didn't have any money. Eventually, he started to miss his bus up to Woodstock more and more and he started to hang out—I lived right off Sutton Place at 56th and First. And the cars. I remember I had a new car from Capitol that Michael borrowed and when it came back, the stereo was missing. I remember when he brought it back, it was all banged up. And I had my Stingray that I bought Linda for her birthday. I was a poor kid that had just got rich. And Michael was a rich kid that was playing poor. So it was an interesting combination. I loved him. He has that way of getting into you.

JOEL ROSENMAN: Eventually, we wrote up a shareholders' agreement among the four of us. Some of it was not too well conceived, as it turned out later. But I remember that they were especially keen on getting into that contract our promise that we would take the proceeds of the festival and build a recording studio. In their minds, the whole thing would be a waste of time if we didn't.

JOHN ROBERTS: The basic agreement that we came to was that Joel and I would provide the seed money. I think we agreed to provide up to a hundred and fifty thousand dollars. In those days, you could sell tickets and use the ticket proceeds to finance your undertakings, so that we never would actually have had to take down much more than that hundred and fifty thousand from the bank in seed capital. We would be responsible for all of the business of putting this thing together, up to and including ticket sales, advertising, procuring equipment, fencing, what have you. They would get the talent, do the site planning, do the promotion, set up the outlets, and essentially do the production. And do the lion's share of the work. It was all spelled out. And we would get our money back first—actually, we weren't putting up anything but guarantees to the bank initially—but in the event any money came out of our pockets we'd get it back first, and then we'd split the profits fifty-fifty. Or the profits would go into the recording studio. That was to be the plan, if there was anything that was left over. We figured that we would be able to throw the festival, finance the recording studio, and pocket some money too—all in the space of one year.

JOEL ROSENMAN: Stock ownership in Woodstock Ventures Incorporated was provided for in that agreement. We split the stock twenty-five percent apiece. And by the same document or a similar document, we incorporated four other entities, because we had evolved, in discussion, a master plan for controlling all of the products of this festival and the recording studio and the groups that we would have under management—both at the recording studio and at the festival—and the songs that would be written, so we had a publishing company. I think we had a total of five corporations, including Woodstock Ventures. The original corporation, Woodstock Ventures, was the production vehicle for the festival and the others were for ancillary activities in and around the music business, including management and publishing.

JOHN ROBERTS: I think we had a very modest idea that maybe we'd have

twenty-five thousand people, at six bucks a day per man—that's four hundred thousand dollars—and two hundred thousand in costs. A ridiculously small amount of money was needed to build a recording studio in those days, compared to these days, and this threw off enough for that, and then some, as I recall. There was a pie-in-the-sky budget that showed if seventy-five thousand people could be induced to attend, that we would all be on Easy Street forever. But none of us seriously believed that could happen.

Michael and Artie, I think, were just like two kids in a candy store, at least for the first month of this thing. "We've got partners with deep pockets who believe our rap. Let's just see what we can do—something good might come out of it for all of us." And I think there was a genuinely benevolent feeling on the part of Artie—and possibly on the

Artie Kornfeld

37

part of Michael—for all of us. But it began to go south pretty quickly in terms of getting the job done.

MICHAEL LANG: Initially, Artie was going to handle publicity and press, public relations. I was going to do the festival in physical terms, produce the physical event. John and Joel were going to do the business administration, ticketing, and make whatever deals had to be made. That's kind of how it went from the beginning—I mean that was its intent. But I guess communication problems started instantly.

JOHN ROBERTS: We began to see that Artie was not much of a performer, pretty quickly—that he was charged with doing something and it wouldn't get done. And then we would find out from someone else that Artie had decided something totally at odds with what we as a group had decided. Michael looked like a get-it-done kind of a guy and he came to us sometime I think in April and said, "I need another office." He said, "I can't work around Artie. It won't happen if I'm working here around Artie." And at the same time he went to Artie and said, "I need another office. I can't work around John and Joel. It won't happen if I'm working here around John and Joel. They're too much like business cats and they turn my people off. If they see these guys behind desks over there, they are going to be turned off. I need a production office."

That was sort of the first statement—I remember Artie and Joel and I comparing notes about this at one of our, sort of let-your-hair-hang-down meetings later on. It was the first sign that there were real rifts developing there. Artie said, "You've chased Michael away out of the office." We said, "*We* have? *You* have!" And we all recounted this thing and Artie said, "That son of a bitch. When he was starving I took him in," etc., etc. "Well, let's call him right now and we'll have a meeting tomorrow morning and clear all this shit up, because I'm not going to put up with that for a second." And I remember walking into the meeting the next day with Joel prepared to have an honest expression of opinions and Artie acted as if it had never happened. "Michael is my best friend. You can't drive a wedge between us, and this is a lot of misunderstandings." Michael said, "I never had any problem with Artie, I never had any problem with you, I just want the gig to be done." And Joel and I sitting here trying to figure out why this thing was going south because Joel and I still had the sense that there was essentially goodwill and a communitive interest among the four of us.

MICHAEL LANG: At the time, my handling of it, my method of handling problems, was to avoid them. And so the first thing I did was to move the production office downtown, away from the rest of it. Isolated and away to give it breathing room. Which I think was a good idea. I think it was one of the factors that helped make it a reality, because I think if we had gotten everything caught up in the internal insanity that was going on for those six or eight months, it wouldn't have happened.

JOHN ROBERTS: To this day, I'm not entirely sure what the dynamics of the relationship between Michael and Artie were then, continued to be, and are now. I don't know. Artie does not speak with great kindness of Michael these days, but he could tomorrow. I don't know.

Rock Dominates '68 Golden LPs

Rolling Stone
March 1, 1969

ARTIE KORNFELD: Joel and John were like the thorn in my side, which Michael sort of placed there because it took the heat off him. And he had to have—and righteously so—he had to have a free hand. Looking back, I could see how he felt—that I had the strength and was also vulnerable enough and believed in him enough to go along with his trip. Which I didn't know at the time; that's why Michael was so clever. Michael has a way of manipulating people. He's charming and he has his Butch Cassidy-James Dean charisma that he's carefully honed. Don't get me wrong—I don't say that negatively because I love Michael. And I think deep inside Michael loves me, if he's capable of loving anybody but himself. And I think he does love me, you know. And I do love him. Now I do. There were ten or twelve years after the festival that I really despised him and he didn't care for me, either. But I guess that comes with anything when you do something so tender and so touching and so raw emotionally. It's like a divorce. You come out with some bitter feelings.

MICHAEL LANG: The problem that I felt was that no one had a grasp of what the thing was—what we were creating—and maybe there was a problem for me to express what it had to be. I mean, you could express it graphically what it was that we were doing—putting a festival together, putting a show together, and so many people were going to come. But I had another feeling about it: I thought it was going to be more spiritual and special. I had grown up in the midst of the whole sixties movement, and was in the middle of a lot of issues, and my values were a bit different from theirs. And I knew that people that were going to come to the show were in the same frame of reference. So it had to have certain things to make it work. It had to have a certain feeling, it had to ring true in certain ways. It was hard to explain, impossible to explain to John and Joel at that point. So while I wasn't afraid that they were going to hurt the project, I also knew they would not really know how to express properly what it was supposed to feel like. Maybe I was wrong; that was my feeling.

ARTIE KORNFELD: I don't know. It might have been me, you know. It could have been just paranoia on my part. But I felt trouble coming the day we met. It was the first time I saw or felt that I was some sort of psychic—I've been tested for being psychic—and I felt it. "Trouble ahead, trouble behind, don't you know that notion just crossed my mind." And that's when it crossed my mind, the first meeting. But it was O.K., because it was a start to get something done and nothing comes easy and there's always trouble—no pain, no gain. There's always a price to pay. I didn't know it at the time, but I was prepared to do it, whatever it was, to get the thing done. It was an obsession by that point.

• C H A P T E R   T W O •

"You can fake it every day of your life, but this was a major fake with a lot of money involved."
—*Penny Stallings*

STANLEY GOLDSTEIN: In the early spring of 1969, I had left employment with Criteria Recording Studios in Miami, Florida. I had a job offer on the West Coast with Wally Heider, who had taken over United and Western Studios. Wally was the king of remote recording, and what he offered me was an in-house engineering operating position at the studios, which I was not interested in. I was more interested in doing remotes with him, so I elected to come through New York, hoping to connect up with A&R Recording Studios here—Phil Ramone is just an enormous talent—hoping to gain employment here rather than go there. I had essentially given up on the position I wanted and was about to go to Los Angeles when I got a telephone call from my then wife who was living in Florida, saying that Michael Lang was trying to reach me, that he wanted to do a festival of some kind. So I called Michael, and we arranged to get together. I met him and Artie Kornfeld up in that room off of Artie's offices at Capitol Records in New York and had some brief discussions about what it was that Michael was doing and what he wanted me to do.

I was not terribly interested in doing a festival. The project as it was presented to me at the time was that he had found some relatively wealthy people and they were going to build a recording studio and this festival situation was one designed to put the recording studio on the map. And that I would be heavily involved in the recording studio and would assist in gathering together the people for the festival and in helping to design it; and once that was done, I would concentrate on putting together a recording studio.

MICHAEL LANG: Stanley I had known from Florida, from Miami, when we had done the Miami festival. Stanley was one of those guys who in a desperate situation could always come through, really to the point where he worked better in a desperate situation than when things were going smoothly, I think. He was just a real good utility guy, Stanley, and he knew everything that I knew, plus he knew sound backward and forward and was very bright. I liked him a lot and so he was one of the first people I got a hold of.

STANLEY GOLDSTEIN: Criteria was the major studio in Miami at the time and I was the senior mixer on the premises and became involved in a lot of record projects and with the rock 'n' roll musicians. I was not a rock 'n' roll person per se; I was a professional working in the field. Some of the musicians I knew—in particular, a fellow named Don Keider and another fellow named Pete Ponzell—were living in the Coconut Grove area and knew Michael. Don Keider, in addition to playing vibes and drums, was an artist and was a participant with

Michael's then girlfriend in some poster art, which Michael was representing; I'm fuzzy on the business details. As I understand it, Michael became their marketing representative. Michael had come to Coconut Grove and created a head shop and had all kinds of hassles; he was the first head shop in the area down there. And I believe that he was representing their line of posters, which went into national distribution. You may remember there was "Lucy in the Sky with Diamonds," which was the one that received the widest distribution, I think—a day-glo poster of a girl's face and hair just kind of swirling off with sparkles and things. And so the jazz community, the hip community, the underground community all kind of came together there in Coconut Grove at that time. It was a way station in the Greenwich Village/Boston/Sausalito circuit of hip people. Michael had a place that you could buy rolling papers and other implements and impedimenta. And so as a result of those mutual acquaintances, we met, though we established no particular relationship.

In the meantime, I knew quite well a fellow named Marshall Brevitz, who had developed a couple of rock 'n' roll clubs in the area. Marshall was in competition with a fellow named Harry Levass, with whom I'd also been working. It was a small community; everyone eventually got to know everyone. Marshall initially approached me— I had done some development work with Marshall when his first club was closed and he found a new location, and I did some sound work and eventually helped him put his joint together.

Michael had the finance and some elements of the scheme. He and Marshall made a deal with a racetrack in Hallandale, Florida— Gulfstream Racetrack—and decided to put on a show and came to Criteria to talk about sound and staging and acts and recording. And so the studio made a deal to provide the sound and recording services and, for practical purposes, I wound up as technical director and general factotum of that event, as well as helping to select the acts. The major acts had already been selected but not necessarily booked, though some of them may have been Jimi Hendrix, Arthur Brown, Blue Cheer—or Blue something or other—and a couple of others. I opened them up to the booking for Chuck Berry and John Lee Hooker and some others along those lines, and we did the show.

The show was a financial disaster for the participants for a lot of reasons—everything from counterfeited tickets to terrible weather problems that caused some of the shows to be canceled and unhappy crowds and so on and so on. Nevertheless, we held it together, did some recording. And so I became very involved with and got to know Michael, at least in a working atmosphere at that time.

I never got to know Michael well. My impression of him at that time was that in difficult circumstances, he managed somehow to be the person in that group most capable of going forward and addressing real issues and getting to the heart of matters. We didn't do any hanging out. We never developed a friendship; we developed a business relationship of some mutual respect. It was tempered by a certain element of not quite trust on my part. We just came from two different cultures. I came out of a world of music and that was where my interest really lay. Michael came out of a world of commerce, was devoted to rock 'n' roll, thought Dylan was the answer to the world's problems,

Cheers and Tears as Beatle Paul Marries

Times
London, England
March 13, 1969

41

Stanley Goldstein

and did not fit in with this world that I lived in and cared about. I didn't think Dylan was the answer.

I agreed to work for Woodstock Ventures for two hundred dollars a week. Boy, did I work cheap in those days! This was going to be a maintenance salary, something just to keep me afloat while this venture came together. I would have an eventual piece of the studio action. Somewhere along the line, and I don't remember exactly when, but it was shortly thereafter, my salary went up to three hundred dollars. It wasn't something that I asked for. It just came along, and it remained that way throughout.

I was going to assist in pulling together the staff for the festival, and then I was going to deal with the studio and the creation, design, construction, implementation, and so forth. That was my mandate. That was it. I was divorced from the festival except that I might come back in to fill a hole during the actual operation of the event. I hired people to do all the jobs that I was interested in at the show.

I was there in the early councils as a technical reference point and took on certain elements to provide within the company an understanding of the technical magnitude in cost so that the other proposals could be evaluated; to do some basic sizing; to gather information, schedules, costs, resources; and to help decide the tone. It wasn't as though there was a formal structure, though I tried to create one. The early-on decisions of whether it would be a one-day or a multiple-day event were decisions in which I was a major participant—sometimes, I think, wielding considerable influence. In general, I was a bit older than the folks that were putting it on. I was about to turn thirty. I had some technical expertise that no one else possessed in a nuts-and-bolts way. I had a fair amount of experience in putting together shows over the years and being involved in musical presentations. And so my opinion was valued, I guess, and influential.

One of the first people I called was Mel Lawrence. I knew Mel because some time after the event that Michael and Marshall staged at Gulfstream Racetrack, I got a call from a group that wanted to put on a show at the same place and had gotten my name and wanted me to get involved in one way or another and to tell them a little bit of this and that. Mel came in as the on-site person for that, and Mel and I spent some considerable amount of time together over a period of months. I wound up not really being involved with the show to any great extent, but plugged in a developing friendship with Mel.

MEL LAWRENCE: The Miami Pop Festival we did had probably the best lineup of any show in the sixties, everyone from José Feliciano to the Iron Butterfly to Chuck Berry to Marvin Gaye to Joni Mitchell to the Grateful Dead to Three Dog Night—I mean on and on. It was a dynamite show.

STANLEY GOLDSTEIN: The only actual direct involvement I had with Mel's show was to be the stager of the walking catfish races. Someone had imported from Africa a species of catfish that had developed a lung capacity in adaptation, and they would leave their drying-up ponds and rivers and travel some considerable distances to find water. These catfish had the normal protrusions and spines and so forth, and a particularly virulent substance—poison of one kind or another—and someone had brought them to South Florida, turned some loose. They were breeding and had become a cause in the area. They had to be gathered together; they were dangerous to the populace. And Mel wanted to stage some walking catfish races, so I had some contacts at the Seaquarium there and we went down and got some catfish, set up a pond, and kept them within this pond. Unfortunately, my studio did the backup recording and audio services for the Orange Bowl parade, and so I was the technical manager of all of that at the same time and was delayed because of some technical hang-ups at NBC. I was delayed in getting out to the grounds of the festival, and the catfish cooked in the sun.

MEL LAWRENCE: We had some other maniacal kinds of things that we thought festivals ought to have because it was a festival. It wasn't just a concert, it was also an art show. The celebrated sculptor Duane Hanson had his first public showing at the Miami Pop Festival of his piece called the *Motorcycle Accident*, and it was a very, very beautiful show.

Stanley Goldstein: So anyway, I called Mel Lawrence to talk to him about being director of operations of this event. His show had been very, very impressive.

Mel Lawrence: After the Miami show, I got back to L.A. and rented an apartment in the canyon and sort of didn't know what was going to be happening next. Then I got a phone call from Stan saying that he had heard from Michael Lang—who I knew of, because he had produced a show in Gulfstream Racetrack probably a year before I did, which was Jimi Hendrix, and it wasn't a big festival like this thing, it was just a show. Stanley wanted my partners on the Miami Pop Festival and myself to come up to New York to talk about this festival that he thinks can't miss. I forget what it was called, but it wasn't called Woodstock; I think it was called "An Aquarian Exposition." We did end up coming to New York—Tom Rounds, a guy named Tom Driscoll, a guy named Tom Moffatt, and myself, all of us being principals in a company called Arena Associates.

We looked at this site, and I was turned on because I was just turned on by another big project—I'm project-oriented—but my partners were not so turned on because they had their own businesses. So they passed, and we talked about it and I said, "I think this is great, I want to do this. I really want to do this. I don't want to stay in Laurel Canyon." So I actually quit over that. I liked Michael, I liked Stanley, and I wanted to get into it. I knew that I could have a good influence on it and of course, I had the right experience. None of these guys had the experience that I had.

We talked about salary and what the responsibilities would be.

Mel Lawrence

My mission was to design, operate, plan for all of the functions of the festival aside from the actual show, but that included sort of a coordination of all the things that got built, and that basically was it. It wasn't like hiring talent or promoting, but it was coordinating all of these aspects—water, sewage, you know, this and that.

STANLEY GOLDSTEIN: And so Mel came in. I was doing the scurrying after the technical folks. I didn't know any of these people myself. Well, I had met them because some of them were involved in Mel's event, and so I sought them out. They were all associated in various ways with the Fillmore East at that time. We met at John Morris' apartment down on, as I recall, 12th Street, and one thing led to another and that's where the initial meeting with John Morris took place, which eventually led to John becoming a part of the organization. I'm not positive whether it was John or Chip who wanted to know what my job was, and since I didn't have a job and was trying to avoid taking one, we came up with the fact that in some ways I had taken the position of Holy Ghost in regards to this venture. No one knew what I did, but you knew you had to have one.

CHIP MONCK: I don't really recollect what I was doing in those days. If it were anything as usual, it would be going back yet again to rebuild the stage at the Village Gate in New York on Thompson and Bleeker Street, to then go out on the road with something like an Odetta, a Josh White, a Shelley Berman, a Belafonte, a Makeba. Still probably working Newport folk and jazz for George Wein, when it had made its move from Freebody Park to the seaside. I was the stage designer, and I hung all the lighting and operated the lighting from a funny little trailer on stage left, and Bill Hanley would come in moments before with his soldering iron and a roll of zipcord under his arm and a couple of the speakers and that would be Newport. So, I was still doing the Newports and the Village Gates and, I think, perhaps the more central New York-located things before Woodstock had come up.

I was doing my usual Friday trek to William Morris and I was sitting in Hector Morales' office; his office was probably no bigger than our largest filing cabinet here. I was sitting there and saying, "O.K. Hector, what's going on this week?" or "Who's designing what?" in the usual fashion. I've always sort of pecked at agents in order to find out, since I had no real legitimate promoter ties or connections. He said, "Have you heard about Woodstock?" I said, "Woodstock what?" "Well, this funny little guy, Michael Lang, came to see me and I was the only one that would see him, so he's trying to book everything in the agency for this thing." So Hector gave me Michael's number.

MICHAEL LANG: Chip was pretty much the best-known lighting tech around at the time and charming and nice and seemed to have a good grasp of what we were trying to put together at the time and was unflustered by anything.

CHIP MONCK: John Morris and I invited Michael down to Morris' apartment, and we started discussions on Woodstock. Michael would put his hands in front of him, as he was wont to do, and wave them

45

Chip Monck

slightly like this in order to describe the shape of something. Of course his hands were moving in such a way that was neither a sphere or a square. He had a very good idea of what he wanted to do as talent and the feeling that was to be there, the overall control that he wanted the collective mind to exhibit. He had no other idea nor did he necessarily care who was passionate about what shape and what containment, what load-bearing capacity any of the structures would be, upon which someone either performed or through which someone was heard. He was really more interested in the overall feeling and, perhaps, the sense by which or through which everybody would be connected to each other. He was the major purveyor of that type of guideline that Woodstock would take. There was the money, there was Michael, there were the structuralists, there were the people who were hanging from the rafters, and there were folks like myself that were most concerned with the design, the installation, the operation of something that would never get done properly.

Michael is very bright but what you normally think of Michael is that he's so flaky he'll never get something together. But that's not the case with him. It's always difficult when you go into a situation like that when you're working with somebody who works on different levels or perhaps a different plateau than you do. I'm very nuts and bolts. I went towards nuts and bolts because it doesn't talk back, it never changes. A number-two Phillips will always fit a number-two Phillips, and that's very simple. And a three-eighths bolt will ne'er go on nothing else but a three-eighths nut. So, dealing with Michael and having Michael try and explain to me his feelings was not an easy thing. But

Michael didn't need anything from me other than perhaps structural integrity or the design element or perhaps the limited plateau of control that I could exhibit for him on his behalf.

My mission was for thirteen weeks at seven thousand dollars. That was one important aspect of the mission. The other mission was to look over a design to be generated by any number of different people for the stage house and the load-bearing roof, to cause that to be erected, to be basic production manager, to be the lighting designer, to be the operator, and only to find out at seven in the morning that they were shy a master of ceremonies. That was the mission, and that was not a bad price for that mission. I think he got what he paid for.

JOHN MORRIS: I had been running the Fillmore East for Bill Graham. I think it was Stan Goldstein and Bert Cohen and Chip Monck who came to my apartment in New York and told me about this idea to do this festival. And I had left Graham and I was out of the Fillmore and I thought, "Why not?" I mean, it sounded fascinating. My father was chief of staff of a logistics outfit in the United States Army. He was a reservist, but he kept getting called back in. He was fifty-two the last time he went back into the Army. And so I'd grown up with that sort of logistical-planning-type stuff. It was interesting. And I remember they came and talked to me about it and then very quickly there was a situation where there was going to be a separate production office. And I went to my landlady, who I think now is probably no longer around, and rented a couple of floors over her offices on Sixth Avenue between 13th and 14th. And we just went to work. It was that simple.

I'd known Bert Cohen from before, when he was living in

John Morris

47

Philadelphia and doing concerts. Chip and I, of course, had worked together on a bunch of different projects. I didn't know Michael, I didn't know John, I didn't know Joel, I didn't know Artie in advance. I was the only one who could be sort of considered a pro or a hired gun at that point in that I was the only one who'd been producing concerts and been doing it. Everybody had been peripherally involved, or whatever, with the exception of John and Joel, who'd just taken an ad and gotten the ad answered. So my job was to help put together the booking, and to help sort of pull together the design thing.

MICHAEL LANG: John sort of talked his way into a job I think. John was very nice and familiar with most of the acts and familiar with the business in a way that I wasn't, and I felt it was a spot that we needed filled. His mission was mostly to work with the agencies and the industry so that when we figured out who the acts were going to be that we wanted, John could help put that together and bring in the logistics of bringing in the talent and equipment. He had done that kind of role at the Fillmore. So it was talent coordination.

JOHN MORRIS: One of my conditions was that we bring in Chris Langhart. Langhart was the head of the theater technical department of New York University, and it was a total accident how it happened.. I bumped into him when we were doing shows at the Anderson. Here all of a sudden was this Ichabod Crane-looking genius who could do anything to anything, anywhere in the world, under any circumstance. There was always an answer, and there was always a solution, and it worked. And it came in generally under budget. And so it was a condition of mine that he had to be brought in. He had to come in.

Michael Lang (left),
Chris Langhart

CHRIS LANGHART: I was working at New York University, with the Fillmore next door. There was this sort of undertone about Woodstock, and ultimately they had an office somewhere. Chip was already part of the situation, and he had anchored the staging and lighting aspect because that was his specialty at the time; still is. I had never met Michael much but I came highly recommended from everybody else at the Fillmore because I had solved a lot of problems over there. My general role at the Fillmore was to deal with things that people wanted that had to get actually executed—fix the air conditioner because someone wants sixty grand to look cross-eyed at it, hang the light bridge up in the middle of the house, hang the speakers up for Hanley—because those were the things that had to be rigged and suspended and welded and rearranged and engineered. And so that was the role that I had and they were happy to support it in any way that they could. Somehow, it fell into place that I would be dealing with all the parts of the festival that nobody else wanted to deal with—the toilets and the communications and the supply of the power and the performers' pavilion.

CHIP MONCK: Chris is probably one of brightest people I have met, with the exception of my wife, who also believes he is one of the brightest people she has ever met. He's an absolutely marvelous, indispensable person to work with. There's always a depth of structural integrity that's considered. He's brilliant, he's absolutely brilliant, and I would never involve myself in a major project without a Langhart type, preferably, if available, Chris. And if not available, I might postpone the project.

CHRIS LANGHART: There came to be salary negotiations. Michael was very streetwise. I had not met him much but we finally settled on a figure—a low and a high—having argued it back and forth. And he announced that he would flip a coin. As far as I was concerned the low and the high were a little far apart, and I was shooting for the high and he was shooting for the low. I said, "Well, we're not having that flipping-of-the-coin routine because I have a student in my class who can flip a coin reliably twelve times out of thirteen or so, more or less, and he's also named Michael and he's streetwise and you probably are one of those that can flip a coin, too." This wide Cheshire-cat smile comes onto his face; his bluff has been called. So we settled at the higher figure and the coin flipping was out of the picture and from then on we pretty well got on straight ahead.

JOHN MORRIS: It was a semi-organized disorganization. It was Stanley Goldstein and Joyce Mitchell, who were sort of their own operation. There was Chip and Steve Cohen and their operation. And then there was Langhart, myself, and a couple of people who were working with me. And then there was Michael going back and forth. John and Joel were sort of uptown somewhere. Artie was—I do not remember Artie at all from the preparatory stages. And it was, I guess, primarily a matter of all these disparate things starting to accidentally fall together.

MEL LAWRENCE: I made a checklist that blew everybody's mind because it showed everybody the really tremendous amount of detail that had

Troop Cut in Vietnam Is Ruled Out

*Post
Washington, D.C.
March 15, 1969*

49

to be coordinated for an event like this. And then we all were stuck with this reality, and I think we approached it in a really good way because I had festivals under my belt and so had Stanley with Miami Pop and maybe even Michael with his show, but it wasn't quite the same deal.

The checklist was pages and pages. I wish I still had that checklist; it was really a work of art and it all came off the top of my head. It was things like water, the different types of water that we'd need—down to drainage for the receptacles of the hoses, storage tanks in case we didn't have wells. It was a comprehensive checklist, everything from roads to fences to food to transportation, fire access, security—where the different security people would go—headquarters, communications systems, lines of communication.

At that time we were just setting up on Sixth Avenue and Chip built us these incredible desks, handmade—overnight they appeared. They were sort of drawing table-type things, but whole rooms were filled with them, very comfortable, a nice atmosphere in that particular building.

There were different floors. I think there was like a talent floor. Michael and John Morris were there and they were doing their talent numbers and everything. And then there was like the operations floor, which included staging, so there were all these different designs of stages that were being presented to us, and some of the nuttiest designs you've ever seen—flying buttress, trestle jobs, and things made out of giant logs and just all different kinds of things, and we had to pick one design that everybody agreed with, everybody from Steve Cohen to Chip to Michael to Stanley and—some of the names are fuzzy; they're like brothers to me but I forget their names.

CHIP MONCK: Sixth Avenue was the place that John Morris, I believe, found. It was a little upstairs office and we started to work. John immediately leapt into extending his agency contacts and working with Michael and I immediately contacted folks like Langhart, Steve Cohen, all those folks, and Steve made a stage design, as did Chris Langhart.

Steve's design was adventurous and I thought it was neat, so I decided that ought to be the one; John Morris, Michael, and myself decided that. I should have had the sense, honestly, to go with Langhart because Langhart has never had anything fall down, and it may not have been much more completed than Cohen's design, but it was simple enough—it was almost, as Langhart often is, too homespun. I don't think either of them were the correct choice, but we chose one and we went with one and it never got completed, but it was an interesting look.

CHRIS LANGHART: There was a competition, such as it was, that Michael had organized for what the stage ought to look like. And at that point I had seen some Japanese ice rink drawings, various cable structures with kind of an involuted cable with tangent pieces coming off of a spiral curve. I thought that was kind of exciting looking, and so I made a design that was related to a tension-structure kind of framework with a couple poles stuck up like a wishbone. There were these two involutes that came down on another, leaving a kind of an ellipse in

50

Steve Cohen (left),
John Morris

the middle. It was covered with a different color fabric.

They somehow came to the idea that I should make this model, and so it was made and I took it up there to their office. And that model just shocked them because I was not really in the Bob Dylan end of the music and I wasn't into heavy metal music. I really hadn't thought much about what the sensibilities of the people were at that time from the standpoint of the music-goer. I had worked in the Fillmore and I had seen these kind of audiences for a year or more. But it didn't occur to me that along with this kind of music Michael felt that there was a definite log cabin, woodsy, outdoors kind of idea, which definitely had to be part of the stage. He saw it like under a tree.

I didn't understand where he was coming from. I thought it was some kind of new festival of music and art, and so I was looking for something new. And I designed this modern, whiz-bang thing and they all just went, "Oh my God, what are we going to do with that?" They all decided it was really quite out of order, but I was concentrating on something that could be done.

CHIP MONCK: It was a competitive field at the moment and Langhart was competing against Cohen in the stage design and was fairly relegated to the back burner. The problem with Chris is that he can't be used properly, because his in-depth solution is so deep that he will get bogged into something, and he needs a force of fifteen people who do nothing more than run around with the wrench and the torch and the arc welder.

51

Mel Lawrence: On the other floors there seemed to be more of the real world, because they had to deliver talent, they had to make the deals, whereas we builders and designers and artists had a different thing. So their floor was contracts and schedules and that kind of thing. When I say "their" and "our" it wasn't like that really—it wasn't one against the other or separated philosophically.

Penny Stallings: Life in the office was fabulous. It was great for me because I come from a world where everybody punched the clock and was very straightforward and serious about their work and their families and their lives, very structured lives. And I came into that world where nothing was real, only it became more real than anything that I've ever done since. It was just this tremendous dream that actually came to pass. It was sort of like one of those drug reveries—*and then, man, we'll get all these people together and we'll have, like, every star, man, and it will go for three days . . . .* And it happened to come true. I think it was as much the time as anything else.

Penny Stallings

I had just come to New York from Dallas, Texas. I had just graduated from Southern Methodist University and had left Dallas to come and live with the person that I would marry many years later, Barry Secunda. He was managing the Electric Circus at the time in the East Village, and he had a high school friend who had been one of the site directors at Miami Pop, Mel Lawrence. And Barry negotiated the job for me because I was losing my mind in New York. I was just wandering the streets at the time because he worked all night. And slowly but surely I was becoming a night person, too, but with nothing to do at night except go and try and be heard over the music at the Electric Circus. I was very much out of place in New York. Very much a Texas girl, I had not found my way, to put it mildly, in the city. So, I became Mel's assistant and began working at a little office on Sixth Avenue, trying my best to be terribly efficient, not understanding at all what we were doing.

I was just a gofer at that point, basically—a college-educated gofer. I didn't have a clue as to what the point was, and actually didn't really believe it, either. If I did know I didn't buy it, because the office was filled with con men. There was absolutely no question that these guys were not for real, in my mind. John Roberts and Joel Rosenman had another office at that point. They were not there. But I wouldn't have had a lot of faith had I seen them, either. I think Michael was keeping the two factions apart. I don't understand to this day what the psychology was there, but they had an office uptown. And the only contact I had with those guys was when I would watch people forge their names. They would hold a check up to the window and forge John's name on another check. And that was really all I knew of John.

The guys there were and are guys with no specific talent or training other than making things happen. And at that time you could bullshit it, and it came true. It's not nearly so easy now in the eighties as it was in the sixties. Everyone there was long on hype and short on credits and skill. And I was very overeducated. I was just the opposite: with no experience, except I had worked all of my life in Texas at minimum-wage jobs. These were guys who just came in and kind of stirred things up. I remember Steve Cohen building a model stage out of cardboard, and he would kind of play with it as with a doll house. He moved the little pieces around. And for the most part the guys were very surly—at any given time anxious that they not be questioned about what they were doing there or about what they would be doing, because we were all faking it. You can fake it every day of your life, but this was a major fake with a lot of money involved.

JOHN MORRIS: It was everybody pulling in. Everybody had a friend. Everybody had a friend who could do something or put something together. A lot of the influence came from the experience that I had with the Fillmore. It was like you got up in the morning and you made a list of everything you could think of that we might need. And then everybody would have at the list and try to put something in. And even that early there was probably a feeling of—I don't think there's anybody who can say they trusted everybody else and thought it was all working together like a finely honed, well-oiled machine. There was a lot of personality and ego, and I was as guilty of that as anybody

53

else. But there were all sorts of different things going on.

Because there were four partners, there was no clear single person to do it, to be the director. Michael was the curly-headed—I mean, Langhart's the one that named him the "curly-headed kid." But Michael was the one with the vision and the idea and the waving of the fantasy. He probably, if anybody, understood what—or if it was anyone's dream or intention that we were aimed at, it was Michael's. And Michael's energy, no question. But he wasn't the single, sole boss. And John and Joel—Joel especially—were trying to run it on a business-like basis. So there was a—I don't want to say a conflict, although there was, but it was more of a mishmash.

STANLEY GOLDSTEIN: When I came up to New York, I had no real dollars in my pocket, so I had to live cheap and was sharing a hotel room in a crummy hotel on 49th Street with a drummer named Joe Gallivan. Neither of us had any money and it was really a sleazy hotel. Dollars weren't flowing in from Woodstock Ventures, and while things were coming together, the initial site was lost almost instantly upon my joining the organization. And it wasn't at all absolutely certain that there was something going on until there was a site. So I didn't rearrange my life or find a place to live; I just continued to live in that hotel. I was making a vast volume of calls and since the switchboard service was so crummy, I just went down and took over the switchboard and made my calls and received the calls and operated the place for a period of time. It was a little weird because I was in contact with some fairly high-powered people, talking to them about doing a fairly unique event, and that was going to take a great deal of money to put on. There was certainly no question about that in anyone's mind. And so I spoke to the fellow who had done all the electricity and all the lighting, for instance, for the Montreal World's Fair, who of course made a special trip to come see me. I don't know exactly what he thought, but he had to think that it was rather weird to be talking about spending hundreds of thousands of dollars while meeting in this sleazy hotel where I was the switchboard. Nevertheless, we moved forward from there.

JOEL ROSENMAN: I think Michael got good people. He wasn't sure, I think, whom he needed, and so he got maybe twice as many people as he needed and we paid maybe a lot more than maybe we had to pay. But I think it's to his credit that he put together a group of people who overkilled greatly what was necessary to do the project.

STANLEY GOLDSTEIN: There was no budget until Michael and I sat down in a hotel room one day and began sketching things out just shortly after bringing John Morris aboard. John tried to stage some kind of palace revolt and take over the gig. He said that Michael was incapable, that Mel Lawrence didn't know what was going on, but that he and this coterie of New York hotshots really had a handle on everything that had to have a handle on it. And, also, I was quite dissatisfied with what John and Joel were doing. They were incredibly concerned about the fact that the ticket printing costs were going to be so high, and they had found some cut-rate way to do this, which was immediately counterfeitable. After all the discussions, they still were not moving in a direction.

I had a general impression that we were not getting anyplace in terms of gathering the gig together. Organizationally, there was no organization. There was no delineation or definition of responsibilities and authorities—who was doing what and what it was that they were capable of doing. And that there was some momentum being developed. There was a staff being gathered together, and there had to be some kind of outline, some framework. And then John Morris staged this attempt to cut everyone out but him as the promoter and producer of the event. And so Michael and I went to a hotel room, what was then the City Squire Hotel. We took a room and worked through the day and night and drew up some organization charts. We put some names in the blocks and drew up a rough, rough budget. So rough— this was all done in pencil and paper in a hotel room after being up day and night for two days or something, working our way through this. I remember very well, we inadvertently misplaced a decimal point and wrote down "security" at $40,000 rather than $400,000. But that was the first budget cut that there was on the event.

But it wasn't at all absolutely certain that there was something going on until there was a site.

JOHN ROBERTS: The first thing that I think Joel and I noticed was that after a month of all this corporate-forming and office-getting and preplanning—planning the tone and the idea—the first problem Michael had been unable to solve was that he couldn't get a site. Michael had told us we had a site up near Woodstock, in Saugerties actually, but then we all went up to negotiate with the landholder, and he had absolutely no intention of letting us use his property for this purpose at all.

JOEL ROSENMAN: I think even the Train didn't shed any light for me on this partnership and on the relative capabilities of the people in it. But that first conversation with a party named Schaler, I think, up in Saugerties was the revelation for me. From that point on, I started being concerned about this project.

MICHAEL LANG: I went out with a friend of mine named Jim Young to find a site initially, before I met John and Joel. There were a couple of sites we found that were suitable and the thing started to grow in terms of what kind of audience we thought we'd have. And so the first couple of sites, in Woodstock, were not really suitable. And the first site we thought was really workable was one in Saugerties, about five hundred or six hundred acres alongside the Thruway, which was, actually, a perfect place for us; it still would be. So, we negotiated on that site for a while. And as time goes by, John and Joel came into the picture. It was owned by a guy who manufactured hot dogs, I think. Initially, they expressed willingness in renting it to us, and I think John and Joel went to close the deal and suddenly the deal disappeared. The guy decided he had heard something, or whatever, and just decided he didn't want to become involved at all.

JOEL ROSENMAN: The way John and I would work we would figure out,

55

"Well, what do we think we can get the property for? What are the things we really need? What can we give away in the negotiation?" Maybe we didn't do it as thoroughly as we do it now, but we did it to prepare for negotiations that way. We walked into the room and were essentially stonewalled and kicked out by this guy, who seemed to be amused by our request to rent his property. He had a little fun and then kicked us out. It was so different from what Michael had prepped us with that we thought we were dealing with a partner who might not be in the same time-space system that we were operating in on the planet earth. And I became concerned then about a number of things we had sort of assumed were "going down." That maybe they weren't ever going to go down as he had suggested. After that, John and I went into a kind of yellow alert—which became red alert later on.

MICHAEL LANG: That was really the first site we counted on. We never really got a site in Woodstock that seemed like it was going to work. There was one possibility, which was an abandoned golf course, but the access was just too difficult. And then we just searched the areas out from Woodstock—we went further and further out looking for a suitable place. We did some helicopter surveys and then we drove to whatever looked feasible.

I think John found the Mills site. I think they were riding back from someplace upstate and there was a sign along Route 17 that said HOWARD MILLS INDUSTRIAL PARK. I think that's how we found it.

JOEL ROSENMAN: We got a call about the Mills property. It was listed. It was being developed for an industrial park.

JOHN ROBERTS: We hopped in the car on Monday or something and drove up and met Howard Mills, who was a farmer, I think, who was turning his land into an industrial park. But before it was going to be industrialized, it was cleared; there was nothing on it. He thought it would make a perfect site for our folk festival.

Joel and I met Howard in his kitchen. He had a small, unpretentious home on the property. We told him that we were part of a group from New York that was thinking to put on a music-and-art fair that summer and that we were thinking in terms of twenty-five to thirty thousand people over a three-day period. He was interested in what kind of music we were going to be having there and what our financial bona fides were and would we clean up the property after—you know, practical questions related to our use of it.

JOEL ROSENMAN: It went exceedingly smoothly. It was the opposite of the reception that we had gotten on the Saugerties property. In fact, I was stunned by how easy it was to get land. I don't remember him being too concerned with what all we wanted to do with his property as long as when it was finished it would be suitable for continuing his project as the development of an industrial park. We talked about ten thousand dollars.

JOHN ROBERTS: Seventy-five hundred sticks in my mind. It may have been ten thousand.

JOEL ROSENMAN: As soon as he got the feeling that he was going to get this money for a very short period of time as a rental, he went right on to extolling the virtues of this land. And for us, these were virtues that we thought would be inescapable and just overwhelming.

JOHN ROBERTS: The land was not enormously attractive. It had enough size to it, and it was cleared, and it had pretty good access. It was flattish. It was not meadows rolling—dipping meadows and glens. There was no water that I recall. Maybe there was a stagnant pond somewhere. I remember stepping out and looking at it, and off in the distance you could see a shopping center. It was suburbia, but here was this rather nice tract of land.

JOEL ROSENMAN: There was power and water. The utilities were supplied, but I think there was aboveground power and it was smaller than what we eventually ended up with. It was two hundred acres. It had great access. He had planned this for an industrial park so—in fact, in retrospect, and I'm sure one of the reasons that Michael didn't like it, was because it wasn't remote enough. It wasn't enough of a remote retreat.

JOHN ROBERTS: Here it was April, and we were starting to sign acts, and we had to tell them where we were going to be throwing this event. And we were starting to plan the ads and buy advertising time. All of this had a certain momentum to it so we were not exactly in a buyer's market at that point in time, so we told Mills that we were interested, that we would have to consult with our partners. And we came back to New York and we told Michael about this. Michael, being frugal, of course immediately hired a helicopter and flew up and over the land.

MICHAEL LANG: I was horrified by it. It was as far away from the flavor and the feeling of what I thought it had to be as you could get. It was hard, ugly, cold. It did not feel relaxed; there was a lot of tension in the land. You know how you just walk into some pastoral scenes and they are beautiful and calming and open and you feel comfortable and at peace? This was the opposite. It was just ugly and dirty and it felt someone had just sort of ripped the land apart and left it. Taken what they wanted from it and left the debris. And I knew it had to feel a certain way for it to work. It was not something I could describe, but it was something I could recognize.

JOEL ROSENMAN: He pronounced it unfit, a bummer, a downer, and we can't use it.

JOHN ROBERTS: So we said, "O.K., fine, Michael, but at least it's the fallback position. I think we should set a date certain, and if we haven't gotten the land by such a date then we just make the best of this land." So Michael then proceeded to bring Stanley Goldstein up and Mel Lawrence and a couple of the other techies and they pronounced the land workable.

JOEL ROSENMAN: They liked it much better than Michael because it had

225 Radical Students Picket 8 Buildings at Columbia Univ.

Times
New York, N.Y.
March 26, 1969

57

already accomplished a lot of the things they were afraid they were going to have to do. We all agreed with Michael about the look of it, but we felt that we had less wiggling room than we had a month earlier or two months earlier, when we thought we could get any site we wanted.

MEL LAWRENCE: The site was pretty good. I would say the site, topographically, was beautiful, and logistically or trafficwise was located perfectly in a really good spot next to Highway 17, I think. And there was—maybe it could have been better, but we were going to try and politick like another exit or something for our purposes.

MICHAEL LANG: I gave in. I was pressured into it. Their arguments were not unreasonable—we needed to get going, we needed the site—and I felt fairly comfortable after talking with a bunch of the people working on staff that we could transform it into something that would be all right. I mean literally: we'd plant, reseed the whole area, and create a park where none existed. I was never sure enough of it politically to plant anything permanent. When we did our planning sessions for that site, I made sure that everything we were doing to the place could be moved—that the stage wouldn't be planted until all the permits were issued.

JOEL ROSENMAN: Michael continued to look for property because he was convinced that he could find a better piece of property than the Mills property and nobody was contradicting that because nobody was bananas over the Mills property; it was a bird in the hand. And I think that after a while he gave up looking because it was a nuisance for him to have to spend the time to go up there.

MICHAEL LANG: It never felt comfortable. It never really felt right. It never felt friendly. The town itself and the surroundings were kind of hostile, to say the least.

CHAPTER THREE

"I had kind of a hint that someone would think it funny to drop some acid and see the security chief freak out."
—Wes Pomeroy

WES POMEROY: In the summer of 1969, I had just recently left the federal government and started my own consulting business. And some guy named Stan called me and said they were going to put on this rock festival and it was three days of peace and music and wanted to know if I would be interested in heading up the security. And I told him no. But I told him I would be willing to try to find someone who would.

There were several guys I had in mind, and they were all busy. One was John Fabbri, who was then chief of police in South San Francisco out in California, later became chief of Fremont. An extraordinary guy; he died about ten years ago. Another was Ben Clark, who I think is now retired as sheriff of Riverside County. He looks like a real tough guy, but has a marvelous holistic concept of where he is and where law enforcement ought to be, and of peacekeeping. I checked around and I couldn't find anyone I really trusted. And since I was recommending, I wanted to be sure.

STANLEY GOLDSTEIN: I had asked a lot of questions of a lot of folks. I talked to some local police authorities and eventually worked my way around to the International Association of Chiefs of Police and had a talk with the head of the association, who gave me a list of names of people to contact. I was pretty direct in discussing what I felt were the criteria for the head of our public safety presence. In the meantime, I had worked my way through a lot of other possible sources. I talked to Pinkerton, talked to Burns, talked to all the private security agencies. I discovered who did security for conventions. Miami was a big convention town. I came from Miami, and I had certain contacts there. I contacted Rocky Pomerantz, the guy who was at that time the chief of police of Miami Beach. I pulled some other names out of the hat who were in the headlines. That was a time that there were conflicts all over and the names of chiefs of police were often in the news columns. Who managed conflicts? What towns didn't burn? You know, if it didn't burn, someone must have been doing something right. And if it did burn, how was that contained so it didn't spill and people weren't abused? It was library time and telephone call time.

But there weren't very many folks to whom you could speak who could address the concepts and the concerns with which we were attempting to deal and the attitudes that we had. I must have interviewed personally fifty high-powered guys and cut that to ten or twelve, then reduced those to three or four to go further with, and presented to Michael my conclusions.

MICHAEL LANG: The philosophy in all areas was to get the best people available, people who carried the most weight in whatever their spot

59

was. And who also understood what it was we were trying to do. In terms of finding a cop, it was sort of—I mean, those were pretty tricky times. And it had to be someone who had a good-guy credibility in the police world because we felt that less is more. We did not want to have any armed anything around, internally or externally. I went to every other big show in the country, and most of them had problems, and you could always see that there were confrontations set up. I mean, there was a squadron of guys with shields and bats and tear gas waiting to use them, and things like that went on. And it was kind of a game and everybody sort of got into the spirit of the game, and it wasn't really fun unless you got gassed. So I tried to arrange to avoid all that.

WES POMEROY: I was very interested in a couple of things. Most importantly was how they viewed the use of violence and control. I made sure that they didn't want security with guns and physical violence. And when I thought they were ready to do that, then I said, "O.K., I'll work with you because I believe in what you are trying to do." And I believe, generally anyway, that whether people act well towards each other or don't is a matter of a whole host of social contracts, most of them tacit, where they don't want to hurt one another, they don't want to victimize one another. I won't go into that; I can give you a whole philosophical treatise on that. But it's true. People see neighborhoods where there isn't a police car for days and there's no crime because people don't want to hurt each other.

STANLEY GOLDSTEIN: This was 1969. We were in the middle of a war in Vietnam. We were in the middle of a civil rights revolution. The youngsters were—I use the term advisedly, youngsters—but there was a vast awakening of some kind of political action, I think inspired by the civil rights movement. The police were in general considered the enemy. *Pigs* was the common parlance for police. New York was a hotbed of social action and reaction. The Yippies and the hippies and marches protesting the war, marches for civil rights, marches for gay rights, marches for women's rights, marches for the Pink Panthers and Black Panthers and White Panthers, and John Sinclair was in jail for possessing two joints or something. Only months earlier, Lyndon Johnson had divested himself of the presidency and Robert Kennedy ran for president. Norman Mailer and Jimmy Breslin ran for mayor and president of the City Council of the City of New York, respectively. They had buttons printed, black buttons with white lettering that said NO MORE BULLSHIT. It was an exciting time. The world was in great flux.

There was conflict everywhere you looked—there was Them and Us. Vast assumptions were being made as to who Them were and who Us were, who represented "the People," and who those people were. And certainly the police didn't show a lot of hesitancy in using their billy clubs in trying to enforce the rules of society that were being rejected and overturned, willy-nilly. They were the enemies, the enforcers of all of these discarded attitudes.

It was obvious on the face of it that Woodstock was going to be a traffic problem if anything approaching the numbers of people or even a lot fewer were coming. There was going to be a traffic problem. And it was to some extent the telling argument with people who didn't wish to deal with police, who wanted to ignore the police, to find some other way. Cops stand on street corners in the middle of the worst weather in the world and wave their wands and point the traffic around. That's what they do. I don't know why they are willing to do that, what that commitment is, but they do that for low pay in the middle of all kinds of horrible, horrible circumstances. And you need to have some of those people around, folks that you can depend on. And so, since no one seemed to be able to suggest anyone else to do that, it had to be cops, or at least folks that had that kind of background and training, that had those kinds of discipline.

WES POMEROY: I had been in law enforcement since 1942, twenty-seven years. I started as a California Highway Patrolman and had taken military leave in the Marine Corps for two and a half years during World War II. I came back to the Highway Patrol. After almost ten years I left the patrol and went to work for the San Mateo County Sheriff's Department, where they had a new sheriff and a reformed kind of an approach. I moved up through all the ranks. After eight years, I was the undersheriff, or the chief deputy in the county.

Bomb Plot Is
Laid to 21
Panthers

Times
New York, N.Y.
April 3, 1969

That was in 1960, when I became the undersheriff and it was a great time and a great place. San Mateo County is and was a rich county. The politics, whether liberal or conservative—it didn't make much difference—people had enough goodwill that they wanted to do good things. And so there were a lot of things going on. And of course, San Mateo County was the same as the rest of the United States in those years, and we had all kinds of challenges and opportunities and problems because of the emerging of a new reality in the civil rights movement. I've always felt, and I did then, that the police really ought to be at the forefront in that. They ought not to be dragged along by it. They're in a unique position in our society, and it's just essential that they be the leaders in what's happening out there.

Dick Gregory is a good friend of mine who put it so well then. He said, "If you're not careful, the cop is going to be the new nigger," because what happens is you get a school integration problem or housing or jobs, or whatever it is, and it's a problem of disenfranchised minorities trying to assert what they'd like to have. And then the police get involved because of the demonstrations and so forth. And if you're not careful, the clash between the police and the minorities—it becomes a police problem, which lets everybody off the hook, except the cops, who ought not be there in the first place. So what I said to people for years, whenever I had any influence over my commands, is, "Let's not let the Romans put us in the arena where you can't tell the Christians from the lions because it's not our beef. What we need to do is be more advocates with the people who we have so much in common with. We're out there with them twenty-four hours a day, seven days a week."

So that's what I'd done during my police career in the sixties. I was on a school board in a changing ethnic neighborhood. I was the president of a board that ran a halfway house for tough felons out of jail. The '64 Republican convention in San Francisco gave us a whole set of dynamics, and we ran that. Then Ramsey Clark offered me a job. He was attorney general under Lyndon Johnson. And so I went to work

Wesley Pomeroy

for him as Special Assistant for Law Enforcement Coordination. I was able to take the job because I was a lawyer also; I'd gone to night school and gotten a law degree and passed the bar. I was appointed by Johnson at Ramsey's recommendation as one of the three men to head up the new Law Enforcement Assistance Administration. And we got that thing cranked up, and then Nixon was elected. In April of 1969, I resigned and started this consulting business, and that's where, several months later, I met the people involved in Woodstock.

Oh yes. In 1968, I was the advance person for the Justice Department and the coordinator for the federal presence at both national political conventions—the Republic convention in Miami and the Democratic one in Chicago.

STANLEY GOLDSTEIN: I went down to Washington to visit Wes. I wanted to go to Washington anyway because I had been chasing again—sanitation and so forth. The Army knew about that stuff, and I wanted to get some advice from the Army about field conditions and how you keep from polluting water supplies.

Wes picked me up at Dulles Airport. I deliberately—well, this was a time Abbie Hoffman had just been on television wearing a flag shirt and had been blanked out on the air and there was a big deal being made. And so I went out and purchased a shirt that was blue with white stars all over it, so that when I walked off the plane I would be able to see how Wes reacted. He just went on. He was very straightforward, very direct. The shirt didn't faze him.

I outlined what it was that we were doing. We had a relatively brief conversation there at the airport, and then he took me into town and we continued that conversation. Of all the people with whom I spoke, he was the one who most grasped the concept. He was the one who understood most directly that we had a community-relations situation to deal with and that we needed someone who could be our face to the community who was not Michael Lang and who was not John Roberts and who could cover a lot of areas. And so it was immediately a structure and organization that made sense. Unlike others, he understood full well the concept of unarmed public safety and he didn't have any problems with that; that instead of being a *police* force it was going to be a *Please* Force—a disciplined force that knew that a crowd of that size presents, just by the sheer weight of numbers, a potential danger to itself.

WES POMEROY: Stan was this young man with—you get a sense of a lot of energy in him. I suspected he was idealistic, or at least espousing idealism. I always program for my natural, almost an instinctive, bias against New Yorkers. And I think I do it pretty successfully because if I didn't I wouldn't get through to a lot of decent folks. But Stan wasn't arrogant. And I thought it was an interesting idea. I just remember a lot of talking. I had to slow him down a little bit to make sure that I was understanding him. But it was a pleasant experience and I took him on face value and he meant what he said.

STANLEY GOLDSTEIN: I think Wes was in his late forties, but very youthful. Stocky, strong, a good listener, and one who had the ability to zero in on important points, to discard the nonessentials, and get right to the heart of matters. I arranged for Wes to come up and meet Michael.

WES POMEROY: I met Lang and John and Joel. Kornfeld didn't seem to be much of a presence one way or the other. And I liked what I saw. I liked John and Joel right away. These were really interesting guys— idealistic, all that sort of thing. They were smart; they were intelligent. They had a lot of big ideas that didn't scare them and they thought they could do something. I thought, "Well, yeah, maybe they can." And I kind of liked them. You don't see people like that very often. And you never know if it's real. But they were willing to try. They had a lot of bucks they were willing to put behind it, apparently. I didn't know anything about the financing at that time. And Michael seemed to be someone that they all respected.

> I don't know a damn thing about rock music. Well, a little bit. I traveled with Led Zeppelin after Woodstock. I was doing security. And it's not my kind of music, but I like music anyway and I get turned on by it. On that tour, the opening song was "Immigrant Song." When Robert Plant is starting off with that high-decibel thing and the whole place is shaking, I would be thrilled, too. But rock music is not my kind of music.

MICHAEL LANG: I was surprised that someone who was working for Nixon, I think, at the time, would have such an open mind about the politics of the time. He seemed less concerned with being judgmental and more concerned with being prudent. And really, I thought that was the key for me. Not so much that he agreed with what our politics were or anything else. His concern and his perspective was that these were still kids and people and this was still America. And he was very cool. He had a good overview, a good perspective on things, and seemed to get a kick out of what we were doing and it seemed to be impossible anyway. And that seemed okay with him. I mean, it wasn't so okay with him, but at that point it was okay with him.

WES POMEROY: I trusted the people there. One thing that kind of struck me, because I never thought about it before, was how young everybody was. You get used to looking for talent and ability only in older people. Well, these people didn't seem to wait around for that. It was a very exciting kind of dynamic. But I was still—I resisted any effort to make me look like something else, either. I remember saying, "I am what I am. And that's a plus. You don't want to have a hippie security director. He's not going to be doing anything for you. I'm a policeman. I may be a liberal policeman, but I have respect in the field and that's going to be a lot of plus for you." It wasn't an issue really. I wasn't sure if it was, but I had kind of a hint that someone would think it funny to drop some acid and see the security chief freak out.

I got the word out very clear: Don't do this; it wouldn't be funny. I wouldn't mind personally if we were in a big vacuum someplace, but it's not smart. Besides, there's a lot of money tied up in this and we don't want to risk it. I used the same argument about don't be smoking joints all over the place because some deputy sheriff will make his reputation by knocking this thing off.

STANLEY GOLDSTEIN: I took Wes up to the Mills site and looked at roads. I think he was pretty much intrigued by what it was we were doing and what the attitude was as expressed by me, and wanted to do it. It would give him an opportunity to demonstrate some of what he really believed in terms of the way that police and the community could interact and relate to one another and what were the important and essential elements, and I think it offered an intriguing kind of challenge to him. Wes was not limited in his imagination. He could conceptualize and was intrigued.

WES POMEROY: I was very comfortable in my role. They were comfortable in who I was and it was a very exciting thing to do.

I brought some people on board. I had Lee Blumer as my assistant, who was a very energetic and talented gal. They called her secretary. I didn't know anything about her except they said she had been a secretary to Bill Graham at the Fillmore East for about a year at least, and knew her business. She knew a lot of things I didn't know. They said, "Here is your secretary," and it turned out she was a highly talented person, knew a lot, and was able to function as a secretary very well. But she was more than that. She was just a damn good executive assistant. She had a phone in each ear. She did a lot of business on the phone; I don't know how she did it. And full of energy, a lot of hyper-energy.

LEE BLUMER: They paid me two hundred dollars a week, which for 1969 was good money. I mean, it wasn't a fortune, but it was for a secretary, or whatever I was; I was never a secretary, because I couldn't type. But I was like some administrative assistant at that point. So, two hundred dollars a week, plus they were paying all the other expenses that we could supposedly invent. I mean, we didn't know that at the time, but that was what it worked out to be. I hate to say this, but they were paying for my Tampax. I mean, I didn't spend anything of my own money all summer.

WES POMEROY: I got John Fabbri to start giving his time at so much per day. He was a tremendously talented guy, and he did things well that I didn't do. I never bothered to learn all the technical aspects of some things that I need to have done because other people could do them. And he just was a very talented guy.

I brought Don Ganoung on board, who was an Episcopal priest and I met him on the line at the '64 convention, because he was the head of the Christians for Social Action. We had become good friends and I trusted him. We called him an executive assistant. At the beginning, his role was to help us get permits. And he turned the collar

Thousands March for Peace in Cities Across the Nation

*Post
Washington, D.C.
April 6, 1969*

64

around when he needed to, that sort of thing. And it was to give an air of respectability to what we were doing. Also, he had quite a background. Before he was in the priesthood he had been, I think, a warrant officer with a criminal justice bachelor's degree in the CID, the Army's Criminal Investigation Department, during Korea. So he had a lot of wide range, and he also had this ability to understand the holistic dynamic of social interaction under stressful conditions. He understood all of that. He was able to cut across at his priesthood ecumenical lines and other things. He was a humanist and a decent guy and smart.

STANLEY GOLDSTEIN: Don was a unique character. He has since died at an early age of a heart attack. Don couldn't seem to decide where he properly belonged in life. He was a priest and he was a cop and he kept going back and forth between these two professions. He was an Episcopal priest and represented the church. I don't know the exact title, but the essence of it was ministering to youth and the disenfranchised—the Hispanic community, the black community. And he was a cop. He had been a cop for a while, then became a priest for a while, then he took a leave of absence from the church and became a cop for a while, and became a priest for a while.

LEE BLUMER: Don was special. I'm really sorry Don's dead. We didn't know anybody else like Don that summer because Don had hung out with Bishop Pike, the Episcopal priest who later died in the desert; he

Lee Blumer

65

Don Ganoung

was his administrator. And Bishop Pike was out there in another place. Pike was not your average Episcopal bishop; he was very metaphysical. And Don was defrocked somehow—he drank, he was defrocked; I don't know what happened. He may have told me and it was probably less significant than he thought it was, but it never stuck. But he gave it up and he never could forgive himself for giving it up. He really had a calling that he couldn't quite satisfy in the real world. We loved each other very much. I mean, we really came to love each other that summer. At one point I even entertained the notion that he should be my boyfriend, but that wasn't right. We just loved each other. Because we had just gotten so close; the experience was so, you know, forceful. And also, because he was so sad, and I'm so compelled towards tragedy. He just dragged me right in.

WES POMEROY: I arrived in New York and went to the office we had near Greenwich Village before going up to the site. I think we were all a little uncomfortable with that first site. We were trying to make it something it wasn't, and John and Joel thought that there was an overpass that had to be completed or it was going to be a disaster. And they had thought they knew people in Albany that were going to get that thing going and all cured and it would have helped a lot. But it still didn't feel right. I hear people talk about vibes and I don't talk about vibes, but I know it's the same thing. If it doesn't feel right and you're not comfortable with it, it's not right. I trust that kind of feeling I have in myself. But we started working.

66

LEE BLUMER: I remember walking off the property—I was pacing the property to figure out maps. I mean, it was that kind of silly stuff. I was trying to figure out what the perimeters of the property looked like. We—Don and Wes and I—were trying to get the physical lay of the land, how were going to secure it. We were like cowboys.

• • • •

STANLEY GOLDSTEIN: As a group of very limited size—the group being the producers, promoters, and the direct employees—we felt that there was a combination of needs in addressing the folks that were going to be coming to this event. And one of them was that we needed a communication interface with the crowd; some means of addressing what our interests and philosophies were—pardon the use of so grandiose a term. And just stepping aside from that, I think that was one of the major reasons for the success of the venture in those terms. There was, amongst some of us anyway, this very real concern for addressing our audience, making them feel comfortable, welcome, safe. I was not part of the 18-year-old crowd, but certainly I was not part of the norm of society, as it were. We were all to a certain extent outlaws. Not criminals, but outlaws anyway. The language was different; so much of it was appearance. Two people saying exactly the same thing, but one of them in a necktie would create an atmosphere that wouldn't work. We were very concerned with what it was we were saying and how we presented that in atmospherics.

We knew certainly that most of the crowd would be urban, most of whom probably had never spent a night under the stars, who had no idea how to survive or what to bring to an outdoor event that was going to be night and day. We had to demonstrate how to survive under those circumstances and maintain an attitude. It was obvious as well, because it was endemic to the culture, that there would be a lot of drugs around, and there would be a lot of people who couldn't handle whatever it was that they were going to take. And we had to find some means of addressing that problem, and doctors were not the answer. And so, we felt very strongly that we had to find a group that had its own integrity, that was large enough to be the core of our direct relationship with the people who came, who were a part of the culture, who understood the problems and how to relate to them and address them in very real ways.

It was Michael Foreman who raised the name of the Hog Farm, which rang a responsive bell with me. He knew that at least some of the group was in the area—in New York City—of which I was not aware. I called Howard Smith of the *Village Voice*, figuring that if anyone would know how to find them, Howard would know, which was the case. I arranged to meet Gravy—who at that time was not known as Gravy; he was Hugh Romney—and then went to a meeting with the balance of the group that was in town in a loft downtown. I showed up—and this was prior to my getting together with Wes—but in the same way that I costumed for Wes, I costumed for the Hog Farm. I wore a white shirt, formal slacks, and I remember carrying a business-like Wall Street briefcase. And I got together with this group of people in a semi-confrontational type of meeting.

ROTC Foes Seize Harvard Hall

Globe
Boston, Mass.
April 10, 1969

67

WAVY GRAVY: The Hog Farm was in New York City, the Cement Apple, our destination of choice when we uprooted and left California doing this traveling show across the free world. It turned out we got busted for a quarter-gram of marijuana ashes in Montrose, Pennsylvania—a little house of students that the Living Theater pointed us to, and we went in there and they thought it was the big dope drop. And we were surrounded by hundreds of police. Of course, we had nothing, traveling in a caravan of eight painted buses, but they searched and searched and searched until they found a dusty bag, and in the bag was a pipe that some hitchhiker had left on the bus. And they scraped it, woke up a guy sleeping in the back, said, "What's this?" And he sneezed and they arrested him for destroying evidence, and they scraped it again and took away that guy and the registered owner. They were put in the Dallas State Penitentiary in Pennsylvania. And so we were in New York attempting to pay lawyers to spring them. We were doing everything. We were doing security at the Electric Circus. We were tearing down walls and redoing lofts and baby-sitting and anything that came up that we could get bucks for.

So we're in New York and this guy Stan shows up looking like Allen Ginsberg on a Dick Gregory diet. He shows up at the kitchen table, which was enormous. We're famous for long kitchen tables that

Wavy Gravy

68

occasionally disappear into sight lines. And he says, "How would you guys like to do this music festival in upstate New York?" We had lived in campsites for years and years and years and in buses and were very good at survival. We said, "Well, we're going to be in New Mexico. It's a great idea, but like Bob Croppin said, 'Cities should be built on one side of the street,' and we're evacuating." And Stan says, "Well, that's all right, we'll just fly you in in an Astrojet." And we suggested he take another—we were smoking flowers at the time—and offered him a few more of those. We just thought, "Oh, God, another loony."

BONNIE JEAN ROMNEY: It was really humorous because we were raiding the backs of grocery stores for thrown-out vegetables and if we didn't have our hundred-pound bag of rice we would have starved to death. And we were very far from a world where a hundred of us would be given a plane ticket. It was really amusing. But this guy was here in the midst of us and we sort of just said, "O.K., sit down and party with us. Sure, buddy. What chemical have you taken this weekend?" That was kind of the way we treated him. But he was a very persistent fellow. And he kept talking to us and he seemed to be completely ready to participate in what we were then doing at the level that we were doing it too. So he wasn't just somebody who didn't fit in. He walked right in and started playing with us. And so as we got to know him, we started listening more and more to his fantasy and sort of incorporating the possibility that even that far-out weirdness could be real.

STANLEY GOLDSTEIN: Woodstock was a profit-making venture, and some members of the Hog Farm couldn't believe that I was quite sincere about what I was saying our interest was. They assumed this had to be some sort of a capitalist rip-off of the culture. And in the same kind of vein, they didn't do things for money; I wouldn't let them do it otherwise. This *was* a capitalist venture. We intended to make money, but we intended to make money our way. There were certain things that had to be done and that we were prepared to do them because we thought they were the right things to do. But we had every intention of making money and that people were not going to work for free.

We were asking them first of all to be our interface with the crowd. Secondarily, to provide certain specific services. I presented it to Wavy—I remember it well, and Gravy has subsequently written of it—that if we succeeded in gathering together one hundred or two hundred thousand people in any particular place, crowds are volatile and, as I said before, they present a danger to themselves. If a hundred thousand people all suddenly start moving in any particular direction at any time for whatever reason, someone could get trampled, people can be hurt, aside from property damage and so forth. And we well knew that tear gas and mace and such things were not the answer, that Jeeps with barb wire and machine guns were not the answer. What was the answer? I did not know what the answer was.

Gravy was the only one who came up with a reasonable alternative. His suggestion—it had something to do with twenty pretty girls in T-shirts and a couple of truckloads of chocolate cream pies and seltzer bottles. And it was the most rational suggestion that anyone had made, and was within the attitude of the event.

Jury Finds Sirhan Guilty

*Post
Washington, D.C.
April 17, 1969*

69

The conversation went very directly to such things as, "Well, people are going to come who aren't going to have tickets. A lot of people live on the streets or crash around. We need to address those matters." And the Hog Farm was right there—the idea of a free kitchen and being prepared to feed the crowd and care for the needs of those who didn't get through the fence or who didn't have tickets was all part of that conversation and discussion. The size of the group—the fact that there would be drug situations that had to be dealt with—that they were not a police force—that they had an obligation to themselves to be true to their own attitudes and ideas and if there was conflict we could discuss these things. But very clearly, we were what we were and we were hiring them to do a specific job. That was real, that was contractual, and we had to understand that.

There were other concerns: showing people how to survive, digging fire pits, acquiring wood, setting up a campgrounds area. We would need an advance crew to come in and prepare the campgrounds area. The Hog Farm was very concerned about the picking up of garbage after the event. It was part of the understanding that there had to be an environmental consciousness and the area had to be cleaned up, and they wanted to do that.

We reached a kind of common intent, I think, with some concerns on both sides: their concern that we really were sincere and that this could happen and that we weren't ripping them off and so on and so forth. And our concern that they really could and would be able to fulfill an agreement. And there were folks there who simply thought that I was a great con man and that they were being sucked in and that it was a grave mistake to listen any longer or discuss it any further.

We didn't necessarily make specific arrangements, because I had to go back and talk to Woodstock Ventures, and the Hog Farm had limited presence at the meeting; there were other people who had to be spoken to. They wanted to get out of New York City. They were there only because someone had gotten busted, and they were there trying to get the money together to make someone's bail and fines and so on and so forth. They were going back to New Mexico or wherever and had other things to do. So there had to be future discussions. And I spoke to other groups as well, trying to find some alternatives. If they were not going to be in town, I preferred to work with a group that lived and operated in this area. My recollection is that we still didn't have a site at that time, or that we were about to lose a site, so the gig itself was somewhat up in the air. We didn't yet have a lot of the staffing done; the initial conversations had not yet taken place with Wes and some of these other folks. There were a lot of things up in the air, but we had at least an intent of trying to put something together.

BONNIE JEAN ROMNEY: I made an agreement with him to be our phone contact person. Which meant that at some point I had to hustle a vehicle or hitchhike into a place where there was a pay phone at certain times and stand there and make arrangements with him. I was sort of an administrative type of person in the middle of this wonderful zoo that we were living in. And so I ended up becoming very close friends with this guy, who went back to New York. And we would deal from roadside pay phone to his office.

Tom Law: I was living in the mountains of northern New Mexico. And had actually been sort of a liaison person for the Hog Farm just because I knew Hugh Romney, who is now Wavy Gravy, and had known the Hog Farm people from its inception and always had a lot of fun with and respect for them. A friend of mine and I had been sort of instrumental in getting them out of L.A. and into buses and out to New Mexico, where we had spent a year or so traveling around New Mexico doing free-form environmental shows anywhere and everywhere we felt like it. And even though I had long hair, I grew up in a family that was full of cops and my father was a detective for the sheriff's department.

Bonnie Jean Romney

I sort of knew how to relate to people and I always had a great fondness for what was going on with the counterculture. And I was a part of it but I was also the kind of a person that wanted to help nurture that kind of spirit at the time because, as you may know very well, it was a very bad time for America and I considered myself very driven by the purest spirits of what America was. I really was brought up to be sort of your right-on kind of American believer. Before then I had gone to Europe and I traveled around the world and my eyes had been opened many years before. And I knew about Vietnam since 1962; I knew what was going on. So in the light of what was going on with the country, many of us had retreated to the hinterlands; that's what eighty-two hundred feet in the southern Rocky Mountains was. And the Hog Farm was out there, and I sort of was the person who would talk to the police and talk to the local officials and try and tell them that "Really, these funny-looking people are quite fine. Let them do a few things and don't get in their way and you'll see everything is good." And sure enough, we had a number of really interesting events out in New Mexico and in that general area.

STANLEY GOLDSTEIN: In mid-June, I went to New Mexico to finalize the arrangements and to satisfy my own feelings. Wes knew a gentleman named Jim Grant, who was the head of the Crime Commission for the State of New Mexico, an associate or acquaintance of his, someone that he knew and whose opinion he respected.

The occasion was that the Hog Farm was going to be getting together with a few other groups of people for a summer solstice celebration in Aspen Meadow outside of Santa Fe, and that seemed like a good time to get together, see how life was conducted out in the field. So I jumped on a plane and went out.

WAVY GRAVY: We were having a summer solstice celebration—summer solstice being very sacred to the *hip-eye* tribe—and it was also just after Ken Kesey had shown up with all this beer with screw-on tops and they had just invented screw-on tops, so it never occurred to us that he could unscrew the tops and electrify the beer. And we had planned to do this bus race.

STANLEY GOLDSTEIN: I landed in Albuquerque and, to the best of my recollection, I rented a car, drove to Santa Fe, went into town, went to Carmen Anderson's store—Carmen being a lady about which there is a great deal of information to be spread; unfortunately she is dead now. A marvelous person. Carmen wound up coming as one of the concessionaires, selling Mexican handicrafts, and brought with her flower dolls that are generally stuffed with candy—piñatas. And so she had a booth with piñatas and other things, which, of course, when the rain came was utterly destroyed. And so she cried for about five minutes and then started serving food. Carmen was pretty neat. Anyway, I saw Carmen, got directions, went out to Aspen Meadow, found the group, hung around for a while, came back down, met Jim the next day. I stayed there Friday night, met Jim on Saturday, and we went back up Saturday afternoon.

There were a number of details to be settled, specifically how many people, what kind of dollars were involved; the chartering of the airplanes was going to cost us as much as a major chunk of wages would have. And so we had to reconstruct and consider what the financing was going to be. There was the site situation going on, which meant that our plans were not as fixed as we initially thought they might be. And Wes wished to have this evaluation, and I had no reason to hesitate in proceeding along those lines.

TOM LAW: We didn't necessarily think that our presence at Woodstock was a good idea, but Stan was such a genuine and persuasive person. There was a lot of dissension about whether we should even contemplate doing such a thing. They offered to pay us for our time and energy, which was an interesting offer we rarely got. And we sort of as a group tossed it around. I wasn't per se part of the Hog Farm; I was kind of a field marshal for Wavy Gravy. I would sort of expedite

Censors Muffle Smothers Bros.

Rolling Stone April 19, 1969

72

things and get things going. And so would the people I was with. But I wound up being the person that came along with them.

STANLEY GOLDSTEIN: There were just an enormous number of people up there in Aspen Meadow. It was not just a Hog Farm situation, or just other communal groups who had gathered together. One of the super-swamis had elected to come up with a band of followers and it may have been—I don't know where the crosscurrents were. The folks from the communal groups who knew the swami wanted to do some things with him, involved him, and got him to come up. In any event, somehow the swami seemed to have had an advertising campaign out and so there were a lot of folks who came to see the swami. And, indeed, on Saturday the swami married—I'm not positive whether it was Saturday or Sunday—the Swami married Tom Law and Lisa in a Hindu ceremony—I guess it was a Hindu ceremony, though I'm not certain—and about six or seven or eight or ten or twelve other couples.

I got up there Friday evening and had come relatively ill-prepared. I had not really planned on camping out or staying out, and wound up deciding to do so. Some of that may have had something to do with the fact that I may have found it a little difficult to leave that evening. The thought of driving down the mountainside in the dark given my state of mind was not a great idea. I remember lying on the ground out there near a fire while Paul Foster danced, what seemed to me at that time, almost maniacally. The picture I have in my mind is almost of that famous Lautrec poster of the can-can girls with the man's silhouette in front of that, and that just went on for hours and hours and hours, and folks dancing and getting high and dancing and dancing and dancing all night long. Very little real conversation.

I went down the next day and got Jim, or Jim got me or something like that. We went back up and spent a major portion of the day. We were there for what later became the famous bus race. I don't know if you are familiar with it. It was exciting, it was exotic.

WAVY GRAVY: Well, actually it started out—I think there was a woman, a couple of people, that had been exposed to bubonic plague and I'm sitting on top of the bus with Kesey and some cop runs up and hands me this note, and I'm tripping, right? I look at these two words: BUBONIC PLAGUE. And down into my DNA, "Holy mackerel! What are we dealing with here?" So the idea was that we would all drive the buses and try and find them, and get them inoculated. But then the cops came running up saying, "It's all right. They found them! They found them!" So we had these buses all revved up and we figured we'd just go around the place and see who won. And everybody had to put stuff up, like, you had to risk something as your entry fee.

STANLEY GOLDSTEIN: The meadow was filled with sinks. I don't know what it was. It may have been vegative matter that rotted out big stumps underneath. Large chunks—fifteen feet long and the same wide—of earth that just collapsed down five, eight, ten, twelve feet. And they were all over this place like potholes going down Broadway or Seventh Avenue. And so Gravy had thought that the thing to do was to send the buses out in individual and timed-lap competition. And eventually it was decided that it was going to be an all-out race of these mad schoolbuses painted and covered with people out of their minds, berserk, hanging on them, racing up and down this meadow with all these other crowds of people. It was an extraordinary event.

Anyway, Jim and I spent the afternoon together and I understand, though I don't remember ever seeing it, that he wrote a letter back in which he had some reservations. He was not unfamiliar with the Hog Farm. When Wes had spoken to him originally he had known of them and known of some interesting good works things that they had done, and he was somewhat disappointed when we got up there and, as I understand, he later wrote a letter in which he had some things to say about the fact that the campgrounds were not well managed and that it was somewhat scuzzy. And he was right. It was not well managed, it was somewhat scuzzy, but the fact was as well that it wasn't a Hog Farm gig. But that's neither here nor there.

BONNIE JEAN ROMNEY: We were interested in Woodstock for the purest of reasons. I don't really know how to say it without sounding foolish. We were very interested in sort of our whole generation coming to operate in a more loving way with each other. And we had been raised in the fifties, most of us, where it was pretty repressive and the police were pretty mean. The Hog Farm spent a lot of time traveling across the country just going into neighborhoods, introducing ourselves to the Episcopalians and the straight folks, and then introducing ourselves to the left-wing folks and saying, "We are harmless to all of you. Let's get together and party. Do you have a rock 'n' roll band? Do you do birdcalls? We've got a light show in a tent. Let's have some fun." And that's sort of what we were doing. And somehow, we managed to keep eating and buy gas while we did all of this. So we saw the opportunity to do that on a large scale and make the planet we thought a friendlier place, a safer place, a place where there was more cooperation, more lovingness. And I think most of us still feel exactly the same way about why we do what we do.

SDS Presses Campaign to Infiltrate Industry

Post
Washington, D.C.
April 21, 1969

74

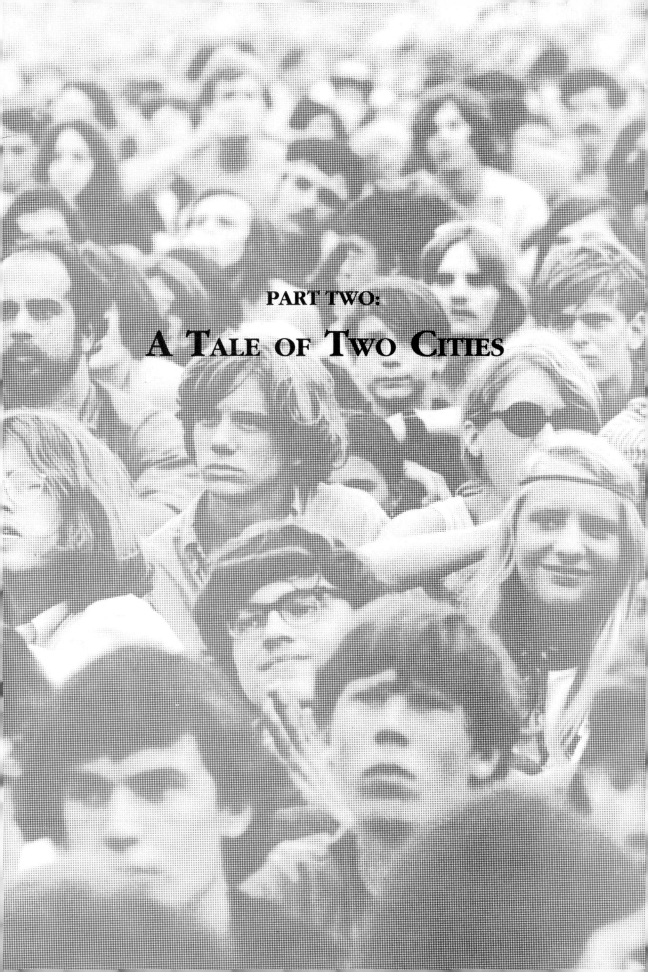

PART TWO:

A TALE OF TWO CITIES

• CHAPTER FOUR •

"It was horrifying for me, horrifying.
Because I had to cook for these people."
—*Carol Green*

MEL LAWRENCE: In Wallkill, we set up operations in a barn and the barn had a hayloft where I made my office. The reason I made it up there was because there was a great window so I sort of looked out on things. And downstairs we set up these big tables. I believe Joyce Mitchell got us this furniture on the East Side of New York. One day a big truck arrived with all these desks and everything. It was a nice working space, it really was. And Penny was there and myself and some guy we hired—I forget this guy's name—but what I wanted was a topographic diorama of that site and he said, "I've gone to architectural school. I know how to make that." And he started to make this giant diorama thing. Some friends from the Miami Pop Festival came up to work. The Miami Pop Festival supplied a bunch of connections to Woodstock: Bert Cohen, Michael Foreman, Chip Monck, Stanley, and others. And along came Linda—we called her Linda Pinda Dinda, but I forget her real name—and she had met a guy at Miami Pop and they were together, and when Linda came to work, he came. And he was one of those guys who cleared land. That's the first thing we had to do—clear the land and do horrible things like take down poison ivy and stuff.

We had the topographic map and we were making our diorama and we had our stage position, we had our facilities position, the trouble areas. We built a bridge over this sort of stream, a wide bridge. And the next thing you know, we started getting it together, cutting down grass. It was a beautiful site because the condition was good and we were ready.

PENNY STALLINGS: I would just sort of walk around with Mel and take notes. I wanted to work but I had no idea what kind of contribution to make at that point. And mostly I was just trying to soak up what was going on and trying to at least be able to answer questions about it. And at that point, every sort of semi-famous scene-maker in the Village— in the world—showed up. They all came; they all smelled it. And that was delightful because a lot of times they were people you've read about or people that wanted to be read about. There was just a tremendous amount of psychodrama played out with everybody kind of auditioning for a part to play. And it was really fun.

One person who was really great—I don't know what's happened to him—but his name was Tom Edmonston. A very handsome guy who would describe all of the magical environments that he was going to build and create for the festival and one of them involved a large globe that everyone would touch and it would pulsate and it would be a communal experience. You know, it was that kind of stuff. And perfumed pools and things that couldn't have been built under any circumstances, and certainly couldn't have been used by anything

77

resembling the crowds that showed up. I mean, there was just no way. But it was fabulous. There was a lot of that, ". . . and then we'll do this, and then we'll do that," with each thing bigger than the next. And people just coming and going, with no one having any idea of what actually should be done.

RONA ELLIOT: After the Miami Pop Festival, which ended in December of 1968, I decided to take a trip to Europe by myself. It was good old backpacking days and so I went to Europe. I went to France and I visited my family. I went to England and I went to Spain. I decided to hook up with a girlfriend of mine who was also traveling and I met her in Morocco where we were two nice Jewish girls dumb enough to be traveling alone. I mean, we really had amazing adventures. And she had a sort of a boyfriend who worked with the Peace Corps in Algeria, and so we decided to go to Algeria, which was really crazy for two Jewish girls in 1969. And there we were in Algeria and I got a telegram from Mel Lawrence, one of the other people I worked with at the Miami Pop Festival, that basically said, "Come home. Festival in upstate New York." And my intuition said, "You should really do this." So really within a day or two I flew to New York City and found myself driving to upstate New York.

I pitched Michael on doing the local and community public relations. I had background in promotion, public relations, radio music—broadcast side of things—and Michael agreed, and I think I

Rona Elliot

was making what I thought was a lot of money. What was a lot of money then was about a hundred seventy-five dollars a week.

My own job was dealing with local radio stations, local newspapers, local TV. I don't remember much of it other than speaking to local community groups, and I regret to say that I lost this wonderful thing, this diploma. I spoke to the Elks club or the Kiwanis club about why this festival would be beneficial to their community; in retrospect, I'm screaming thinking about that. You know, a twenty-two-year-old girl standing up in front of the Kiwanis club or the Elks club, whichever it was, explaining why it would be beneficial to their community. It was a riot. Little did we possibly anticipate what was really going on.

PENNY STALLINGS: I cannot emphasize to you how little was known about how to do a festival, and certainly not by these people. Everybody was trying to accumulate enough jargon to be able to fake it as well as they could. And when Lang would show up, you'd just sort of go into a spiel of some sort. He just would sit quietly and people would try and sound like they knew what they were talking about. And I can assure you that Mel, who was the senior person at that point, knew nothing about this stuff. He knew about promotion and he knew how to get some good people in to do things, but the entire construction crew was middle-class kids who were on summer vacation, you know, who maybe could hammer a nail in something. Until Chris Langhart from the Fillmore showed up, there was no plumbing, none of those things existed.

STANLEY GOLDSTEIN: Mel had, at his festival at Gulfstream Park, done an extraordinary job of decorating the premises by throwing money at the University of Miami, underwriting projects that the students might not otherwise have been able to undertake—enormous sculpture and so forth. There were nine-foot-high Blue Meanies behind hedges, and other Beatles imaginary characters sitting out in the parking lots. And to break up the unbroken expanses of macadam, he commissioned artworks. There were a couple of replicas of open half-pint cardboard milk containers that were laying on their sides with the spouts open, so that thirty, forty people could walk inside and get into the shade. This was all at Gulfstream Park. So he now had an intimate relationship with the art department at the University of Miami—Bill Ward and others. So Mel again contracted to bring in this group of art students and instructors from the university to sculpt and to prepare the grounds.

BILL WARD: We all got along very well in Miami and they promised me money and actually came up with it, and we went out and bought materials. We bought metal and plywood and paint and stuff and the kids got interested, and myself and a guy named Ron Liis, who was also teaching at the university, got interested in it, and we built some stuff. After it was all over with, Mel and I continued to stay in contact. Mel called and said, "Big festival. See if you can find all of your sculptors and people there and get an art crew together," which I did. And then I guess Jeannie and I and Ron and Phyllis Liis all flew up to see this thing that was going to happen.

Princeton Will Admit Women

Times
New York, N.Y.
April 21, 1969

79

MEL LAWRENCE: We gave them the jobs, four of them—Bill and Jean Ward, and Ron and Phyllis Liis. And then they were going to pick up people. That's fuzzy to me because—it was like people would arrive when they had to. If we needed a lumberjack, a guy would walk in, say, "Here I am, I'm from Massachusetts. I'm into lumber, man." That's the way it was. It was kind of an organic crew.

CAROL GREEN: I was living in Pennsylvania with a guy named Steve and we were kind of looking for our next thing. We'd lived in New York; he had been an usher at the Fillmore East. I had met Steve Cohen and Chip Monk and Josh White at a festival; a friend of mine was a roadie for Country Joe and the Fish. And I got friendly with Steve Cohen and he was real nice to me.

I remember going up with Steve to New York to go out to Chip Monck's house—I didn't know who Chip Monck was—out in the Hamptons, and then we went to the Fillmore East to get money and had breakfast, with Bill Graham serving us orange juice. Anyway, Cohen liked me, liked my cooking, was trying to think of a way to get me into his festival, and said he designed this wonderful stage for this gigantic, outrageous festival. It would be a great way to spend the summer—get out of the city, get out of whatever you're doing. String beads and things like that, odd jobs, and this is going to be wonderful. And I could be the cook for the people who were going to crew it, and my boyfriend could work with Cohen on the stage crew.

So we were traveling around in a Volkswagen bus with paisley—literally, paisley—curtains, and I remember on June 16, driving up from Philadelphia to Middletown and following directions in this sleepy little countryside to a psychedelic mailbox; I think Penny had given those directions. We got there right around sunset—we found the psychedelic mailbox with no other identifying marks or scars—pulled in, there was this barn, and out in the middle of the field there was a horse running free and Jean Ward trying to operate a tractor.

BILL WARD: We got a David Brown tractor, because Jean and I both had raced cars at this point and David Brown was the one who made the Aston-Martin race cars. So we found a tractor made by David Brown and we said, "That's for us." Jeanie was out there operating the mower.

PENNY STALLINGS: I found a role model at the festival in Jean Ward. And as I saw her do all of the things that the men did, and in many cases better than they did, that's when I thought—this is prefeminism, pre-anything, the Stone Age—that's when I began to think that's what I want to do. I want to be as crucial to this operation as I see her being because, in fact, she really did a great deal of Mel's job. She drove the tractor. She used the posthole digger. She built the booths. She commanded a little group of longhairs who built these jerry-built booths. And that's when I began to say, "O.K., that's it. That's what I'm going to try and do here." And slowly but surely I began accumulating some bit of knowledge that only I had, and consequently would make me important in a small way.

WES POMEROY: The person I remember working harder and longer than

NFL, AFL to
Merge Into
One League

*Sunday Star
Washington, D.C.
May 11, 1969*

80

Jean Ward

anybody else was Bill Ward. He and his wife Jean were up there and they were working morning to night. They really cared about what they were doing, you could tell that. And they didn't take time out for any kinds of relaxation and weren't sitting around rapping when other people were rapping. They were working like they didn't have enough time to do everything that they wanted to do and kind of a feeling that if they had a whole year, it wouldn't have been enough time, because they wanted it to be perfect. I never talked to Bill except to say hello; he's not much for small talk. He was too busy. But I remember being very impressed with him and with his wife, too. They were obviously a team.

LEE BLUMER: The very first part of June, Penny and I and a group of I think eight or nine people went to the Rosenbergs' in Bullville. And it immediately became surreal. I mean, we got out of the car and it was already surreal. It was in a bungalow colony with a bunch of old Jewish people, and I knew exactly what that was because I had been raised in all that. But there was Penny from the South and there were other people who were virtually thrust into Mars. It was really bizarre.

MEL LAWRENCE: I used to go up there as a kid to visit my aunt and cousins. I was real young, I remember that, and we would take out the car—I lived in Brooklyn—we'd take out the car and drive up there and visit the Rosenbergs. It was like a dairy with dairy food and it was kind of a health farm in old Jewish days. And I remembered that it was in this same area, so I called a relative and I said, "What was that place?" and they said, "It was Rosenbergs'." So I went up there, I think me and Penny, and we just talked our way into renting all their bungalows.

I don't know what I told them; I just made it up on the spot,

81

whatever it was. I just talked. "We're having"—I can imagine what I did tell them—"we're having a big show, like, it's a big music show and these people are coming from out West to help in a big art festival. And these people are artists and these people all are coming from New Mexico and they are going to be staying here." Not anything about that they were Hog Farmers or freaks, of course. They discovered that when they landed. But, they were such wonderful people. We got along great.

PENNY STALLINGS: I feel so lucky to have seen that place because I think they are all gone now. It was a bungalow colony that served three meals a day and basically very large people sat around waiting for the next meal; the kids might play Ping-Pong. And they had huge meals and there was recreation. I went there with Mel and I'm sure he was familiar with that kind of thing because he'd worked with Barry, my husband, in the mountains in the Catskills. I was just remembering— this isn't funny to anybody but us—but Mel said he was the only person who went to the mountains to get a nicer room than the one he grew up in, because they all slept on cots. But anyway, having heard these stories from my husband, I was really excited to see the Catskills. It was the end of that kind of thing.

Rosenbergs' probably accommodated a hundred and fifty to two hundred people, and there were kind of cabins and when we were staying there, there would be a table or two of our group. They were the craziest-looking people on the planet at the time. And there were people from the time warp—from what seemed like the forties—and it was not friendly at all, as you can imagine, but it was wonderful to see those two worlds come together.

CAROL GREEN: Each little cottage had a name: "The Apple" and "The Berry" and "The Cherry" and "The Grape." I remember these Jewish families where the husbands come up on the weekends and the kids with the yarmulkes. I remember the social activities—basketball, shuffleboard with no stick—this was our recreation. And we were not really well received in the area because we were these horrible hippies that were going to rape and plunder.

BILL WARD: They used to come and say, "Can you make the kids wear their shoes and their shirts to dinner?" And I said, "I'll try." They were glad to see us in the beginning because it was early in the season and it was going to be two or three weeks before anybody came up, so they were real happy to have us. Then when the families started coming up they had their choice and they didn't like us very much.

• • • •

CAROL GREEN: Rona Elliot was very good with people, so she got to relate to the townspeople. She would go around and make nice and represent us as these nice little boys and girls. We had to do these things like have square dances with the local people, and we would get these directions: "You have to be on your best behavior, you have to look nice, O.K.?" It was almost like when I was a little kid and my parents would say, "Now, wear your hat, gloves, and bag." We laid low. I remember trying to appear like the all-American kid, except that we were obviously a little bit different. We were right smack in the heart of hippiedom and the love generation and all of those names that we carried. And I know any countryside in America is going to be a little reactionary and a little scared. I remember making friends with the local Dairy Queen people and telling him, "They hate us, they hate us!"

WES POMEROY: There was great attention to good relations with the community. Quill, which was sort of a house band, was doing fundraising things for them if someone wanted them; they were available for no charge. Everyone was working hard at it. And there was an honest effort to pay people fairly for acreage that we thought we needed for parking. We did need it for parking, we just didn't get a chance to use it. And caring about people's boundaries. If someone had a field of corn, we tried to help them protect the corn before and during the festival. I thought that it was a town that was not hostile. Some people didn't like us and they never changed their opinion of that, but all in all it seemed like a relatively compatible place to work.

Nixon Asks Draft Lottery With 19-Year-Olds First

Times
New York, N.Y.
May 14, 1969

BILL WARD: A lot of people came and brought friends. And I had a crew. I had my crew from Miami who came up and there were about six or seven. And then there was the crew that was already there when I got there and they had come from all over. They were just kids who were from New York and California, from wherever, and they were out cutting grass and getting poison ivy and all that stuff.

We took a look at the place and said, "It's a big mistake to go ahead and build big steel sculptures around this place." And we, Ron Liis and I, sat on the hill and decided that what we really needed to do was play around with what was already there. We had to decide how to lay the whole site out. And so somebody got an idea that a quick way to do this would be to send me up in a helicopter with a camera and photograph this stuff and we could get stuff developed real quick and get blowups done real quick. If we had to wait for site plans and topographicals, we could be six weeks getting that stuff. And every day a new helicopter would appear and I'd say, "Oh my God." And I'd have to go up and sit in a helicopter with a 35-mm camera and, of course, in order for me to get a picture of all of this thing, he's got to turn the chopper on its side. We'd get stuff developed, come back down, and I'd do a big layout of the whole thing. We'd say, "Well, there are trees over here. How do we want to do that?" It was nice because you could see stuff happening day after day. It was really unfolding. It wasn't simply an idea that people were talking about. We were making it happen.

CHRIS LANGHART: I didn't have much of any chance to figure out what the Mills site was made of because they had already bulldozed it up so badly that it was just a sea of mud when I saw it. It wasn't a logical approach to it—it wasn't aerial maps and all that kind of thing. It was just zoom in and attack. They had done a lot of attacking; it was kind of a contractor's approach, which I'm surprised Michael tolerated, except that I think he was just advised or he didn't really exert any

83

control. It was not his sort of thing to tear up the whole land and then make it into something else and then try to use it. I would have figured him to use a site that was already pretty much the way it was naturally to be.

BILL WARD: So we cut paths, we built roads, we went and found all kinds of old farm machinery—old John Deere stuff, beautiful stuff—and we got a flatbed and we hauled it all in and we put it around in strategic places. We made it look like an old farm with a lot of abandoned stuff. And there were wild strawberries on the hill. We were going to plant some things so that when people came there would be more wild strawberries and some other things. We also planted some grass around. That was what we had planned to do as far as decorating the place—and forget about the sculptures—but we had to send crews out every day with machetes and all kinds of stuff to clear these paths. Well, there was poison ivy everywhere and first one or two people got it. Eventually, everybody got it, and I don't remember the doctor but somebody said it was Bob Dylan's doctor who took care of everybody. We paid him, of course, but he was the one who looked after everybody.

Ron Liis (left),
Mel Lawrence

84

CAROL GREEN: I remember my boyfriend coming home. I mean, these guys couldn't move, they couldn't fold their fingers or anything. They had white stuff all over them. We were in the Rosenbergs' at the time. We couldn't play shuffleboard, either.

BILL WARD: There was plenty of money, always lots of money for stuff. And when we went into town to buy things we just had all the money we wanted. I wasn't even used to it. I was careful buying stuff, you know, and Mel would say, "No, go ahead. You need trucks? Go get trucks. You need equipment? Go get equipment." I remember going into town to shop and we found a nice big hardware store there. And we had already gotten trucks. We went one weekend to Brooklyn and rented three trucks, three U-Haul trucks of some sort, and came back out. We had our trucks, went into town to get machetes, rakes, axes, and stuff like that and I had three or four of the kids with me from the field crew. And I remember they got really upset at the local kids, because the local kids were beginning to look like they did and they were upset because the local kids didn't earn it. They had sort of earned their look for their generation and these people had come along and just taken their look without really earning it, and I remember there was a big brouhaha about that. The townies were looking like them and they hadn't earned it and it was a problem.

CAROL GREEN: I think we got too big for the Rosenbergs'. And after that we moved to this little motel, uninhabited by anybody. Red Top.

JOEL ROSENMAN: I took a lot of rooms from time to time. We rented rooms by the dozen, by the hundredweight. We rented whole hotels, because we were housing a transient population. I don't know why we rented rooms for them. They all worked around the clock.

PENNY STALLINGS: Red Top was just this old, funky, single-story motel. And that's a lot of people's favorite place, Red Top, and I believe that Mel found it. At that point, I was rooming with Lee, as I would do later

85

at the Diamond Horseshoe, which was my favorite place. Red Top was a place where we'd all sit outside—where there used to be a swimming pool—and talk every night and it was just a dream. It was wonderful. Everybody was so funny and I just laughed constantly at the people and the developing drama and at what was coming to be more and more a reality—the festival. There were too many people there for it not to happen, too many people were on the payroll. And I guess Red Top was when we began to believe it, that it might actually happen.

RONA ELLIOT: The thing that makes that hotel stand out in my mind was the fact that the swimming pool was drained, and mad and wild sex took place in the swimming pool often at night. And the night before the festival someone set the hotel on fire. It was the scene of everything that you could possibly imagine. Everything you think ever happened did take place in that hotel.

I was living with Mel Lawrence. We lived a little bit closer to the site and in a regular motel. It was a little more for the solid citizens, which is not to say *they* weren't solid citizens; I just couldn't have lived at the Red Top.

CAROL GREEN: I remember from the cooking point of view. I was going to be the cook, which I couldn't do at the Rosenbergs'. Then there was this other woman, Linda, who was from Miami, Linda and Michael— they got fed up and left early. Anyway, Linda and I were going to co-cook when we moved over to the Red Top. We started out with thirteen

people, I guess, when we moved into the Red Top, and by the time we moved out of the Red Top I think there were eighty-five people.

STANLEY GOLDSTEIN: I'd been looking for a place to stay while all of this was going on. There was this cottage up on top of the hill and I rented it and made a deal with the guy. I rented all these other cottages down at the foot of the hill for the Hog Farm advance crew and then they would live on the land when the rest arrived and this would be available as a private place for the Woodstock group staff. And of course, I had the house at the top of the hill.

BILL WARD: The thirteen stayed there for a long, long time. And then all of a sudden—I kept hearing about the Hog Farm and I didn't know too much about the Hog Farm; I knew it was a commune. And then suddenly one day Mel was in New York, and everybody was gone, I get a phone call from somebody, probably Mel, who said, "The Hog Farm is coming. You gotta get somebody down to meet them." I think maybe Linda was the woman who was there with us and we sent her to New York to meet the Hog Farm, and also at that point there were advance contingents from the Hog Farm arriving at that time—they had a bus—and they suddenly appeared at Red Top, after first being delivered at a motel down the road. They went to this motel and the guy from the motel called and said, "Get these people out of here. They've only been here twenty minutes and they've stopped up all the toilets." So we moved them from there to the Red Top.

RONA ELLIOT: One of the highlights in that period is the moonwalk. We all sat around after dinner one July night and watched it together. I can remember being in the room with Bill Ward. It was really wonderful. I mean, we knew something was happening even though we were in this abandoned and temporarily renovated funky place in the Catskills.

STANLEY GOLDSTEIN: As it happened, I had some friends who had been living in my place in town who came up to visit and stay with me for a couple of days—Joe Gallivan and Dee. And the Hog Farm arrived just as I was leaving. So I said, "Hi, my friend Joe is over there. Go move in, we'll talk in a few days." And I went off. Well, first of all, no one had anything to do; I don't know exactly the things that they did for the next few days—I did not see them at all. Well, it turned out that since the instructions were not there, no one knew that I had rented out the whole motel so this whole advance crew moved into this one-bedroom cottage, while these ten or twelve or fourteen cabins remained unoccupied. And so it turned into Tobacco Road because the septic tank for that one-room cottage couldn't take it. My first great Hog Farm disappointment: one of the reasons that Joe came up was to bring me a pound of grass and it was going to be stashed over there. And I got so pissed because when I came back to the place, they hadn't left me a joint.

People's Park: Newest Battlefield in War at Berkeley

*Post
Washington, D.C.
May 19, 1969*

CAROL GREEN: It was horrifying for me, horrifying. Because I had to cook for these people. They would steal food out of the refrigerator. They would come and they would bargain with you, or whatever. They would say, "Hey, you have a joint? You have a joint?" I'd say, "Well, my boyfriend has a joint only I don't want to touch it because he's saving it for a special occasion." There was drought that summer; nobody had any drugs. "Well, I'll give you a hit." And then twenty-five Hog Farmers would appear and wipe you out from whatever you had.

Linda and I would take cash and go over to the local supermarket. Now, when you shop for eighty-five people for food every day and you don't have a lot of storage you buy food for those people for three meals a day. I remember spending seven hundred dollars a day.

I'd go to the store with Linda—Linda Dinda was pregnant—she and I would go to the store with seven hundred dollars every day and get followed by store detectives. And one day I turned around and said, "*What?* You see our money every day. We're not paying you with bum checks. We are here, like anybody else, for food. We're not shopping for any illicit stuff. We're not carrying anything." We would get stopped and searched. Linda and I would drive down the road in her Volkswagen van, and I remember getting stopped by police and searched, and she was obviously pregnant. And I remember thinking, "Here we are, the most wholesome kids in America." And it was scary, it was scary. Especially because there were rednecks around who would drive down the road, like we later saw in *Easy Rider*, with shotguns across the back, and we'd get names yelled at us. And I remember certain, just scary stuff that went around, like KKK stuff—it wasn't KKK, it was local.

JOEL ROSENMAN: The presence of longhairs in town brought some reality to the theory of the Woodstock festival to these people. I think that stirred things up a little bit, and it may have been marijuana that upset them most. At one point, we were advised in New York that they were—"they" meaning our group up in Wallkill—were under surveillance or being scrutinized by locals for drug use, and we hit on the ingenious plan of circulating a memo that announced to all of our staff that it was company policy to discipline strongly anybody caught with illegal drugs. We thought this would calm the locals. In fact, it just gave them further evidence that we were a bunch of criminals with long hair. Druggies.

JOHN ROBERTS: I did the "No Smoking" memo, I think. This was part and parcel of the Wallkill political problem. And as soon as we realized that it was a real problem, and that Wallkill was keeping a very close eye on what we were doing, the one thing that we couldn't have anyone see us do was drugs. Drugs, as you will recall, were fairly routinely taken by people of our age and generation in those years, particularly if you were involved with the music business. So I thought the most important thing that I could do was put out a memo that would bear the scrutiny of the Wallkill people, should it fall into their hands. Or send the memo and see that it fell into their hands. And so I wrote this memo saying—with the full knowledge of everyone I was writing it to—that we didn't allow marijuana smoking and I was shocked to hear that some of it had been going on and this was not the image of Woodstock and that if anyone continued or was found smoking it they would be discharged from our employ forthwith. I sent it off. It landed with an enormous thud, I think, in Wallkill.

JOEL ROSENMAN: It got out by design. We intended for it to get out; it was one of those planned leaks and it didn't work very well.

JOHN ROBERTS: The staff of Wallkill had a big laugh over it but they knew it was coming and they knew why it was coming and that there was no resentment there as far as I know. Although I think Artie Kornfeld misunderstood it, didn't realize it was a put-up job. And he announced, "That's just what's wrong with John Roberts."

CAROL GREEN: Fortunately for our venture, for Woodstock Ventures, it was a dry summer, and until the actual festival happened there was very little grass. Bob, the dishwasher, had some. The Hog Farmers were scrounging themselves. I remember, however—we didn't know from cocaine then—but I remember somebody dispersed some cocaine, a little tiny bit of cocaine out in some looseleaf notebook paper or some white paper. And it was so humid at the time that it all melted into the paper. I remember people standing around chewing the paper. I just remember people eating paper that had originally been cocaine and I remember seeing it practically dissolve before your eyes. I had never seen cocaine in my life and people were opening small packages of stuff and going "Aaaah!"—it was just so wet that it ended up being in the paper.

CHAPTER FIVE

*"It's weird, but at some moment,
these conversations always come back to
the subject of shit . . ."*
—Stanley Goldstein

Wallkill to Get Rock Fete—20,000 Expected

*Times Herald Record
Middletown, N.Y.
June 11, 1969*

JOHN ROBERTS: Early on, when we first got the Mills site, we had to go before the zoning board in Wallkill—the ZBA, the zoning board of appeals there—and tell them what we were planning to do and get their blessing. Which we did.

I think it was a classroom. In my mind's eye I see kind of a classroom setting with maybe a raised area and some desks or a long trestle-table type thing and four or five people sitting behind it. And there were maybe seven or eight people in the audience. One of the guys would be saying, "Now,, Agnes, we've told you about that sewer line and you gotta get it covered up." And someone would say, "The siding on your house is just a disgrace, Milt, and you know you're going to have to . . ." It was that kind of a setting—homespun, nice, concerned. It seemed like a zoning board that cared about the people that came before it and knew the people that came before it. After about three or four of those cases that came before them, we came up and one of them said, "I see this Woodstock Ventures outfit from New York is proposing to rent Howard Mills' parcel and, it says here, for some kind of a music fair. What do you boys have in mind?"

JOEL ROSENMAN: The case before us was with a guy who wanted to put a big billboard on his gas station property and everybody complained it was going to be an eyesore, except this guy, who, of course, wanted it. And they worked out some kind of compromise, which made me feel that they were going to be able to work with us. He asked us what kind of a project this was going to be, and we described it as kindly as we could without deviating too much from the truth. We said it was going to be folk music and we said it was going to be a crafts fair. So it was going to be arts, crafts, and music. And I guess when you put the music in there with the other two it sounded a lot better. In fact, that's what we eventually produced, more of a cultural exposition than just music. Nevertheless, we knew that there was a possibility that at some time or other in that weekend there was going to be loud rock music. We did not stress that. And I knew that we weren't stressing it at the time.

We were asked how big a festival did we think it was going to be. Cognizant of the fact that the biggest festival prior to us, the Monterey Pop, had drawn somewhere around twenty-seven or twenty-eight thousand, we figured—we jacked it up twenty or thirty percent and said that we expected to see our crowd go into the thirty-thousand range. That gave them a lot to chew on. That was a big project as far as they were concerned, and they weren't really clear on what that would mean. They were not alone; we weren't that clear on what it would mean either. It sounded relatively benign to them, I think.

John Roberts: They were a little concerned because they have a fair there in August every year, the Orange County Fair, which was going to be down the road a little bit. And they wanted to make sure we weren't going to be the same weekend as the fair, which we weren't. And they talked a little bit about traffic for the fair. Someone said, "We can handle the fair, this shouldn't be any big problem." And they said, "I guess it's O.K."

Joel Rosenman: They were pleased that the Mills property had a lot of the infrastructure that one needs to support people. And that was in our favor. And as far as we knew, since nobody knew that hundreds of thousands of people were going to descend on this little spot, it was pretty much an unexceptional proposal. And we were approved.

John Roberts: Wallkill felt a lot further away from New York than fifty miles. It was the kind of town that you would not be that surprised to encounter in Tennessee or Missouri or Idaho. It felt very small town, very provincial. Sort of lower middle class, I think. There wasn't a big white-collar group there. I don't think there was much of a commuter group from Wallkill to New York. For 1969, people seemed very conservative, religious. It felt like you had to play down the fact that you were from New York, because if you didn't they'd immediately assume you were a city slicker. They probably wouldn't have been terribly pleased to think that you were Jewish. And having seen *Easy Rider* that summer it had a wonderful resonance to it. It just felt like we were in that kind of environment. When we were up there I was always aware of hostile glances and suspicious looks from people. I was very unused to that in my life. But whenever we were around there if you were associated with that Woodstock group, you created a great deal of enmity.

Stanley Goldstein: The first day I went up there, I went up there with Don Ganoung. First, I took Don over to my place in New York so that I could get a bag, or that he could drop off some things off, and then we were going right up to Middletown. By this time, I had sublet an apartment in Greenwich Village over the site of what is now Sweet Basil, and I also had acquired a lease on a loft down on Canal Street. My friend Joe, with whom I was living in the hotel, was supposed to be living in the Canal Street loft and watching over my apartment on Seventh Avenue. But when Don and I got to Seventh Avenue, we discovered Joe in bed with two girls, and naked bodies flying around.

Anyway, Don and I then went up to Middletown, introduced ourselves around town to various places, met the city editor of the newspaper, Al Romm, then met subeditors. One of the fellows was past middle age and he and Don immediately struck up a relationship because of Don's priest background. But we were just up there to touch bases and get a sense of the community and introduce ourselves around and about. I don't really remember whether we came back to New York or stayed. I think that we decided that Don would remain in the area. We found a room for him to rent on a short-term basis next to what turned out to be the hot bar in the area. Middletown had a substantial college population—Orange County Community College is

Wallkill Faction Girds to Block Folk Festival

*Times Herald Record
Middletown, N.Y.
June 12, 1969*

91

in the town—and this wasn't the college bar; this was the other bar. And he was raided that night and it was suppressed because he was getting high with—it may have been the mayor's daughter, who was in some state of undress when the police burst in. Which probably didn't endear us to the mayor.

We went in to meet the Wallkill town fathers. And it was obvious that we had a problem. I moved up there almost immediately and commuted between there and New York City.

JOHN ROBERTS: They started having some meetings. There was a group, put together by I think a local policeman, called the Concerned Citizens of Wallkill, which had mobilized because they didn't like the looks of the people who were working on the site. They didn't like smoking, they didn't like loud music, some of the neighbors were concerned about music wafting over the property lines onto their property and disturbing their rest. They were legitimately concerned about traffic, they were concerned about a variety of logistical preparations that we were making. But I think they were irrationally concerned, or what later turned out to be irrationally concerned, about the sense of young, long-haired kids in their midst doing the mischief.

We tried a variety of things to calm them down. Don Ganoung preached a sermon in the local church one Sunday—a couple of Sundays, I think. We invited a lot of local kids out to the site to watch us work, to meet the people. I think Don and some of the other guys tried to get involved in weekend softball games. We really tried to practice good community relations. But the Concerned Citizens got wind of it and they were not about to listen to reason or logic. They just had a real sense—it was a real kind of *Easy Rider* sort of thing.

LEE BLUMER: We did a lot of visiting. We visited people. We set up this tour of a band called Quill. We went and did this tour of the New York State justice institutions, where I learned, back in 1969, that a child who was admitted to the Warwick School for Boys had an eighty-five percent chance of graduating to the prison at Elmira; that they were not really in the business of rehabilitation of twelve-year-old boys. That was very depressing, actually.

We were there to make people feel safe about us, because they were feeling that all of those people were ruffians. And Don came on as a man of God. All I remember seeing was people's kitchens. I don't remember accomplishing anything, but I do remember seeing people's kitchens.

We took Quill around the state entertaining the troops. We were trying to get good press, goodwill. There wasn't a lot. There really wasn't. But there were John Birchers. There was a very big contingent of John Birchers in Middletown. And I think Wes really believed that there was a real potential for violence. That was the impression I got. Wesley had been sheriff of San Mateo County for like twelve hundred years and had never pulled his gun. He was a peace officer, not a law-enforcement officer. And I think he thought that people could really get hurt, and he wanted to get away from it.

92   **JOEL ROSENMAN:** When it was first presented, the Woodstock festival

was described as a cultural exposition featuring arts and crafts, music of all kinds—folk, I think, maybe classical, folk-rock. We didn't say that there'd be violins there, but you could have guessed that there might be, the way it was presented to the zoning board, and the emphasis on heavy rock music of any kind was played down. I don't think we told any lies but we certainly did not prepare them fully for—nor was anybody prepared fully—for what eventually assembled. In the construction phase at Wallkill, all they saw were the sort of archetypical rock musician, either hammering and sawing or driving around in a jalopy or walking with an equally hippie-looking girl. And they heard about marijuana or smelled it and they heard the music—and it never seemed to have violins—and they started thinking to themselves that maybe what was coming. In fact, it was what was coming. In addition, they may have heard, and I don't know if they knew this, but they began to guess that more than twenty-five to fifty thousand people might show up.

Is the Earth Safe From Lunar Contamination?

Time
June 13, 1969

STANLEY GOLDSTEIN: Somewhere along the line, and it must be admitted—I was not a participant so it's very easy for me to point the finger—but in the original representations of Woodstock Ventures to the local planning board, there were some fudgings of what the plans and intents were and what the expectations were. Some of that was because people really didn't know. If we hoped to attract X many thousands of people, every indication from everyone, professional and otherwise, was that was a forlorn dream and that couldn't possibly happen and that we were madmen to anticipate anything of that nature. And so some of the representation was not necessarily deliberately misleading; some of it was tempered by what reasonable expectation might be. They were truly trying to avoid presenting some issues.

The town didn't seek to clarify any of those things. From everything that I was able to gather and that I can remember, the town fathers kind of had these fellows walk in, tell them their story, said, "Well, everything you are proposing is well within the ordinances of the community. There's no need for us to act. This has nothing to do with us. If you want to do this thing on private land, the regulations of the town don't prohibit it or require us to take any action. So go right on ahead, boys. Do it." I'm not suggesting that a community doesn't have a concern and that the fact that you are naive doesn't mean that you don't have the need, upon achieving information or acquiring intelligence, to question these things and go back over them. But it clearly was none of that which eventually caused the community to rise up in arms and for these folks to make their decisions. They wielded the power, bowed to some political influences. We were just incredibly naive. All of us were incredibly naive.

When I finally saw what the zoning board decision was and what the representations were, I said, "We'd better get some legal counsel." Everyone said, "Well, go out and get some." So I went out and I got Sam Eager.

Sam Eager was a local attorney who had been recommended to me by a number of people and the fact that we didn't have local counsel I thought was astounding, was simply incredible. And that we damn well had better have some real quick. I spoke to a number of people in the community. By this time I knew a number of folks. Sam's name came up, and Sam's name came up, and Sam's name came up, and so I sought out Sam.

SAM EAGER: I honestly don't recall how they found me. I had done considerable zoning work in those days and still do. I'm one of many attorneys, however, in the community, and that may have been as much a fluke as anything else. Generally speaking, I might be a little less volatile then some lawyers; I'm calmer and quieter, but otherwise no different from any other fellow who graduated from law school and passed the bar exam.

At that time, my father was a justice of the state supreme court. He may then have been on the appeals court—the appellate division; I don't recall. But he was a justice of the supreme court. My family had been residents of Orange County for over two hundred years. And we were a conservative, quiet family; that may have been a contributing factor also.

STANLEY GOLDSTEIN: Sam was quintessentially a Yankee lawyer, well placed and well connected within the community, highly respected, highly regarded by everyone to whom I spoke. When I mentioned his name to people—you know, "You got *Sam Eager?*" There couldn't have been a more ideal representative from the community than Sam, and acquiring him gave us an aura of respectability.

JOHN ROBERTS: What Sam basically did was coach us. He'd say, "Look, this is what you've got to sound like, this is what you've got to look like, this is who you're up against." He was a pretty good coach. I mean, I think Sam maybe instilled in us a certain—because it was quiet confidence—a certain false hope that we could overcome this thing. Not that he ever promised us that we could, but you got the feeling with Sam Eager on your side that you had the best possible shot, you had the best possible representation up there.

SAM EAGER: The situation that the Woodstock Ventures people were in when I was consulted was that they had come to the town of Wallkill, negotiated with the owner of a parcel of land that they thought was suitable for their purpose, and talked with some municipal officials about the prospect of a music festival to take place on the premises in question. By word of mouth, a general understanding had been reached as to the terms of the leasing of that property, and the Woodstock Ventures principals were led to believe that the town would afford them the necessary permits.

This area had no experience with anything like a major music festival and had no ordinances that were designed to handle whatever zoning and public health and public safety problems one with experience might expect to flow from such a project. But the town did have zoning and the zoning limited the uses to which property could be put. In effect, a special permit had to be obtained to use the proposed festival site for that purpose, and building permits had to be obtained. And again, some officials of the town indicated there would be no difficulty in obtaining those.

But at the time that I was called, there were indications that this was no longer so. The town had started to give some trouble to the Woodstock Ventures people and the proposed landlord of the site— Howard Mills—also was indicating some change of heart as to some of there terms of the proposed lease.

There were the negotiations with the town, with the town planning board, the town attorney. There were preparations for hearings—and frankly, I suspect that the town would not have been able to prevent the staging of the Woodstock festival in the town of Wallkill if the town had not determined that they were going to adopt a new regulation for the purpose of regulating such exhibits, such shows, in the community. So, even while the Woodstock Ventures personnel in the area were working with the town officials to comply with the requirements of the town officials under their present regulations—and finding means of complying—the town was working on a new law. The adoption of that law was really the death knell for the Woodstock festival in the town of Wallkill. There would be no way that the festival could comply with the requirements.

STANLEY GOLDSTEIN: The first town council meeting that was held, I was there solo. I just went in to quiet and quell and present ourselves as reasonable human beings and discuss what it was we planned to do. It was a lot of name-calling. And then Mel and I attended another meeting, and I believe Don was with us, and then the whole crew came up for another, and then there were special hearings of the zoning board, to which we came with experts and lawyers and so forth.

MEL LAWRENCE: We would be in a meeting hall, say like in Middletown, and a guy would get up and would say that this is a meeting about getting a special permit to allow this music festival to happen, in front of—I guess it was the town council, or they may have a different structure, but it was the leaders of that community. Then guys would be saying "Gee, they can't have this. They are going to bring in motorcycle gangs and you know those kind of guys. We can't let our daughters be out here." There was kind of really like asinine reasons— you know, they called them longhairs and hippies. It was like being discriminated against. Like, they didn't want to hear any other part of it. They didn't want to hear from the music aspect of it, or this is what's going on for people right now. They just didn't want it in their place,

Folk Rock Festival Promoters Defend Intentions, Expertise

Times Herald Record
Middletown, N.Y.
June 17, 1969

95

because it would cause too much confusion and disruption.

JOHN ROBERTS: Mel Lawrence gave as good as he got in that environment. Mel was short-haired also and looked like a fellow who'd been outdoors a lot and worked with his hands and knew construction and farming and a variety of things that these people knew. And when he spoke, he spoke with a lot of authority, a lot of firsthand knowledge. Someone would say, "Well, how are you going to drain that thirty acres you're thinking of as a parking lot?" And Mel would say, "Jesus Christ, haven't you guys ever drained some land? Don't you know that when the pitch of the land is a certain level and you build a catch basin here and a drain there and a French culvert here, that it's a snap in two days, no matter what the rain is? It's going to be great. Don't you guys know that? Come on, you know that." "Yeah, well, he's right." There was a begrudging respect for him and I think by the time Mel got through, most of these people had only their emotions to fall back on and not a sense that this was not in the hands of professional people. But Mel gave a strong feeling, and Stanley did too; they were both articulate and knowledgeable and no one came away from those meetings feeling that we hadn't hired good professional people. We had.

But they were traveling on emotion, too. We'd get up to speak or Mike would get up to speak at some of these meetings and you know, with long hair, and they would say, "Is that *Mister* Lang or *Miss* Lang?" And you know, there would be cries from the audience, that sort of thing. I don't recall speaking personally at that meeting myself, but it was a hostile audience, and they didn't like us one bit. I don't know whether it was because we were young or long-haired or from the city. I don't know what it was. There was an us-versus-them feeling there.

MICHAEL LANG: It was pretty impressive, I thought. I mean, I would make the presentation and have everybody there, head of security and Mel and Chip and everybody present their areas and try and allay everybody's fears and then once in a while we had to make speeches about our generation. Those happened, too. But they were kind of a stereotype redneck town reacting to this thing coming and invading. They got pretty nasty.

JOHN ROBERTS: It wasn't that we didn't have our supporters there. There were people in that community who felt that—and of course these were usually people who had some commercial interest on our being there—but I think who also genuinely felt that what we were doing was interesting, we had a right to do it, that we weren't hurting anyone. We were taking considerable professional care to get it right. People who were fair-minded about it. People who went and listened to the presentation usually came away impressed. "Well, these guys know what they're doing." People who walked into the room with that kind of unreasoning feeling about young people, long hair, rock music, and all that implied to them, wouldn't listen to anything that was being said. They couldn't have cared at all. They just didn't want us in their community.

LEE BLUMER: There was real hostility—there was open hostility to us, if

Festival Pic Bright; Woodstock Adds Day

Cashbox
June 28, 1969

96

people had long hair and stuff. People who were hostile were extremely hostile. And I remember—and I'm not sure if I remember this being at the meeting or at the court—but I remember that there was a real ominous threat that said, "The first hippies who set foot on this property will get their heads blown off."

STANLEY GOLDSTEIN: We brought in plots and plans. They demanded that we address very specific concerns and present our plans. How were we going to deal with sanitation? The town had a law that privies were not acceptable within the town limits of Wallkill. What were we going to do about sound? What were we going to do about this and that and everything else? How were we going to get the water? And so we tried to address those concerns. We brought in drawings and plans and plots and quantities and exemplars of contracts, and so forth.

There was a lot of name-calling. There had been threats made that the Millses were going to be bombed out of their house, that there were going to be shotguns and pitchforks, and run the hippies out of town. That we were coming up to infect the whole community with hepatitis and who knows what all else.

When these threats began rolling into the Millses, I sat down and wrote a letter to the community which, in order to get published, had to be placed in the Public Notices column. It couldn't be as a letter to the editor at the Middletown *Times Herald Record*. It had to be placed as a public notice and had to be placed within a certain period of time. So I went running out onto the street to find someone to whom I could dictate and who could type. I found a wonderful girl who was just coming down from an acid trip. I found her on a street corner, and I hustled her into a car. We worked through the night writing this thing. Her mother got up and made us coffee and eggs, and she typed like crazy. Very capable, very confident.

JOHN ROBERTS: We were trying everything. Miles Lourie's father was a fellow named Felix Lourie and Felix had connections in Albany. He was an old clubhouse politician I think. Nice, gentle man. When we finally got to meet him he was perhaps past his glory but he was a lot of fun, Felix, and he had known all the backroom boys from the smoke-filled rooms. And we had hit on the notion that if we got a welcoming letter from the state and the endorsement of the state, that the supervisor of the town of Wallkill was a Republican and this could stand us in very good stead.

So Felix offered to take us to Albany and shepherd it through the corridors of power. But on the way to Albany, he thought that we should stop off and meet his old friend, Lieutenant Governor Wilson here in New York, which we did—Joel and I and Felix. And Felix was very, very concerned about the protocol in these particular meetings, very concerned that we call Malcolm Wilson "Governor Wilson," not "Lieutenant Governor," not "Mister Wilson," you know. We were young kids to Felix. Who knew what impropriety we would commit as soon as we were in the presence of this great man? As we were strategizing, I would say something to Joel or he'd say to me, "Well, now if Wilson says . . ." And Felix would say, "Not *Wilson*, boys. *Governor* Wilson."

Boosting Peace: John & Yoko in Canada

Rolling Stone June 28, 1969

97

The Times Herald

RECORD

Weather: Warm   Middletown, N. Y. 10940   Thursday morning, July 3, 1969   10 Cents

Wallkill votes to curb

Aquarian rock festival

--Page 3

Group wants court to KO rock fete

-- Page 3

The Times Herald

RECORD

LATE FINAL Edition

Weather: Warm   Middletown, N. Y. 10940   Friday morning, June 20, 1969

Rock fest opponents to take iss

A. Rosenstein said it
ry hearing

SILVER LAKE
the

THE TIMES HERALD **RECORD**   Friday, June 13, 1969

guests and area residents.
He cited past successes of his compan
in organizing similar events in Florid

Ruckus erupts as rock fete rocks Wallkill

Supervisor Jack A. Schl... said the
board was "planning to pas...
... public assembly

firm to supervise details of the exposition.
...ill be handled, he said, by

Battle rages

ER LAKE
its first
onths

Festival to sue Wallkill

festival promoters

Up the showbiz ladder

tentions

By EDMUND P. KLEIN
MIDDLETOWN
The promoters of the

THE TIMES HERALD **RECORD**   Tuesday, July 15, 1969   **3**

Show will go on, rock fete promoters boast

warning that about 40,000 holders of
... have already been sold
... Aug 15

thrown in their way, backers of the
"Aquarian Exposition" appear convinced
that the event will go on as scheduled.
... Monday even to discuss the
... do it if

court to try to get it back if the festival is
banned.
For the first time Monday
conscientiously polite relations between
residents and festival organizers broke
... as the ZBA hearing wore on for
... own hall

We were ushered in to see Malcolm Wilson and we had no more
than begun the first sentence of why we were there when Wilson
launched into some really tedious reminiscence of some conversation
he'd had with Cardinal This or Monsignor That about youth and its
ways and music and what have you and—you know, your eyes began
to sort of glaze over. And I think we began to weave and Felix was just
sitting there just as pleased as can be that we were sharing this
confidence with Governor Wilson. And finally Joel and I could stand
it no longer, and I don't know which of us was rude enough to interrupt
the great man and say, "Yeah, that's very interesting, Governor Wilson,
but about our festival up in Wallkill . . ."

Felix was practically out of his head. "Boys, the governor was in
the middle of telling you an important anecdote." Anyway, it went on
in that vein for a while, and when we finally got to explain to His
Eminence what we were there for, the fog cleared long enough for him
to say, "Gee, I don't think the state could possibly . . ."

SAM EAGER: The upshot of it was that a local law was adopted and it was clear that Woodstock Ventures would not be able to comply. They had to make a very serious decision: whether to litigate the issue and try to compel the town to permit the festival or to look for another site. Well, when that point was reached, the only sane alternative was to pursue both courses at least until another site could be located. So there was a frantic search for an alternative site while things were being prepared as though the matter were going to be litigated.

STANLEY GOLDSTEIN: It's weird, but at some moment, these conversations always come back to the subject of shit, and what you are going to do with it: where are you going to gather it together, how are you going to provide sanitary facilities, and how are you going to get rid of it? At the end of time, for all that there were objections to this or incomplete that or we didn't respond to this or that, the one area in which they could really claim that we intended to break the law was this matter of privies.

Now, it happened that on the Mills site, in this industrial development, there were privies that had existed there for the construction crew. Lining the road in front of the Mills site where the state was doing roadwork, there was a line of privies. Right down the street from there where there's now a major shopping center with Sears and so forth, there were more privies. There were privies all over the township. And so it seemed to me that a very strong case could be made that while that may have been the rule on the books, that the town knowingly accepted these things and that they were making a very specific exception in this case and beating us up; that we could, in most cases, find good reason to claim that they were not even-handedly administering the law and so forth; and that to abandon that site at that time was not in our best interest. I was overruled.

JOEL ROSENMAN: Our lawyers never felt that we had much stopping power with the zoning board. Legally, we could bring them to trial sooner or later, probably later. And we might win but probably not, especially in light of subsequent events. And then to prove damages— I mean, the whole thing was very difficult, and they may have been judgment-proof anyway; it's hard to tell. So I think legally we never really had that much ammo. I don't think they were ever in doubt as to the outcome of those final meetings. They were trying to put together enough concrete information to justify what they had already decided.

JOHN ROBERTS: We, in what was probably a mistake, took our partners at Media Sound out for a celebratory dinner at the fanciest restaurant we could think of in New York in those days, which was Four Seasons. We were sitting there having a jolly old time and knowing that the town board would be probably rendering their decision that evening—it was a Friday night. I asked Stanley or somebody to call me there to let me know the verdict. And shortly before the main course or dessert, Stanley called me and told me that we no longer had a site. And here it was, July 7 or 8 or something like that. And it took a lot of the fun out of that particular dinner. It was a mistake, a nasty moment.

Ticket Sales Boom—Expo Extended

*Daily Freeman
Kingston, N.Y.
June 28, 1969*

**Preachers
to Offer
Counseling at
Festival**

*Times Herald Record
Middletown, N.Y.
June 30, 1969*

JOEL ROSENMAN: He tried to drown himself in a chocolate soufflé. For me, I think I was enough of a lunatic at the time—obviously, to have gotten involved in this at all—to think that it was going to work out. I wasn't sure who was going to work it out. At that point, I think I had become disabused of my belief that Michael was going to work it out. We had found the first site. I thought, "Well, we'll just have to get in our car and find another one." How were we going to build another site in a short period of time? I thought we would. I thought this was a tremendous pain in the neck, but I thought, "Let's finish dinner and we'll get to work."

MICHAEL LANG: I don't remember ever losing hope. There were moments of depression and moments of reflection and times of sitting outside of town halls wondering about the American dream and those kinds of things, and, "Do we really have a system of justice and laws for everyone?" You know how those things get you. But I never lost the attitude, that positive attitude. Never. I knew we were going to do it always.

JOHN ROBERTS: I didn't share any of that. I very quietly said, "We're ruined, we're ruined." I thought our remaining asset was a lawsuit against Wallkill as of that moment, because I thought our constitutional rights had been violated. And then I thought Wallkill probably didn't have much in the way of assets to seize, so I thought we were in very deep yogurt and I didn't know that we could have a site ready in time. I thought it was worth finding out, trying if we could, but I thought the chances were kind of small. And then I was thinking, "How do we tell all the people we have sold tickets to that they're not going where they thought they were going—you know, what kind of massive publicity effort is that? And do we have to offer those people tickets back? And how about the acts who were specifically booked for Orange County we were now proposing to move somewhere else? And what credibility will we have with ticket buyers if we start advertising a new site, even if we get one as early as next week?" And all I could think about was all of those kinds of things.

It turned out that it was just as bleak as all that.

100

"I wanted to see a good presentation of the Woodstock Nation that showed that all these people could come together and weren't going to stab each other . . ."
—*Abbie Hoffman*

JOEL ROSENMAN: We were not exactly flying on instruments here, but there were elements to this project that we were learning as quickly as we could. Our partners seemed to know a lot more about what moved the entertainment world than we did and what was important to the press and what was important for our image. And lots of times we would have these brainstorming meetings. I felt I was learning a lot more than I was contributing in those meetings—about the new consciousness, the Aquarian Age, and essentially, a good deal about LSD and marijuana and cocaine or whatever it was that was the popular drug that generation was taking.

JOHN ROBERTS: Things got very, very busy. A day at the office in May of 1969 would consist of a thousand and one things, ranging from preparing to make presentations with the town board to dealing with P.R. people. We were dealing with the lawyers and agents for acts, we were dealing with hundreds of different ticket outlets. We had to check to make sure the tickets were being printed properly, were not counterfeitable, were distributed to the outlets, the monies were collected, that it was deposited, it was accounted for. We were getting rain insurance, we were talking to people about portable toilets, about the gates, about programs being made. I mean, it was extraordinary. And here were four guys essentially who, including Michael, had never done any of this before. And every once in a while, things got away from you. Artie and decorating the office was certainly an excellent example of something that got away from us. Artie got very involved in decorating our offices. He had a big room in the back and he had this guy Bert Cohen come. And Artie spent all of this time with Bert Cohen, decorating his office in the back, which looked like sort of a headquarters for a harem. It was most bizarre.

MICHAEL LANG: Uptown, it was going to be very groovy. Bert Cohen was going to do really psychedelic stuff. And it was horrible, actually, the designs he came up with. In any case, he was going to make very sort of hip offices for this hip little business we were putting together. And I guess we were all going to have offices up there. I remember I used to go up once in a while for a meeting to see Bert's latest creation. He was quite a character, Bert.

It was awful. When I had the head shop, we had blacklight rooms with posters and things like that. They were nifty in their own little way. He was creating these total environments. The Electric Circus was around then with those kind of environments, created with lighting and color and painting. I can't really describe it to you. They were just in bad taste, from one room to the next. I never used an office there. There was one front room—maybe it was going to be my office—that had these sort of steps that were chartreuse, I think. Instead of having couches, there were these different levels—platforms—in the room, with chartreuse carpet. And I think all four of us realized how absurd this was getting. But old Bert was out there.

JOEL ROSENMAN: It was a multilevel environment, carpeted in soft enough rugs so that they could be used as seating. And there were pillows thrown around and, as a concession to us, they had included some desks. But for the most part it was free-form. And the ceiling, instead of what's called a drop ceiling these days where you put in fluorescent lights, they had—it was a hung ceiling or something. It was some diaphanous cloud-like fabric hung at varying levels to simulate I-don't-know-what. Ultimately, it seemed a little depressing in some ways. Very colorful. Lots of purple, as I recall. Artie was into purple.

Artie's part of the office in the back was sort of like the throne, where he would receive. I think Artie in a lot of ways regarded himself as the potentate of this venture—the author of it, the originator of it—and less and less as a functionary.

This is how every one of these items got processed, from the Train right through practically the end of the festival. We would go into a conversation—you could fill in the blanks with anything, but it would essentially be: "Guys, we need to authorize an expenditure of X amount of dollars for Y activity"—in this case, Bert Cohen. This is Michael or Artie talking, although Artie less and less. In fact, Artie was virtually phased out of the operation at a certain point some months before the festival. But Michael, or one of Michael's lieutenants, would say, "We need this expenditure." In this case, let's take Bert Cohen. We would say, "Gee, do we need to hire a guy to do that? Why don't we just pick out some nice paintings, we'll put them on the wall, put a rug down and everything will be fine." "Well, you can do that, but if you do that, what you've done is signal to the world that Woodstock Ventures is the least important thing to happen in 1969. Everything has to support this attitude and the image and the fundamental approach to life that we're trying to get across to people." And John and I would stare and say, "For ten thousand dollars—or for five hundred dollars or for fifteen thousand dollars or whatever—do we want to have that be? And these guys are telling us that is one of the most important decisions that we can make in this week of preparation for the festival—do we want to be on record as having said, 'No, we're not going to do that,' and have it come back later on as the flaw in the plan, the chink in our armor, the thing that pulled the rug out from under our entire presentation, just because we wanted to spend four hundred dollars instead of ten thousand dollars?"

MICHAEL LANG: That was really one of the problems—"What's Artie doing?"—as far as John and Joel were concerned. "Is he sane?" Artie was kind of in a transition between—I mean, what is his world really like anyway at that point? He had a great sense of public relations. And as far as the rest of it goes, I don't know exactly what function he was performing. I never really got that clear, either, except for that the three of them were in that office, handling press, ticketing, publicity, financials, contracts, permits, things like that. And I think that what Artie was performing mostly, between Artie and I, was keeping everything off the back of the downtown office. I think he was really performing a function of letting us work. As far as I was concerned, that's what he was doing. He was handling whatever problems came up, or whatever misunderstandings came up. Artie was going to handle those things initially, so that we could get on with doing it.

STANLEY GOLDSTEIN: I didn't have a very high regard for Artie from the beginning. He seemed otherworldly and so ego-driven that I saw no particular use for him. Michael was very committed to Artie but nothing that Artie touched seemed to work and everything was groovy and wonderful but nothing hung together and he had no concept, to me, of putting a deal together. Artie was going to be the deal maker. He was supposed to be the guy who knew how to deal with talent, get the releases, put together a record package, put together a movie deal.

ARTIE KORNFELD: I saw at the beginning that there was a slight resentment that I was probably egotistical at the time and knew I was Artie Kornfeld and successful in the music industry. I was the only one that was probably ego-ed out a little bit, and that turned them sort of against me.

JOEL ROSENMAN: John and I started to turning to some of Artie's functions that we thought we could discharge ourselves, because we felt that, for example, if we didn't promote and advertise this thing, it was just going to be an exercise in—a waste of time. We had some fun doing that in a way. I don't think we ever really pulled it off as hippies, but we tried. We grew long hair, we went to what were called head shops in those days and bought hippie clothes.

You had to have bell-bottoms, each leg of which could pretty much accommodate both of your legs. Some of them had stripes and very colorful stuff. The shirts were really big and blousy and open at the collar. I'm afraid to say that I wore beads. I would go down to the Village with a pad and a pencil in the pocket of my fringed leather vest, and I would hang around in the Village and listen to kids talking about what was hassling them, what they were happy about. They'd walk by and be getting stoned. They'd talk about the music, they'd talk about their parents, they'd talk about—a lot of them were going to the country for the weekend and a lot of them thought the pigs were going to hassle them, the pigs being the police. And you would hear phrases like, "This is a capitalist rip-off" or "This is fucking capitalist hype" or one thing or another. And we started to get a feeling for what the kids were really into and what they really feared, what their dreams were made of essentially.

It's very much like a focus group in advertising. That's what it reminded me of. Years later, I found out what focus groups were and that was what I was doing down on the corner of 8th Street and Sixth Avenue.

And it translated itself into what we wrote for the advertising copy. We decided that we would slant this festival in such a way that

Many States Enacting Laws to Curb Campus Disorders

*Post
Washington, D.C.
June 2, 1969*

103

Joel Rosenman (left),
John Roberts

it gave the kids what they were dreaming about. It was easy, because it wasn't so hard to find a place in the country; they all liked that. It wasn't so hard to promise them that they would be free from hassles from their parents because their parents weren't invited. And on and on like that. There was something exotic that they all wanted. They had simple dreams, pleasant ones.

STANLEY GOLDSTEIN: From the very earliest stages there was this attitude towards overall concept: How do you present yourself? What do you want the thing to be? And I think that's best expressed really by the poster that was developed for the show—a dove sitting on the arm of a guitar and large, large, large letters saying "Three Days of Peace and Music." The listing of talent on the poster occupied no more space than the description of the camping and what facilities there were going to be. But what we were promoting was "three days of peace and music." Now, obviously, we were interested in selling tickets. Radio advertising listed talents larger; all that hoopla about the music groups that were going to be there. But that presentation that said "Three Days of Peace and Music." It didn't say "Jimi Hendrix." It didn't say "Janis Joplin" or "Jefferson Airplane." There was an expression of an interest there.

JOEL ROSENMAN: Michael came up with the phrase "An Aquarian Exposition." We didn't like it. I didn't like it. I didn't even know what it was. An exposition sounded like something that would take place in Paris in the nineteenth century and I didn't think we could attract

104

many ticket buyers with that. And Aquarian, as far as I could tell, was something that had to do with water, but I wasn't sure exactly what, so he kind of left me behind with that one.

JOHN ROBERTS: Michael and Artie were into astrology a little bit. That's where that came from: the Age of Aquarius, from *Hair*, that song. Our contribution to the poster was "Three Days of Peace and Music" and the copy that talked about fields and streams and lakes and crafts bazaars and a little zoo and that whole sensibility that we thought would sell this weekend. I think that is, in fact, what charged people up. I don't think people remember that tag line, "An Aquarian Exposition." But as you can see from the poster design, we thought "Three Days of Peace and Music," particularly in the late sixties, was a very important concept.

Mail-order information

Joel and I bought into the three days of peace and love and music and the kind of sappiness of it; it really was appealing to us. And we would get a lot of correspondence in those days, particularly with the letters which ordered the tickets. It wouldn't just be a check in there. The outpouring of love coming from people—peace signs drawn on it. "Love and peace forever, Little Raven," or some bizarre kind of late-sixties nickname. And we were seeing this, and maybe there really was something going on there. It was very strange and very lovely.

• • • •

MICHAEL LANG: We had lots of confrontations with the underground press, or just members of the underground in general. They were confronting this big rip-off. And it wasn't a rip-off, and I knew it wasn't. And I never had much trouble with any of them—ever—once we talked about it. Because I was aware of the same things they were aware of, and we were dealing with it. I remember Bob Fass called— I think he was on the air—and he was talking about what a big rip-off this was. It was like three o'clock in the morning. We were still working. And so I called him, and said, "Listen . . ." And we had it out on the air. Because we really weren't trying to rip anybody off.

The attitude was we were giving for everything we were getting. I mean, we were really dealing with all the problems that would exist in a very conscientious way that would enable everybody to have a great time and for everybody to get what they should. I mean, people

A poster that was
never used

were investing a lot of money; they should make money on it. I was not concerned with making profit, but I knew that John and Joel should make some and I knew that we should too for all our work. But I didn't feel it was wrong or negative. Had it been a rip-off—had the acts we claimed were going to be there weren't going to be there, the place wasn't going to be what we said it was going to be, the facilities weren't adequate, you know, whatever—then there was a right for people to bitch about it. But as I said, it wasn't being planned that way. It was being planned as a cultural event, for the culture and of the culture.

JOEL ROSENMAN: I recall that at one point we were having a meeting and Michael said—he was impatient, we were talking about the site or one of our routine problems—he said, "This is not as important as something that's just happened to me, and something real heavy is about to go down and we gotta do something to handle it." And he told us that he had received a call from the underground and that they wanted a forum, preferably on stage, at the festival from which they could announce their radical policies. This was entirely antithetical to what we were trying to present in the festival. We were trying to make it be a) nonviolent and b) artistic. And we certainly didn't want political statements.

Number one, stylistically, it wasn't what we wanted in the festival. We wanted to be arts, not politics, although we knew there was going to be some politics no matter what. But the major reason that we didn't want it was because we felt that it greatly heightened the potential for violence. A lot of decisions that were made about how to style and construct the event and what talent to hire and not to hire had to do with keeping the potential for violence down to a minimum. It would surprise you how many decisions had that as a factor.

JOHN ROBERTS: Whether or not to try and get the Rolling Stones was one.

JOEL ROSENMAN: We chose not to. Their hit song at that time was "Street Fighting Man." And we just didn't want street fighting in our festival.

JOHN ROBERTS: Or what kind of security force.

JOEL ROSENMAN: Whether to put our security force in uniform, and if so, what kind of uniform—a plain and friendly uniform or one that reminded kids of the pigs. And along with those decisions, the decision about whether to have radical literature passed out at booths, whether to have radical speakers on stage haranguing the crowds. And we just made up our minds early on that this was going to be peace and music and that it was not going to be stirring oratory about political causes. Although we felt that those were important causes, we just felt this wasn't the event. We were frightened, I think, basically. We were frightened to do so.

ABBIE HOFFMAN: I was at a Youth International Party powwow or conference in Ann Arbor, Michigan, when I first heard about Woodstock. And I remember a lot of people—this was about June—were talking about this big music festival that was going to take place at Bob Dylan's farm and I said, "Wow, that sounds pretty interesting." Now, by the time I got back to New York City and started to check out what was actually going on and knew it wasn't Dylan's farm—it wasn't even in Woodstock—I knew it was going to be a huge event because its mythology was so big that people were making up these amazing stories about it, and it was at that point that I approached the promoters.

Nixon Says
Rebels
Imperil
Education

Post
Washington, D.C.
June 4, 1969

MICHAEL LANG: Abbie was a crazy kid at the time. He called out of the blue, thinking that there was some sort of culture rip-off. He called demanding this and that: "We want money from you; we're going to screw up your show. We're going to fuck this up, that up. You guys are in big trouble." I think at first I didn't really pay a lot of attention to it. Then finally, when it was getting time to deal with it, I said, "Listen, if you want to talk about it, we'll get together." And so we went to see him. And there was a whole coalition of people somewhere in the East Village.

ABBIE HOFFMAN: I said, "Look, you're going to have a lot more people. It's going to be hectic and everything. This culture belongs to the people in the streets; we're trying to build a counterculture. I'm going to put together a coalition of Lower East Side groups and we want to come back for meetings," which they had agreed to. And we came up with about eight or ten groups, everything from the Medical Committee for Human Rights to Up Against the Wall Motherfuckers to Yippies to service organizations that took care of bad trips and runaways on the Lower East Side. Community-based groups. Anti-war groups. All of which were centered in the East Village in the Lower East Side of New York where I was living and was certainly one of the key organizers.

JOEL ROSENMAN: Abbie thinks that everything that the establishment is doing—from capitalist rip-offs, from the military industrial complex, from the oppression of the poor, from exploitation of them to our foreign policy—is just plain old wrong. Being done as badly as it can possibly be done. And there is really no reason for restraining yourself when it comes to changing things around. Do it as quickly and as nastily as you possibly can because it's the only way you're going to achieve results. It wasn't violent overthrow of the government, in that many words, but it had overtones of that and I generally did not pay too much attention to groups like that and wouldn't have this time except Michael was paying a lot of attention to it and was visibly shaken by it.

Abbie Hoffman

JOHN ROBERTS: I had more of a view of Hoffman as being sort of witty and not a threatening figure. He threw dollar bills on the floor of the Stock Exchange, which I thought was very funny. That was a funny prank to do. And didn't he nominate a pig for president? Some of his pranks, I thought, poked fun in a sharp and clever way at our conventions. I didn't have a vision of Hoffman as a threatening person. But I didn't give Abbie Hoffman much thought one way or the other.

JOEL ROSENMAN: So at this meeting Michael said, "I think we're in some kind of trouble here. If we say no to these people, it may not stick. We can say no but we can't control them once they're there. We can deny them a booth, we can deny them access to the stage, but we can't tell what they're going to do." And I said, "Well why don't we just call them up and talk to them or whatever?" And he said, "It's not going to work. What we have to do is go down there and somehow reach some sort of agreement with them." And I remember Michael wanted me to go down there and talk to them. He did not want to go himself. And I thought to myself, "If there's one person that can talk to them on their level, so to speak, it's Michael. He's a creature of the counterculture." But Michael somehow didn't feel that was appropriate. He thought that I could do it much better. And I think that he just didn't want to get in that situation. It was one where he—when we finally arrived there it was clear. It was one in which tap dancing was not effective. And Michael's specialty was tap dancing. I convinced him to go along with me. I said, "I'm certainly not going to walk down there by myself." The

108

two of us went down somewhere in the East Village.

I dressed sort of casually. I thought they would beat me up less readily, I don't know. By the time I got done talking to Michael and seeing the expression on his face, I thought this was likely to be a dangerous meeting. I didn't wear a tie and jacket. In those days, especially in the presence of Michael, I felt that I could only look silly trying to look like a hippie. Because if you try to look like a hippie and fail, it's almost worse than not trying. So I think I wore just slacks and a turtleneck, or something like that. And Michael was dressed as Michael, which was kind of a Florida/California hippie. It had flair to it. The right kind of faded jeans and the right kind of leather vest with fringe, and so forth. The Yippies were not nearly as well done up as we were. The Yippies didn't give a damn what they looked like.

We were into an office. You walked up a flight of stairs and you were in an office that was no bigger than this room. Maybe a hundred or two hundred square feet. And it was furnished in a very Spartan way—there was a typewriter here, a couple of phones. There were disheveled people around, a lot of them seemed to be overweight, not ill fed. This was not a beautiful bunch of people who were doing this for their image. They fit my stereotype of deep political thinkers who were anxious for a radical change. And it kind of reinforced what Michael had warned me about: that we were in for some "heavy shit," as he put it.

I had a little agenda that I was hoping to get across to these people. In fact, I had worked on it a little bit the night before because I had a hunch from the way Michael had been acting that he wasn't going to be an ardent spokesman at this meeting. And so I had prepared. Number one, I was going to tell them what we were about, and that we were not doing something that was opposed to any of their views, but rather alongside of, and that the two things didn't really mix as an event. And I would offer them something, like someplace where they might pass out some of their leaflets or whatever. I would give some concession at the end. I thought that this would be sort of a peacemaking kind of a negotiation.

And I think the meeting lasted about thirty seconds. I had no chance to give my agenda, no anything. Hoffman was abrupt and sort of very powerfully and menacingly—not quite angry, but just sort of, "I don't give a damn about you. I don't give a damn about your platform, your agenda, or whatever. Here's what we need." And what he needed was money. He said, "We don't give a damn about your festival. We don't give a damn about whether you want us or not. We're going to bring this whole thing down around your ears and if you don't want us to do that you'll write a check."

He wanted ten thousand dollars. And I started to talk about—I had this whole preparation—and as I started to talk, he sort of leaned over real close to my face. He said, "Can you hear me? *Ten thousand dollars.*" And at that point Michael began to cough sort of to get my attention, and said, "Well, we should be going now." And we left.

I said, "Well, we'll think it over. We'll be back to you." This wasn't a discussion. I had been hoping for some kind of a talk. No interchange, no exchange of views or anything like that. The price was named and that was it, and we left.

Hearing Reveals FBI Tapped Rev. King

*Post
Washington, D.C.
June 5, 1969*

109

It was a shakedown. There was enough vehemence in it and enough profanity in it so that I was meant to take him at his word. Something along the lines of, "We'll bring this motherfucking festival down around your fucking ears if . . ."—you know—"unless you meet our demands." And so it was kind of like, "Make my day. Go ahead, don't write the check and see what happens to you or to all your grand plans."

Michael was absolutely quiet about this. We took a cab back to the uptown office and I said, "Michael, do we have any room in this? Does this guy mean what he says?" "Yes, he means what he says." I said, "Michael, what kind of maneuvering room do we have here?" And Michael said, "We don't have any room." And I essentially trotted out all of my arguments and my negotiations on Michael, which was sort of a futile thing to do, but I was frustrated and a little frightened because these guys sounded like they meant business. And I said, "Michael, why don't we go to the police?" He said, "You don't understand this at all, do you?" And I said, "What am I missing?" He said, "You just don't understand this. You don't get it, do you?" And he invoked things that were beyond my grasp, although I must say that they did vibrate and play on that fear that I had that they were capable of unimaginable disruption and violence in a situation that I had always felt was susceptible to that. And, of course, history proves that such events are susceptible to that. We didn't conclude that we were going to pay the money, Michael and I. It was clear that Michael wanted to. I was uneasy about it. I still thought, and I talked it over with John, that maybe we should go to the authorities, but we were afraid of blowing something sky-high by doing that.

ABBIE HOFFMAN: I've seen this meeting referred to in subsequent dissections as kind of a blackmail and all this, but I don't particularly remember any bad vibes at all. I remember it as them thinking that it was a good idea, that it was worth it, that it would help the whole event, and I remember that we would agree to publicize it, too, through our various organs of communications and, you know, give it the Lower East Side stamp of approval.

MICHAEL LANG: It was a funny meeting. A lot of what went on in those days were theatrics. And I think the idea was to intimidate us. I think the whole thing was to intimidate us from the beginning, knowing Abbie.

I didn't want to give him money. I wasn't into buying him off but I did want to eliminate the heat, in essence. We offered him a deal, basically, to do something positive. His concern seemed to be that all these kids were going be out and not be properly taken care of, etc., etc., etc. I told him, "If that's your concern, why don't you figure out a way you can help make sure that they are taken care of?" He had proposed some sort of a press thing that he wanted to do, some sort of a newspaper screaming about this or that. I had to personally agree with a lot of the things he was saying, but that had nothing to do with what we were doing. So I said, "Help put out a survival sheet." So they agreed to that and we settled on an amount of money that we figured they would rip off so much and put so much in—or enough in so that they could do a sheet like that, which I thought would be helpful, everybody thought would be helpful. I don't remember the details. I remember that it was kind of ritualistic that morning. My impression is that there were certain rituals that everybody had to sort of sit through while they did whatever it is that they were doing.

JOHN ROBERTS: I think Michael probably overestimated the importance of Abbie Hoffman in those days, or at any time really. Hoffman was largely irrelevant. He was very good then and has continued to be extremely good at self-promotion. You hear a lot about Abbie Hoffman. But you have to search pretty hard to figure out—at least I would—how he changed much of anything.

JOEL ROSENMAN: I think that you're highlighting one of the things about Michael, too, and that is that he knew less about this stuff than I did. What he knew about was music and particularly the kind of music that his group was into at the time. And he knew kind of on the surface what people were thinking and feeling. But he hadn't been into what was going on in Vietnam or the radical politics of Abbie Hoffman or Bobby Seale. He didn't know what these people were about, what their power was, or their lack of it. He just knew he could tell me that he knew more about it than I did and would probably find an agreeable listener. So we paid them the ten thousand.

ABBIE HOFFMAN: A certain amount of bargaining went on and that's O.K. It's kind of collective bargaining, you know. I mean, I know people are not used to this, but by '69 I was twenty-eight years an organizer. You usually approach people in authority with some terms and you reach some agreement and we reached some agreement, so I don't see the point of hashing through the procedures, except to say that there have been mass rock concerts ever since that have known about this and there have been, whether it's a food bank or a local drug abuse clinic or whatever that have gone up to the concert and said, "Hey, look, we'd like you to kick in a little because it's our people, the people that are out in the audience that we care for," and they do. So, you know, I'm glad that we did this and as you will eventually find out in the narrative, I believe it's what saved Woodstock from being a disaster.

I think once the terms are agreed upon, it's ridiculous to go back and look at how you did it. It's enough to know that there was a negotiation session, that the reason for it was that there were people, there was a community at the time, that community felt that the music had grown out of its bowels, and that it was in conflict with mainstream society, with the police who were working for mainstream society, with the war in Vietnam, with racism being practiced by the society. That it was, for all intents and purposes, a revolutionary community. And so this would seem quite natural, if we're going to have this kind of event, to try in some way to inject some kind of political content into it—which, of course, rock promoters and the rock record industry, because this is the part that got them in trouble with Southern record distributors and with the government—always, always tried to separate the politics from culture as, of course, the movie *Woodstock* bragged about doing. The producers bragged to my face that roles that

Nixon to Reduce Vietnam Force, Pulling Out 25,000 G.I.s by Aug. 31

Times
New York, N.Y.
June 9, 1969

111

I and other political activists played were deliberately cut out of the movie, and they explained why and I understand.

Columbia University had a famous slogan at the time, you know, "The man can't bust our music." They were taking the energy from the streets and using it for a commercial value, saying, "If you are in the revolution, what you got to do is buy our records," while we were saying, "You got to burn your draft card, you can't go to Vietnam, you have to come to the demonstrations and the protests and wear your hair long, you know, drop out of school, etc., etc." It was a conflict and we called their process co-optation: that they were able to co-opt those parts that were commercial, and the parts that were radical they were able to reject quite easily. They were able to turn a historic civil clash in our society into a fad, then the fad could be sold.

I'm not an antagonist to sex, drugs, rock 'n' roll. I wanted to have a good time. And I know many of these performers personally and I wanted to see as many people as possible have a good time. I wanted to see a good presentation of the Woodstock Nation, of an alternative lifestyle that showed that all these people could come together and weren't going to stab each other, could enjoy the music. And I also wanted them to be able to know at the proper moment that they were supposed to be raising fists and not "Vs", and it wasn't all love, love, love. It was about justice, too. It was about ending a war. It was about changing our society.

CHAPTER SEVEN

"There was a moment when it was like being on a roller coaster that had just crested the rise—you know, before that first enormous plunge . . ."
—*John Roberts*

MICHAEL LANG: Wallkill died hard. It was less of a surprise than I thought it would be when I finally heard. As I said, I was sort of half-expecting it. I was hoping against it, but I was still half-expecting it. It was not a shock. It was a drag, but it was not a shock. And it was, "O.K., let's go find another one."

MEL LAWRENCE: The morale wasn't good. But things were happening so fast and the date was coming up so fast and to tell you the truth, I know this is true, but I never just thought it wouldn't happen. I always thought it was going to happen, we're going to make it happen. Because I liked the idea of it in the first place, and I know that everybody that was involved in it had their energy going to make it happen. And I knew that all that energy was going to happen. So, I tried to keep up spirits and say, "We're going to find some place." Michael and I must have looked for a week or maybe ten days—going to places and renting helicopters, and going here, and going there.

MICHAEL LANG: I think we put some ads in the papers, local papers upstate. And then I think we started making phone calls to everybody we knew. Wes and I and Ganoung and Stanley had developed different community programs, community projects. We called out through some of those programs to people that we contacted in various communities around. And then we also went out on the radio I think.

STANLEY GOLDSTEIN: Mel had been, all along, recommending Sullivan County. He felt that was the place to go, before the Mills site was acquired. Mel got a call from Elliott Teiber, who was the son of some people that owned a motel.

I know that it all happened pretty fast. I believe that Elliott called us and offered us a site, that there was some land down behind the motel that his family owned, and Mel and I went up there to this hotel— the El Monaco perhaps? Elliott pointed out the site to us. It didn't look great, it was overgrown, and Mel and I walked down into this bloody swamp. It was terrible. It was utterly unsuitable, and he took us down into it. And we had to get back out of it, as we tromped through looking for some piece of ground within this area that might be suitable.

MEL LAWRENCE: Stan and I go, "Oh God, maybe it will work. Maybe if we cut down all these trees." And then we thought that was horrible. Anyway, we went down to the bottom, and it was swamp marsh— impossible—so we really were dejected then, because this one really sounded the best.

113

Stanley Goldstein: Elliott, I think, wanted to become involved. He thought that he would get to cater the event, that if he could somehow get us up there that his commercial attitudes and instincts would be satisfied, that they would become the caterers to the event, provide food, that the motel would be busy, that it would be the center of activity and so forth, and that if he could be instrumental in causing it to happen that he would wind up making money. The area up there was one that was not doing well. The community was really quite depressed. And Elliott had been trying to attract a different kind of crowd and attention to the area. The motel occupied a corner piece of property and behind it there was another old inn and attached to the old inn was a barn and there was a theater company that was installed there. Elliott wanted to create kind of an arts colony atmosphere in that community, feeling that that might revitalize it. Yes, kind of a Woodstock. And he wanted to have bands up there and little concerts and so forth, and so this was furtherance of his dream and goal and what he felt was the proper course to follow. And so it was two dreams coming together.

Bill Ward: We got some addresses that were sent down by telephone, I think. And these were addresses of a whole bunch of people who had other sites for us to look at. And then the helicopter came. We had to go out to the airfield to pick up the helicopter, and I think Jeannie drove us out there and put us on the helicopter, and Mel and I flew away with this helicopter pilot in this old World War II helicopter. We started going to different sites to interview people. It was pretty spectacular. We came in a helicopter to these places and we met some of the sleaziest people in upstate New York. They were all trying to sell us a bill of goods and they were promising all kinds of things. I felt like kind of a rock star.

I remember one place that we went was a big summer camp-like thing for families and there were lots of kids and people around and it was in a huge open field—the most unappealing thing you ever saw—and a giant swimming pool and some buildings. And there were people everywhere; you couldn't hardly see anything for all the people. I remember all the vivid colors, all the oranges and yellows and reds and stuff like that. It was like a polka-dot village. The whole thing was so strange. We were ushered in and lots of kids came out when we landed the helicopter, and people followed us around all over. And we were ushered into this guy's office, and his desk seemed to be an old bar top or something. It looked like an old bar that was sort of reduced in size, and there was a huge fat man sitting behind it, and they told us all of the things that they could give us and promised all of this stuff, showed us the site. But it wasn't nearly big enough.

So we listened to him for a while and then we flew somewhere else and did the same thing and the pilot didn't quite know where we were going—because *we* didn't know where we were going—but what we had was addresses. And we actually flew—there are all those little hills in upstate New York, and he would fly over a hill and then dip down—and I had the brown bag over here ready all the time. I was getting so sick and Mel was a little queasy, but Mel was holding up pretty good compared to me. And the guy would dip down with the helicopter, get out his Texaco road map, I swear to you, spread out the Texaco road map all across the three of us and try and find out where we were. He would go down and read road signs, and that's how we were finding all of this. And finally at one of these places, the helicopter expired. It would not start. It started to rain. And I was so happy it wouldn't start. I remember the guy's famous quote: "This has never happened to me before." We had a taxi come and we were still about seventy-five miles from the next place we had to go. I was so sick from the airplane and then we had to go through these mountains with this guy driving really fast like this, up and down. It was terrible.

MEL LAWRENCE: I don't know how it happened, but the next thing was the Yasgur farm. Oh, I know how it happened: there was a middleman who somehow got wind of this—Morris Abraham. The middleman, in the old Central European tradition, is the guy who put deals together; he just keeps his ears open. I think that's what he did. And through Elliott, we get a call. It was a rainy day, foggy day, when we met with Abraham in that little hotel with Elliott. We sit and talk at the table, really weird. "Okay, I'm going to take you to the guy and the guy's farm." So he takes us to Max Yasgur's house and Yasgur comes out and he hops into the car and we're off, and Yasgur takes us to this big field. Flat. "There it is," he says. Michael looks at me and I say, "No, it's going to be hard to see. It's very big but it's flat. It would make a great parking lot, you know. This ain't the site." And we look at each other and he says, "What do you mean?" Yasgur says, "You want"—I forget what he said—"you want something that has an angle?" "Yeah, do you have any kind of hills?" "Oh yeah, come on." And then we hop in the car again.

Now it's raining and we're going through and it's misty and we're on this back road. We drive onto the top of that hill, drive right onto the grass, get to the top and get out, look out. And all of a sudden the rain stops and the mist is, like, breaking up.

And there it is. It's like a lake and a natural amphitheater and roads and woods. So we say like, "Oh, how much of this is your land?" "It's all mine," he says. "All mine, except the lake's not mine," he said. "That side of the road is not mine but I know the guy . . ."—you know, this and that. *Whew.* Michael and I looked at each other and said, "This is it." We were happy, we were smiling.

MICHAEL LANG: It was made in heaven. It was a bowl with a rise for a stage. What more could you want?

STANLEY GOLDSTEIN: Upstate New York is one of the prettiest areas of the country. It doesn't have the rugged beauty of the Rockies, it's not the spectacular beauty of the Grand Canyon, it's not the Black Hills; there are a lot of things that it's not. It's just lush and rolling hills and—pretty. There's a softness to upstate New York that's repeated in very few parts of the world. Fortunately, we have a few of them in this country, the Shenandoah Valley being another one. I've traveled extensively and there are few places in the world that are quite so lush and inviting, that there's contours sufficient to satisfy the eye and to keep bringing new vistas into view. But none of it is assaultive; none of it challenges you. It's very welcoming, warm, lush.

Show Will Go On, Rock Fete Promoters Boast

Times Herald Record
Middletown, N.Y.
July 15, 1969

115

Max Yasgur

And Max's land was manicured. He was a farmer who cared about his land. His fences were painted. Everything was in good repair. There's a relationship between a real farmer and his ground. If someone has been farming a piece of ground like that for that many years, there are no pebbles, there are no rocks, there are no broken bottles. The land had been tilled and turned and all obstructions removed. The land was just gorgeous. Max had a lovely, lovely farm. And all of the folks up there—it was not a new community. Max's farm was surrounded by other farms. Real development had not struck. So it was unending. Max grew hay, the folks next door grew corn, and so as far as the eye could see, there were fields and fields and fields. Those areas that couldn't be farmed because they were swampy or rocky or too hilly or whatever were left forested and treed so that wherever you looked there was green and shade. The particular area for the performance site was about—approximating—a hundred twenty degrees of natural amphitheater. It happened that a road cut through a portion of it, so there was a piece of it off from across the road, but without the ability to contour the land yourself, it would be very hard to have found a more ideal site than that. Now, as it turned out, some of what we thought was Max's land turned out to be other people's land, across some of these roads and in various places, and some of that had to be negotiated, and those tales are well told: that we paid more for two- or three- or five-day rental than the land had been for sale for just moments before.

116

Chip Monck (left),
Michael Lang

MEL LAWRENCE: We talked money with Max. I forget the conversation but it was decided very quickly and we shook hands. And Max only had three fingers on his hand. I'll never forget that, shaking a guy's hand that has three fingers. We all, like, shook. Michael and I shake; if it was now, we'd probably high-five, but I think we just shook, you know. And driving back we were elated. We thought we had a deal.

STANLEY GOLDSTEIN: And so Michael and I went there and I went with the roll of drawings and prints, all this data that we had gathered to present to the Wallkill community. I was the possessor of paper, and I was also the relatively articulate spokesman; I was presentable. And so Michael and I met with Max and showed him and described to him what it was that we had done, the vast amount of work that had been done, and the fact that we weren't fucking about, that we had hired really competent and capable people that had taken this seriously, that we were not simply Mickey and Judy and Donald O'Connor—*You can play the piano, I can write the words, you can sing, so we'll get together a show and we'll take it on the road*—but that we were a little bit more sophisticated than that.

MIRIAM YASGUR: My clearest memory is of this young man coming up the lane on a motorcycle wearing very long, curly hair—something I had not seen on a boy up to that date—a pair of jeans, I think, and a black leather vest, highly decorated, over his bare chest and arms, and boots. And he came to the door and I was a little hesitant as to whether

117

to let him into the house or not, and it turned out to be Michael Lang. And our first impression—you know, we felt very negative about the whole thing, having seen Michael; we weren't going to get involved with "those kinds" of kids. But it takes Michael about fifteen or twenty minutes to charm you, and having spoken with him for a while, he really put us at ease, despite his appearance. After that, it was a matter of discussing whether or not we really wanted to get involved in this thing, whether we wanted our land to be abused by almost ten thousand people a day for three days, which is what we were told it would be. We didn't feel that the compensation would be the issue at the time. We didn't want any damage to be done to the farm. So we hesitated about it and they kept trying to convince us, and there were discussions in our lawyer's office and subsequently in our home, I believe, and Max and I decided that we would take it under advisement; we were going to sleep on it and decide whether we really wanted to get involved or not. They were putting it on the basis of these young people who had no place to go, and they sort of appealed to Max's sense of fairness because why should young people be denied a place to go where older people would not be?

Michael Lang: I remember that Max was sympathetic, but he was also from another world from any of us, and I also remember he was pretty sharp. He kept sort of licking his pencil and taking notes about how much this was going to cost us. And he was trying to make a good deal for himself as well. He had that motivation as well. I mean, I think at the first meeting his main motivation was that we were willing to pay and that he was willing to make a deal on that basis. But he also was kind of intrigued by the idea.

Miriam Yasgur: Michael has a way of ingratiating himself that's really— I think it's born in him. He's a born con man, Michael. And you can't help but like him. Even though you know you're being had, you can't help but like him. Anyway, once we met John, we had a little bit different feeling about it, too, because John comes across as a very straight person, and he's probably one of the most honorable young men I ever met, John. And we were still hesitant, though, because we didn't want to get involved with this possible damage.

We were sort of iffy about the whole thing and we went to sleep thinking about it. My concern basically—Max was always the one to wade in with both feet; he was a person who got very involved—but my concern was for his health. It was not good and I didn't want him to have any added strain over and above what he was doing in the business, which was strenuous enough.

Max had his first heart attack when he was thirty-nine years old. He started working on the farm as a youngster. His father and mother had a farm and a boardinghouse; he preferred the farm and he worked the farm. His father died when he was seventeen and he became the man of the household in the sense that he kept the farm going, he helped his mother as much as he could with the boardinghouse. He had a brother who was six years younger than he was and he had a sense of responsibility and he grew up very young.

118   When we were married he was, I think, twenty, and I was

nineteen. And so, we made the choice to live on the farm instead of staying in the city, where he had family with whom he was very close, who were all in the real estate business. And he had gone to NYU and studied real estate law and so forth for a couple of years, but he wanted to go back to the farm. He didn't want to stay in New York. So I went back to the farm and it was a thirty-five- or a forty-dollar-a-month milk check and put-the-pennies-in-the-jar-until-we-had-fifteen-cents-apiece-to-go-to-the-movies kind of life. It was not easy, but it was what he wanted, so it was what I wanted and we kept building the farm. Eventually, his mother sold the boardinghouse and we left that farm; it was sold and we went to Bethel in order to be able to get more land, because in the area where he was born and raised, in Mablewood, we could not expand the farm and he wanted to grow.

We started increasing the herd and shipping milk to a commercial dairy. Eventually, we got a license to pasteurize milk and bought some routes which were then existing and then sent people out to canvass for other routes. And in order to then supply the customers that we had, we bought additional farms, we increased our herds, we became known as breeders of fine cattle, we built a pasteurization plant and the office, which was down right on Route 17B. And we had the cooler and we produced, pasteurized, and delivered our own products, both to retail customers and to some of the larger hotels like Grossinger's. And in the mountains we manufactured some products—cream and sour cream and the best chocolate milk anybody ever tasted. People came from all over just for our chocolate milk. The name became known in the area as a quality product. And he was very proud of that. He wouldn't put his name on the bottle if he didn't think he had a good product. Max was a man of great pride, very hard-working. He was as hard, maybe I should say, on the rest of us as he was on himself because he demanded that things be done right and he was that way with employees, too. And sometimes they didn't like it but they all respected him. And he was a man who, if he shook your hand and gave his word, you didn't need a contract. But nevertheless, he would take out a matchbook or a piece of paper and write a contract and it was iron-clad. And if you tried to break it later you found out that he knew more law than you thought this quiet farmer did. He played with a pipe and he thought it out while he was reaming the pipe. By the time he answered you, he knew what he was doing. He was a bright guy.

So we started with a farm and we bought adjacent farms as we could and we worked through the years that way together. But it took a toll on him and his heart was always a problem, and at the point when the festival occurred he had already had a subsequent heart attack or two and I had an oxygen tank in the boat and in the car—these little porta-tanks—and we had a big one up in the bedroom where he would go if he felt that he could not breathe or he had pains. He was taking medication and yet he was functioning in business and socially. A lot of other people who were in good health wouldn't have done that much, but we tried to be sensible. If he was overtired, he would sit down and relax, he wouldn't push. We wouldn't go out in the evening, even though we had planned to, if he came in and said he was tired. We both loved boating and fishing and so on and we had a place at that time already in the Florida Keys, and we would spend some time

Battle Rages— Festival to Sue Wallkill

Times Herald Record Middletown, N.Y. July 17, 1969

119

down there out on the boat and it was—we tried so that he would take it easier and easier; we had enough staff at that time so that we could do that. And so I felt that he was undertaking something that might be detrimental to his health. That was my hesitance.

So, we were fifty-fifty or sixty-forty or whatever and went to bed and got up in the morning. Apparently, the talk was around town at this point because several days of discussion had been going on. Morris Abraham had probably talked to other people about it and maybe some of the principals, and it doesn't take long for things to get around in a small town. And there were a group of people apparently that were very distressed at the idea that this might happen. So we got up in the morning and in our bedroom we had a balcony off our bedroom window which faced 17B, the main highway. There was a big field between the house and the highway, and down at the end of the field we saw a sign had been erected. Now, we knew we didn't have any signs down there. Eventually, of course, we checked it. On the sign it said something like, DON'T BUY YASGUR'S MILK, HE LOVES THE HIPPIES. And I thought, "You don't know Max, because we're going to have a festival."

That did it. He said, "Is it all right with you? We're going to have a festival." We always made joint decisions after he decided what he wanted. Most of the time I said yes because I agreed. If I said no, we then didn't or discussed it further. But I knew that he was not going to get past this sign. And he was leaning toward helping the kids anyway, so I said, "I guess we're going to have a festival." And he said, "Yep, we're going to have a festival." And maybe we wouldn't have if not for the sign, I don't know. I won't ever know.

JOHN ROBERTS: Joel and I went up to see Max and get some kind of a handle on the town politics. We sure didn't want to get into the problem there as we had in Wallkill. And this town looked like it would be an easier nut to crack. They just didn't have enough time to organize. It was really a question of could we insert ourselves with enough momentum into White Lake before they could mobilize.

We drove up to Max's with Michael Lang and Max was very matter-of-fact, very casual, told me he thought a great wrong had been done, gave me a little bit of history about his life as a dairy farmer there, spoke about the town, what he saw as the problems of getting this thing through to the town, wanted to know what we had in mind, how much damage we thought we would do, asked us a few questions about our backgrounds. Came off as very matter-of-fact. He just said he was doing a good thing, he felt, but he was going to be paid for it, by George—quite a lot of money, actually—and told us what that would have to be, and there was a sense that he wasn't that open to negotiations. You know, we tried—at least I tried—and failed; I think we got him down somewhat from his original. And he basically sort of opened up his property to us and said, "This money covers everything I'm going to need. Whatever you gotta do to the property you do. I just expect you to restore it. And I'll give you all the cooperation I can, all the favors that I can, to get this thing done."

Max and I got along very well. I think Max thought Michael was bizarre. He didn't dislike him but he didn't know what to make of him. He knew what to make of me; met my type before, I think.

STANLEY GOLDSTEIN: Max was just Mister Solid Citizen. Max was a businessman and Max made a good deal and Max got his dollars and so on and so forth. But the real telling thing with Max was that he felt, after we made our presentation, that in fact we had been mistreated, that we had not had a proper hearing, that we had not had a proper forum, that there was nothing that we were doing that was un-American and not right, that people deserved to have their say and their moment, that we were entitled to that as folks. And, by God, he was going to see that we had our chance. Max was just straight, solid, and upright. Not that he was a paradigm, but Max was quite a guy.

MEL LAWRENCE: Max was very handsome. He looked like sort of an old Sandy Koufax. He was very strong, you know—not too tall, but you could tell he was strong. He was a total farmer, but businessman farmer, you know. He'd managed to build himself quite a business with his dairy farm and he owned quite a bit of property. He was an intelligent man that gave the impression he was well read, and he seemed to be a religious kind of guy, although I never saw him in any kind of a religious activity, but he did seem to me to be a religious kind of guy. He liked Michael and I. We hit it off, not in a formal kind of way, but you could see in his eyes when he would talk to me or to Michael. And he kind of liked the craziness of it and the lark of it and he also liked the big money of it—he loved that part. We were, I mean, you know—we were doing everything for this guy. We were giving him money, we were going to bring him back his land to the same condition, leave all the wells that we dug there, making his land even more valuable, and we promised all of this, we oathed that we were going to like clean it up and bring it back just the way it is, you know. Which we did, and which was a nice thing. And did improve that land.

MIRIAM YASGUR: Max dictated what terms he wanted, they discussed what terms they wanted, and since they really didn't have too much choice, I suppose he got mostly what he wanted out of the thing. I'm sure he tried to be fair—someone else might have pressed them harder—but he was as fair as he felt he wanted to be. They had a choice of yes or no and they settled the deal. The terms that he put in were that they could not use certain parts of the land and so forth until we got the crops off and he was just trying to make sure that the land wasn't damaged in any way.

STANLEY GOLDSTEIN: Max made a good deal, or a relatively good deal. But Max didn't need the money. Max was not driven by greed as so many other people were. Max's basic decision was, to him, a moral decision. Max was not stupid. Max had value; he was going to get real value for it. He wasn't going to give his land away to prove a point. Max ran a very successful business enterprise. He was not giving anything away; he made his bucks. He made a deal and he hung to that deal. There were lots of times that a weaker man would have and could have canceled the deal. And we didn't uphold all the levels of our contract. We had agreements with him about how we would begin to occupy the land, that he had to get his hay out, and so on and so forth. And we wouldn't dig trenches here, and we couldn't cut this, and we

Aquarian Exposition May Move to Sullivan

Times Herald Record
Middletown, N.Y.
July 19, 1969

121

wouldn't do that. Max had lots of opportunity to impede us, to demand more dollars, and he didn't, he didn't. I believe that he made a commitment based upon what he felt was the right thing to do, what was the American way. He was a strong believer. Max was really a firm, firm believer in people's rights. And so while he screamed and he hollered and he went into his oxygen tent and he sucked oxygen and he beat us up about this and he beat us up about that, he was just true-blue all the way. Once he made that commitment, once he agreed to do this, he was committed to seeing it through and seeing that we got a fair shake. The end of it was seeing that we got a fair shake, and a straight forum.

JOHN ROBERTS: He was a good guy, Max, and I think he had a strong sense of goodness in people and looked to that and was always surprised by reality. That was my sense of him. Not a hayseed, not uneducated in any way at all. Homespun, likable. After the festival we became very friendly. He invited me up there to help him milk the cows and live with him for a few months, actually. He was a father figure type. I think he liked that role. I think he found a real cause or reason to be living through this festival.

JOEL ROSENMAN: I think that it was a sense of adventure, a sense of wanting to do something other than what he was doing, that motivated him to invite us. And I agree with John that his businessman's attitudes made him charge the limit for the rental. And he knew he had us. But for a farmer to do anything, he has to get behind it emotionally, I believe; very few farmers would do it just for the moment, especially in those days when I don't think they were as financially behind the eight ball as they are now. He was a romantic down at the bottom, fundamentally, and this had so much appeal for him in a romantic way that he couldn't resist it.

MEL LAWRENCE: But we hadn't heard the last of the White Lake community, either, because they started fucking with us. But this time we had Yasgur. This time we had a member of the community who wasn't a wimp like Mills—who was a nice guy, you know, but not a man of stature or a guy who can be a key element in a historic time, in an event that was almost meant to be.

This time, it was the Hasidic community and, again, a community of country people, that did not want an influx of people. We always talked lower numbers than what we expected, but even with

Rock Rumble in Rip Van Winkle County

*Saratogian
Saratoga Springs, N.Y.
July 19, 1969*

those lower numbers, they didn't want to have any part of it. But Max was an important part of the community and, I suspect, somebody who supported a lot of the politicians in that area in one way or another. And his influence overrode the rest of the community. He started appealing to the democracy of it all, you know. I'm sure he was working behind the scenes because he always indicated to me that, "Everything's going to be all right. Don't worry." But there were times it was pretty hairy, many times where Michael and I were outside, not knowing what was going to go on. But again, there was always this sense that I had that it was going to happen.

JOHN ROBERTS: We felt excited about the possibilities of the new site, but there was a lot to be done. We didn't want to repeat a lot of the same mistakes that we'd done at Wallkill, so we paid a lot of attention to the politics of this particular site—who we had to know, what we had to do, who we had to convince, who we had to stay clear of, you know.

STANLEY GOLDSTEIN: Michael and I debated about going to see Max because a real estate agent came to us looking for some money in a bag and claimed that he was going to use this money to grease the town fathers, certain specific town fathers. We really debated at that moment whether or not to pay the man off. And I think that it was in keeping with our attitudes—and I think it was one of the things that was telling with Max as well—that we decided that we were playing it straight-arrow. Michael and I decided that we didn't want to do that, that we wanted to talk to Max. If that's what we had to do, that we would do that, but that we didn't want to do it, and that we were coming to him to say, "This is what we've been offered. We don't want to do it, we don't think it's the right thing to do. Do we have to do this? Is this the way to survive in this town? Is this the way things get done?"

We described to Max these circumstances—God, Max was incensed—and he said that no one was going to have to pay anyone off in that town to do the thing. That was the right thing to do, and if anything, committed Max more to our cause. For all of our failures to abide by agreements, for all the niggling details that went on later, it was the fact that we had come to him and said that we had this offer, we didn't want to buy our way into the community; that wasn't the way we wanted to do the gig.

MIRIAM YASGUR: I don't remember the exact details, but Max very firmly told them that he was not interested in getting involved in anything like that and as a matter of fact, some funds had already changed hands and Max insisted that this money then be donated to charity, otherwise, you know, he would blow the whistle on the thing. And as I recall, this individual was deeply distressed, angry, whatever, that the money did not get into his hands and/or anyone he intended to share it with. But Max insisted that he would not allow anything like that to happen.

JOHN ROBERTS: When we found Max, the first thing we did was try and direct this juggernaut that was heading towards Wallkill to White Lake. We took out this great ad—have you ever seen that ad with the guys with the blunderbuss and the jowly hillbilly looks that said, "Certain

Ted Kennedy Escapes, Woman Dies as Car Plunges Into Vineyard Pond

Globe
Boston, Mass.
July 20, 1969

123

citizens didn't welcome us to Wallkill"?

JOEL ROSENMAN: We talked about that ad for a long time. Did we want to thumb our noses at Wallkill?—it was the same kind of decision that we had to make throughout the festival—or did we want to do something positive in the statement? And it's kind of nice to look back on it and think that we made the decision to do something as positive as we could, given the circumstances, while at the same time acknowledging what everybody knew, which was that we had been evicted. I

think the ad came off very pleasantly, very positive, and actually reinforced the tone that we were trying to set for the festival, and made everybody comfortable—may have even made Wallkill comfortable, I don't know.

JOHN ROBERTS: There was an enormous amount to be done in a very short period of time. The major hassle, of course, was building the site, building the stage, getting the lights and the sound system up, the fences, and, of course, we were in the last throes of contracting with food concessionaires, with the small concessionaires who were going to be putting together the shops and the booths. All of the logistics. We had to rent some outlying pieces of property for parking lots. We had to meet those people and convince them that this was going to be a good thing. Security forces—we were getting down to the last what we had hoped would have been just sort of topping out at Wallkill. We had to do the topping-out process while at the same time do all the substrata work too. So it was a time of incredible frenetic activity.

MEL LAWRENCE: We hadn't really built anything in Wallkill except the bridge; most of the work that we had done was clearing work. So we started to lay out what the grounds would be, where the concessions would go, where the art park would go, where the camping areas would be. We'd do a lot of walking around, finding the best areas. Then we discovered that down at the bottom that we had a drainage problem and we had to tile it—we had to put these tiles so that the drainage

124

would drain away from the stage. That was considerable work to do that. We had to acquire some property, like for the backstage area—we had to acquire that property next to the lake. Mister Filippini—that was a guy we worked with. I remember a lot of negotiating about what we needed and there were other players now. I mean, now we had, God, maybe a hundred people that were involved with us. We started our own lumber operation—that's one thing from Wallkill that we did. We had a lumbering thing that we were cutting down these sapling trees to build concession stands and things like that. And I believe we started doing that in Wallkill, so we had those sapling trees that we brought to White Lake. We had to establish things, like you can't drive all over the site. I mean, that was a must because I knew we'd destroy it in like three weeks; it would be just like total mud from guys just taking the shortest routes and everything. Of course, now we're talking about we gotta bring all this power, because we didn't have the right power on site, so we needed all this electricity to come; I forget how many miles it had to come.

JOHN ROBERTS: There was a moment when it was like being on a roller coaster that had just crested the rise—you know, before that first enormous plunge—and I think as we were going up there we were always calculating this and that number of tickets and how much the acts cost and what the fences will cost and all that. But there was that moment after we crested that hill—and I would date that moment from Max, the day Max entered the picture and we closed the deal with him and we made that first enormous payment for his land, which I think was seventy-five thousand dollars. From that day, things were going past too quickly to think in terms of profit or loss. I swear I never thought of profit and loss. I just thought of getting it on. And the reasons, I've determined in retrospect—why I was so careless in my thinking about it at that point—were that I had contemplated the abyss of a total wipeout a week earlier where the three quarters of a million we had spent as of July 1, let's say, was gone; plus, we'd have to end up refunding about six hundred thousand dollars' worth of tickets. So compared to a million-three-hundred-thousand-dollar bath, everything else seemed like an enormous windfall.

So once Max entered the picture, it kind of freed up a generosity impulse on our part, and so we just started spending. It was just if you were going to throw it, then you had to pay to move certain things to certain places, you had to pay to make sure that people knew to come to White Lake instead of Wallkill, you had to pay to reprint the tickets so they said the right thing. You had to pay. Otherwise there would be no festival and you could hope that whatever the ancillary rights were, whatever number of tickets you would sell, would pay you back. The original budget was out the window.

'The Eagle Has Landed'— Two Men Walk on the Moon

Post
Washington, D.C.
July 21, 1969

125

• CHAPTER EIGHT •

*"If Jimi Hendrix was running across that bridge,
chased by as many groupies as could get
on that bridge, and they were all coming down
on one foot at one time, what was the weight load
for the bridge?"*
—*Chris Langhart*

MICHAEL LANG: A lot of thought went into the program—who would follow what and how you build through a day. I mean, you have kids that you have to keep there for three days, or at least a day at a time, as we were originally thinking. And you wanted something that moved them through the day nicely and climaxed well.

Prior to the festival, I had stayed in Hector Morales' office for six months, learning the business of booking acts. Hector became a friend and we spent a lot of time together and I used to stay in his office, morning till night, before this project happened, just learning how to book and what the business was about. So I realized that in order to create instant credibility for the show, I had to book the major acts in the industry first—two or three or four of them—and pay them what they asked. And then we'd be in a position where we'd at least be considered a real entity. People would take us seriously.

That's pretty much how it worked. I think the plan was a good one in that sense. We set a limit of what we'd pay an act, which was fifteen thousand dollars, and stuck to it. The only one that negotiated beyond it was Jimi Hendrix. He had a booking a week before for a hundred fifty thousand dollars in California, and I still wouldn't pay him more than fifteen thousand, but he insisted on it being thirty. And I said, "Fine. We'll pay you thirty if you'll play twice—the first day and the last day." It never really occurred; we ran out of time. But he was the only one who was paid more than fifteen, and it was for two shows.

I booked it by the day. I had planned to build it so we'd ease into the festival on Friday. I didn't want to become feverish too early. So there were a lot of folkish acts booked on Friday. Friday was supposed to be easing into it. Saturday was, as I recall, supposed to have been more of a getting-into-rock day and West Coast acts. And Sunday was just, blow it out.

JOHN MORRIS: The idea of the booking, the philosophy of the booking, as it eventually became, was that the first day would be soft, would be the Incredible String Band, Joan Baez, Richie Havens, Ravi, that kind of thing. That the second night would be sort of America, and then we'd go England. And so that really was the only booking philosophy to it. We were damned lucky—the things that we got and the prices that we paid. I mean, of course, by today's standards. When I think of everybody that was listed on that program, I think about a third of the people are still performing.

I hadn't done all the booking at the Fillmore—Bill Graham had done most of it—but I knew all the agents and everybody. We did some funny things. The Ten Years After concert we wrote for nine thousand, eight hundred seventy-six dollars and twenty-three cents, or some comparable figure, just because nobody had ever done that. Everybody talked in terms of twenty-five hundred, five thousand, ten thousand dollars. And just as a joke we decided to do an odd contract.

MICHAEL LANG: We came up with the concept of alphabetical billing, which simplified a lot of the ego problems. And then we did a lot of early bookings. We booked Crosby, Stills, and Nash before they were a band. David Geffen came into Hector's office, I remember one day, and played the record. He said, "Wait until you hear this." We heard it and it was fantastic. So we did a lot of interesting booking that way. We booked a lot of people early on who started to come into the public eye around the time of the show. I booked Sly Stone three times and canceled him twice, as he started to do more and more no-shows. But he was a friend. I had known him. I was talked into it, I think, mostly by him. He really wanted to do it, and he was serious about making it. Which he did. It was one of the high points, I felt.

Rock Fest Wins A-OK From Bethel

*Times Herald Record
Middletown, N.Y.
July 22, 1969*

JOHN MORRIS: I'd seen Joe Cocker in London and he'd done one show at the Fillmore and Cocker was just potentially the greatest. And that was a steal at twenty-five hundred. I'd seen Santana because I'd been out to visit Graham and I called two or three record company presidents that I knew to "get down here and sign this guy." He was playing with Elvin Bishop first and it was wonderful.

BILL BELMONT: In early 1969, Bill Graham conned me into going to work for him. I worked for Graham in his San Francisco office on and off for like two or three or weeks. He asked me to fix his management company, Shady Management. Shady Management at the time managed a whole bunch of unknown bands. But it also booked and kind of managed the Grateful Dead. The Grateful Dead had an office in the back room on Union Street. And through that I heard in May that these guys were trying to put together Woodstock, this festival in Woodstock, New York.

The person that was doing most of the talking and most of the booking and most of the negotiating was John Morris. John did almost everything. Michael Lang appeared to be a principal only later on as the summer wore on. In May, Santana went back East for his first Eastern trip. And Graham was still negotiating to get the Grateful Dead at Woodstock. The only way Graham could give them the Grateful Dead was if they took Santana, and that's how Santana got on the bill for a thousand dollars. Michael Lang was like, "Who the fuck is this band anyway?" I remember. It's true that John knew the band and liked them, but Graham forced them on as a way of solidifying the Grateful Dead. The Dead didn't get very much money to play Woodstock. Santana got a thousand dollars, I remember that.

JOHN MORRIS: There's the story about The Who and Frank Barsalona. I booked a lot with Premier Talent, because I knew them very well. Barbara Skydell and Frank were good friends. And we needed one more key act. To get The Who for Woodstock, Frank and I had Peter

127

Bill Belmont

Townshend to dinner at Frank Barsalona's house. Frank's an insomniac, and I was pretty good at staying awake in those days because I was almost as much of an insomniac. And we wore Peter down to the point where he agreed to do it. Finally. This is after him saying for hours and hours and hours, "No, no, no, I'm not going to do it, I'm not going to do it." Because they didn't want to stay in the U.S. that long. They wanted to get back to their families. Or he wanted to. And Frank and I finally wore him to the nubbin that he was at that point. He was sitting in a corner and finally he said, "O.K., all right. But it will have to be fifteen thousand." And I had to look him straight in the face at six o'clock in the morning and say, "We only have eleven thousand dollars left. That's all that's left in the budget." And I thought he was going to kill me, but he was just too tired. He just said, "Oh, all right, if you let me go to bed. Whatever you say."

Frank was furious that we didn't—he couldn't believe that I would book Country Joe and the Fish and an unknown band from California named Santana for twenty-five hundred apiece—Cocker also got twenty-five hundred—and not take Jethro Tull. Frank would give me a lot of, "Who are these guys? They're a bunch of guys from California. And you won't take Jethro Tull!" And were we not really good friends, he would not have talked to me for a long time. Frank was and is probably one of the most powerful agents in the business, and one of the nicest human beings that ever existed.

BILL BELMONT: A month before Woodstock, I got hired by the Doors to do a South American tour with them. I grew up in Mexico and I speak

128

Spanish. So I went to L.A. on and off. And Michael Lang himself was trying desperately to get the Doors to play Woodstock. You know why the Doors didn't play Woodstock? Jim Morrison was convinced he was going to get killed. That was the only reason they didn't play, because Jim was convinced that someone was going to shoot him, assassinate him. And he didn't want to expose himself to that. A couple of the Doors showed up at the festival and I arranged to get them in.

Earlier in the summer, I was in New York City, visiting Woodstock's fancy office in the Fifties. I joked with them a lot about the fact that Country Joe and the Fish were not scheduled to appear, and someone made a comment that Michael Lang didn't like Country Joe and the Fish. There was a political problem about it. They didn't want any politics at Woodstock. And that's that. We figured it was a fait accompli. So when I later went back to work at Woodstock, I was entrusted by my colleagues—we wanted them on the bill—with the mission of getting Country Joe and the Fish on the bill.

So Jeff Beck canceled and John started pressuring Michael about Country Joe and the Fish. Beck was supposed to get seventy-five hundred dollars. Michael—probably because he was pressured into it and probably because he really couldn't get anybody else he wanted— finally agreed to pay Country Joe and the Fish forty-five hundred dollars. And we called the agent; everything got settled. He got both Country Joe and the Fish and Paul Butterfield. So there were two draft choices for one running back. For the same seventy-five hundred dollars.

JOHN MORRIS: I don't remember in the booking there being any terrible booking problems. I don't remember us having sort of our hearts in our throats with the exception of The Who. Once we had The Who—we had Hendrix before we had The Who. Once we had Hendrix and we had The Who—again, not having any conception of the size or scale of what we were doing—we had a pretty rounded-out schedule. We'd managed to fill it.

• • • •

MEL LAWRENCE: Every day was involved with meetings—with the electric company and with our electrical contractor and with the plumbing contractor. And on our side there was always an expert in that area. It was a lot of getting our shit together, ready to coordinate it all into place in a certain time. And the weather was not good; it was raining quite a bit. You know, this all compresses sort of, but I remember it raining quite a lot. I also remember outfitting everybody, buying them these yellow slickers. Also, people were coming down with colds and we were getting these B12 shots. Every three days, everybody would go to this doctor in White Lake who gave us these B12 shots that really worked great, because they were like speed for everybody. And little did I know, they were resisting colds. I was giving them, really, for speed—and I was taking them myself. But they resisted colds.

BILL WARD: It was always my view that Mel held everything together.

Promoters Claim They Can Handle 150,000

*Times Herald Record
Middletown, N.Y.
July 22, 1969*

129

The guys in town were playing with booking dates and stuff like that and making deals and doing all that stuff, and it was all on paper. But Mel was doing everything in the field. Mel had a hard job, and he had to cajole people. He had an incredible thing to face every day. He was making deals with people about toilets. He was trying to make people do their jobs that had come and agreed to do jobs and were not doing jobs. He had to make that whole thing work, and he wasn't real popular with some of the people. I always thought he was the one who made the whole thing work—other than maybe God—because nobody really knew how it all came together. It all just sort of came together mysteriously one day.

LEE BLUMER: Because we were moving closer to Monticello, we had to go out and find permanent housing, and Penny and I found the Diamond Horseshoe. I guess Penny found the Diamond Horseshoe— I was eventually with her—which is the place that caught fire the night before the festival. I remember that was the weekend also that I found out about John Lennon marrying Yoko Ono. And that was very distressing to me at that time. I was quite upset with him.

CAROL GREEN: Penny and I drove up to the Diamond Horseshoe where she took me on a tour. It was a condemned hotel. As we were looking at this place—it looked like *The Money Pit*—Penny says, "Isn't this fabulous? Isn't this gorgeous?" It was crazy. We moved into this hotel. There was a pool in the back and there had been stables and I think the deal was that this had been a very posh hotel in the twenties and a horseracing thing; the horse track was nearby.

We moved in, and we had a plumbing crew put in the plumbing. I remember sitting in—I think it was breakfast that we were trying to eat in the dining room—and the ceiling went *creak, creak*. And we thought, "Let's get out of here." We lost a few rooms. People would have to actually evacuate their room, because the ceiling would cave through. We didn't have any plumbing for I don't know how long, like twenty-four hours or so.

It was nuts: we had like one toilet, I was not getting along with my boyfriend, some girl came up to sell everybody heroin—that was fun—and was making it with my boyfriend. It was a mess, and there we were in this crazy mess. And I remember finding a gun in the kitchen with Penny and going "Aaaahhh!" It was a gun for starting swimming races and stuff like that, but I thought for sure there had been some terrible murder here, and this place was so crazy that anything could have happened.

CHRIS LANGHART: That place needed a hell of a lot of renovation, and we ended up having to do a quick-and-dirty to get all the lavatories in there working, or even some reasonable part of them. The place was just beat. They had let all of the galvanized pipes freeze over the years, and there just wasn't a stick of plumbing outside the kitchen that could be made to work on upper floors, and you couldn't have everybody running downstairs all the time. So we spent about a week with a separate gang in there just in the most grotesque fashion: Take the Skil saw and saw up an ugly section of the hall floor where the water seemed to be squirting and look after the pipe and then whip out a braising torch and then braise closed the crack. Or braise the fitting back on, or whatever was wrong. It wasn't real plumbing, where you actually replaced things. You just put bandage clamps around things and radiator-hose clamps and did one thing and another until you could make it so that it dripped less and worked more, rather than dripping more and working less. And that's where everybody stayed until the actual thing, when it suddenly became impossible to get back and forth anymore.

LEE BLUMER: That's when the tensions actually began—when we had

131

to move and we had six weeks. Tensions within the organization. I mean there had been camps in Wallkill. Michael already had his Porsche in Wallkill, but then we moved to White Lake and he went out and got horses. And that sort of solidified a certain kind of—"Who the hell does he think he is?" Well, it was so pretentious for what we were doing. It was completely so unconnected to what we were supposedly going to be doing—or what, supposedly, his vision was. He rode the land like a land baron. Like there were people picking the corn and all that, and he was riding the land, wearing this fringe—I mean, I'll never forget it—this fringe vest and no shirt, so his muscles popped through, and he had this curly hair and he always looked like he was listening to a different channel than everybody else—and I think, in fact, he was. I mean, I was very ambivalent about it because I thought he was just so cute. He was just so funny, so odd, and very charismatic. But his responsibility level was just—he was like one of those guys who could drive his car eighty-five miles per hour on the freeway and not get killed; but if you did it, you'd get a flat tire, your car would turn over, and your mother would get you or something. He had such this false sense of courage. But it wasn't courage—it was stupid. I mean, everybody likes to think he had a vision. I think he had an idea about how great it would be—far out, man. But I just wonder if he really believed himself to truly be an instrument of it, or he just, as I said before, took the next logical, abstract step once it became available.

MICHAEL LANG: We had horses that we used a few days while we were building. I didn't have a horse that festival weekend. I didn't get around on a horse. But it became a little bit much. There was a stable down the road so a bunch of us rented horses to ride; especially in the mud it seemed like a good idea. The image was a little difficult for everybody to take.

Michael lang

LEE BLUMER: Michael was pretty much an icon to the Woodstock festival. He was the religious artifact. He was somehow going to "glow" this thing right, and he was completely incomprehensible to me. He never said anything. I do not remember full

132

sentences from Michael. We did have a few staff meetings where he would say something, but they never appeared to be full sentences to me. And he just seemed to glow. That's true. He had this cosmic aura about him, and I don't mean to overdo this, but he always had this little smile on his face like he knew something that none of us knew. Which, as it turns out, was not necessarily true. And he smiled a lot and anybody who walks around like that, you get the feeling that he must know something, otherwise what would he be doing? As it turned out, that wasn't necessarily the case. But he managed to glow a lot of things into existence that I don't think any other one of those people, given the personalities—none of them could have done that. He also glowed himself a Porsche. And he glowed himself a horse. He somehow became like the icon of the festival.

How Now, Aquarians?

Herald Mail
Fairport, N.Y.
July 23, 1969

And John and Joel were considered to be just so outside—"Uh-oh, they're coming again." But because I was with the grown-ups—Don and Wes—I was more inclined to be around them and hear what they were going through and listen to their tortured tales. So I was. I mean, I actually got close with them in the end. And I still have very strong feelings for them. But they were seen as bumbling fools who had lots of money and who had not a clue—nothing—about any of it, and would never really hang around to find out. When they did hang around, they hung around in sports jackets; you could never quite forget that they had just graduated from wherever it was—Princeton, I think—and that they were very Ivy League, while all the rest of us were absolutely not. There were no real Ivy Leaguers in that group. Their sort of quasi-announced reasons for being involved with Woodstock—I think maybe this is myth now, I don't remember—was that they wanted to get laid. This was like the big idea that that's what they were there for. And they weren't doing that either, so it was like, "What *are* they doing here?" They were almost like Steve Martin and Dan Akroyd, except not quite. But at the same time, you couldn't quibble with their hearts. They were trying hard to be good guys.

STANLEY GOLDSTEIN: We had to expand our staff enormously. All of our plans, everything that we had done, everything that we had laid out just went right to shit from being on an industrial site, where there was plenty of power in close proximity and everything could be done pretty easily, and being in-line for telephone communications easily. We suddenly were off in a not just rural—we were remote—and there wasn't the ability to get the electrical power. Instead of being concerned now with whether or not we were going to light the campgrounds and roadways, we were concerned with how we were going to get power there at all on any kind of stable basis.

CHRIS LANGHART: There was a lot of stuff to be bought. Jim Mitchell, who had been at NYU as the TD/administrator of the scene design department for a while, was one of the ones who was doing all of the buying of pretty much all of the stuff. He was in charge of buying fire extinguishers and supplies for the food people—not actually the food, but pretty much everything else. During the course of arranging the office trailers and arranging the rent-a-cars and all of that stuff, I guess we ended up—although I don't know the exact story—with almost all

133

of the Alexander's rent-a-cars that Alexander's had. And so far as I can tell, after the job, all of the Alexander's rent-a-cars just went off to the four corners of the earth and Alexander's went out of business.

WES POMEROY: We could talk about all the problems we wanted to and nobody quite had a solution. But everyone knew, everyone was an expert on toilets. They understood that. Everyone had that experience. In the beginning, it was kind of a joke, sort of a place to retreat was to a Johnny on the spot, or to talk about it.

JOHN MORRIS: A lot of Woodstock was planned from U.S. Army field managers. Go to a library and try to find out how many toilets you have to have for how many thousand people and how you set up food and how you do the rest of it. About the only source that there is, I mean until the Mass Gathering Act and all the stuff that came afterwards. But that was about the only place you could look was to look to the military and get an idea.

We needed resource. We needed a library to figure out, "How do you figure out how many toilets you have to have for how many people?" And the only data was little brown U.S. Army field manuals. So Langhart and I went and pulled them out and there are some general rules. It's not all just guns and the rest of it. But that was the only source there was.

Until we realized that it was a resource, we were trying to figure every way we could. Stanley would go take a clipboard and figure out the traffic patterns or something like that. There was no real precedent. You could call people who built buildings and see how many toilets per floor and this kind of thing. But it wasn't going to help you. So everybody was doing things their own way. All that data sort of came in. And Mel and Chris had their confluence of ideas and information, and that's where it came out. That was all you had to base it on.

STANLEY GOLDSTEIN: We knew we'd have to have a lot of toilets, but no one knew how many, so I started making telephone calls to folks and no one apparently knew much about it. They could approach it from the point of view of construction sites, but no one had any real feeling for how many toilets you needed for how many people for how many hours, and so forth, and how long people took. I began going to events with stopwatches and clipboards—Madison Square Garden and baseball stadiums. I went to the airport—any place where there's a lot of people—and I'd time people going in and coming out and going in and coming out and so forth, at all kinds of hours, and developed my own criteria for toilets.

I took all the information I gathered, took the information provided by experts, read all the building codes for public gathering places, and threw a dart at the board and made some guesses. When we took the numbers it was just too outlandish. Some of that had to do with the fact that we were talking of crowds of unknown sizes so we just took various size crowds and created some numbers that said, "How many people can crap in how much period of time?" and I multiplied and divided and presumed twenty-four-hour use and divided how many people could use one john in how long and then

134

divided the size of the crowd and came up with outrageous numbers of johns. Tens of thousands. Impossible numbers, particularly in view of the calls that were made to toilet vendors who had fifteen or twenty or sixty-five or a hundred-ten. And it always turned out that the number of toilets that we would need, according to the experts, were *exactly* the number of toilets that they owned or expected to have free at that time. You know: "Hey Joe, how many crappers we got?," as they covered the mouthpiece with their hands, hoping that I wouldn't hear what was going on. And then Joe would shout from the back, "Sixty-five." And the guy would get back on the telephone and say, "Yeah, for a hundred thousand people you're going to need sixty-five toilets."

Part of the problem was that when talking to people, if you dealt with numbers of a hundred thousand or greater, first of all they considered that you were nuts and to do an event of this nature out in the woods was the proof that I was nuts—we were nuts, all the people involved were nuts—and that it couldn't possibly happen. So I was potentially just simply wasting their time and that even if we were crazy enough to do this that no one was going to come, so we really didn't require much in the way of resources. And if you took the number up to two hundred thousand, or two hundred and fifty thousand, that was proof positive that we were crazy and that it could never, ever, ever happen. And so we dealt with more moderate numbers to just get any kinds of answers at all and then extrapolated from that and then decided that nobody knew and that we were going to have to create our own sets of numbers and do a best guess.

FRED DUBETSKY: I don't remember how the call came to us about Woodstock, but since Port-O-San is perhaps the largest or most well-known company in the portable toilet business, I'm sure we just got the call from whomever the promoters were. And it sounded to me at the time like it was going to be a pretty big deal. Of course, my interest in it at that time was largely because it was going to be business—that's what we're in business for. So I remember going up there and going over the area and having discussions with the promoters, whose names I don't remember, about what kind of attendance they anticipated. And based on what they told me and my experience in specifying toilet requirements for special public events, we came up with what we thought would be needed.

Now, you should understand that specifying toilets for public events is far from an exact science. We have some experience about how many toilets should be for so many people. But this was a new kind of event where people were going to be camping out. They were going to be staying there twenty-four hours a day. Generally, a special public event is something that's a few hours or a day and then it's over. So we had to calculate how many toilets to put up there, how to get them cleaned, and all of this had to fit within some kind of budget. They had to be able to pay for it. And essentially to pay for it in advance, because dealing with special public events you have to get paid up front or there may be nobody to chase afterwards.

CHRIS LANGHART: Well, the health department now imagines that you should have a toilet for every hundred persons. In point of fact, it will

135

hold together about three times that—just—so that gives them a bit of a safety factor and the honey dipper manages to find someplace locally where he could unload whatever toilets he could unload and clean and so on. A honey dipper has this big hose and they just stick it down there and clean it right out. That is the way it's handled. It's only a question of where the truck goes and whether it can get there in time, and some of them were accessible and some weren't. It's just a question of where they're put and you just cannot—I mean, in that situation, it's the first time that kind of an event had been done and nobody could reasonably predict, except for Stanley's experience in Florida, which was nothing like as solid an impact as this thing was. It gave a little test case.

STANLEY GOLDSTEIN: Where do you dump the stuff? They did not have any concept. They only knew that if you pumped out these temporary shitters that they wanted it out of their town and they wanted it taken to a site that could accept all this stuff, which was a million miles away, and the toilet guys just were not quite prepared to provide service that many miles away with those many toilets. There had been some conceptualizing that, well, sure, if we don't have enough toilets, we can always bring some more. Well, just the cartage, the additional miles to bring all that stuff up there, just made the contracting that much more difficult because it took everything out of everyone's service for that much longer.

CHRIS LANGHART: Everybody kind of had their dibs in there. It was a difficult area. It was a question of coordinating the honey-dipping trucks and getting enough toilets there and dealing with the health department. Mostly it was a matter of dealing with the health department. The actual contracts for the toilet contractors were not in my area. But the actual man-to-man defense of the health department was in my area. And what we ended up with was I was kicking the problem around with somebody or other at the Bora restaurant down there on Second and 9th. This is the restaurant which at that time was run by the Ukrainian Boy Scouts. And I was talking with somebody at the counter there about this problem and there was this interested chap across the way, and he kind of had his ear perked up and I invited him over to find out what he knew about what we were up to. His name was Gene Meyer and he's a biologic research chap.

He did know about all these things—more than I knew about them. I mean, I know about purifying water a little bit and filtering and dealing with piping and size and flow and all that. But that's all engineering stuff and not really biology stuff. And the health department was more into the other. So when I caught on with him I thought, "Right, this is the body. We just put him in with the health department and he can communicate with them. We set them all up in a trailer and he just keeps them sort of at bay and when there's a problem he'll come around and we'll get it dealt with. But that way they will always have somebody to deal with and my being constantly pestered by everything else will be able to be continued without that erupting as a difficult problem."

I could see that more and more they—the health department—were being given the chance to decide whether this was going to happen or not. And ultimately, the Mass Gathering Act of New York State, which most other states copied and adopted, was a health department regulation. And so, indeed, mass gatherings in all these different places now are regulated by the health department. When somebody wants to know whether you can do a festival, what you have to deal with is the state health department, because they're the ones that get to decide whether you can have all these people in one place or not.

That was kind of the way it was on all fronts. You saw the problem coming and you found the Gene Meyer or the Tom Grimm or whoever it was that was going to put the fire out and you got it in place before the fire got started and it just kept on going. The power company by that time was there pretty much on a constant basis and so you would say, "All right, in a couple days this is going to turn into a campsite and we're going to need a transformer here, and you plant a pole and bring your high line over here and do this and that and give me a box on the pole and I'll work it from there." And you'd get Harold Pantel lined up to get the secondary of it taken care of. And then, at some point, while you were on some other errand, the green Porsche would drive up and Joel would be there, and he would say, "Well, what can we do?" I would say, "Well, over there in Mrs. So-and-So's yard we're having a pole in her front yard with a transformer on it and it's going to turn into a campground. You better go over there and make some kind of an arrangement with her because there's just no way that's not going to happen." So he wouldn't resist—it wasn't the usual promoter's aggravation of, "Why do we have to do this?" He would just go off and deal with it. And then he would come back and say, "Oh, that was bad. I had to pay her seven thousand dollars and I could have had this whole farm for less than that and now I've only rented it for two weeks for that much money." But it was done. And on we went like that, just ever increasing the diameter of our little city as it was necessary from whichever direction it would seem most reasonable to attack it.

And there were many other things that were in need, like how shall we handle lighting around the heliport so these helicopters can come and go in the middle of the night, because they can't see where to land all of a sudden, and that kind of thing. So we put in Christmas tree lights. We must have had most of the normal, worldwide supply of Christmas tree lights which could be bought in the summer already installed, swagging through the forests to the camp areas. But there were still a few more, so we put a red ring around the snow fence and that was an easy marker for the drivers of the choppers and they could easily see their way in there.

STANLEY GOLDSTEIN: It was an enormous construction undertaking. There had to be water, there had to be this, there had to be that, there had to be a thousand things. Time. There was the political situation, that negotiating and trying to come up with acceptable road plans, sanitation plans, coming up with these things but, again, so much of that was a function of time, to suddenly have to do all of that.

For example, you can't just take garbage and throw it anyplace you want, you have to find a place to put it. Ordinarily, you deal with a carting company. Carting companies are weird people to deal with. All their names end in vowels, you know, and they're very territorial, and they have their own peculiar relationships and standards and forms, and Mel was the guy who was primarily doing that. So Mel was trying to contact and contract the very best garbage guys around and available who had the largest, the best, the biggest equipment and so forth. And those guys didn't have the connects up in that area, didn't have the dumping grounds in that area, and they also just didn't understand the volume that we were discussing.

MEL LAWRENCE: There was a company that was going to do the trash hauling, they were called New York Carting, a guy named Chuck Makalooso, you know, the New York Carting Company. I mean hard businessmen in a very competitive field in New York, you know. And I asked them for a bid, amongst other companies, and I'd interview these guys, you know, and see what kinds of guys they were and check out the company and everything, because that's a responsible job and plus it's pretty expensive. Finally I decided, "O.K., this is the company, New York Carting Company." I liked their facility, their trucks, how many trucks they had, and they had these containers and shit. So I called the guy and I told him, "O.K., you're the guy, Chuck. Let's meet." So I think we met in Middletown, and had a little contract and everything, and he said, "What do you want for *you?*" I mean, it was like from so far left field for me, it never even entered my mind for me, you know, but that's the way business is done. He was like, "You deserve this. You're giving me this big job. What do you want?" And what I'm saying is that it never entered my mind to even think that this would even be open. And this was not the first—I mean, the fence guy too, and this other guy, too.

Sen. McCarthy Won't Run for Re-election in 1970

Post
Washington, D.C.
July 25, 1969

STANLEY GOLDSTEIN: There continued to be, for us and for them, this very hard situation of how many people are coming, what do you really have to prepare for. If you said to someone a quarter of a million people they said that you were just absolutely nuts; if you said a hundred thousand, they still didn't understand the scale of it and what the impact could be, what the sheer volumes of material could be. Water, finding satisfactory sources for water. We eventually ended up digging a lot of wells very, very, very fast, and installing an above-ground water system on Max's property. Left him a lot of wells. I don't remember how many; Chris Langhart came in and got really involved up at that site.

CHRIS LANGHART: Max Yasgur and I got on quite well because he wanted to talk about the dairy and I was interested in the dairy, because it had ice cream-making facilities and bottle washing. He had some refrigeration problems and I could talk refrigeration because I had done it at the Fillmore, fixing the air conditioning and doing all that stuff. So we hit it off pretty famously in terms of getting on. He would come by while we were working during the early stages and we would shake hands and walk around on the grass and see what there was. Sort of then, after explaining to him what the water system in my mind was going to be made of for Woodstock itself, I talked with him about the few ditches that I would have to have here and there and I hired all his recommended contractors and the next thing you know the poor dear was in an oxygen tent because I had cut a slot right across the field in such a way, according to him—even though it seemed to be going across the slope perpendicular to the travel of the water—he was sure that it would bring about tremendous erosion and all kinds of troubles. It wasn't what should have happened. But, indeed, for the use to which we had to put that field, there was not much of any other approach.

Basically, there were six or seven wells there—some of them were the producers and others sort of not worth the trouble to drill. But

139

between that and the lake and four ten-thousand-gallon tanks, we managed to keep water there all the time. Things got a little low on the second day—that is to say those tanks might have been down to a couple of feet—but still that's a lot of water, given that the usage never ran them out. Also, things got off to a slow start because the health department had us putting philozone tablets in every twenty-foot length of pipe that was assembled. These are like you use for campers to purify water, kind of chlorine stuff. And it was a difficult problem because it was super overchlorinated and it made everybody not use any water. Which sort of was handy—that wasn't the intent of the use of it, but it ended up being that way.

MEL LAWRENCE: There were some excesses, but I think excesses in spending money, the excesses were to get it on. I mean, sure, we had to pay Harold Pantel, our electrical contractor, three times as much, because we wanted it in one week, you know. We wanted some miracle in one week, so we had to really pay. And that was excessive, but it was all to get it on.

HAROLD PANTEL: I told them that either we would do it all or they could get somebody else. So they were just going to use the pole-line work—the street lighting, the yard lighting, and bringing the feeds into the various areas. Anyhow, they seemed to go along with me. I said I was going to be able to perform—after all, we were going to build a city there in a couple of weeks; we never knew how big it was going to be, though.

I sent my men over and we started to work. They had it very well organized as far as I was concerned. They had blueprints, maps, projections for the whole area. So then it became a question of logistics once we got the work, to get enough materials at the job site so we could perform. I started to pull supplies from the three local supply houses in the area and they had nowheres near enough, so we got stuff from Albany, from Binghamton, from New York City, and we got it there on time.

On the site we had about thirty electricians working, and even to get that much manpower I had to drain my other jobs and put men on double shifts; you know, they'd work on one job to meet our regular obligations and then they'd come after work for six or seven hours at the site. And I had no problem. Everything went along fine except when the people started to come up. Nobody had any idea that there were going to be that many people. So it became difficult to gain egress or exit out of the property—to get tools in, to get trucks in, to get supplies—and eventually, we were using the helicopters. We flew from there, landed in my backyard over here, went out to the warehouse and loaded up, and got the stuff back and forth.

The supply houses—we had them at their wit's end trying to get enough equipment in. And luckily we had some large switch gear that we had purchased when the New York World's Fair finished up. We bought a lot of that equipment up and it just fit in fine here. So, some larger stuff that usually takes three or four months to get on hand—because they have to be factory made—we were able to alter the stuff that we had and use it for the facilities there.

140

It was like wiring a city up, actually. We probably put in a couple of hundred poles, strung wires, put in these large services, many of which were not ever used because they were installed for the parking lots so people could get in off the road. I think there were ten areas that we put in four-hundred amp, three-phase service, eight-hundred amp, and one place two thousand for the stage. Like I say, it's enough to light a town up. And it did. Of course, we had more work when all of the sudden they realized they had to have a heliport to take out the people that weren't feeling too well. As far as the material goes, we probably used maybe fifteen miles or so to go in and out. It was just unreal; we couldn't get the stuff, but we managed, we had to. Some of it's still here, believe it or not.

I'm in the movie also, in the stage area. I used a little foul language, if you hear somebody hollering out there—"Get the f--- out of here . . ." You know, that's me.

CHRIS LANGHART: It became apparent that we needed telephones. I thought we ought to have a lot of pay phones so that all the kiddies who had worried parents could ring up home and announce that they were all right or they were not all right or they needed this or that or whatever. So we organized this big panel with sixty or eighty pay phones on it and we figured we needed twenty lines for ourselves on the site itself, more or less. So in round numbers, we ought to have a hundred lines. But the phone company wasn't willing to believe it. And they were hanging back until the very last moment.

I don't know exactly what happened, but at some point, I got my college roommate from Carnegie, Tom Grimm, involved. He had worked for the phone company and had a better understanding of how their processes went, and either by contacting the FCC or some other means, succeeded in convincing them that we were, indeed, the customer and they were indeed the purveyor in this area and they'd better hop to and get some phone lines in there. And when they finally made the decision they did come in droves. They had six or seven trucks down from Canada, each with a giant roll of cable, and they put in seven or eight miles of phone line in nothing flat and wired up all those pay phones. Somebody in the office cut a deal with them whereas we got part of the coin box and they got all of the reverse-charge calls. They will not yet, so far as I know, divulge how much money they made on that weekend. But it must have been staggering because there was a queue of sixty or a hundred feet on every one of those phones for the entire duration of the entire time that anybody was around there. Of course, it's much easier to charge it to Daddy at home. So it was all reverse the charges. I don't think anybody ever came near trying to get the coin boxes emptied, because who had any money to waste on calling home? You'd call and reverse the charge.

CHIP MONCK: I think I was probably there about a week and a half, two weeks prior to the show. And I don't think I ever stayed there in any sort of accommodations that I thought I was supposed to. I know I opened an account in the local bank, which was about the size of a postage stamp. And I think I brought some thirty-six-foot piece of construction trailer up, and I remember it had two wrought-iron

Auto Thrill Show to Compete with Rock Festival

Times Herald Record
Middletown, N.Y.
July 26, 1969

141

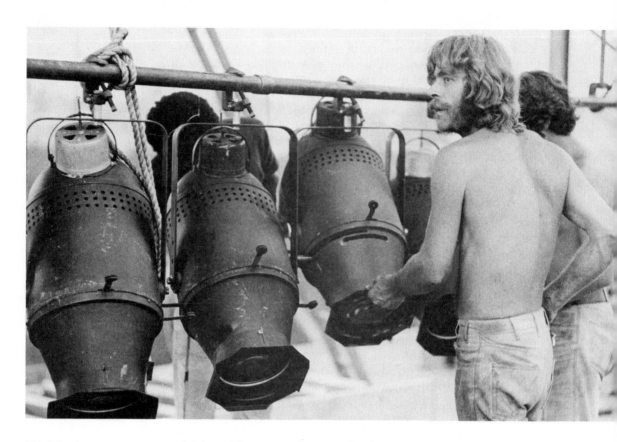

Chip Monck

candelabras. They were about six feet high and I brought those in with lots of furniture. I think I stayed in the trailer then, down near the lake, for most of the time that I was there. Made showering a little bit of a slight handicap.

The stage we built was about seventy-six feet across, with a sixty-foot turntable. The downstage of the section stage from the center line of the turntable, which was some thirty feet, was up about nine and a half inches high, the vertical depth of the turntable. So you had some ferry slip or surround on either side of the turntable and around the face of it, and it was at the same height of the turntable. The depth of the deck, I think, if I'm not mistaken, was also some seventy-six feet, about eleven-foot-six off the ground. The barrier fence was eight feet in front of that and was about six feet high. There was an eight-foot barrier behind that and upon that was the camera platforms. Two stairway accesses, only one of which I remember, and the bridge were upstage right to go across the road to the performers' pavilion. Somebody said to Langhart, "Build a bridge," and he said, "Oh, okay." And numbers of telephone poles and four-by-fours later, the bridge sort of sprung up, as if there wasn't any problem with getting a bridge over a main road.

JOHN MORRIS: Langhart came into my office one night and said, "How much does Jimi Hendrix weigh?" And I said, "Huh?" And he said, "How much does Jimi Hendrix weigh?" I said, "Well, I don't know. He was a paratrooper, he's in pretty tight shape, he's not that tall, he's maybe

142

about five-nine. Maybe a hundred thirty-five, a hundred and forty-five. Why?" "Never mind." Langhart disappeared and went over to his trailer. He came back in a while and he said, "What does your average groupie weigh?" I said, "Langhart, have you lost your mind? What is going on here?" He said, "What does a groupie weigh?" I said, "Chris, there's no such thing as an average groupie." "John, just give me a number." I said, "O.K. Well, actually probably about the same as Hendrix. Some of them are sort of chubby and overweight but my image is small, say a hundred and thirty, maybe a hundred thirty-five—between a hundred twenty-five and a hundred thirty-five. Langhart, what are you talking about?" "No, it's O.K., it's all right. I just need to know." You just leave Langhart alone. So he went away.

Three or four hours later he comes over and he shows me the technical drawings for a bridge. And this bridge is built out of four-by-fours and telephone poles—we're talking a solid bridge. I think it was four feet wide. I said, "Langhart, what's the story?" He said, "Well, I had to figure out the loading. I had to figure out how strong to make this bridge." It was a long span, it was an eighteen-foot span. And I said, "Yeah, what has this got to do with Hendrix and groupies?" He said, "Well, I figured if Jimi Hendrix was running across that bridge, chased by as many groupies as could get on that bridge and they were all coming down on one foot at one time, what was the weight load for the bridge? Then I doubled it." The end of this story is that it took two D-6 bulldozers with steel hawsers around this bridge half a day to tear it down, and they destroyed the road surface doing it. You could have driven one of those bulldozers, if it was four feet wide, across this thing.

CHRIS LANGHART: My job was always to be the "Oh well, consider what would happen if" kind of person. And that was the sort of general construction approach which we took all the way through. And it paid off because, though the system did endure a bulge, we never actually stopped or had any disasters which were extreme.

CHIP MONCK: He built the bridge, and it had the same sort of interesting, perhaps funky, fit into the area very nicely because it wasn't made all out of steel, it all was just wood. No plans, just paste this here and screw that here. And it worked out just fine.

143

Chris Langhart: The performers' pavilion was another interesting problem. After we got done with the futuristic stage, which competition I lost, so to speak, it was then decided that I should design something. Or it was suggested, I think, mostly by John Morris. So then understanding more about where Michael's head was at, I went after doing the performer's building. Here again, what I thought should be a modern flavor mixed in with this rustic aspect that Michael had—after all, rock 'n' roll music, Jimi Hendrix, and the like could not exactly be considered rustic in my view. And with all of Chip's brightly colored lighting, it didn't seem to me that it was hardly plain white light and the German Brecht theater. So thereafter I thought, "Let's have something with modern angles but which is relaxed-looking but is not so simple as a rectangular kind of cubicle log cabin."

So I organized a kind of a not-too-accurate circle of posts, each of which had an off-center "T" on the top that pitched at an angle, so there were all these verticals with these kind of sloping logs, with the smaller diameter part up at the top and the larger part down at the bottom so as to make them kind of balanced. They put a couple of metal struts up on the side of the phone pole and cut it off at an angle and set this other thing on top of it. I had a model built on a wooden platform that was on a hill and we photographed it from the top with graph paper set underneath so that they could position the poles, and Harold Pantel came around with his posthole truck and plunked all the poles in. And they bought a load of poles somewhere, used, and we put all these angled pieces on the top and then Dick Hartman, who was

the sort of resident rigger-type, came up there and put cable loops through the groups, so that the thing had like three or four coincident apexes, where poles from varying sides would come up and join here and then other ones would come up and join underneath but off from where the first lot was. So there were three or four different tops to this thing. Maybe five; I don't exactly remember. At any rate, John rigged up a kind of roof underneath it with kind of a canvas button that fit down below all the apexes.

Bill Hanley

The pavilion worked fine and Michael liked it a lot in the end, having sort of set himself up as the artistic director, if you will. And he insisted after we had torn out and torn down most of the things that it should be left up, even though it seemed to me that there might be some legal problems surrounding it. And ultimately, that land was owned by this gent who did tear it down or got it torn down somehow. But it stayed there quite some time after the job, maybe a couple of years. I guess people went back to see the site where it was, and it was still standing there. I think he envisioned it standing like that, a monument kind of thing. But it was obvious that this guy was going to build his ranch there and it just wasn't going to stay.

JOHN MORRIS: The performance pavilion was a testimony to Langhart's brilliance. Al Aronowitz, who covered the festival for the New York *Post*, did a whole series of articles leading up to the festival. I guess a day or two before the festival he had pretty much run out of things to write about. And he said, "John, tell me something—what can I write about?" I knew most of the press from the Fillmore and from being around New York and being involved in theater and all the rest of it. And Al needed a story. I said, "Why don't you go follow Langhart." So he wrote this wonderful thing about Chris. It was a great piece about how Chris was repairing what he was doing and everything else. And there was a typo and Chris Langhart came out *Christ* Langhart. And it was one of the great accidents—a great, almost true thing. The article was about "Mister Christ Langhart."

STANLEY GOLDSTEIN: Another problem was that we weren't quite sure when the sound system was going to show up. Bill Hanley was the hardest guy to make a deal with and to get a real commitment from. He said he would do it, he wanted to do it, but to find out what it was he was going to do, what he was *really* going to do and what he could really deliver was just fucking impossible.

CHIP MONCK: Hanley was always marvelously schlock. He is an absolutely darling man. If he gets you in a corner, he'll talk you to death and you're gone. He was at that time just about the only contractor available. He had more RCAW boxes than anybody else had. He

145

actually could woof and tweet what was an appropriate estimation or resemblance to the actual sound. Numbers and numbers of tube amps and early Macs and Altecs and some gorgeous equipment that would be fun to have nowadays, because it would make a guitar sound lovely. But beyond that, it was a really small, nice, cute little system that nobody in their right mind would have used for a gathering of that size.

Bill Hanley: Stanley called up looking to do the sound for this humongous event, trying to pick my brain. That's the first thing I remember hearing about it and it sort of lie dormant for quite a spell. I was the most experienced person in doing large events, doing large sound systems. We pioneered in that whole field. We were the first people to put in large, high-fidelity-type sound systems, with speakers weighing tons and a lot of heavy equipment. He was proposing having a lot of people at this event. I can't remember specifically how many people that he was expecting. I had done President Johnson's inauguration in 1965. I was doing these kinds of things all the time, all of the anti-war movement stuff with large groups of people. So we were the most experienced people that there were at the time.

Mel Lawrence: He and his brother and his business manager, Judi Bernstein, were people who had developed some of the first big P.A. systems. I remember first meeting him through Chip Monck and Bert Cohen and his company when we were setting up the Miami Pop. That's how I met Stan. I was looking for a sound system for Miami Pop and Stan was an engineer or a partner or something in a studio down there, and Stan didn't have the equipment that we needed or that Chip, who was the staging director, wanted. And he knew Hanley and Hanley had this equipment and came down from Massachusetts.

Hanley was kind of a square guy—I mean, he wore white socks and black shoes and kind of nondescript suits. And his brother Terry was very different from him. I remember Hanley had dark hair and Terry had red hair or light hair, and they were completely different guys. Terry was like a hippie and Hanley, I think, was a hippie in his head, but he certainly didn't look like one or ever give that impression. And Judi Bernstein was a trip too. These were kind of movement people. Many times, Hanley would donate his sound system to the movement for various shows that went on in the sixties. At that time, the festival biz was a small biz and I personally had been involved in most of them—I think all of them, at that point. So all the same people sort of worked in positions. We worked as a family, and Hanley was really a good guy.

Judi Bernstein: Perhaps the connection for most of those people at that time was the fact that we had the sound system at the Fillmore East, which was the focal point for all the rock 'n' roll in the city of New York. We were the largest mobile sound company in the country and the only company that had much experience in large outdoor events like this.

Bill Hanley: We started mixing the Newport Jazz and Folk Festivals back in the late fifties and took it over in the early sixties. So we were doing large events for a long time.

JUDI BERNSTEIN: In terms of the discussions concerning Woodstock and putting all the pieces together, that's something that I remember being very concerned about from the point of view of the fact that I managed the company. In managing the company, this was a question of having eight or ten or twelve trucks on the road at the same time and getting them to the right place, having equipment in the right place. And I always had great concerns for the fact that the entire Woodstock operation was such an amorphous mass and that it was constantly changing. It was nothing you could pin them down on. Bill and I went down to New York and had a meeting, and it was an amorphous meeting. It never really took place.

We stood in the offices and just watched people moving from place to place. No meeting ever took place. No six people ever sat down and went through this production from beginning to end to say, "This is what we expect." Part of the problem was that it was coming close to the time where they ended up moving sites. And the whole thing became a series of histrionics. But the intent was that there was going to be a concert come hell or high water. That was the goal. I was beside myself when I left there. I just didn't envision how any of this was going to happen, how we were going to get paid, how we were going to prepare. Because you couldn't pin anything down. Everyone would have these grandiose ideas and they unrolled these huge plans. It was wild. The cast of characters was incredible.

STANLEY GOLDSTEIN: I don't want to give the wrong impression. At the time, Hanley was—there were a lot of guys competing and there were a lot of guys who did a pretty decent job given the fact the equipment just didn't fucking exist at that time. These were tubed amplifiers.

What people were using were Altec Voice of the Theater speaker cabinets. Not the small Voice of the Theater, the enormous Voice of the Theater cabinets—nine feet tall, four feet wide, with two fifteen-inch loudspeakers in them. They were just enormous. They had been designed to work inside theaters. They were enormous, they weighed a lot but they could not take the power; they were driven by tubed amplifiers and the best amplifiers in the world, McIntosh, but they were not designed to travel. They were not designed to be beaten around on trucks at high speeds over roads and out into fields. P.A. was really in its infancy, and Hanley was capable of putting together a large system. Maybe not large by today's standards, but at that time, Hanley was—there was nobody else. There were other people who claimed that they could do it, but there was no one else. And Bill was doing as many gigs as he could possibly do. He was in a lot of ways very innovative, very creative, and very sloppy. His equipment didn't get the maintenance that it required. But Bill was extraordinary. He put together what was not a bad P.A. system of relatively enormous size, and he hauled the shit all over the country. Bill was the original tractor-trailer man. He created touring sound of magnitude. But the equipment was falling apart around you, and he had used it on gigs and gathered it from here and there and pulled it out of Madison Square Garden and pulled it out of a theater in Boston. It was simply lashed together.

HAROLD COHEN: At Hanley Sound, we did something that was very

Kennedy Weighs Quitting; Pleads Guilty to Charge

Times
New York, N.Y.
July 26, 1969

147

unique for the time. And that is, we used very directional speakers: we would put speakers where the people were. If you look at any of the pictures of the sound systems at Woodstock, you'll see there are multiple levels. The speakers that were down low were for the front people. The speakers that were up high were to shoot and project all the way back. The purpose of doing that was so you weren't blasting out your front rows and you were carrying your back people. We also used multiple compressor limiters at that time. There was more compression on things going long distances because you wanted to reduce dynamic range. Dynamic range being the difference between the loudest and quietest portion of what you are hearing. If you were setting up a large speaker system such as what we had there without having some form of compression, the people in the back would never hear the soft passages. They'd only hear the loud passages. So, consequently, what you needed to do was you needed to remove the dynamic range.

The system was approximately ten thousand watts RMS in audio into eight ohms. It would be the equivalent of a sound company today going out and doing a hundred twenty-five to a hundred fifty-thousand watts. There weren't ten companies in the country like there are now that would be capable of being able to amass that kind of power. We did all of this using equipment that was owned by Hanley Sound. We didn't pool it with five other companies. And we did have not only the main stage covered but we also had small systems available for the puppet theater and also the other free stage that was to be set up at Woodstock, even though the sound systems were never erected on those stages.

By the way, most of the things that I'm talking about now are pretty commonplace to what people are doing in sound reinforcement and they are certainly doing a lot more. But at the time we were doing it, no one was doing this. We used to have everything in black boxes because we didn't want people to know, for fear they would go out and buy the stuff or copy it and go into business for themselves. We kept things as trade secrets on an ongoing basis.

MIRIAM YASGUR: Max admired so much the zeal that these young people were putting into it, and he sort of became their booster. The only thing he would keep an eye out was to make sure that they weren't doing anything that they weren't supposed to or destroying anything. But he would go up there and show them how to run a machine once in a while or send someone up to help them. But in the main, they were working round the clock like beavers and he began to feel a strong admiration for their zeal.

MEL LAWRENCE: Max was starting to get a little upset because we were going very fast and I was making decisions very fast—decisions like, "Where shall we put this road? The guy is here, the gravel is here. This is it." "There, put it there." You know, like, "Hey, this is where we're going to put it. And that's it. We gotta commit. This is it. The gravel is here. Do it." Then he'd come out and say, "What are you doing? You can't put gravel there," like that kind of thing and then hold his heart, because he had a heart condition. Oh, it was a trip. And then I would have to calm him down. "Max, Max, we're going to clean this up, every piece of gravel. If you don't want it here, every piece of gravel is going to come up. If you don't want that, don't worry, Max." That's the way it was. There was a lot of that kind of thing.

MIRIAM YASGUR: I don't recall that it was a major thing in our lives because, you know, I would be going down to the office in the morning and working in the office with the women. I worked in our dairy office during those years and until probably about 1970 or so. But Max and I were still in business together so to speak; by that time he very rarely, if ever, went on any extended trip even to see someone on business for two or three hours that I did not go with him, and more often than not I drove the car in order to spare him physically. He would never admit to the world that he tired but he did; his heart was giving him problems. He was six feet tall and he had shoulders like this and he had muscles all over. He had worked hard in his life and he had this sense of not wanting to admit that he had any weaknesses physically.

We would drive up once in a while and look at it with amazement, this what was going on, and they really were very careful, they did not do any damage—no more than they had to—and I thought to myself, "How are they going to sit ten thousand kids on this hill?" But they said they could so they would.

• CHAPTER NINE •

"My God, we're the cops! I can't believe it."
— *Wavy Gravy*

LEE BLUMER: Once the Hog Farm and all that started pouring in, it was just hard to tell fact from fiction a lot. Who was working and who wasn't. And that last seven or eight days was—I mean, I couldn't tell one day from the next. We really did not sleep. We really didn't have a chance to do anything else but keep trying.

Right in the middle of all that was when we lost our cops.

WES POMEROY: One of the things that we were doing was recruiting the members of the Peace Service Corps. Jewell Ross, a retired captain from the Berkeley Police Department, a longtime friend of mine, came up with the name. And I hired Jewell to write a procedural manual and to fill up the rules for this Peace Service Corps we were having. That whole thing was done rather carefully, I thought. We got permission from Howard Leary, the Commissioner of Police in New York City, to go down and put notices in all the police precincts. Or at least from his office. I never got anything signed by him. And that's where we met Joe Fink, because he was one of the good guys.

JOE FINK: I was assigned down on the Lower East Side at the time of the advent of the hippie movement—I was the precinct commander in the Ninth Precinct—and among the people that we dealt with were business people that were involved in providing entertainment and merchandise for the people in the area. The Fillmore East, you know, and Bill Graham were outstanding people in that entertainment community. And I think it was through Bill Graham or people that worked for him that I got a call asking me if I would be interested in handling security for the Woodstock festival. They told me what the setup was going to be, and they said because of my reputation they would like me to handle all the security arrangements for the Woodstock festival.

I was working in the police department at the time and it wasn't an easy thing to do. We were prohibited from doing outside work that had any semblance of security or police operations, and I think I told this to whoever contacted me at that time. I told them that I couldn't do it. It wasn't something that I could leave the police department to handle and I had no intention at that time of leaving the police department.

In the city of New York we had lots of cops. At that time I would say there was something like thirty thousand policemen more or less. And we came up with the idea that if we could get policemen who were off-duty to work at that festival, you would have experienced people, you would have people who were knowledgeable, you would have people who had some sort of background and understanding of what the problems involved would be.

I contacted the Patrolmen's Benevolent Association, and we

discussed the possibility of their being the agency through which we could reach all the police people and find out who would be off-duty at the time and on vacation. We were trying to use only those who were on vacation, so there wouldn't be a question of a fellow on his day off being called back. If he was working up at White Lake he couldn't return quickly to the city. I eventually got to see the chief inspector, who was then George McMannis, and we discussed the situation and we delineated the fact that

Joe Fink

policemen—who would be on vacation at that time, who had the right to leave the city and do whatever they wanted practically—would be asked if they would work on a per-diem basis to help solidify the security situation there. Because if there were going to be a big problem, it would be better to have experienced people, knowledgeable people, rather than those personnel that they can pick up and hire without any in-depth investigation into their background—mental capacity, physical capacity, etc. Nothing was clearly defined, nothing was established as a special procedure, but we were given the okay to go ahead and to do this.

WES POMEROY: We advertised for people to come and work for us, and we said if you can be content with a nonenforcement role and work unarmed and become members of the Peace Service Corps, we'll pay you fifty dollars a day plus room and board and transportation. That was a pretty good salary then; not bad now for a lot of folks.

JOE FINK: We held interviews in a catering hall right next to the Fillmore East. We set up a couple of sessions there where we had the policemen come up to be interviewed and to explain to them what was going on. We worked through the Policemen's Benevolent Association. We posted notices on all the bulletin boards in all the station houses—and there were some eighty-eight precincts in New York—requesting those that were interested to come down and apply for a job. And we had a tremendous outpouring of people. We had to find people who were younger and who had the physical stamina to do something like this. We had to interview people to see if they would be amenable to

151

policing kids without hassling them too much for minor peccadilloes. We had to find people, knowing that there was going to be grass smoked up there and everything else, that could understand this and see if they could help to provide safety for the people around without making a big production out of little matters.

LEE BLUMER: I want to say that we interviewed a thousand cops. It probably really wasn't a thousand, but we did it for two days where Ratner's used to be. We sat there all day, interviewing cops all day. I think they were fairly obvious questions about young people. I wish I could remember the specific questions, but I do remember coming away knowing, from the questions, that I knew who was going to be too rough and who was going to be too physical and who was going to be upset by drugs and copulation, or whatever little things might occur as a result of this little soiree we were throwing. I can't accurately remember questions. But we talked until the cows came home and came away with, I think, over three hundred policemen who all fit Wes's very-well-drawn-out profile.

WES POMEROY: As part of the screening process we showed them the uniforms they were going to wear, which was bell-bottom jeans and red T-shirts with "Peace" on the front and the Woodstock emblem on the back, and the jacket, which was a nylon jacket. And a pith helmet. Showing them what they were going to wear—that in itself would be enough to screen people out. We told them, "It's a rock festival and there would be kids up there who were relaxed and easygoing and they're going to be dressed in lots of different ways and you have to

Peace Corps

be comfortable with that." We just wanted to make sure they were comfortable. "And your role is going to be to help people. That's what you do most of the time anyway as a police officer. If they need to know how to get help, you help them. We don't expect there to be any violence up there but there might be people who may become ill or disoriented, so we want you to take care of them like a cop would."

JOE FINK: I would say that there were people that came who were attracted by that money because it was good to be off-duty and make fifty dollars a day and have a weekend in the country; it seemed to be a very fascinating thing. There were a lot of the older fellows that came in and walked out because they were ready to go up there and just ride rough-shod over anybody that crossed the line from what they considered acceptable behavior, and were looking to be stringent law enforcers. We found enough younger men on the force, men with a good deal of experience, who understood what the requirements were.

We had plenty of volunteers to serve with us and everything went along great, and we hired a large number of men—I would say it was between three hundred and four hundred people. We started making provisions for housing them and moving them and assigning them. I went up a couple of times to White Lake to survey the area with Wes and Don Ganoung and other people. We laid out posts and we laid out all the requirements and set up whatever provisions had to be made. We put everything on paper and established schedules and time frames for moving people in and out, since these fellows had to be fed, they had to be lodged, and they had to be transported. One of the stipulations was that there were no weapons up there.

The hippie community in the Ninth Precinct was a very volatile one. There were a number of different factions that were fighting for control. You had Abbie Hoffman and his group in one corner. The Up Against the Wall Motherfuckers. You had bikers who were in a whole different thing; they were threatening and violent, were milking the community and the kids for all they could get out of it. The Up Against the Wall Motherfuckers, I think, were the real virulent faction of the community, because they kept stirring up the problems; they kept handing out brochures complaining about the cops and complaining about the lack of freedom they thought they were being subjected to.

Shortly before the festival the Motherfuckers distributed a leaflet saying, "Let's all go to Woodstock and greet the New York fuzz who will be up there unarmed. Let's give them a real warm welcome." When this was brought to Police Commissioner Leary's attention, we said, "He's not going to let his cops go up there and be overwhelmed by thousands of hippies and people who were looking to get even with them." In fact, he issued a memorandum directing that an order be issued on the teletype to all the precinct station houses saying that it would be a violation of regulations for anyone to go up to Woodstock where they may be subjected to the threats of a mob.

And that created a consternation with us because we were all set for our security people. Everything was ready, and here he says anybody that does it will be in violation of the rules and regulations and could be thrown off the job or punished. If it were a question of losing their job or making fifty or sixty dollars a day, there was no question of what would happen.

The department order banning police involvement hit the papers just a couple of days before they were supposed to go up there, and the New York *Times* blasted Leary in an editorial. And that cooked my goose with Leary, of course—but they blasted him for at the last minute depriving this operation of their security force, and that could create quite a safety problem.

Lower East Side flyer

153

Howard Leary

WES POMEROY: I felt angry and I felt betrayed, and I tried to get ahold of Leary. And he wouldn't answer my phone calls so I tried to get other people to get ahold of Leary. Nobody could reach him. I even knew someone who was one of the top guys in the state correctional system. I said, "Can I have some of your correctional officers?" He said, "Well, I really like you, Wes, but I don't think I can do that."

So then we got word that a bunch of cops wanted to talk to us. They just showed up. They showed up at the place that we had said we were going to have them anyway. Several buses, they said, "We're here, we want to work."

JOE FINK: What we did was to tell the men that were involved, the men that we hired, "We're not taking any names. Any name you give us is all right." They were going to be paid in cash, for one thing—all they had to do was show up and work and they got paid, and that's what happened. A a lot of people decided to come up.

WES POMEROY: I sent Don Ganoung over to talk to them and he was talking to guys with names like "Robin Hood" and "Errol Flynn." They were all using aliases. They wanted to be paid cash and they didn't want the right names used and they wanted more money than we'd promised—one hundred dollars a day, twice what we had promised them. And this was just before the thing was to begin, and we had had strong commitments by our lawyers that we would have cops. We were dealing with a whole bunch of anonymous people we didn't know. Don came back and he said, "Wes, those guys scared the shit out of me." I said, "What did you do?" And he told me the agreement that he made. "Oh, shit." But I don't blame him. That was how we came out. We felt like we were being extorted and that we had no way out of it. We didn't know what would happen if we didn't. And there was no control over it if anything did happen. I could have taken that chance, but I didn't know what they would do in retaliation. They may not have done anything in retaliation, but I don't regret my decision. So, I was very angry about that whole thing, but there was nothing I could do about it.

STANLEY GOLDSTEIN: The loss of the cops put a lot of things right into a cock's hat, aside from

Organizational chart

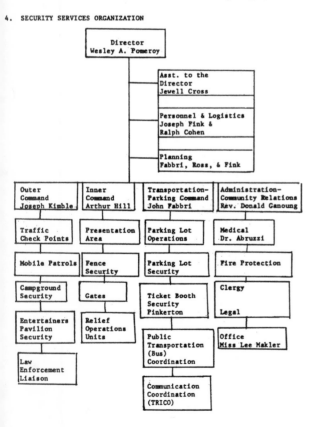

4. SECURITY SERVICES ORGANIZATION

- Director
  Wesley A. Pomeroy
  - Asst. to the Director
    Jewell Cross
  - Personnel & Logistics
    Joseph Fink & Ralph Cohen
  - Planning
    Fabbri, Ross, & Fink

- Outer Command
  Joseph Kimble
  - Traffic Check Points
  - Mobile Patrols
  - Campground Security
  - Entertainers Pavilion Security
  - Law Enforcement Liaison

- Inner Command
  Arthur Hill
  - Presentation Area
  - Fence Security
  - Gates
  - Relief Operations Units

- Transportation-Parking Command
  John Fabbri
  - Parking Lot Operations
  - Parking Lot Security
  - Ticket Booth Security
    Pinkerton
  - Public Transportation (Bus) Coordination
  - Communication Coordination (TRICO)

- Administration-Community Relations
  Rev. Donald Ganoung
  - Medical
    Dr. Abruzzi
  - Fire Protection
  - Clergy
  - Legal
  - Office
    Miss Lee Makler

the fact that we now had to hire whatever could be hired under whatever conditions they could be hired, believing that we had to have some kind of disciplined cops—someone would stand on a street corner that knew how to maintain radio control for communications. You get a bunch of people chattering on the radio and you can't maintain some level of discipline, you're just lost for communications.

WES POMEROY: You just go with what is all there. It's what a good friend of mine, Ralph Siu, who was a Dallas philosopher and a chemist and a lot of other things, and an author, calls "the instantaneous apprehension of totality." He says that's where you have all your—you've been gathering information in your brain all your life and if you're in a position of command, you are an important person, you know something. He said, you'll never have all the data you need to make a decision; you'll never be perfect. When you get to the point, trust what your feelings are and make a decision.

We had planned several strategies for defusing problems we might encounter. One thing that we'd planned was to get people when they first came up there, as they were coming off the buses, and ask them if they wanted to earn some tickets, those that didn't have tickets. We'd give them a briefing. From then on, as each bus came in, they'd be the guys who said, "Welcome to Woodstock and this is what you find. You have the presentation area over here and you're expected to clear the presentation area every night. But the woods are full of places to camp and a place for kids." All that sort of thing. The plan was to do that and also take a chance that those people, if we gave them tickets, would continue to work for us. It was a trusting thing, O.K.? You knew you'd lose some, but what the hell.

Another was that we made a deal with the Merry Pranksters and they brought their bus, the famous bus, and we parked them right up against the fence. And there was a hole dug under the fence and the idea was they'd quietly let out the word—"You can sneak in if you want to"—for people who had to rip us off, let them do it. And another deal was made with Abbie Hoffman and his folks—that was multifaceted. One was that he could park his truck right near the gate with a printing press and crank up anti-establishment and maybe anti-Woodstock stuff all this time—that was O.K.—in exchange for his diffusing the real wild guys from New York City. Nobody else could get close to them. There was more to it than that. He had lawyers who met our lawyers. We had lawyers hired as a legal defense, and they were integrated with Abbie's lawyers. We had our own medical people, and we had ordered a whole bunch of medical supplies for the facilities we had there at the festival. And Abbie had a doctor or two, or people who thought they knew this stuff, and they were really looking over our list of stuff we had ordered. And what they were looking for was stuff to treat people who had been gassed, because they didn't trust us. I also—I had some trouble in my own staff but they very quickly gave into it because it was no longer participatory management—gave them a couple of radios so they would be on our frequency. Completely open, so they were able to see what we were doing and be able to help us out.

So we were just diffusing them, that's all. That's what we were trying to do. That's the way we handled the Hell's Angels. We knew

Crashers, Cops, Producers Spoil Newport '69

Rolling Stone
July 26, 1969

155

when they were coming because my New York state police contacts were telling me. We couldn't deal with them as a group, so we picked up several of them and made messengers out of them. We needed motorcyclers for messengers. The only thing you could use was horses or motorcycles. I think we hired two of them. But our plan was that if we got a lot of them we'd hire them individually and get them on individual tasks.

• • • •

STANLEY GOLDSTEIN: The idea of the campgrounds, just the idea, was very, very, very early on, that if we drew the kind of crowd that we anticipated drawing for X number of days, there was no place that those people could have stayed, whether it was Wallkill or Monticello. There just wasn't the housing in the area. But more than that, it was in the spirit of the times to get out and commune with nature and so on and so forth—be ecologically sound, live off the land, be a part of it. So, the camping idea was just a part of the plot.

The idea was that we would do as little as we possibly could, but that the Hog Farm and associates would do essential campground living demo and be available as the experts. At the Yasgur site, the Hog Farm went back into the woods, studied the swamps, laid trails through the swamps, built bridges over streams, created the interconnecting paths, learned the territory.

It also came to pass that various other groups of people showed up. The realization of that was that there had to be some means of identifying the Hog Farm. They didn't have guitar-and-dove shirts, they had their own costumes. They were not part of security, they were not part of stage crew, they were not this or that, and they were not uniformed services. But nevertheless, there had to be some means of identification. So, we stenciled—Paul Foster, as I recall, did the sketch and stencil—we got some red polyester rags and tore them and stenciled a flying hog on a rag that was handed out. And Gravy's idea was to stencil thousands of them. There weren't going to be eighty-eight arm bands for the eighty-eight people. There would be thousands and thousands and thousands. The idea was to get everybody to be a part of this group that was picking up the trash and supporting their neighbor, and doing all of these other things. And that worked from the very beginning.

Other communal groups showed up, moved into the area, the movement folks showed up. People were moving in a week and a half before the show, so more and more and more people were showing up. There was a group from the Orson Welles Theater in Boston that came down and said, "What can we do?" We said, "Well, you guys seem pretty together. What you need to do is not hang out over here. You need to go down over there, and set up a campsite and show people how it's done."

We were going out and we're buying fifteen or twenty or thirty-two cords of wood; I don't remember how much. We bought a lot of cut firewood and brought it down to the site and stacked it in piles all over the place so people wouldn't have to cut down trees, green trees. And the Hog Farm dug fire pits and lined them. Not enough for all the people that would be there, but enough so that people could see how it was done and these were large enough to be communal fire pits.

And so, what has come to be called networking actually was working and in place from the beginning. And that had been the concept: that people of the community were going to be there in advance, who had shorter lines of communication, and as people got plugged in they would then be in this chain. And people seemed very rapidly to find their level and choose whether or not they were a drone or a queen bee or a worker bee, and sometimes they changed roles for a little while—they'd work in the freak-out tent for a while, or they'd work on the serving line for a while, then they'd go over and listen to

THE WHITE LAKE DAILY
WEIRDNESS

VOL I NO. I   S UNDAY AUG 9th

88888888888888888888888888888888888888888888888888888888888888

BABBY RACES IN TROUBLE: Inclemante weather means muddy moppets and mean mothers however, as they say in the mysterious east, " We'll see what happens when we get there."

DORK IN WIND BLOWS FIRE INSPECTOR: Please cover up. Any nudity at this time -in the wrong hands- could close the entire operation.

BIGGER CIRCLES: The large benched circle in the field of last nights circle bong will be the work recruiting center. Please hang there if you are free. We will provide joys and toys. The Hog Farm will feed everybody something . The workers will be fed food.

RULES FOR TOOLS: All right you tools ...stop over at the tool shep and see Tool Man (Paul Fleming) who is trying to get you all on a piece of paper. Calling all flashlites for a check off.

WHO TO GET FOR WHAT: Rick Sullivan   Pro cure er
                        Lou todd   Coordenation
                        Lisa Law   Kitchen Show
                        Evan Engbar   Information
      get stan   Buffalo Bob   Wood
      soldain for him Tom Watson & Will   Happy Trails
                        Fred the Fed   Firepits
                        Red Dog   Your money or your herbs
                        Tom Law   Healthy Happy Holy
                        (Yoga classes each morning at the sound of
                        the conch .)
                        Dave Rocket   Carpenter Commander
                        Hguh yenmoR   Please Department

Hog Farm publication

157

the music or they'd find a pretty girl or guy that turned them on and did whatever they did.

The major contingent of the Hog Farm didn't arrive until four or five days before the show. They got up and moved in and began doing some of this, some of what began to spread out because there were evening campfires and baby races. Wes came over for the baby races, and the sheriff and the mayor were out for the baby races, and some of the other Hog Farm family stunts that went on.

WAVY GRAVY: One of my fortes is I put together a bulletin board. I'm very quick with a staple gun and paper. And we cut a hole in the side of the bulletin board so you could stick your head through it and make four- and five-D announcements. Suddenly instead of being two-dimensional, you'd be three-, four-, and five-D. I would stick my head through and blow bubbles and make an announcement or something. That's the bulletin board. And as I stuck my head through to make an announcement, there was Max Yasgur and his whole family. And so we brought them over. What I was announcing was a baby race. Just before we went to Woodstock was when the men landed on the moon. We had a celebration called Gonk Day where we had all these TVs that we'd collected from all over New Mexico, watching the thing. And one of the things that happened was a frog race. And it was a big outer circle and the frogs were all let go at the outer circle and whoever got to the middle first won. So we set up the same ground rules with babies in this big circle and an inner circle and let all the babies go. And just the grass-roots human revelation that came to Max Yasgur from that really opened him up. I mean, it was just gorgeous—all these little kids crawling away and their moms rooting for them and everything. It was a real just-folks kind of a vibe that he locked into.

• • • •

JOHN MORRIS: I had gotten into the Indian project as an ancillary thing because I suddenly pointed out that we had an arts and craft fair and what were we doing for arts and crafts?

Baby races

The Indian project was an accident. A friend of mine, an art collector whose daughter I knew, called me up and said, "You have to go visit this man Lloyd New in Santa Fe, New Mexico. He runs the Institute of American Indian Arts and was a very famous fashion designer in the fifties in Scottsdale. He actually started Scottsdale, Arizona." I had been involved and interested in Indian things all my life since I was a kid, a Boy Scout. And I think I needed to get out of New York. So I got on a plane and flew down to Santa Fe. And got off the plane at sunset with an electrical storm, rented a car, and started driving up out of Albuquerque with an electrical storm with horizontal heat lightning going over the tops of the mesas. I pulled off the side of the road and sat there on the side of the road and just thought, "I've never seen anything like this in my life." I'd lived in seventeen states and five countries and the Caribbean and Europe and I had never seen anything like this.

Rock Fest Moves Ahead Despite Protests

Times Herald Record
Middletown, N.Y.
July 30, 1969

I came up to Santa Fe and met this absolutely phenomenal man. He is—for twenty years—one of my best friends; he's like a second father. I came and saw this school this man had. It was a government-run school, but basically his philosophy in running the school was if you were more than one-eighth Indian and you could say "I want to be an artist," he would give you a junior college education with the exposure to some of the best painting teachers. Those who came out of it were T. C. Cannon, Kevin Redstar, Bill Soza, Earl Biss, Earl Eder, Delbridge Honannie, Hank Gobin—the best Indian artists of our day.

And we came up with this idea of bringing the whole group up. My idea was that to take this experience that existed down in Santa Fe and mix it with the East Coast penny-loafer, prep-school thing that I had come out of, would be a mind-blowing experience. And it was.

BILLY SOZA: At the time, I was an art student at the Institute of American Indian Arts as a painting major. And the arts director called me up on the phone and said, "There's a guy coming in by the name of John Morris and he wants to talk to you about taking a bunch of artists to this festival." He said it was being coined as the largest outdoor festival ever in the history of the world. Everybody you can think of is supposed to be there, every popular group. I said, "Sure, I'll meet the guy. What can I lose?"

So John and I had a meeting. We drove around town and I showed him some of the artists' galleries. I said, "Is this for real? You want twenty-five Indian people to go to this festival? What exactly do you mean by that?" He said, "Well, we'll fly you there and anybody else that is away from here now that you can't find. We'll send them a ticket and we'll fly them from wherever they live—bus, plane—if they can get to Albuquerque. If not, we'll fly them in from wherever else they're from."

This is like the hippie days and you go, "Well, is that really real?" There was Lisa Law and the Hog Farmers and a bunch of other people around. There were always rumors flying around and you never knew what was real and what wasn't. There was a lot of drugs around there then and you're kind of unsure whether the stories are real or not. So John was very honest about it. He said, "Well, here's the date. Do you have access to the phone? Call people and have them in Albuquerque."

159

I got people from South Dakota, New Mexico, California, Arizona; the ones that were in and around upstate New York were going to meet us there; Oklahoma people. We had like a whole troop of people because we had anticipated that it wasn't going to be that big and that we would have access to playing some songs perhaps.

• • • •

TOM LAW: The Hog Farm arrived at the Albuquerque airport and loaded up a couple of sets of tepee poles up the rear door of a 747 and flew off to New York, where we were bused up to the festival.

Businessmen Throw Weight Behind Exposition

Times Herald Record
Middletown, N.Y.
July 31, 1969

LISA LAW: That's when Albuquerque was a real small airport and, in fact, that section is Cutter Air Force Base now. And it was just a little waiting room and everybody was taking acid that was in wine that were in botas. They were going to this little ladies' room and they were spraying it into their mouths. So I just sort of stood—I didn't take it because I had a baby and I was pregnant with my second child—and watched them in awe as they all got loaded and were sitting around waiting. I ran outside when the tepee poles were about to be loaded and shot a few pictures because that was amazing, too, that they would take tepee poles. In fact, it was pretty amazing that they would send a jet for us. That amazed all of us. We were all surprised and we decided they were really for real when the airplane arrived. And to have a whole plane to yourself, a bunch of crazies, was interesting.

BONNIE JEAN ROMNEY: There was this big question of who was going to go. Suddenly, there was a free ticket on an airplane, which we hadn't been on for a long time. We were really living very grass roots. We didn't have anybody coming in and donating food or stuff. It was just very hand to mouth, and it became a big deal to be able to go to this rock festival in New York. And who was going to go? There were some representatives of an American Indian group who would go. I think there were ten places on the plane for them and we were trying to decide sort of politically in the family. There are various other families we were related to. One was the New Improved Jook Savages, which was Tom and Lisa Law's family. And a certain amount of places for them seemed appropriate. And then things like: How we were going to get to the airport? Were we really going to do a kitchen? Were we going to buy pots and pans here in New Mexico or we were going to get them in New York? Just a whole mass of details about a real chartered plane. I spent a lot of time at different pay phones dealing with Stan. I was very much involved with who was going to go and how we were going to get the gas money to get ourselves to the airport and who was going to take care of the dog and stuff like this.

Going out there, I remember the Native Americans that had joined us as being very separate from us, and sort of a little distanced from us. They didn't know—I guess we probably looked pretty wild. And there was a lot of excitement and a lot of, "I can't believe this is really happening."

160   **PENNY STALLINGS:** The first word I got was that they were all flying in on

the same plane and they had to have goat's milk on the plane and they weren't going to come if they didn't have goat's milk. So I had to have goat's milk waiting for them because they had a lot of babies and they were either nursing or they had to have milk. So I took care of that.

TOM LAW: We arrived at the airport in New York. We were a pretty funny-looking group in those days. We were having a good time. There was press to meet us at the airport and I came off the airplane with the earphones in my ears and the tube in my mouth talking to myself and interviewing myself. It was just fun. We were always having fun. We didn't take the media or the government or anybody very seriously. We really thought we had a much better way to go, which we did, actually, as it turned out. And I don't know how many people realize that, but we really did.

BONNIE JEAN ROMNEY: There was a big press scene at the airport, which really surprised us. None of us had ever seen anything like that. We were suddenly celebrities. I mean, really, just out of these funky buses we were living in in New Mexico. We had to find a place to put the pig when we left. And suddenly, a phalanx of press pressing in on us. I guess that's when I really heard that what everyone else thought we were going to be doing was security.

LISA LAW: I don't think I could ever forget when we got there, because I felt this light. Everything was lit up as we walked off the plane. There

The Hog Farm arrives

161

were cameras every place—microphones, booms—and they were just rolling. You know: "Here they come!" And that's when they said to Wavy, "We hear you're head of security," and he hadn't known that up to that point.

WAVY GRAVY: I'm going, "My God, we're the cops! I can't believe it." We had no concept of the magnitude of the thing until we had first hit the airport and there was just all this world press, just a wall of it. And they're telling me about that we're doing security. And just off the top of my head I said to a reporter, "Well, do you feel secure?" And he said, "Well, sure." And I said, "Well it's working then. Must be working." The guy says, "Well, what are you going to use for crowd control?" And I said, "Cream pies and seltzer bottles." And I noticed they are all writing it down.

JOHN ROBERTS: As Woodstock gained certain notoriety, up until its final explosion of notoriety that weekend—there was a picture in the *Post*, I think, in August of '69, showing our security force, the Hog Farm, arriving at La Guardia Airport. I think my father called and said, "Nice cops you've hired."

BILLY SOZA: When we landed in New York City there were three limousines and a big Trailways bus. The Hog Farmers—being as famous as they were, with the Pranksters and Ken Kesey and those guys—they thought, "Well, the limos are for us." Well, that wasn't the way it was; the limousines were for us, the Indian people. John really treated us as if we were like rock 'n' roll stars—by today's standards anyway. They were really nice to us. They said, "Don't worry about the luggage, we'll take care of it. Are you hungry?" So we went somewhere and we all ate. We got in three limousines—all of us packed in three limousines—took off from La Guardia Airport and drove all the way to Woodstock that same night, all the way. All kinds of drugs again, you know, little boxes. "Whatever you want, it's all right here." And I was in the front limo on a little walkie-talkie saying, "Whatever you guys want, it's there."

And a lot of them, this was their first experience with any kind of narcotics, drugs, hippies. I mean, they had seen hippies in Santa Fe and stuff, but they had never really been around them. Being an artist, a lot of us were already used to all the sixties stuff that was going on, the pop art. We were involved with that.

WAVY GRAVY: I always think it's peculiar when somebody else is driving the bus. I think, "What straight buses. They never have any collages on the ceiling."

TOM LAW: Going up on the bus, this line came to me that I wound up saying on the stage actually, but I was really trying to tune into what this was all about that we were asked to do. And this line came to me that, "God really doesn't give a shit. It's the good in you that cares." And for me, that was a piece of poetry I remembered that came through my head. So I got a chance to say it at the festival. I said it from the stage when I was leading some breathing exercises.

LISA LAW: We brought our tepees and we set that up right away so we had a really nice place to stay. And the other people stayed in the buses or in tents. I guess everybody brought their own thing. And the Hog Farm group that had been there before us had set up a kitchen with a plastic roof. It was like a dome with a wood floor. And they had it filled with vegetables. Yasgur kept us supplied in yogurt, milk, and eggs. I think there was cottage cheese, too. But he kept us supplied. We'd get these flats of eggs every day. We were purchasing them from him, but it was right there from his dairy farm, so it was really nice.

And right away the campers started arriving, so we were cooking continuously and trying to get our act together for what we were going to do. And that's when they told us we were going to do the free kitchen. I think the Hog Farm had discussed it before I got there about doing the free kitchen.

I know that I got real pushy in saying that we shouldn't have aluminum. I had done all this study on aluminum cooking and how it poisons you and I was having all these babies and I didn't want poisoned babies and I didn't want anybody poisoned, so I really came down hard on them for running around scavenging aluminum pots. I said, "You gotta be able to do it a better way than this. You can go right to the people and ask them for money and go get the equipment that you need."

I remember kind of looking up and thinking about the vibe that was coming down from the place and I got really religious at that moment and I said, "There's going to be a lot more people here than we think." I just felt it. And I recalled saying that I would like to be the one who went out and purchased the food. So I was the one that went out and decided to do the shopping. I went into one of the trailers and asked for three thousand dollars.

I remember getting the first three thousand, going into town with Peter Whiterabbit, getting a truck. I think we actually had a truck there, and then we got another. I think we somehow got a refrigerator truck, too. But when we went into New York to buy, I spent that within a day and a half, and that's when I went into the office downtown and I said, "Listen, I've already spent this for the free kitchen and I need another three thousand." And they just handed it to me. There wasn't any problem at all. And I've fed people at other concerts afterwards that always had trouble handing the money out. But these guys had no trouble handing it out.

I think I used the money frugally. I went out and got good cooking pots and good utensils so that we could do mass food-making. It's very important to have large knives for big jobs, rather than tiny little knives; they're going to drive everybody crazy. I bought fifteen hundred pounds of bulgar wheat, and fifteen hundred pounds of rolled oats, two hundred twenty-five-pound boxes of currants, a bunch of bags of wheat germ, sunflower seeds, dried apricots. I bought kegs of honey and kegs of soy sauce. And almonds. Plus the pots, the pans, and I got a great onion cutter that worked on a spring so you put the onion in and just go like that and it cuts it. I got thirty-five plastic garbage cans—big ones—so that after you prepared the food and cut it, you put it into these garbage cans, moved it over to the stove and then dug out of those. We'd cut up an entire garbage can of onions,

Opposition Mounts in Sullivan to Aquarian Expo; Hearing Slated

*Times Herald Record
Middletown, N.Y.
August 5, 1969*

163

Lisa Law and daughter

for instance, and mixed our museli in that. That really came in handy. We bought two hundred fifty enameled cups for the Hog Farmers because of ecological reasons. I couldn't see them just throwing away paper cup after paper cup and I knew I couldn't buy one for everybody at Woodstock so I just bought it for the Hog Farmers.

So I sort of thought out the whole process of how it was all going to work, spoons and serving utensils—I bought a hundred and sixty thousand paper plates and cups and knives, spoons and forks, plastic. And I bought a Buddha, a jade Buddha, which is still here, the kitchen Buddha which we put in the kitchen to bless the kitchen.

Bonnie Jean Romney: We had big battles between Lisa and I as to whether or not there could be brown sugar. We finally settled on a certain kind of honey that was pure enough for her taste. I was demanding that it be sweetened. And then we had another battle over whether we could have milk on the granola. And what it ended up being was museli, because there was such a tremendous demand for the food that, in truth, what we served was plain raw oats with milk on it—powdered milk mixed up—honey and raisins. Because there wasn't any time to toast the oats. We just threw the nuts and seeds and raisins in it and served it to people. And then the evening meal was bulgur wheat. And there were big debates. I was unfamiliar with bulgur wheat at the time and I was arguing for brown rice. Thank God Lisa Law won out and we had bulgur wheat because bulgur cooks in a few minutes—you just practically put hot water in; you could almost just throw boiling water in it and let it sit and put something else on. Almost that quick it cooks. And it was bulgur wheat and vegetables.

Lisa Law: My job was to make it as easy as possible for the people in the kitchen so they could produce the biggest amount of food. And I had helped design the kitchen so that there was a cutting space in the middle for chopping and then tables all around the outside of the tent for serving and for cooking. And then we had a small tent in the back for storage. That really worked well. You could pass on two sides of the server so each booth served two lines of people. And we were serving over a hundred at a time, or more. They'd be lined up.

We got back and unloaded and stored everything, and the guys set up the stoves. I think they had gotten the stoves. And they had set them up when we arrived. Everything fit right into place. The volunteers just walked right up to the booth and started cooking.

Hog Farm arm band

WAVY GRAVY: I remember starting to actualize the security situation and the production people having a meeting with us and we're deciding on the arm bands. Ken Babbs wants to know how many people they are expecting. They say they're expecting a couple of hundred thousand and we said, "We'd like to have that many arm bands." We just thought if everybody was a cop there couldn't possibly be a problem. That was the logic. What we'd try and do is take the hard edge away from the concept of security, which is people helping each other out. I remember one time I had to bail somebody out and I was psychedelicized in a cop station and I read the policemen's code. It was as psychedelic a document as I've ever read, ranking with the Magna Carta and the Lord's Prayer. It's lovely. If those guys actually behaved like that—I mean, everybody would want to grow up and be one. So we decided to call it the Please Force. And we developed a password called "I forgot" so if you forgot you could get in anyhow. You'd knock on a door and somebody would say, "What's the password?" and you'd say, "I forgot." Come on in.

BONNIE JEAN ROMNEY: Security seemed like the last thing that was needed in this group of us fellow citizens—human beings—coming together to party. But we started talking about security. How are we going to do security? And Wavy or Tom Law came up with the idea of doing the Please Force; I don't know whose idea it actually was. And they presented it to us. So we made a bunch of arm bands. The idea was that when we saw someone who was taking responsibility in a really excellent way that we would have an extra arm band in our pocket and would say, "You are part of the Please Force. Help out wherever you can." And while there was some abuse of that, mostly it was excellent. It really worked well. I remember that as being a good idea.

WAVY GRAVY: I also had several meetings—myself and Tom Law—with Wes Pomeroy, who later became the police chief of Berkeley, which was kind of a treat. In the Land of One Thing Leads to Another, he went on to Washington to become a top cop. I thought Wes was nifty. He

165

also read the same piece of document—not necessarily in the astroplane that I was looking at it from, but certainly he seemed like he was. Lenny Bruce used to be my manager in the ancient times. And Lenny said, "You know, there's pigs, there's police, and there's peace officers." And Wes was a peace officer.

WES POMEROY: I adapted my style for them. They would never adapt it for me. First of all, there was nobody in charge. They said, "We're all equals and there is nobody in charge and no one speaks for everybody else," except obviously there were some who were leaders. So the way I dealt with them was that they always had some kind of yoga in the morning and contemplative kinds of things. I'd get up there when they were there and sit on the—I'm not very good at it; I didn't try to be—but I sat on the ground and I was just there. I wasn't going to say, "Hey, everybody, come together." I went up there and sat down along with them and it was obvious they knew I was there, and after a while we'd start talking. Maybe someone would blow on the horn—on the conch shell or ram's horn; I'm not sure which one it was—and give a blast on that and people would come wandering over. And we'd all just talk.

One thing we had to talk about was the fact that they were all going to leave at one time when it was sprayed for mosquitoes. Mosquitoes were a problem so we had hired someone to come in and spray once for DDT, and the Hog Farmers were going to leave because we were killing living things. They were ready to go. And we were all working on that. So that was an opportunity to go up there and sit and talk. Their roles were clear, but the parameters were ambiguous. And to try and instruct them any more was a piece of work. It was not like getting a bunch of people together to have a drill every day. It was an entirely different dynamic. When I did want to talk to them, and it was only several times, I would just go up there and kind of wander around and hang out and just shoot the shit. Just like hanging out on the corner.

• CHAPTER TEN •

"Chip Monck, he's about the right age. I mean, he could be Custer or somebody."
—Henry Diltz

HENRY DILTZ: Sometime in July, Chip Monck called me in L.A. I was a rock photographer at that point. I had finished with the Monkees. I was doing Crosby, Stills, and Nash. We'd just done the cover of them sitting on the couch for their first album. And I'd done the "Sweet Baby James" album cover with James Taylor and I did some Mamas and Papas. So I was doing rock record album photos and publicity stuff. And Chip called me up and said, "Henry, there's this incredible festival that's going to happen, this big music thing, and you should be a part of it. So I want to find out if you can come out and I'll speak to the producer and see if we can try to hire you and have you come out." And so I said, "Great! Great!" And the next day he called and said, "You're on. Come on out."

So I flew out and then I was put up in this little boardinghouse in White Lake. I remember the first day was kind of a rainy day. I don't remember what exact day it was, but I went over to where they had some production trailers and I discovered my good friend Mel Lawrence was in there. Mel was just a real good friend from back in my college and coffeehouse days in Hawaii, just part of a karmic group of friends on the West Coast. I just remember people out there with rain slickers and bulldozers and stuff.

So I started taking black-and-white photos. I still have the proofsheet of Mel with his feet up on the desk that rainy day, you know, making the phone calls. I just kind of started taking pictures of all the stuff that was going on. I didn't think of myself as this incredible photojournalist. I didn't even think of myself as a photographer that much; that's what I was doing. But I'd been a musician. I just liked people. And I liked to hang out and I liked to take photos. I always took photos of anything that was happening around me. So I started taking these photos.

I enjoyed going down every day to where they were building the stage. It was like a huge battleship or something because it rose off the ground, you know, this big imposing thing. And at that point, it was just a big flat wooden deck. It reminded me very much of a battleship. A big flat wooden deck and these long-haired guys with their shirts off hammering nails and putting the planks down and just building this big deck. It looked over this green field and the blue sky and it was really like an ocean. There was nothing else there. And then these hippie girls who ran the kitchen would bring lunch out to the site where the guys were all building this thing. And then there was Chip Monck and Leo Makota and Michael Lang, driving bulldozers and tractors and stuff. Michael Lang had some kind of an old motorcycle that he'd come riding on through the alfalfa fields with his leather vest on and his curly hair. He looked sort of like this cherub, you know.

I was fascinated by the way that all this was progressing in such

167

an orderly way. It was like an army. I mean, Chip Monck seemed like a young general to me. And I remember thinking one day, "Chip Monck, he's about the right age. I mean, he could be Custer or somebody." We were in charge there. There were only people like me in charge and it was no adults. It was no businessmen. There was no guy in a suit, you know. There was just Chip Monck and Mel Lawrence and Michael Lang. Mainly those three, as far as I was concerned. And they were like brigadier generals. I thought, "Well, yeah, Mel certainly was a brigadier general." This is silly, but that's the way I thought. There were the captains and the lieutenants and the guys up there—the corporals, you know—pounding the nails, and shit like that. And there were the various engineers. There were sound engineers and young boy genius-type guys who were setting up all this sound equipment and all this stuff. They were like warrant officers or something, specialized guys. And definitely sergeants, the guys in charge of the different teams, the head carpenters and stuff like that. People were issuing orders and getting stuff done and there was no saluting, but things were carried out in a very crisp and efficient way—but a very friendly way. It was during the time of love and peace and brotherhood and there was certainly that feeling there of all this happening. There were certainly no hassles. It was all very beautiful, very nice.

Henry Diltz

BILL BELMONT: In July, I came back from Mexico and I had a call from John Morris. He wanted to know what I was doing. I said, "Nothing." He says, "Well, you want to come back and be in charge of artists, logistics, and accommodations and read all these contracts that somebody's screwing up?" So I said, "Yeah, O.K." I went back there and I got picked up at the airport and there was this house in Liberty, New York, and I got a room. John, as usual, had a bunch of girls around. My job was basically that we had all the hotel space in the known world and we assigned people to hotels. And we also tried to figure out when they were arriving and whether or not we were going to pick them up, whether or not they were going to get there on their own.

Leo Makota

The stage progressed incredibly slowly. The backstage area was progressing slowly and the thing that happened that was truly bizarre was that in the late afternoon everyone would stop working and go horseback riding. That's what happened. Everybody would stop working and go horseback riding. Chip Monck and Steve Cohen; I went a couple of times. They would go up to this Jewish resort—what they used to refer to as the Jewish cowboy—and rent a bunch of horses and go horseback riding. That's what everybody did. It was funny.

CHRIS LANGHART: We were hiring like crazy. I had my army. There were two trailers side by side and the payroll operation was in one and the drawing and figuring out what to do was in the other. Anne Morris, John's wife, ran the payroll across the hall. So every morning there would be ten or fifteen more guys out in front of the trailer and I would just sort of have an instant interview and ask them what they'd done and where they'd worked or what sort of trades they had and look at the sizes and shapes and try to pick from nothing. What they looked like and how they smiled. So we just said, "All right, it's this one, this one, and this one." She'd take all their social security numbers and sign them up and they'd start. And the people who had been there before would be elevated into crew heads and the new people would come on underneath them and put in the piping joints and string the wires and do this and that. And the army is right. That's one thing I did discover about their conception of supervision. The nine or ten people that you can watch with one person is about the real limit, maybe twelve, if it's really organized. Because I could go out on the way to the campgrounds and there would be people screwing in Christmas tree bulbs and some of them would be just sitting under the trees looking into space. That's because you just couldn't watch as many people as had to screw in as many Christmas tree bulbs as there were to screw in. And one guy couldn't watch as many as it took to do that. So you just had to spread it out as best you could, and there were a few lost-time accidents, but basically it all got done.

CAROL GREEN: We had some crazy guy who showed up—he was a local

169

kid—and got down on his hands and knees to me and this girl Linda and said, "I'll do anything for you. I love you. I'm so glad you came to my town and you're bringing rock 'n' roll. I'm dying for you, I'll do anything for you." He held onto our legs and cried and sobbed and hugged us. And we hired him to be our dishwasher and that night I cooked spareribs for about eighty-five people and he cried. He stayed in the kitchen, scrubbing pots and pans.

JACK SCALICI: I was an unemployed actor in New York, practically starving to death in those days. And a friend of mine, Holly, was a scenic artist who had another friend, Nick Prince—Nick was the son of the actor William Prince. So I met him at Holly's house and he said he was leaving for a few weeks to work at this festival. And even though I was a young person at the time I wasn't into music so much so I had no concept of what they were talking about. "A festival, what is that?" I mean, I didn't even know. What I was interested in was that it was a *job*. So he said there was a job before the festival, making preparations for the festival. Our job would be to lay water pipe, and he was in charge of the crew more or less, Nick was, and he said would I like a job and it pays a hundred twenty-five dollars a week and room and board. I said "Yes!"

So I had a beat-up old station wagon I drove up there. It was just marvelous, this rolling hills with grass and trees and this stream that went right through it. And I just was in heaven.

What we did—and it was the first time I ever saw it in my life—was connect plastic water pipe. It's real simple: there's a joint and you

take the glue on the joint and you stick it together. It's like a little jigsaw thing and you just lay it. And that carried water. The plan was they were going to pump the water from this water hole to various places. We laid pipe to the Hog Farm and various other places and there would be drinking water, fresh drinking water supply.

So what we did was we'd just get out there in our jeans and take our shirts off and we'd be digging ditches all day, and it was very lax. We had long breaks. We'd break for lunch and then the guy would say, "Hey, it's too nice a day to work. Let's just take off." And we would go to this water hole and we would swim. It was just a bunch of guys at first, so we took off all our clothes and we'd go in naked. And then all of a sudden you'd look up and there'd be some *girls* there. And they took their clothes off and they were naked. It's the weirdest sensation I've ever had in my life. For the first thirty seconds, you're like, "Wow, a naked person." And then it didn't matter after that. It was just so natural and the setting was so idyllic that you didn't even think about it. But you know, you just swam naked and you put your clothes on and you went back to work. I guess probably a lot of publicity was, "Hey, there's a lot of naked people and orgies and things," but it was nothing like that. It was just simple and pure and beautiful.

I still was in the dark as to what I was doing there. I mean, I just didn't quite understand it. I noticed the carpenters building, this huge platform and this huge stage. And then there was also a film crew. They said, "We're going to make a movie of this whole thing." I said, "Oh, what kind of a movie could they make out of this?" And they were riding around with cameras and they had convertibles and I kept being an actor. I kept trying to get on film. Every time I went by I'd be smiling and jumping up and down, but I guess they weren't too interested in what we were doing.

CHIP MONCK: There was obviously so much to do and so little time in which to do it, and we had all come to realize, unfortunately, that all of our individual jobs were going to be left somewhat undone. Everybody ran over and helped Josh White get certain things together but then we had this horrible realization that there wasn't going to be any light show screen because you couldn't put that wind loading on the roof, so why help Josh? So everybody left Josh and went downstage and started doing something else. We all kind of banded together in one sort of SWAT team, trying to run around and finish, with everybody's help, each project, and taking it one by one instead of having three or four tired souls continually working on such and such—what they had done for the last three days—which probably would be terribly boring and not very rewarding. We all banded into a group and ran around trying to do all the rest of everybody's projects.

STANLEY GOLDSTEIN: There was just not enough time to do what we had to do. Some of it was quite ambitious. The overhead lighting scheme with these poles in a rig of cables. You've seen photographs of that I'm certain. Well, they never got the lights on it but it was a very ambitious construction. The soil was not of the right kind for the original supports. They had to redesign all the poured concrete widgets, to which the guy wires would go that supported these things.

Crosby, Stills and Nash Add Young

Rolling Stone
August 9, 1969

171

I think there was a great, great sense of commitment on the part of everyone involved that one way or another, by God, we were going to do this thing, that it was a good thing to do and a worthwhile thing to do and the right thing to do and we fucking-A well wanted to do it and we were going to do it somehow. We were going to do it no matter what the obstacles; it was going to go on.

JOEL ROSENMAN: I think I arrived at the site from New York on Monday, just a few days ahead of John. You know, in spite of my confidence on the night in early July when we had been evicted from our Wallkill site, I must say in the last week, if you were up there at the festival and saw what was going on to prepare for the arrival of half a million people, you were immediately aware, even if you knew nothing about the business of throwing a festival, that you couldn't possibly be finished in time. The phrase triage comes to mind. One of the victims of triage, I guess, was the gates. I am sure there were plenty of others. In fact, an elaborate system that we had, or we had planned to have, for busing people in from the parking lots, for example, was one victim. Remote TV screens was another one. There were all kinds of schemes that, had we had enough time, might have been instituted. But at the time that I got up there on Monday, everything was in a state of preparation, roughly on target for a festival to be thrown some time in November. Not for one that was supposed to begin within four days. Everybody was in a high state of panic.

It became clear that we couldn't do what we had hoped the festival would be. Everybody knew we could get the speakers working and that is, in fact, the way it was approached. We all sat down and figured out what were the essentials. "Well, we have to have water." So, I spent a lot of my time with the Commissioner of Something or Other—either water or health or something, from the area, assuring him that there was no danger of bacteria or something in the water and that he could certify us as safe for our crowd. And then we had to have communications and we had to have electricity. So we put in the basic systems and made sure that they were done. And not too much more than the basic systems actually got installed. There was enough to survive. I think ultimately, the fact that that is all there was, gave Woodstock its charm. It certainly wasn't overproduced.

STANLEY GOLDSTEIN: Our building permit got yanked just days before the show. I don't remember what the specifics of it were in terms of the mechanics of how it got yanked, but someone insisted that there had to be some kind of a review and until there was a review of a specific site plan or something, that the building permit had to be canceled. And so somewhere along the line it was decided by the local government that our building permit was canceled, and there were continuing meetings with the township.

There was a local building inspector, a nice young fellow, although probably at that time he was older than I was; he was just young in his job and young in relation to the rest of the people that he was working with. But he understood very well—he was a very bright fellow—that if we didn't proceed with the construction and get the permit, and accomplish everything we possibly could, that we would be fulfilling that prophecy that we wouldn't be ready. And so we arranged the night before that when he went down the following morning that we would meet at a particular road intersection—this was something like five or five-thirty in the morning. We were meeting just as the sun would begin to dawn because he was going down to put up "Stop Work" notices all around the site. And we met and then I followed him. We separated so that no one could say that we actually arrived at the same time and that he saw me do it, but he would post a Stop Work notice, and I would tear it down, and he would post a Stop Work notice, and I would tear it down, and so on and so forth. We knew—"we" being John, Joel, Michael, Wes, Mel, myself—that this was happening and what were we going to do and certainly decided that we were going to continue working; we indeed were not going to abide by this notice. I don't know that it was ever exactly an official decision but we certainly felt that there was every possibility that someone was going to go to jail, someone was going to get arrested over this.

MEL LAWRENCE: It was like an unending thing. I mean, if it was needed, try and get it for the cheapest you could get it, but the marching orders—my marching orders to other people and Michael's marching orders to me—were, "Get it on." And getting it on meant sometimes spending more money.

Of course, now we had all these new guys. We had these guys from Cambridge. They were designers of traffic systems and signage. They had a sign shop and they were from Cambridge, near Boston— Intermedia Systems. They set up the sign shop and they were setting up traffic coordination, parking lots. We'd had these meetings all the time about how they were going to do it. And actually, if I remember correctly, one whole parking lot, I think the first one we ever looked at, was never opened. For some reason the cops—something went wrong out there and they didn't open this huge, huge parking lot and that's what started it, started the traffic jamming up.

CAROL GREEN: The last few weeks building up to it had gotten more and

173

more and more intense. These guys were just—where there's a will, there's a way. And most of them were not, as far as I knew, professional carpenters. They just did it. They had a telephone pole hung from a crane swinging over the ground and wires—they were holding wires to balance this thing, to steady it and stick it in the ground. And then Jay Drevers climbed up to the top of this pole himself and put the steel cap on it, and that was the thing that held the lighting trusses, these two poles. As that happened, a woman, like a Jewish lady, wandered through. "What's happening, darling? What's this?" And we were told, "Stand back. Somebody can really get killed."

Yippies, SDS Reported Bound for Rock Festival

Times Herald Record
Middletown, N.Y.
August 14, 1969

LEE BLUMER: I mean, the whole summer up to that point, everybody was working towards a festival but it was amorphous. Michael all along had a vision. All the rest of us had only smaller segments of that vision, I think. We had our jobs to do, we knew that people were going to show up, but none of us could even begin to get what we did. When all the people really came, you know, it's like you have a party and you invite a lot of people and you say, "Gee, wouldn't it be nice . . ." But then everybody you invited in the entire universe showed up. And then more. And they were all like banging on your door trying to get in, and it was really quite an effect.

HENRY DILTZ: There was no real sense of—at least in my mind—of what was going to happen. And I think in a lot of people's minds. I mean, you kind of got into this blissful summer, almost like a summer camp—this project, you know, right here in upstate New York. Everything was kind of really nice, everyone had a job to do and there was plenty of activity. Zip over here, zip over there, check out the Hog Farm and the site where they were building. But there was no big anticipation of crowds. I mean, nobody pictured that field full of people because the day that happened was like, "Look at those people out there in the field. Who are they?" A few thousand people were kind of sitting out in the field, and it was really odd. It was sort of a sense of, "God, they're here a little early aren't they?" I remember thinking, "They're going to have to clear them out and have them reenter or something."

CAROL GREEN: I knew the guys on the stage crew had taken acid for days to stay awake and hang up in the air in these cherry pickers. They would fall out of the cherry pickers and catch hold of the trusses and be hanging there; somebody would have moved the scaffolding. Somehow or other, none of them was killed. Somebody got a truck backed up into him—the truck stopped at his knees—and so there was an intensity. By that time for me, and for most of the people on the crews, this was "our" land and we didn't want anybody there. We did and we didn't. We were very protective. We were pioneers who had staked out this land and these people were just coming up over the rise and here's fifty thousand people, camping in *our yard*. I remember that afternoon going, "What have we done? What have we done?"

BILL BELMONT: A week before the show, things went into an all-night phase. The stage kind of got finished. Three days before the show, Hanley finally started getting the sound system hooked up. And I remember having a phone conversation with lots of road managers, all of whom couldn't really believe it was going to happen. But I had to call everybody and be sure that they understood it was happening. We had to make sure that people's deposits were in, the money had been sent to their agencies and stuff. A few of them had curious requests. The Who always got paid in cash in one-hundred-dollar bills before the first foot hit the stage. Other people had curious little requests like that. That they get picked up at the airport and they have their own dressing room. The kinds of things that bands were just starting to get into then.

Wednesday or Thursday before the show I get this phone call and somebody hands me the phone and says, "Here, talk to Steve Stills. He doesn't want to come." So as I'm talking to Steve Stills, they're playing "Suite: Judy Blue Eyes," testing the sound system. I stuck the phone out of the window of the trailer and he says, "Wow, man. Really—it's going to be O.K.? It's going to be all right? I'm not going to get killed, man?" I said, "Sure, it's going to be fine."

STANLEY GOLDSTEIN: On Wednesday and Thursday, I was spending a lot of time with Wes and John Fabbri and the security people because we had indeed lost the New York cops, and we already had thousands and thousands of people living there. There was no show yet—I mean, the construction crew was busting its ass to get the show together—and we were tending to five, ten, fifteen, twenty, twenty-five, forty thousand people. And they kept arriving—more and more people— and there were already serious traffic jams in the area, and there were a lot of negotiations going on and conversations with state cops about, "We got to put on the road plan. The road plan that's supposed to take place on Friday. You got to do it now. If you don't do it now, we're going to lose these roads." And, of course, we lost the roads because they never instituted the traffic plan.

WES POMEROY: We knew a week before—seems to me it was a couple weeks before it began—that we wouldn't have to advertise. There was stuff coming in from all over the United States. Everyone was talking about coming to the Woodstock festival or the Aquarian Exposition. Several days before the festival we thought we might have a hundred and fifty thousand people there, which would make it about three times bigger than anything anybody had ever had. But we were comfortable with that, because we had planned so that there were no outside parameters.

One problem, though, was that the state police didn't believe us. I was talking to these guys about the traffic patterns—the rate of flow of traffic, how much per lane and under what kind of a highway. The New York Thruway was one kind of thing and secondary roads were another and so forth. They were talking to me about all of the lanes they had moving up here and talking about thruways and all of that, and I said, "But when you get to the last few miles you only have two lanes." So we had to plan for that because that was all we were going to have—and maybe two extra lanes, because they would be using the shoulders where they can. They just didn't hear it. I had a firm commitment from these guys that they would have their people up

Security Chief: Rock Fest Won't Lack Guards

*Times Herald Record
Middletown, N.Y.
August 15, 1969*

175

Directing traffic

there at a certain time, and they didn't show up there until almost eight or ten hours later. We had over five hundred acres for parking and we had people at those places to direct people in. But the police were not there to get the traffic flowing as they came up, and they got up to where they ought to have traffic control and there was no one to tell them where to go. And they just parked. Of course, once that was jammed—Route 17B—it was just one parking lot. So our five hundred acres, that we had rented at prices we could have bought it for, was blocked and useless.

JOHN ROBERTS: On Wednesday, August 13, I decided that I should go up to the site and spend the rest of the time up there, that whatever ticket operations we had going in New York would be transferred to White Lake, and we had all our ticket takers and ticket sellers and various paraphernalia removed to White Lake. And I'd been in touch with Joel a lot by phone and knew that he had his hands full up there in a variety of other things. So I decided to go to White Lake and I needed a lift. My older brother Bill, who had been following along with these exploits of ours, had known that I was going up to White Lake and he offered to give me a ride and I said "Great." He said, "We can talk about what's going on, what your expectations are, if you think you're going to make any money, and just have a nice chat."

So, he showed up and my father was in the car and it was a limousine. And I was not real prepared for this, because my father was fairly intimidating to me at that age. My mother had died when I was very young and he was a kind of cold and distant guy throughout most of my youth, very skeptical of all of my various hair-brained schemes, as he thought of them, this being the most hair-brained.

176 I knew that we were in deep shit up in White Lake and I wasn't

sure what I was going find up there. Joel had kind of filled me in on the state of the site and some other things, so whatever I knew, it wasn't going to look like Aqueduct Racetrack on opening day. It was going look a lot less prepared than that, and I didn't really want to hear it. So, we rode up together in kind of a moody silence. Me, very monosyllabic, my father very inquisitive, but somewhat sarcastically so, and my brother trying to keep peace in the car.

We got up there around noon and we took a road that went along the crest of the hill behind what later became the performance field, the field where most of the audience sat. We could see this beehive of activity from the car. No gates, or some of the gates were sort of half up and people were working on the stage. There were about ten thousand people scattered around the hillside, sitting there. I said, "Well, you guys want to stick around or go back to the city?" And my father said, "We'll go back. Good luck." That's all he said was good luck. And I must say that from that day forward, he was enormously supportive and, ultimately, quite proud. He thought I had stepped in shit in getting into Woodstock, but he thought that we made a lot of right moves and good moves and honorable moves in getting out of it, so he was very pleased with that.

My recollection of Wednesday is from about noon on, dealing with landholders who had contiguous land. At some point Mike Lang came up on a motorcycle and said, "We have got to go see Mister Filippini about his pond and people camping on his grounds and we didn't rent twenty acres from him. Can we go over and see him?" So Michael and I went over and spent an hour or two with Mister Filippini around his table and talked to him and calmed him out and negotiated with him.

By Wednesday, you realized that you had a lot of local landholders who were not real pleased that these people were here. That these people would start trespassing. I remember one of the concerns we had in hours of conversation Wednesday night with Wes and other people: What if these people arm themselves and shoot? What do we do? Should someone go and speak to them? There was one farmer who had a standing kind of welcome, which was to stand on the porch and fire something in the air if you came near. What do we do about that?

Max had concerns about his neighbors' property, and he was not at all hesitant about calling me and telling me that or calling Joel. He had concerns about his own property, about people being in areas that weren't particularly designated. He had concerns about the gates—they weren't going to be up—we were going to take a bath and lose a lot of money. I remember one time he called me because he was incensed because he heard people were selling water or something like that.

177

JOEL ROSENMAN: I think it was Max who pointed me toward Walter Hoeft, who had one of those little plots of land that slipped through the cracks. That particular piece of land, however, was sitting under the performers' pavilion, which we had already constructed. And I think it was Max who called me and told me Walter Hoeft felt that we were on his land—*his* land still; we hadn't rented it yet—and he was willing to negotiate. At this point, of course, we had already built everything *around* that two or three acres, we had also built *on* that two or three acres, and there was a very short negotiation. More along the lines of "Here's what I'd like," and "Yes, sir, here's your check."

MEL LAWRENCE: The only thing I didn't feel secure about was whether that fence would be finished. We had to build this fence around the perimeter of the site, and we had hired a fence company. A lot of my work at this time was also getting subcontractors, like for trash hauling, like sanitary, the porta-john guys, like the fence guys. So you would talk to ten or fifteen different fence companies to get quotations and tell them what the job was to ascertain whether they could do the job. And we picked this fence company—I forget who they were—but they were these maniac guys who could do like huge lengths of fence in a day, you know. And that was sort of a horserace, it really was, because as people were arriving on those last days, these guys were putting up the fence. Sometimes people would walk in and the fence would go right after them. They'd walk right through and—*ta-da*—a fence was put there.

RONA ELLIOT: As inconceivable as it was, Max was running a number about the cows. The cows, if they were upset, would not give milk and Max would lose business. And the cows would surely be upset if the fences were up. So this twenty-one thousand dollars' worth of fencing,

which was the perimeter of the festival, never got up in time because people arrived there three days before. And so there were the cows and there were the people and the fencing went out the window.

JOEL ROSENMAN: We started to put up gates, but like everything else, we were working at triple time. We had the same staff that we had had, so we only had one third of the people working on fences and gates that we could have had, at the most. People were being dragged off to do what we regarded as more important things. The gates were more a gesture to sanity, a fleeting gesture to fast-fleeting sanity.

MEL LAWRENCE: The fence actually was completed in time for the show. I think it was eight feet high. But the posts were not sunk in cement like they should be so that's why it was—they were sunk pretty good, these guys got it good into the ground—but people started to rock 'em, and like one end would go, and it would, you know, sort of sag. It was really dangerous—people walking over it and like the tops of the fence were jagged and everything. People were climbing over and I started saying, "Take down the fence."

And I remember John was in like shock. "Do you really think so, Mel?" And I said, "You've got to realize that this is now a free festival." And people started making recommendations. I forget who recommended going around and taking a collection from people.

BILL BELMONT: Believe it or not, there was a meeting to cancel the festival. "Do we cancel or do we go on?" My comment was, "You can't stop this now; if we don't do it, these people are going to murder you. They're going to tear the stage down." And I think Michael Lang said, "But they wouldn't do that, would they?" I said, "Why wouldn't they? A crowd is a crowd is a crowd." Having been in Berkeley, at countless demonstrations all over the world, I know crowds turn ugly, especially when things don't go the way they're supposed to. I saw crowds get

pissed off because bands wouldn't do encores. The whole concept of peace and love was a state of mind. It was not a reality. Crowds are always crowds.

JOHN MORRIS: There's a scene in the movie where we're all standing in a group in a circle—Artie, Michael, probably Chris, the guy who sold the tickets, a couple of others, I can't remember exactly—and in the thing you can see, I turn around, walk away and throw my hands up in the air and walk ten, twenty feet away from them. Artie Kornfeld had just made a suggestion. I had just informed everybody that we had no real choice but to declare this thing a free festival. We might as well; it was. We're talking after the fact anyway. But to set the mood and to get everybody up and everybody cooperating with us, that's the only thing to do. What are you going to tell a few hundred thousand people who are sitting in your field when you're supposed to be collecting money from them? "Go back out and come back in when we get the tickets and we finish the fences and the rest of it"? And Artie had just come up with, "But we're going to lose money and the whole thing's going to go and we're not going to make any money. Can't you tell them that we're all going to lose money and can't we get a whole bunch of girls and put them in diaphanous gowns and give them collection baskets like in the Catholic Church, and send them out into the audience to get contributions for us so we don't lose money?" And at that point I turned on my heel and I walked away and I just stuck my hands up in the air. It was the most patently ludicrous sentence I had ever heard in my life. Then I just turned around and looked at him and said, "I'm going on stage and tell them"—I mean, I called John and said, "This is what I'm going to do."

And I just called John up and I said, "This is my assessment of the situation. The kids are there in the field. We're not going to move them out. We're not going to be able to collect from them. There is no time to figure out at this moment whether there's enough money in other places to cover." And I just said to John, "This is what we're going to have to do." And basically what John said to me was, "You're in charge. Do it. I'll back you up. I don't know how. I don't know how you're going to do what you're going to do. But I'll back you up."

You want to talk about the most anti-climactic sentence in the world? But it was a great roar, everybody loved it. It got everybody up. Everybody was into it. There's nothing like telling somebody whose in the middle of a field of a few hundred thousand people for free that they're there for free and it's O.K. But it worked. It was, "Share with your neighbor and if you've got a can of beans and the guy next to you has a can opener, you guys have just gone into partnership." And it was one of the greatest things in the world. That's what happened.

JOHN ROBERTS: Certainly as a business venture, it was dead. When you couldn't collect ticket revenues and had no gates, sometime Wednesday we sort of said, "Fuck the gates." We didn't sort of say it, we said it. We made the decision because we needed every available person on the stage to complete that. And the performance area, by Wednesday night, was already filled with twenty-five thousand people. You couldn't dislodge them. There wasn't enough organization to dislodge

They Arrive
With Fest
Tickets, Little
Else

*Times Herald Record
Middletown, N.Y.
August 15, 1969*

180

them. And the gates simply weren't going to get up. You weren't going to be able to ring about a mile of perimeter with gates. With anything that would stop anyone from coming in.

I also started to see that it was somehow very unimportant late Wednesday. I don't know why, but a sort of curious calm overcame us and it seemed like the gates just weren't really what was important here anymore.

It spelled instant doom, financially. And that didn't seem that terribly important at that particular moment, either. It seemed very important the day before and it seemed very concerning and very worrisome the day after. But from roughly Wednesday night through Sunday night, I would say the financial welfare of the venture seemed very unimportant. I don't understand why—I'm not suggesting that we were saintly or anything of that kind. I think all of us found ourselves in a situation that we had never been in before and would never be in again, with pressures and considerations that don't usually happen to you.

JOEL ROSENMAN: It was like worrying about your portfolio while you were under attack, or while battling your way through a hurricane. It was preemptive. So, it gave us the luxury of not having to be concerned with it.

I think that in the mythology of the festival, one of the most beautiful things about it is that it was a free festival. And there is not one person who would not like to claim credit for it—for being the author of that part of it. But, in fact, it was nobody who produced that part of the festival. That part came. Maybe nobody more than the chairman of the zoning board of Wallkill. After that, we were on a slide that led inevitably to the bottom. We all acknowledged that it had become, sometime along the way, a free festival.

LEE BLUMER: Thursday night, the Diamond Horseshoe—our palace, our palatial home—caught fire. I was in a van getting high with this boy who I was having my summer fling with, and we were at the very end of the property. We were sitting in his Volkswagen van, a white one, and we were looking out at the stars. It was just at sunset; it was that time of the year when there is still beautiful sky at that hour. I heard the dinner bell, but we had already eaten dinner and I was a little confused for a second because I couldn't imagine what the dinner bell was for. Then, in the very distance, I heard this "Fire! Fire!" And we drove back across this immense field and the fire brigade, which consisted of our own personnel, were out there passing buckets because the fire engines evidently couldn't get through the traffic. And I looked up on the fire escape. There was Penny Stallings in her little nightie calling for her dog. "Louise! Louise!" And I called Louise and suddenly Louise jumped into my arms and I said, "Penny, it's O.K., I have her." And that was the only thing we really cared about.

But this fire looked to us like an ominous portent. You know: They couldn't get the fire engines through. That if, God forbid, something really terrible had happened, we would have been at the mercy of something that we had no authority over at all. And it was just very peculiar because it was like beginning; here we are at the very beginning of our effort and it was already up in blazes. We really just did not know what we had created. We had realized that something was really happening here that wasn't a concert only.

JOHN ROBERTS: There's a scene I'll never forget. We had rented a lot of land in outlying areas, anywhere from a few hundred yards to several miles from the actual festival site for parking. We had guys out there with flashlights and we had signs directing people into the parking areas because it had been raining Wednesday and Thursday; these parking lots were a sea of mud. Joel and I got on the Honda 50cc's and we tooled around to all the parking lots to find out if these guys had enough food, water, whatever, and what was going on there. Just to tour them to see if they were filled with cars, were they usable, and so on. Then we could tell the state police later on whether they could direct them there or direct them elsewhere.

At some point on Thursday—it must have been close to midnight—we crested a hill that was maybe a quarter of a mile, half a mile away from Hurd Road, where the actual festival area was. And in the distance you could see what looked like hundreds, thousands of little campfires. We turned off the motorcycles and we stood there. It was like—we both had a sense that there was an army at rest before an enormous battle or undertaking the next day. It was very quiet—you could sort of hear noise and music in the distance. It was really a beautiful moment, and that moment will stay with me forever.

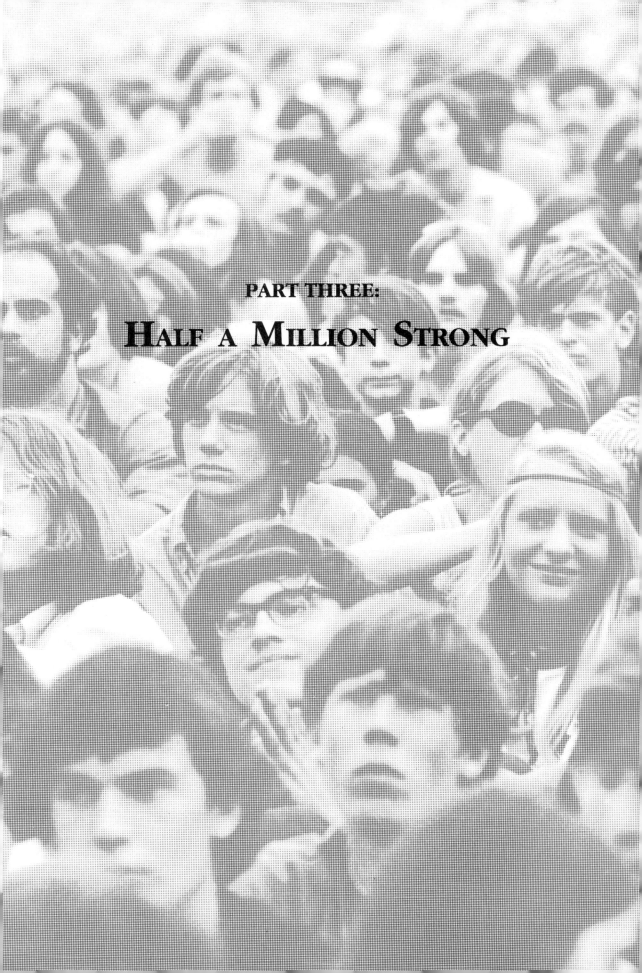

PART THREE:

HALF A MILLION STRONG

CHAPTER ELEVEN

"This is what it's like in Vietnam, only it's guns."
—Richie Havens

CHIP MONCK: I think a combination of frustration and fear kept me going those last few hours. I remember that my knees were chattering beyond my wildest belief when I was told by Michael to go down there and make sure everybody sat down. It was something like seven o'clock in the morning on the beginning day: "Tell them to push back from the fence and get them all seated. And by the way, you can take over these duties because nobody has shown up." What he really meant was nobody else was thought of to be MC for the show.

And so I started my welcome: "I'm delighted to see you all here and I hope you're going to plan on having a lovely three days. We have numbers of things to do. I hope you don't mind if this welcoming announcement is somewhat short. But we'll get back to you with other bits and pieces of information and perhaps the show's schedule as soon as we know it. Do have a moment to talk among yourselves and please enjoy the weather." It was all kind of sarcastic and rather flippant because that was probably the best way to approach it. Trying to present yourself as an authoritarian or something in that particular situation, telling people exactly what to do, I don't think is really the right way to do it. Sometimes you're going to need to say that—to bellow at someone to "get the fuck off the tower" for the last and final time. And I think you need to save that. So everything was kind of flippant and fun—you know: "Oh, you look awfully attractive. Have you met him over here? He's probably attractive, too. Why don't you two talk to each other while you can still have the space to walk around. And then perhaps you can probably tell the guys in between you to sit down that are pressing against the barrier."

The crowd looked pretty raggy. In fact, they all kind of looked about the same all the time. They were sort of smeared with different colors of dirt and they were not particularly interesting. They looked as if they were prepared, at one time or another, to have a nice time, but they wished it would happen fairly soon. They looked even funnier when they were wet. They got a little cleaner, but only for an instant, before anybody sat down and realized how much dirtier they really were.

And suddenly, it was show time. I think that it was a very simple announcement—something like: "Sit down, stand up, do whatever you wish to do but we're ready to start now and I bet you're pleased with that. And, ladies and gentlemen—please—Mister Richie Havens."

RICHIE HAVENS: I was coming back from Europe the second time and getting ready to make my third album. I had heard about Woodstock before that because Michael Lang I had known before I went away, and he had talked about doing something. I had heard that they were going to try to do something like Monterey on the East Coast. That was the image of what it was going to be like.

Now, the consciousness—we have to put it in context, because

Welcome, Aquarius

Editorial
Times Herald Record
Middletown, N.Y.
August 15, 1969

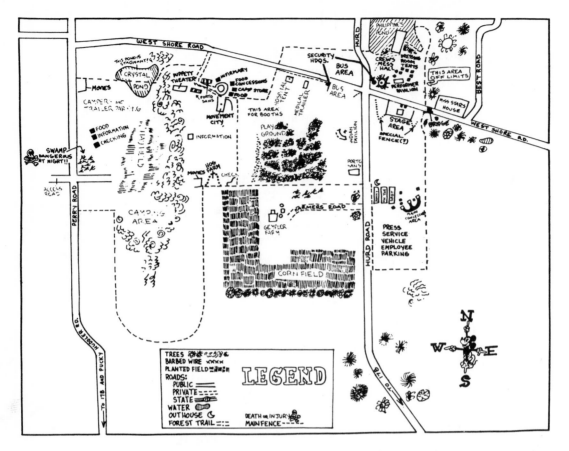

a lot of people do not have the context out of which it came
philosophically. And that is that in California, they had free concerts
all the time—they were called "be-ins"—so this was a kind of a be-in
for the first time on the East Coast. But Woodstock was going to be a
real happening on the East Coast that was more organized and less a
happening for the first time. So it came out of context for the
philosophy, and it had a philosophy base and not just music.

I call it a cosmic accident myself. I call it a media event, created
by the media and not by the promoters, as much as they would like
it to have been more in their control. What happened was created by
the media. When I did come back, I heard on the radio all around the
country about this festival that was going to happen on the East Coast,
and the news was, "Well, they found a place to do it." And the next
two days the news was, "Well, they don't have a place to do it." So,
mind you, all around the country, everybody's hearing this big music
news item. When there was a finality of the location, people started to
leave their places then. There were people from Alaska, from
California—they drove from everywhere.

I went up Friday morning and I had no problem getting there
because actually we left at five in the morning and there wasn't a car
on the road going up. I didn't go to the field; we went to a hotel off
the highway. It was seven miles away from where the concert was
going to be held. There was a Holiday Inn and a Howard Johnson's
on the other side of the road. All of the groups were staying in these
two hotels.

I remember being in the hotel and the so-called stage management letting everybody know what was going on, which was the road was blocked. And as of this point, nobody is going to the field, and since it was already going on the weekend, it was hard to get certain things to happen. So they called out the helicopter help and they came back and knocked: "Helicopter's going to come." And they came back and knocked again: "Helicopter's not going to come." This went on about three times and finally, I'm sitting in my room, watching TV, and I hear a helicopter landing in the driveway of the Holiday Inn, and it's one of these little bubble guys, you know, with four seats in it. And because we only had two acoustic guitars and two conga players, we went over first. That was how I got over there. And there were very few people over there. Tim Hardin was there and maybe a couple of people who weren't going to play because their bands were nowhere in sight. That was how I had to go on first, because they came and asked me to go on first.

MICHAEL LANG: It was a question of who could we get on the quickest, who was ready and who needed the least preparation and the least gear. And it was Richie. I had sent some people back to the staging area to find out what our possibilities were. And Richie came up most possible. Tim Hardin was an idea. He wasn't ready. Tim, I think, was a little blitzed, a little too blitzed. He was a friend, and I was hoping

Tim Hardin

187

that playing at Woodstock would bring him back, because he had been blitzed for a while. And I thought it would be a good opportunity for him to get his shit together, and straighten up long enough at least to get some public recognition. But he wasn't ready.

CHIP MONCK: Tim was absolutely unable to fathom or to deal with the fact of opening the show, fairly delicate if not frail in his own. He couldn't be presented, couldn't be placed in front of that audience without—nothing so formal as an opening act—without some help. So he politely declined. The equipment for the first act which actually was slated, which I don't remember, evidently had not arrived so what we were madly doing was running around upstage trying to find out who in fact would perform. Country Joe's equipment wasn't ready and then it was up to Richie Havens. Richie was in fact ushered downstage, plunked on his stool—or I believe it was a metal chair at that moment— and was thoughtful enough to begin the proceedings.

RICHIE HAVENS: I actually was afraid to go on first, basically because I knew the concert was late and I knew that people paid for this and maybe it would be a little nuts. Flying over that crowd coming in in that bubble, I knew what being nuts could mean. And I didn't want to be trampled by a billion people. So I said, "Don't put me in front of your problem like this. Don't do this to me, Michael. I'm only one guy. My bass player isn't even here." He was walking on the road for twenty-five miles because the cars were backed up. He made it as I walked off the stage, he came walking up to the stage. They'd left the car on the New York Thruway twenty-five miles back and then walked, along with a lot of other people, and they partied all the way down the line and he got there just as I got off.

MICHAEL LANG: Well, Richie was scared, frankly, as I recall. But I think that was a kind of natural reaction to looking at a crowd of that size. But he didn't make it a problem.

RICHIE HAVENS: I just saw color to the top of the hill and beyond. When my eyes went from the foot of the stage up to the top of the hill and beyond, I went right up to the sky, I went right out to where the whole thing was. The best sound that I have ever played on outdoors to date happened at Woodstock. As a matter of fact, they said they heard it ten miles away in every direction, because they put those towers up there, and it bounced through those mountains. We not only did it for the crowd there, we did it for the whole countryside at that point. So it was a modular saturation level of vibrations into the planet. This was not just in that spot, it went ten miles all around, and that's a big circle of sound wave.

CHIP MONCK: Richie sang every song ever written or performed by Richie. He then left the stage because he was out of material. If not completely out, mostly out. There might have been something that he hadn't written, but he wouldn't have thought about that anyway.

RICHIE HAVENS: I did about four or five encores, till I had nothing else

400,000 Flood Site; Rock Crisis Eases Off

*Times Herald Record
Middletown, N.Y.
August 16, 1969*

188

to sing, and then "Freedom" was created right there on the stage. That's how "Freedom" was created, on the stage. It was the last thing that I could think of to sing. I made it up. It was what I thought of, what I felt—the vibration which was freedom—which I thought at that point we had already accomplished. And I thought, "God, this is a miracle. Thank God I got to see it." My whole consciousness of the whole thing was that this was a normal festival, and I had already been too overimpressed by the Newport Folk Festival with twelve thousand people and nothing was ever going to match that. So this wasn't too unusual in its musical aspects, but it was more unusual in the people who came. The people who were up in the mountains who thought they were on vacation in the Catskills who were over fifty to their eighties brought their grandchildren, thinking it was going to be a nice musical festival, and ended up staying for three days and helping everybody out. It was families, it was the policemen in the movie saying, "Leave the kids alone," it was a time when consciousness came about. My viewpoint of it was I finally crossed over the line where I don't have to worry anymore. About the whole planet, the entire planet.

I remember walking across that bridge they built back there, and I just made it because my conga drummer's foot went through and I remember turning around and looking at him and his drums bounced—one fell off and somebody caught the other one—and his foot went through that little ramp that they had that went over that back road, and I just couldn't believe it. He was up to his thigh on one leg down in this hole. That was my picture that I saw, and I just couldn't believe it. Then they got him out of there; he was O.K. and he was worried about his drum that fell off the thing more than he was worried about himself. And we got off and then we came down the stairs and that was when my bass player walked up.

While I was onstage, a few helicopter trips came in with stuff, and

189

at that point it could start. They started rolling the stuff up the minute I was doing my first encore actually, and starting to put it in place for the next band that was going to come on. I spent the night backstage and walking around in the side woods and at some of the crafts area, but spent the night mostly backstage. We all were jamming back there, just hanging out really, and eating a lot.

They flew us back and I got the chance to fly over the whole field in an open Army helicopter, which gave me another point of view. Which was kind of interesting because here I was, sitting against the wall with another band and my group like soldiers in an Army helicopter with our equipment, guitars sitting there. And I look down the row and I flash so heavy, "This is what it's like in Vietnam, only it's guns, right? "And I look out the door and all I see is treetops. I actually fantasized tracers coming up out of the treetops. I actually did, all the way back to the hotel because there was nothing but treetops. There was never an open field from that point back to the hotel highway section and you couldn't see the ground and that put me anywhere in the world, and I was in Vietnam in that sense. And all I could think of was, "This has got to be what it's like, man, for all those soldiers, man, flying and ducking stuff coming up out of the damn trees, you know." And that's where I was at going back.

We ended up getting back to the hotel and packing up our stuff and driving out because I was playing in Michigan the next night, that same night that I got back. So we got into the car, the station wagon that brought us, and we went out to the New York Thruway. And there was not one car on the entire Thruway because it was closed all the way back to New York. We had the entire New York Thruway to ourselves completely. In my lifetime, that's one of the biggest highlights I've ever had, is to have the entire New York Thruway closed and us driving from there back to Newark Airport straight away.

Country Joe McDonald (left), Bill Belmont

JOHN MORRIS: After Richie, there was nobody else. I kept saying, "Play more, play more, play more," because we didn't have another act. There was nobody there with equipment who could play. And Joe McDonald was there and sitting on the side of the stage. He and I had been in Europe together the year before and we talked a couple of times about him doing a solo act.

BILL BELMONT: Joe was wandering around onstage and John said, "Can Joe do a solo set?" And I said, "I don't know why not." "Do you think he'll want to?" I said, "Right now?" He said, "Yeah, go talk him into it." I said, "Me?" He said, "Yeah." "How long?" "Half an hour." And I said, "O.K., well, we can try and see if he'll do it but—" And John said, "Yeah, I know, I know. He's always very cranky."

So I went over and said, "Hey, Joe, you want to do a solo set?" He said, "What?" "You want to go up and play?" He said, "Me? All these people? What am I going to play?" I said, "I don't know. Some songs that you're going to do next month or some solo tunes." He said, "Well, Woody Guthrie songs." We had this nonsensical conversation. He said, "Well, I don't have a guitar." I said, "John, we need a guitar." And then somebody was wandering around onstage with a guitar and I went and got the guitar. We found a piece of rope to tie it up with. We handed him the guitar and he said, "This is a guitar?" And I literally pushed him out there and John said, "Good work, good work. Great!"

JOHN MORRIS: That's when he said, "I need a capo." He asked me to go get a capo and I thought he meant a *capon*, and I couldn't figure out what he wanted with this eviscerated chicken. I had to go ask Jerry Garcia what a capo was and he gave me one. And I went on and said, "Ladies and gentlemen, Country Joe McDonald." And he did it, God love him.

BILL BELMONT: I pushed him out onstage and the audience was bored for fifteen or twenty minutes and Joe looks over and says, "It's not going too well, is it?" And I said, "Sing 'Fixin' to Die Rag.'" He said, "Gimme an F . . . . Gimme a U . . . . Gimme a C . . . . Gimme a K." And that's what happened. And the thing that was so amazing about it was that this entire multitude of people yelled "FUCK!" And it was so loud. I mean, it was just really loud. And it was sort of mind boggling that it was so loud. That's the only time I remember the crowd being intimately involved with something. They roared this stuff. And then he started singing "Fixin' to Die Rag." The people in the front started hearing the song, then further and further and further, and pretty soon everybody started singing it. So after a while, you had all these people singing "Fixin to Die Rag." Joe was really into it. And the festival started at that moment really.

• • • •

CHIP MONCK: As the music started, I felt as if we'd gotten somewhere. I think I was still quite overcome with the feelings that we hadn't completed what I wanted to see. I really wasn't working for them, I was working for myself—"them" being the public. As the public comes into

Ready to Rock, But Traffic Can't Roll

*Daily News
New York, N.Y.
August 16, 1969*

a theater, or however rough an arena or however rough a site, they never know what you had in mind. But you do. And that, I think, is one of the only things that really keeps you going. You don't really want them to know that you're responsible for the perfection that they're seeing, and you don't really want to tell them what the perfection is that they should notice. But you want to complete something the way you had originally designed it. That's been the hang-up for many of us. It's because we have a vision in our heads and sometimes it never meets with the expectations of the management or the accountants or the acts. It's funny that way. And this one was a very—It was nice to have it start, but it was really unsuitable, because it was so rough.

I don't think that I had time to watch anything or listen to anything because the moment that act was on it meant that another one was to be prepared, with Steve Cohen and myself and numbers of other stage-hands and folks that were helping. And so there wasn't a moment's breath there. There was a certain sense of, "At least it started." But when you knew it started, you knew another one had to follow as soon as possible. And without the revolving stage, that was a killer, because then it was going to have to be manually put on. So Richie and Country Joe, being individuals, was obviously a very easy and smart way of starting. Because he could just pick it up and walk off with it. We didn't have to move them off. We would have done a lot more a cappella and individual performers had we known what we were doing.

HENRY DILTZ: I remember the stage—everybody was kind of running around that first day. I had an all-access pass so I was up on the stage a lot and just trying to hang out in all the places where everything was going on. The day started great and Richie Havens and then Country Joe and the Incredible String Band. And Arlo Guthrie. And I was sitting up there digging it, taking pictures in the nice afternoon light, you know. And I loved the Incredible String Band. I loved all of these acts. I was a musician myself so it was great for me to see all that.

John Sebastian

John Sebastian played that first day too, in his tie-dyed stuff. So I took some pictures of him from behind him, with his tie-dyed coat, singing to the crowd. I used some of them in one of his albums that came out. He was a real good friend of mine. I'd spent a year photographing the Lovin' Spoonful. That was my first kind of job that I had, and so he was a real good friend.

JOHN MORRIS: Sebastian was not booked to play. Somebody said, "John Sebastian is here." So I ran over and said, "Please, will you?" And he said, "Sure." And he did it. He was just walking around, casually dressed in tie-dye from head to toe, carrying his guitar, thank God. And we grabbed him and put him on. He was willing. We were just filling until we could get people in and get people on the stage and get them up there.

BILL BELMONT: Sebastian babbled for forty-five minutes. John Morris kept saying, "Oh my God, we gotta get him off the stage." But he was stoned. He babbled for forty-five minutes. That's probably why he doesn't want to talk about it. He was completely stoned.

Swami Satchadinanda

JOHN MORRIS: At one point Friday, I had these people show up in my office and say, "Swami Satchadinanda is outside. He would like to speak to all these people." And I thought, "An Indian guru. A holy man. Why not? We can use anything we can." So I said, "Sure." Also, I was short of acts. And it was true: I really was short of acts. And it was like a little omen thing, or whatever. It felt good. Ordinarily, I probably never would have even considered it for ten seconds, because if you didn't insult him, you'd insult someone else.

They brought him in. All of a sudden there's this teeny tiny little man in a saffron robe with all the people around him. And I thought, "I hope you know what you're doing." And I brought him up on stage and he sat there in his squeaky voice and talked to the people. And he talked about peace—and he was wonderful. It was great. It was part of the calming influence. It was like a blessing. It was like an invocation or whatever. And that was O.K. Don't forget, the energy was still pretty good at that point.

MICHAEL LANG: Friday, the programming was sort of easing in. It was Ravi Shankar and Joan Baez and Tim Hardin and Arlo Guthrie and Sweetwater. And Sly was sort of to build the evening a bit. You needed some sort of excitement in there. Sly provided it. There was some fun things during the day anyway. We needed something that would peak a bit.

193

Joan Baez

JOHN MORRIS: Joan Baez was great. I've done some of the best concerts I've ever done in my life with Joan. I did one in London at Christmastime with Mimi, her sister, and her mother and her father on the stage with popcorn snow that fell in front of the scrim while they sang "Ave Maria" and "Silent Night" a cappella to thirty-six hundred people, and I stood in the wings with tears running down. And Joanie has never failed to give me that. She was good. She was beautiful, she was pregnant, she was radiant, she understood. She didn't talk too much, which is the other thing she'll occasionally do. I have been known, as others have, to whisper loudly from the wings, "Stop talking and start playing." No, I remember her as being very beautiful, very Madonna-like. The voice was as wonderful as it could ever be. And Joanie has a great sense of where she is in life.

ABBIE HOFFMAN: I remember watching Joan Baez and talking to her backstage. I remember she kept complaining—she didn't like rock music, it was too loud, it wasn't political enough. She's sort of not a hedonistic person, not a Dionysian person. She's kind of stiff. I said, "Joan, I want you to hold my knife." She said, "You know I'm nonviolent." You know, like an instinctual response. And I was saying, "Who said *I* wasn't? What do you think—this is for cutting food, this is for helping people at the hospital. I just want to give it to you for a present. Don't freak out." It was just a gift. I had the hots for her.

194   **JOHN MORRIS:** Sly Stone was almost impossible to deal with in those

days. They were using one of the trailers as a dressing room and this "I'll-go-on-when-I'm-ready" type of stuff and the audience was waiting and I did a Bill Graham on Sly. I just grabbed him by the shirt and lifted him up in the air and slammed him into the side of the trailer and said, "You will go on now or I'll tell them you're sitting here and you're too good to go on." He was a real pain in the neck.

MICHAEL LANG: My main concern was keeping the show going and keeping the stage moving. Which to me seemed the most critical part of any show, the entertainment. I spent most of my time onstage, making sure that the deck was—every time the rains would come down—our covering didn't really work—making sure that it got dried and equipment got covered and people got away from live wires and as soon as we got a break in the weather, making sure that the stage was dried out as well as possible, getting the next act up.

Sly Stone

PENNY STALLINGS: I didn't feel that I should be listening to the music. And it was far more entertaining to watch the stuff that was going on with the people who did the festival because Artie was walking around holding his head and he was completely flipped out, and one of my jobs was to try and get him Thorazine, which I don't think that we yet had. As I remember, they had to get that for him; they had it flown in at some point. Michael kept roaring around on his motorcycle. All the bikers were in that area, all the Hell's Angels just showed up out of nowhere, just materialized. And every five minutes, somebody would come in and tell you about the next disaster which had to be dealt with.

RONA ELLIOT: I was particularly freaked out by one of the producers being stoned. I have nothing against people being stoned. It was just that it appeared to me that what was really called for at that time was a major amount of responsibility. Beside the great aspect of it, the producers of the show and the staff of the show were empowered with the necessity of producing a safe environment for these people. It scared the shit out of me. I said, "Wow, this guy is stoned, man, and I'm sitting here doing food drops and blanket drops." I made a big decision then that I was getting out of rock 'n' roll. I didn't want to be in show production. I didn't want to be with people who don't understand what their responsibility is. It was a real turning point in my career, because I decided to go back into news and move away from this. It was not the appropriate response to be stoned on acid if you were a producer at Woodstock, from my point of view.

The environment in general was just wild. Every ten feet, you could see anything. Whatever was in the width of your imagination was there, and things you could not imagine. I mean, I remember—it was

195

Arlo Guthrie

ninety-eight degrees—a woman in a chain dress who captured a lot of people's attention. There was anything. People were doing everything. Anything you could imagine was happening and in a very supportive environment. It wasn't threatening, people were getting stoned and they were doing whatever they were doing. There were children, there were old people, there was everything. And people were really stoned.

• • • •

STANLEY GOLDSTEIN: There was a storm Friday. Friday night was a real whipper. We were confronted with an unusual run of weather. It rained considerably more than what the averages indicated. And there was a couple freak storms, particularly during the show. Now some of it may be apocryphal, because I have not gone back to the records, but my recollection is at the time what seemed to me as authoritative sources—by that I mean talking to the people who were ground control for helicopter flights and the people at the airports—said that this was truly unique weather. I have no other sources for that. But I'll adhere to that; it makes me feel better. We had extraordinarily high winds as well as heavier-than-usual rainfall that made all those construction tasks very, very difficult.

Another thing that occurred was that there had been a cocaine delivery to the stage. I don't know who delivered it. I think I know, but I don't really know. And I don't know how much it was, but it was a lot—certainly a pound, perhaps a kilo—that was delivered to the stage. And the bag was opened up and it was going to be broken down into smaller bags so that it would last through the weekend. That was the stage cocaine; it was in the tone of the times. And the rain came, and in the frantic crunch to get all the equipment back and covered and so on and so forth, someone drained a whole enormous piece of tarp that had been covering things. Tipped it up and drained it into the cocaine and washed it all away. That was one of the things that made Friday night's storm memorable.

JOHN ROBERTS: Sometime that summer, we looked into rain insurance—I'd say, maybe back in June. And we did have some, I think with Lloyd's. The rain insurance requires that you get a virtual monsoon over a very narrow period of time—like six inches in an hour, or something like that. And we got maybe five-point-eight. Whatever it was that we needed, we didn't get.

CHRIS LANGHART: The rain just paralyzed the whole place. But it was warm rain and it never really got cold and what kind of spirits could you be in? There was such community there that it didn't make any difference that everybody's blanket was muddy and wet. Eventually, the sun came out and dried it out. It wasn't what you would have if you were in control of how the *Farmer's Almanac* was written, but who could control it? Just make the best of it. At that point, that was about what you could do. The fact is that the show went forward so nobody was disgruntled or agitated as a result of having come there to see something that didn't happen.

RICHIE HAVENS: The rain made the people interact with each other. The rain made it necessary for us to share whatever we had— the plastic that went over our heads, the coat, or whatever—and it was the natural forces that played a great deal in what happened. So I balance it out as a cosmic accident. It was half ours and half God's.

• • • •

MIRIAM YASGUR: In my innocence, when they finally got this thing going, a few days before

I said to Max, "You know, Joan Baez is going to be there, and I'm going to go up there for the time Joan Baez is there because I have to hear her." Some of the other people weren't as attractive, but she was one, so I had all these nice plans. I was going to go up when Joan Baez was there, maybe one or two of the other people. But, of course, there was no way I was going to get there. That went by the board.

I had to be down at the office and help take care of things. Customers were calling and routes were being diverted, the principals of the festival were getting calls on our lines, and then we had the kooks calling—you know, you would hang up and you would pick up the phone and you would get these people screaming at you and you'd hang up on them and they'd redial and scream at you. It was mostly foul language or "You're ruining the area!" or "You allowed all these hippies in!"—you know, really in more nasty tones than I'm saying. And there were a few people that were so persistent that we called the telephone company, asked them to put a check on our lines and see if they could trace back these calls, because these people were calling up and hysterically screaming on the phone at us so that we couldn't keep our lines open.

So we were involved with that, we were involved with taking food out of the cooler and feeding people, we were involved with trying to keep our business going and I really couldn't push through this. The troopers, when they would go by our office, would stop by, either to get something to drink or whatever—you know, they'd drink orange juice or chocolate milk—and they kept expressing amazement

197

in the fact that they never saw so many youngsters together being so helpful to each other and being so peaceable that their job was really to try and keep things open as much as they could. One car with some troopers got stuck in the road. It went off the road in the crowd, you know, trying to get by, maybe a half a mile west of our office, somewhere in that area. And they said they saw all these kids coming at them and they thought, "Oh, boy." And what these kids did was lift the car and take it and put it back on the road. I had kids come in and say, "You know, there's been a couple of troopers directing traffic on that road for the last few hours. It's so hot; they must be thirsty. Could you give me something for them to drink?" And they would take cartons of chocolate milk and orange juice and go over to the troopers.

It's an Astonisher!

Times Herald Record
Middletown, N.Y.
August 16, 1969

• • • •

JOHN ROBERTS: The White Lake office for the festival was the old telephone building in the center of town, the town having, I think, a grocery store and maybe one or two other buildings and some homes. It was a plain rectangular building with a big front room, maybe twenty feet wide by thirty feet long, and a back room that was maybe twenty by ten. That's my recollection of it anyway. And we had maybe six desks on one side and six on the other in the front and three or four desks in the back, which were in theory the executive offices. We didn't move there until August 13, which was Wednesday, when I arrived at the site. We had in there Wes Pomeroy, who was head of the security; John Fabbri, who had been hired by Wes, the police chief of South San Francisco; Rene Levin, who was the bookkeeper, the keeper of the checkbook; Joel and myself; Lee Blumer; some people doing press liaison work; and about thirty or forty other people who I don't remember.

It had a kind of bunker mentality. Anything that happened came to us first. Anything they said from the stage, any announcements that they were going to make of any importance had to be cleared with us. Anything to do with moving the artists in or out, getting supplies to the stage, people who were sick, security, liaison with the state police, the press, the traffic—all that came through there. Any people, local police figures, who had anything to do with the festival, that's where they came to see us. We got served all our lawsuits there. And I have a memory of being there essentially from Friday morning to Sunday night. I think Saturday I got a couple hours of sleep back at this motel where I was staying. But that's about it, I think.

It will be forever engraved on my mind, you know—the forty-eight hours in that office. Occasionally, we'd go across the street and get a sandwich until I think the food ran out in the grocery store across the way. There was so much input going on, there were so many phones ringing and so many people with problems or concerns or suggestions. It never stopped, never stopped. I'd never been in a situation like that before. I suspect it's like being at a headquarters during a battle—you know, just so much information coming in, so many different divisions that have to get out, and so many rumors that fly around—rumors that range from the state police were on their way to close them down to a bunch of longhairs that jumped someone's

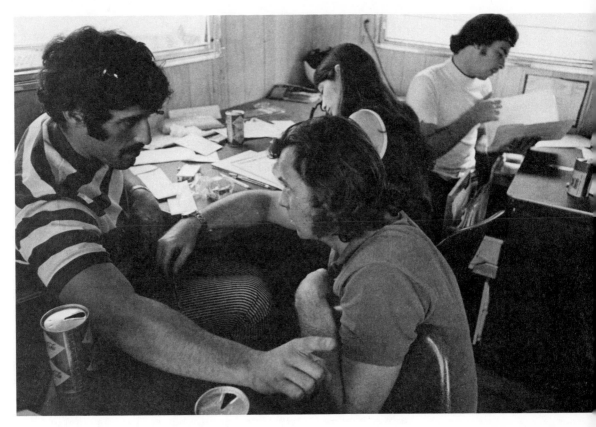

cow and ate it alive. I mean, they were just really from the absurd to the more absurd, and that's where we could be found.

I made it to the festival site. I was at the site most of all day Wednesday and all day Thursday, and Friday morning, but I never made it to the show. I left the festival site about an hour before Richie Havens sang. I could never get out, I really could never get out of that place. There was not one minute that I could remember—and I don't think I've ever had a time in my life where that was the case—there was not one minute when there wasn't something for me to do or someone to talk to or some decision to be made. It's funny because I think Wes and Lee and John Fabbri and Joel and I all felt very bonded by that, because we were all sort of in the same boat that weekend.

JOEL ROSENMAN: I remember being told to get out to the Thruway. The authorities needed me out there. And I went out on my motorbike to the Thruway or to the feeder off the Thruway and I was stunned at what I saw. I mean there were cars everywhere. It was a sea of cars at that point and they were all trying to get to the festival. And there were a few people here and there, including a cop, trying to turn them back, and they weren't having any of it. People who wanted to get to the festival were on a mission. The cop said, "You turn them around. Here's the guy that organized the festival. He'll tell you—there's no way." And I looked back at the cars for miles, as far as you could see, and I went to the first car and the guy rolled down his window and I said, "I'm the producer of the festival and there's no room," and he

essentially told me to buzz off, but not in that language. He said, "I just drove three and a half hours," from wherever he was coming from, "and I'm going to this festival." But the cop was turning them around and they were going down a little ways, getting out of their cars, walking past us—and it hit me that I felt like the Dutch boy with his finger in the dike. We weren't going to be able to stop this incredible tide of people, certainly not this way. As it turned out later, what we did was get on the air and broadcast—we used AM and FM radio—to tell millions of people, "Stop trying to get to the Woodstock festival." They weren't going to make it. The ones that believed us stayed in their houses. The ones who didn't believe it probably got to the festival. And as you know, there were hundreds of thousands that didn't believe it.

Traffic ceased to be a problem after a while at the festival. In fact, sometime on Saturday, the traffic ceased to be a problem for most people because traffic ceased moving entirely and it wasn't even considered as a problem after that.

JOHN ROBERTS: Traffic and clearing the roads was a big concern of everybody's all weekend long. Both clearing the roads to get out and clearing the roads to get in, clearing the roads for safety. When the state police caravan found us in White Lake on Saturday afternoon, they had come over hill and dale on back roads that only the state police knew, when they finally got to the White Lake building. The roads were really quite something.

JOHN MORRIS: I was in constant communication with the White Lake office. We kept a pretty much open line back and forth through Lee

Ravi Shankar

Blumer, who had been my secretary at the Fillmore and was then working with the two of them. God love her. So I called John and said, "Look, this is where we are. The roads are blocked. We're going to have to hire helicopters"—which I had already done. I just turned around to Annie, my wife, and said, "Get on the telephone and hire every single helicopter you can lay your hands on. Go as far as Pennsylvania." In the end, I had the largest private air force probably in the United States. Sixteen helicopters, including the Army helicopters we ended up with. That was it. We're not talking options. We're talking about what do you do to solve the problem fast.

JOHN ROBERTS: Everyone wanted a helicopter. Everyone involved with the festival called us, wanting us to send a helicopter for them. For their dog.

JOEL ROSENMAN: And most of them got it, too. Everybody needed a helicopter. I think probably four hundred thousand people got rides in helicopters. Except for us. John and I were the only two people who hadn't been in a helicopter after Woodstock was over.

MICHAEL LANG: Friday sort of came and went. Ravi Shankar on stage was kind of a special moment. The vibe was intense. I don't know how else to put it. It may sound a little corny, but it was a very tangible feeling in the air. When those spiritual moments would happen, you could really feel them. You could feel everybody sort of coming together at those moments and the energy was amazing. I think everybody felt that, even people who just sort of had nothing to do with the festival, who were just traveling through the area; I've heard those same kinds of comments. There was just a feeling in the air.

Four o'clock Friday was the turning point. I remember the Hell's Angels came in, and got swallowed up. I mean, it was supposed to be one of the moments of crisis. We had finally gotten the show started and I was standing looking over the back of the stage. And someone said that the Hell's Angels were here. And I said, "Oh no, here it comes." Something had to crack, you know. And I saw them get sort of swallowed up in it, in just the whole spirit of the thing. They went off and found their little area and did their thing and it just became neutralized. That potential problem became neutralized. And I suddenly realized how strong this was. And that it was going to work.

• CHAPTER TWELVE •

"Here's a burger, here's a joint."
—Peter Beren

FRANK FAVA: I was living in Saugerties, New York, at the time, working as a roadie. We had this big old Quarrymen's Hotel over in Saugerties and a lot of ex-college friends of mine and other associated hangers-on were living there and everybody was trying to get gigs in the music business. The rumor was around town about a festival; that's how we heard about it. I had done a couple of gigs with Judy Collins at that point and—I'm trying to put it in historical perspective—and I was waiting to start working for Jimi Hendrix. I was on line to go to work for him when the festival started to come together.

I got to meet Len Kaufman in a strange set of ways. Len was working in Woodstock at that time doing real estate and various other kinds of projects. Everybody knew him as an ex-Village person who was basically a hustler and used to work in the carnivals. I think he saw Woodstock from his carnival background as a potential gold mine to make money. I know that at this point I was not really close to him but from hanging around in the fringes, I got to know him. In fact, there was an incident where we had to deal with him on a face-to-face level with a couple of his people because someone had been ripped off and he was brought in to try to find out who ripped them off and recover the money, etc. That's how I got to know Len Kaufman, and getting to know him more and more and hanging around his house. His kitchen table became a place where people would drop by and talk.

I think at that point he sort of got Michael's ear and Peter Goodrich's, and they used to stop by to pick Len's brains. And Len pretty much knew what was going on: they were picking his brains looking for ideas. And he was looking for some sort of an in—to be able to get into the festival and make some dollars.

I guess Lenny somehow convinced Michael that there was a need for a super-elite kind of security force, something that was going to be his cover in case anything disastrous happened. Lenny was always the kind of person who preached from the harbinger-of-doom side. It was like the devil's advocate to the extreme. I think he said enough things to Michael and Peter and other people that were roaming with them to make them see that the downside of this was the fact that a lot of bad things could happen and that they should have some people basically covering their back. Because I had done a couple of things that I guess impressed Len, he asked me if I wanted to work as part of this elite group, and since I didn't have a gig and wasn't doing anything I said, "Yeah, sure. Fine. No problem."

We were asked to be there Wednesday afternoon and we showed up Wednesday afternoon and already disaster had started. There were a lot of people. The fences were starting to come down. We realized right away that there was no way they were going to control this crowd. So we started to make plans within ourselves to cover first of all ourselves, and to do our primary responsibility, which was if something really bad happened, to get Michael and Peter and various other people who worked backstage and were considered key people in the operations area—and I'm talking about backstage operations now, the performers' pavilion—out of there.

We immediately took over two access roads that were on the farm, which were dirt roads, put roadblocks on either end and put a couple of guys on those roadblocks. We had arranged to have this little bungalow colony that was not far from the back end of one of these dirt roads; it led onto a macadam road. That was our place. It was a small place, no one else was really staying there, this was our place, with all the intention that we were going to work shifts. Of course, as things started to develop there was no way any of us were leaving.

You gotta understand this crew of people that I was working with. There was Len, who had worked carnivals and had worked for Wells Fargo in security on an armored truck, done a lot of other various things and run into some pretty crazy scenes in the city. His number-one associate at that point, this guy Bob Braten, used to be somewhat of a folksinger in the Village and I guess that's where he met Lenny, and they moved up to Woodstock around the same time. There was this guy Ralph, whose last name I won't mention because he was from a very heavy Mafia family. He was one of us. There was this guy Al, who was motorcycle president from a big club out in Queens and one of his buddies. There were a couple of people who Lenny knew from Wells Fargo. There was myself. Basically we were all the same kind of people. You know, you could hire us out as bodyguards, you could hire us out as security people. I mean, we knew how to take care of ourselves and we knew how to take care of a situation.

JOEL ROSENMAN: The presence of a Lenny Kaufman—I mean, he was on our side, and he would rumble with the best of them, and he was almost eager to do so. And there was something about that, not that I wanted that to happen, but I felt that if we had somebody on our side who had that reputation, it would be less likely to happen. And I felt that way right up until the time when Lenny showed me what he carried in his paper bag, which was an actual firearm. And at that point I remember thinking, "This is a whole part of life that I want absolutely nothing to do with. If it goes to this, it's gone too far." Lenny had his boys, they all had their pieces and that's pretty much it. It was a security force, the real beefy end and unseen part of the security force. It was the heavy-duty security people. "Heavy-duty security" was what Lenny billed himself as. That was the phrase that he used.

JOHN ROBERTS: It all was tied in some way with Peter Goodrich and the Food for Love people and collecting receipts. Michael had hired Lenny because we expected a lot of cash on hand from the ticket receipts. Lenny and a couple of his friends were going to take over these ticket receipts and make sure they got to the right place.

FRANK FAVA: We started to pull people who we knew from the crowd—friends and associates and people we sort of semi-trusted—into our area, into the compound, which included the entertainers' heliport and the entertainers' pavilion area and backstage. We probably had a group of about forty or forty-five people who we led in there who we just told to listen. "It's nice and safe back here. You're inside a fenced area. You can sit and watch the festival and enjoy yourself. Just be there if we need you."

I was twenty-one years old and I was looking out on a site that was rapidly becoming a city of people all in my generation, and it was pretty intense. Things were going a hundred different ways and we stayed in touch, our group, pretty much by runners. We hired a couple of younger people who we knew and people we had brought in to just sort of run between our different posts to keep us updated as to what was going on. We had walkie-talkies but they were useless. They were eating those batteries up like crazy and you had to cope as best you could. So what we did was just use the old runner method, you know, the most reliable, hoping that your message in translation didn't get changed.

JOEL ROSENMAN: These guys had worked at carnivals and so they knew the tricks that could be played with cups, buns, scrip, and evidently you could make a million dollars look like ten thousand dollars if you did something with the cups and buns. And we didn't know what that was, so Lenny was there to make sure they didn't do that to us. There was a lot of talk about scrip. Peter Goodrich was an expert on scrip. I don't even know what scrip is, to this day, but it can be counterfeited and you could lose thousands and thousands of dollars. It was pretty ugly.

MEL LAWRENCE: It was Peter Goodrich who found Food for Love. Peter Goodrich, he was sort of all our friend—he was very close to Michael and I became very close to him. He was the oldest member of the crew. He'd done virtually everything that a person could do and we all respected him a great deal. And he was in charge of concessions. He had been in that, somehow, in his multifaceted career.

Peter was aiming for Nathan's. "It was going to be Nathan's," he said. This is who he wanted to cater this affair. And he kept coming down to the city, or maybe he was in the city—no he must have been coming out, because he was in Woodstock—and having these meetings with Nathan's, having meetings with the guy who owned Windows on the World, with Harry Stevens Company, Greyhound

Peter Goodrich

International—all the big catering outfits, the ones that take care of baseball parks and this kind of thing. And none of these people thought it was going to happen or wanted to put in the kind of investment that they needed for the food. They didn't have that kind of feeling, you know, that this thing was going to be anything.

MICHAEL LANG: Peter was an old friend of mine from the Grove. He was also a savvy kind of character and someone who didn't rattle. I felt, I remember at the time, that this was such a new adventure and there were so many unknowns that to have people around who just could handle themselves and not get flustered in tense situations was our best asset. So we had a few of those people around, too.

JOHN ROBERTS: In the last days before Woodstock, our staff, I think, went from a hundred to a thousand, because we had to lay on so many hands to get things built and done. I don't think any of us had a handle on where these people were coming from, how they came to us, whose friends they were. I didn't know Peter Goodrich particularly well. I didn't know the Food for Love guys, except through Peter Goodrich, so his vouching for them meant nothing to me. All I could do was make a judgment as to whether we had any alternatives, this all having come down so violently. I mean, two weeks earlier we were close to a deal with Restaurant Associates. Two weeks later, all the legitimate guys had pulled out and all we had was Food for Love, whoever the devil they were. There were three of them, three guys—Jeffrey Joerger, Charles Baxter, and Lee Howard—and they formed this company. I think one of them had some kind of food-catering experience—I don't think the other two did—and they were longhairs.

God, I remember a meeting, I guess in late July, where Peter Goodrich basically said, "They're the only game in town. They've already on my advice made inquiries about hot dog buns and Coca-colas and equipping themselves. I don't think anyone else can come in here in two weeks and do it. They can do it; they can do the job." I suggested that we had a Hobson's choice here—a choice between two bad things—no food or them. So being a pragmatist, I conferred with my partners and we decided that we would work with Food for Love. My sense was that we were probably headed for a major problem, but that if we watched it and if we made sure that we co-signed all the checks and that we bird-dogged their operation the best that we could—at this point, as you could imagine, we had a lot of other things to do—but if we were able to do that the food would probably arrive and be ready for sale. We could probably work that far. In fact, that's what happened.

But it didn't turn out to be a profitable venture for us, and they did not turn out to do a particularly good or efficient job. But had we not chosen Food for Love, there's a reasonable chance there would have been no food at the festival, or drink.

We set them up, we gave them the money to buy the food and we built the booths for them. We were supposed to split the profits fifty-fifty. That was the deal, but there were no profits and, in fact, we never got any of the seventy-five thousand dollars start-up money back, either. They, I think, were very close to being indicted by the local district attorney after the festival, the Food for Love people, for passing bad checks. So they not only maintained they didn't make a profit, they maintained that they lost so much money beyond the seventy-five thousand dollars that they were unable to honor their own commitments.

I spent a lot of Thursday in Monticello with the FBI and Wes. We went to the FBI because the Food for Love people had threatened us. They had threatened, variously, to pull out if we didn't accede to their financial demands and/or to cause mischief if we didn't accede to their financial demands. I told this to Wes on late Wednesday evening and he said, "Well, I take those threats seriously enough, particularly the threat about causing mischief, that I would like to go to the FBI with you in the morning." And we did. They had an office in Monticello and I was met by two G-men. They really looked like G-men. They were very courteous and took down all the information. They ran, I guess, some kind of search on these guys. I knew a couple of the names of some of the shadowy figures who were hanging around the Food for Love trailers. There was some speculation on their part that this might be some sort of organized crime group, or at least that the three guys from Food for Love were fronting for them. But no one proved anything and we spent, I think, most of the morning there just talking about the whole history of our relationship with them, specific conversations we had had, what they looked like—the G-men being very sympathetic and promising to look into this and be helpful in any way they could and essentially advising us to accede to all their demands. "Don't do anything that would cause them to do any mischief whatsoever," they said. So we did, and they didn't. They didn't do any mischief to the patrons of the festival, as far as I know.

WES POMEROY: John had come to me and said, "What should we do?" and I said, "Well, don't stand still for it; you're dead if you do. Inform the FBI and get them on it." The organized crime connection, that sort of thing. Well, the FBI couldn't move that fast. But I had just come out of the federal service where I had been a presidential appointee and also been a special assistant attorney general and that still counted with a lot of these guys. At least they talked to me. The head of the FBI office, the special agent in charge, ended up running the heliport in Liberty City. And he was doing a lot of work for me. I think he was probably justifying it all by gathering intelligence for the Bureau. I didn't care what it was, he did a good job.

FRANK FAVA: Friday, Peter Goodrich had his altercation with Jeffrey Joerger. A lot of it is secondhand. Lenny and Bob Braten were asked by Peter to come up to cover him, to watch his back while he went up to have this discussion with Joerger, that Jeff Joerger was ripping him off. There was this big meeting that was going to be going on in the operations trailer between Peter and Michael and Jeff Joerger and his partners and an attorney and this and that. And he wanted me and another person, this guy Al, who was one of the big motorcycle leaders from Queens, to hang out outside the trailer in case there was trouble and we had to go in and clear some bodies. I remember being outside the trailer and just hanging around and hearing the heated discussions

and "Fuck you's" and "Fuck *you*'s." But of course, at this point, almost all conversation was carried on at that level—it was just loud and a lot of cursing and a lot of people running around realizing that they were in way over their heads. You know, it was crisis time.

Tom Law: There was some major hassle up at the concession stands because all the concessionaires came there to make a lot of money. And some politicos from the city were up there screaming, "Free food for the people," and all that shit. And it was getting real nasty with the concessionaires in a stand-off and all these radicals from the Village. So the Hog Farm arrived in a flatbed truck—about thirty or forty of us— with handfuls of Chinese punk sticks—you know, incense. It was like a smoking truckload of people, and we just filtered into this audience and started handing people these things. "Would you hold this?" We totally dispelled all the action that was happening there. It was a technique. I used it at Washington later on at the March on Washington. We had some crazy radicals trying to fuck up a nice thing, you know. I mean, it wasn't the time for radicals to make their statement, period. It was something else that was beyond them. They didn't know it yet.

John Roberts: Food for Love sort of deteriorated throughout the weekend. In fact, the one credible story of violence that I heard was that they were going to sack the Food for Love stands. They had been doing something horrible, I forget what, but a band of outraged consumers had organized under a flaming torch and were heading up to the Food for Love encampment to, once and for all, get rid of this plague upon the land. Selling them five-dollar hot dogs, or something.

It was a leitmotiv. Every couple of hours there would be a screaming phone call from Jeff Joerger about some thug. I said "Gee, Jeff, you must be selling a lot of hot dogs and hamburgers and they must be really happy." And he would scream something obnoxious into the phone and hang up.

• • • •

Peter Beren: I was at loose ends. I had just graduated from Tufts in Boston, and I had no plans for the summer. I was supposed to go to

207

graduate school in the fall; I'd been accepted at Stanford, but I couldn't see myself going to graduate school. And I couldn't see myself working. My girlfriend had recently left town—her name was Carole—for California. I was living in Boston. She was going to go live on the land and join a commune. I was facing the draft. I didn't know how I was going to get out of the draft, whether I was going to go to Canada or go to jail. I went to see *Easy Rider* eight times and fantasized about joining Carole and living off the land and just—you know, the whole fantasy trip. And while I was experiencing this psychological dislocation in my life I began to hear about this music festival that was upcoming in a couple of weeks in upstate New York. A good friend of mine named Lipschutz—we called him "Lip"—had a sister, who owned an antique store in Manhattan. She had a boyfriend, whose name was Jeff Joerger, and Jeff had arranged to get the food concession at the festival under a corporation by the name of Food for Love. And Jeff had put the word out that he would employ Lip and all of his friends in the food stands and that we could not only make minimum wage, which I think at the time was a dollar twenty-five or a dollar-fifty an hour, but we could get into the festival for free.

We hit the festival site three days before it began and we spent the first night sleeping on the floor in a trailer that was owned by Food for Love. When we arrived, we walked in and the head of Food for Love was on the phone with his suppliers trying to get food, trying to get delivery of his trucks of hamburger buns, hot dogs, and I remember a conversation where he was screaming into the phone saying that he was calling from a skyscraper in Manhattan, and law offices, and he was going to sue everybody in sight if he couldn't get his hamburger buns in. And I thought that was kind of strange because he was on the phone in a trailer in Woodstock and he got off the phone and said, "Hi boys, you can sleep here tonight on the floor. We have to build the food stands."

It was late in the day when we arrived so we went out to walk around and take a look at this because this was about two or three days before the festival started, and we walked around this landscape. There were no structures, it was just like open fields or woods, and as the sun set there were fires built and very strange groups of people being very, very primal, with faces painted up. It was sort

Peter Beren

of like being in Borneo. I remembered seeing a fire, people in sleeping bags around a fire, people dancing around fires with no music, people shouting, people freaking out on acid. I remember one particular campfire we passed. There was a rather large woman with unkempt hair and bones around her neck shouting, wildly out of control. She looked like a witch doctor. And we went from campfire to campfire, and it began to look not like a pastoral scene of hippies, but more like what you would imagine in a circle of hell: fires, people fighting with one another, shouting, people freaking out on drugs.

I had a very eerie feeling. I felt like I was entering another world. I felt like I was going back in time. I felt like I was entering an era that was very primitive—precivilized. I had always viewed that as pastoral—American Indians before the white man came—you know, really loving kind of communal images. But instead, what I encountered was people who were—the only word I can think of is shamanistic. Some of them were experiencing what appeared to be psychotic states of mind. They were kind of performing rituals; they were shouting. There were little groups of people with some playing guitars, and there were some really sweet aspects to this landscape, but the overwhelming impression was one that was atavistic, primitive, shamanistic, as if all the restraints of civilization had been removed and they could do whatever the hell they wanted to. I remember one particular campfire we passed, where a woman who looked like a witch doctor was performing some sort of exorcism on someone who was having a bad trip. And then she turned to me and shook a skull at me and I was terrified by that. They wanted to drag me into their trip.

The next day we got up and we were given wood and a hammer and instructions, and we started building our little stands, which housed grills. And while we were building these hot dog and hamburger stands, more and more and more and more people arrived, an endless stream of people coming from all directions. The food stands were up on the hill. Below the hill was the stage. Ringing the stage was a sea of people. Ringing the sea of people was a column of movement—people moving—and that column never stopped during the entire festival. There was constant traffic in both directions: people going to the bathroom, people going out to their campsites, people going to get food, people going who-knows-where. Some people were just wandering. So there were stationary people almost as far as you could see in front of the stage, and ringing them was an endless procession of people walking and moving.

We were removed from that. We were up on the hill looking down on that. We were there to provide hot dogs and hamburgers to the crowd, which started before the festival opened. So we were flipping our burgers and grilling our dogs, and people learned that there was food up there, and they began to come and get the food. And it never stopped. Endless people, endless hamburgers.

I remember the other weird thing was that you couldn't pay for your hamburgers and hot dogs with money. You had to give the money to the people who ran Food for Love and they gave you little coupons—scrip—and then you gave the coupons for the hamburgers, hot dogs and sodas, and there was no way to make change. So if your tab came to a dollar eighty, and you had two dollars in coupons, we

Hog Farm: Festival's Most Peaceful Area

Times Herald Record
Middletown, N.Y.
August 16, 1969

209

got the two dollars in coupons. After a while, people began to pay for their food with joints, whatever else, and there was a kind of an interplay between us hamburger flippers and the crowd, which was really quite sweet and quite nice.

There was a feeling of—call it brotherhood, you know, a feeling of identification with the people. Snatches of conversation—"Yeah, far out. Wasn't the music great? I love you." A lot of sexual flirtation. There was almost a kind status in being part of the staff working there, even if you were just flipping hamburgers, and everyone wanted to communicate their feelings and get acknowledged, get their feelings validated. So I had the conversations I could and after a while, I mean, I was smoking the joints they were giving me for the burgers—there were joints everywhere—and after a while I got very high. I got into a rhythm and I'd do, like, you know, one for free, one for this, and then after a while we just stopped taking money and we just gave the food away. After that, we ran out of food. There was nothing more to grill, no more buns, no more soda. That was it. At which point we just closed up and joined the crowd.

You know, it wasn't like we were being closely supervised at the hamburger pits, and I think at the moment myself and my fellow hamburger flippers made a revolutionary decision to give away food, we began to become showered with joints. It wasn't like we bartered food for joints, it was like we just said, "We want to participate in this, too. We're giving the food away." Everybody was pressing joints on me—you know, "Here's a burger, here's a joint." I had them sticking behind each ear, in every pocket, and smoking two at a time.

• • • •

GORDON WINARICK: Sometime over the weekend, there was a cry out in the community for food. They said the food concessions and the food stands were out of food, and those with supplies couldn't get them in, and there was gouging going on. So a cry went out that they needed food. It was on a radio: "Bring whatever you can."

The high school in Monticello was the center of it all. People started to bring up food and from there we had to organize getting the food from the collection point into the festival itself. First of all, they sent up some raw food, so the volunteers made sandwiches right there, and then they packed up food and sent it out. I decided to send eggs because it was protein, sanitary. We hard-boiled hundreds of thousands of eggs. This is an egg area. It was easy for me to get eggs from my position at the Concord Hotel, where I was involved in food service. I'd tap people for donations. I said, "Give me cases of eggs," which we boiled here. So we sent out a hard-boiled egg—a whole nutritious package—which is self-contained and clean. So we must have sent six or ten truckloads of food. In fact, my wife went out on one of them, and then we had the president of the high school or whatever—I guess he was the chairman or head of the high school, superintendent—he drove the trucks out and they were distributing. And again, it was a cooperative spirit—everybody helped everybody else get fed.

STEVE GOLD: It began just by word of mouth and all of a sudden the radio stations started broadcasting and, I'll never forget, somebody put a microphone on their car and went to all the bungalow colonies with the microphone saying, like a campaign speech, "O.K. we're here for the can drive. We need food for the people at Woodstock." And people would just come out of their bungalows and shove food in these cars and then they would drive it up there, or however they got it up there. They knew people weren't starving, it's just that they knew there were so many people there—and there was no way in or way out—that these people had to eat. And that human feeling came in, whether they were hippies or the biggest convicts in the world, they were human beings, and that's the way I feel the people felt. They were fellow human beings. No matter what they looked like, we were going to help them. And they became involved in it. It's like being an extra on the movie set. The Woodstock people were starring and the Sullivan County people were the extras, but we wanted to be there, we wanted to get involved. Since we couldn't get there, let's give them the food, so I can say, "Yeah, I gave food to Woodstock"—you know, that whole thing. They wanted to feel that they participated in some type of way.

GORDON WINARICK: Each organization would collect whatever it was that they were going to collect—canned goods, breads, and stuff like that. The food came from everybody's pantry, everybody's stores. It was the church, the Boy Scouts, the Girl Scouts, the synagogues, firehouses—any organization. Everybody put out a cry for food, and it all came in and, I guess, some of them must have sent their own cars out, but a bunch of them came to us. We had to retruck it, you know, from small units to large units, and arrange to get it out to the various places. So it was really a tremendous outpouring.

CHARLIE CRIST: There was the Jewish Community Center, St. Peter's Church people, the Methodist church people, the Presbyterian church people, all of them got together and they made hundreds of sandwiches and coffee and provided everything they could to help these kids out and feed them. As far as any one individual, I would say you could give quite a lot of credit to a fellow named Carl Solomon, who operated the Miss Monticello Diner here. He took a lot of those kids in that time and let them warm up and gave them food and so on. He and his wife were very good to these people.

GORDON WINARICK: It had an ecumenical effect. The nuns came out, there was a Hebrew hospital, every barrier you can imagine was broken. People who would never do things for each other normally, did things together for others. Tremendous. It was ecumenical, it was every phase; every facet came together and worked in harmony, and together. Nobody asked any questions. They saw what had to be done, people's lives had to be saved, care had to be given, they have a problem, we have an obligation, there was care, concern, let's help. And, of course, they were all stunned because when these hordes of people came back in the town, they were all so polite and they would all say thank you, and all be so grateful.

WES POMEROY: We had the big resorts calling us and saying, "Can we help you?" It was like the whole Catskills became a big Jewish mama.

JOSEPH COAKLEY: I remember at one point we picked up food that the National Guard dropped in and I remember they had these big choppers come in and they had sandwiches. I don't know how the logistics of getting this food around worked, but supposedly all the local townsfolk and good farmers of that area had stayed up all night making sandwiches for this invasion of people that nobody was ready for. We'd hand these things out and it was like, you know, seeing something on TV—you know, "Escape from New York" or something. It was basically a near-riot when we'd pull up with this food and all these people would push and try to get to the front. We would try to throw the food out and just disperse it and try to be as fair as possible, but there was really no organization.

BONNIE JEAN ROMNEY: Helicopters were coming in with a thousand little bags of one tiny six-ounce can of olives and a can of tuna fish soup, you know. Some kind of little salad in a plastic thing with a rubber band around the top, little one-serving things. And either you give it to an individual person or you take it all and try to think of how to make something that will feed five hundred out of all these little corners of stuff. That was one thing I was doing, was unloading helicopters, trying to direct the food into a way it could be utilized from what they were giving us.

STANLEY GOLDSTEIN: The stuff that folks sent was a godsend. It served well and it was vastly appreciated, though it wasn't necessary. I don't believe that foodstuffs were required from outside. Except that there were a lot of people who couldn't bring themselves to eat what they conceived as being strange food. They may have been hungry, they may have been wet, they may have been uncomfortable, or they may have been all of that but—*Granola, rolled oats, and vegetables, I never heard of such a thing. I wouldn't eat that! You must be crazy, Jack!* And there were a lot of folks who wouldn't have eaten regardless of the fact that there was food.

If you had walked into the middle of that crowd and said to someone as a reporter, "Well, how you doing?" You'd get, "Oh, all right." "You having a good time?" "Oh yeah." "Well, what's it like sitting here? When is the last time you ate?" "Oh, two days ago." "Are you hungry?" "Oh yeah!" "Well, what are you doing for food?" "Nothing. I haven't got any food." And then someone goes out and they've talked to twenty, thirty, fifty kids and discovered that no one has eaten and that they are hungry. So they put out the word that these kids sitting here in the mud are starving. That they have no food. I know that there were a lot of those kinds of conversations that took place. But the fact is that they were content to sit there in the mud so long as they were in front of the stage hearing the music, and if they had to leave that particular patch of ground to go get some food, they weren't going to do it. And that is why we started running food out to them. It may be that the food condition was not so pressing a matter, because if you're having a good time and you're boogeying and you've been doing a lot of acid, you're not much interested in eating anyway. And so food was not the thing that this bunch of horny-druggie-music-mad kids had on their minds at this moment.

WAVY GRAVY: I was a little embarrassed that so many people wanted to help because actually things were extremely together and it was like we were actually doing something of meaning and having a great soundtrack. Which is what the rock 'n' roll starts to become at these festivals: After a while, it is the soundtrack for staying alive. And these very exciting communities began to develop out of the festival circuit of a kind of positive, creative anarchy that could create this instant little city that could chug along and function. You wish that a government could run as fluidly.

BERNIE WEINSTEIN: My wife and I became very concerned knowing our kids were there and other kids. How could we help? We went into the

Rain, Drugs Ruin Festival

*Tribune
Oakland, Calif.
August 17, 1969*

213

kitchen of our restaurant—Bernie's Holiday Restaurant on Route 17—
and helped to make sandwiches. Everything—turkey, roast beef,
ham—everything that would go in. Fruit, cans of soda. Being local, I
knew how to get there by back roads, which we did, and managed to
get there. When we got to White Lake the kids were there and the
people were there and the police were there and we could hardly give
these sandwiches away or the soda. No one was hungry. They seemed
to be fine, happy to be with each other. I had never seen anything like
that in my life. I was in a war and saw too many unhappy people. This
seemed altogether almost the other way. I never saw so many happy
people. I don't know what was making them happy—the show was
three miles away from where I was—but there they were, they just
seemed to be happy with each other. And we finally left all the food
and the sandwiches and made it home. Our phone kept ringing with
people we had known in New York whose kids had come up here and
showed a lot of concern, and we tried to calm them down. Sure there
were people selling water and selling things, but basically it was a lot
of happy kids doing their thing.

• • • •

LISA LAW: If people wanted to eat, we had the food, if they wanted to
walk over to the Hog Farm. There was this talk about hunger and I
always said, "What hunger?" If they didn't want to get up and walk over
then that was their problem. But there was no lack of food at
Woodstock.

We served museli for breakfast and bulgur wheat for lunch/
dinner. We just kept cooking the two things; they just sort of blended
in together. The museli was the rolled oats and the sesame seeds and
the raisins and wheat germ and honey. The next concerts we used

214

granola, which was cooked. But we couldn't spend the time preparing the breakfast. The dinner was a little bit easier to prepare but the breakfast had to be real quick, and I felt that since a lot of people bought museli like that, why not make it? And it seemed to work. My main concern was the people didn't get sick from being in the wet. And if you have wheat germ and you have healthy things that you are eating and honey and not real sugary things, then you're going to make it.

Dinner was a choice between brown rice or bulgur wheat. Brown rice takes twice as long as bulgur wheat. Bulgur wheat is real good, tasty. So we used a lot of soy sauce on it. And then we'd go to the farms right in that area and buy a whole truckful of vegetables—corn and broccoli and cabbage. We'd get our fruit from there, too. And then we'd throw the vegetables right into the pot with the bulgur wheat. And then we had soy sauce dispensers; I bought a bunch of those. So that was pretty popular, the bulgur wheat. In fact, we only used seven hundred pounds of each. We came back with seven hundred pounds of each. It went a long way.

BONNIE JEAN ROMNEY: We had a separate kitchen for ourselves that had a few other items in it. I remember there was yogurt. About three or four days before the festival we couldn't get out, but there was a place we could get to by driving a truck across fields that had some things, and there was some milk and yogurt available to us and some cheese for the people who were really working. Once again, it was a big debate: the haves and the have-nots. Was it all right for us to have a glass of milk and a piece of cheese when the vast majority of the people couldn't have that, because we were working so hard? And we finally decided it was. But all of these things were like moral choices because we were in a disaster area and we had our own little enclave and all these decisions had to be made.

I run into people now in corporate offices. Once, for example, I was trying to find a lawyer to put together a partnership agreement for our piece of land that we own in northern California, the whole family together. This guy—we were thinking of forming a corporation and he comes out—he's the corporate lawyer for this law firm. And he says, "You fed me at Woodstock and I really would have been hungry. Thank you."

• • • •

FRANK FAVA: There were military helicopters, if you can call them military. I think they were National Guard helicopters; it's hard to remember. What had happened, though, is that when these emergency calls went out for food and water, it was shipped in and it landed in my heliport. What I remember distinctly, were cases of food—but again, so many things were happening, it was hard to keep track of it all. I do remember taking charge of loading frozen gallons of water that were shipped in from some emergency storage facility. Frozen water. And when that came in, we controlled it, we grabbed a lot of it because, again, being in the situation we were, we were covering our butts first. We isolated a lot of cases of the frozen gallons of water in our area and down in the entertainers' pavilion.

One of the interesting things about that water—and this has been talked about with a lot of people, and some people said we were paranoid and some people said we were crazy and some people said there was no way to find out—but we were pretty convinced that water was dosed with LSD. The reason I was convinced was because I had a contingent of two state policemen assigned to me and it was really funny because all these cops were totally lost. They kept turning around to me, a twenty-one-year-old kid and saying, "Hey, you tell us what to do. *You* got the guns, man, you know!" So what I had them do was pull their car inside the heliport area and basically I said, "Hey, just park here and if you hear me scream come running. Otherwise hang by your car." I sent over a couple of ladies, who we had pulled in with that group of people, to keep them company and just hang out with them—hopefully, to just integrate them into what was happening at that point.

Anyway, I sent two gallons of water up to them to put in the car. Now, I know for a fact no one gave them anything else, yet after about three or four hours, these guys were starting to take their clothes off, dance on the roof of the car, and were generally ripped to their gourds. Another reason why I'm pretty sure that there was something in that water is because a group of people who were friends of mine, who I had inside that security area and had set in a corner, the only potable water they had was what I gave them and they had no other food and they had no drugs and they all got ripped out of their minds. Now, whether it was just mass hallucinations that were going on or whether something was introduced to the water, I don't know, but there was another thing that happened not long after we had gotten the water and been given time to distribute it: A couple of jets flew over and cracked the sound barrier. And I guess you know, if you've ever heard it, what that noise sounds like. It's a very loud disturbing noise. It was like a *CRACK*, and then another *CRACK*. Again, we put all of it down to the fact that either the government was trying to mess with people's heads and create a situation or it was just all mass hallucination, hysteria, craziness. We didn't have a whole hell of a lot of time to dwell on it.

• • • •

ELIZABETH BROWN: I was the credit manager and head bookkeeper for a food wholesaler, so we knew about Woodstock ahead of time. John Roberts did come one time and applied for credit because they wanted to have food for the performers at the site. And I had investigated their credit. So we knew probably a month ahead of time that something was going to happen. Of course, we had no idea what the magnitude was. And it was just another summer customer to us. They ordered several truckloads of food, which we took out to the site beforehand.

But by Saturday afternoon we realized that it was a tremendous happening. The roads were closed. They had called for food to be delivered and our trucks couldn't get out on the road anymore. Our truck drivers, each one, would come back, each one more excited because there were more people there. Saturday afternoon, we were getting a helicopter landing in our parking lot, picking up whatever

Drug Illness
Rocks
Hippiefest;
300,000
in Field

News
Detroit, Mich.
August 17, 1969

216

quantity of food they could take and flying it back. And at that point, too, my grandmother and my sister and brother—later on, it ended up also including my two sisters—at my grandmother's house and my grandmother had run her well dry by this time giving kids water and they had run out of food. My grandmother lived about a quarter mile from the festival. So the kids had called my mother in Monticello who called me and we packed up our own care package and they took it out on their helicopter. My father, who was also out there by this time, walked over to the site, met the helicopter, and took food to get my family through the weekend.

About five or six o'clock, we were all really excited about what was going on down there. The guys had this notion: "Well, they needed food. We can't give it away. We might as well make a few bucks. Let's see what we can do. We can fill up a truck or two with drinks and cold cuts and we'll run uptown and we'll buy all the bread we can find and we'll go out there." So the logistical problem was that you couldn't get out there by the main roads. Because of the fact that I came from out there and knew all the back roads, we took two trucks and I was the navigator. We went in through Swan Lake and came out smack behind the stage. I was such a good navigator it was amazing.

We got out there about ten o'clock at night and there was myself, my boss, and two truck drivers, and we parked the trucks next to each other. The first thing that happened was John Roberts' people saw us coming because we came in right by the performers' tent. They came running over because they thought we had brought them more food for the performers and were very disappointed when we said, "No, we hadn't." We couldn't give it to them. We were mobbed; everyone followed the trucks into the parking lot. So we parked the trucks next to each other and we opened up the back and we made and sold sandwiches out the back for a dollar a sandwich, fifty cents a can for a forty-six-ounce can of fruit drink, which is what we threw on the truck. And we stayed there until the concert broke up in the rain Sunday afternoon. We paid the company for the stuff we took, but we made four or five hundred dollars apiece and it was a very interesting thing. And those kids had money. We didn't turn anyone away for not having money, and they were glad we were there.

I can tell you, the people at the general store, they sold out their entire stock of food, which they never would have in their life. John Hector from the bar loved it. He got a tankload of beer in there. He sold beer like crazy. He made money for the first time in his life. Another couple down the road that had a vegetable farm, they actually had all of their crops picked out of the field. But as a result of that, they went into the roadside farm business, so I don't think that they were against it—they got paid for their crops that they lost. But it gave them a new lease on life. They've

been in the roadside business ever since.

CHARLIE CRIST: The price of food went sky-high. Milk went up to a buck a quart and it was selling somewhere in the neighborhood of thirty-five or forty cents. Bread went sky-high. Everything in the stores went remarkably high for this area. Hundreds of watermelons were trucked in to the site. Some people said, "Well, it gave them something to drink; they didn't have water." Others said they were mixing the drugs into the watermelons; it was easier to take. That's part of the reports of what went on, but these are definite facts of the watermelons coming in by the truckloads and the prices of the food going so high.

Seemed to be everybody was selling food at the time. They were selling water. The prices I couldn't tell you because I was not that close to it, and I didn't have to buy water. But there were reports that people were selling water by the cupful, by the bottleful, the whole bit.

ARTHUR VASSMER: When we saw them coming in these hordes, we were scared. I think everybody in the town was scared. We didn't know what was happening. That's like taking New York City, a little portion of it, and moving it up this way. We didn't have the roads, we didn't have the facilities— nothing. So we locked our fence out here. We had that fence locked there, and when they came they started jumping over the fence and going into the lake. And I went out to them very nicely and I said, "I wish you wouldn't jump over the fence." And I never had any trouble with any of them. Then the ones that were in here said, "Sorry, Mister Vassmer," went back over the fence, and on down the road.

Some of the kids didn't have for what to eat. Some of them didn't have cigarettes. But they had money that they could buy a little bit, so we stayed open as long as we could. We opened the store about seven o'clock in the morning and I had three fellows stay at one door. They were all pretty big men, six-feet-two or six-feet-five. I said, "We might as well have somebody up there who looks like authority," and we closed up all the store, just opened the one door. We'd let forty or fifty people in at a time, they'd get their groceries or whatever they need, pots and pans—we had a couple of pots and pans—and things like

that. I said, "All right men, open up the door and let another fifty in."

They'd stand there and talk to them, nicely. I only saw—oh, I saw some that were spaced out a little on drugs—but not bad. But one girl was spaced out, and they told me the boys came and got her and said, "We're sorry, she wasn't supposed to come in here. We'll take care of her." And they took her out. What I'm trying to bring out is that our worries started to cease, you know, less, because it seems everybody was here for a good time and nobody wanted any trouble. If they did, I wouldn't be here talking to you. They'd have taken the store or place apart board by board. There wouldn't be anything left.

I met the Hog Farmers, too. That was my first introduction to food stamps. They didn't wear any clothes very much—very little clothes, and they weren't the cleanest people I ever saw. But they were nice people. A fight started to break out in the store, and this one fellow seemed to be the leader—everyone seemed to carry a knife—they had overalls on or some-

thing, and he took that knife, held it up to the guy's throat, and he said, "There'd be no trouble in the store, remember that and tell everybody else that." We never had trouble. Not a bit of trouble. Well, anyway, I took their food stamps because, "You'll be getting them here soon," he said. They must have had them out West or down in New Mexico, but we didn't have them here yet. But I was so scared I took the food stamps, and outside of that, things went fairly normal.

If you ever hear of anybody that ever has a Woodstock or festival like that, remember one thing you want to buy: peanut butter and jelly. That's the first thing I run out of. I should have put fifty cases of peanut butter and fifty cases of jelly. I found out later that peanut butter is very good for you.

We had a lot of them coming in. Some of the fellows would come in and say, "Mister Vassmer, we haven't any money." Well, that's par for the course. They said, "Can we cash a check?" So, I said, "All right, how much do you got?" Well, the biggest I cashed was twenty-five dollars. I probably cashed, Fred and I—that's my brother, Fred—we probably cashed twenty-five checks. And we didn't have one bounce. Some of these checks were from Texas, one was from the state of Washington—they were from all over the country. One fellow had a Mercedes-Benz—I'll never forget it—and he said, "I don't know where the hell the thing is," or words just like that. Well, we gave him stuff to eat. He said, "I'll be back." And he was. We did that with quite a few of them. There wasn't a one that didn't pay us back. People can't get over that. There wasn't one who stuck us.

KEN VAN LOAN: I think the guy in the general store in Bethel gave the kids a hard time. And after the festival, his frontage by the store was

219

probably a foot deep in debris, probably stuff that he had sold them—you know, soda and whatever. But the debris was there to make a point of what louses everybody was; I think it was about a week before he even cleaned it up. We had the house next door to him, the adjacent property. We had a landscaped lawn, we had roses, flowers growing, and we had not one piece of debris. I don't think anybody picked a flower or touched the property.

At our gas station, we did the maximum that we could do. The pumps run all the time and that was it. We had many people that had no money. At one time, I don't know if they're still around, but we had stacks of letters from students and their parents where we trusted them and they just wrote back and sent the money and thank-you letters for trusting a stranger. Just one hundred percent we were paid back. There's no outstanding debts from them. It's almost twenty years later now, but there probably isn't a week goes by that something doesn't come up about it. I had a guy pay me for a quart of oil not too many years ago—I think it was about two years ago. Said he owed me and he just never had a chance to get back in touch with me. So he asked me if I was the one that was here during Woodstock and I told him yes, and he give me two dollars. He said, "I owe you for a quart of oil." That was probably the last outstanding debt.

CHAPTER THIRTEEN

"Listen, Mother, I'm just down the road from Grossinger's."
—Myra Friedman

JUDI BERNSTEIN: After the first night, Bill Hanley came in and collapsed in the back of the trailer. I was in the trailer and Bob Segal was there and it felt like we had just hardly closed our eyes. All of a sudden there's this smashing on the door. So being the only responsible person who could open her eyes, I opened the door and there's Mel Lawrence standing there, and the rain is dripping off of him in his yellow raincoat. And I said, "Oh, Mel, what do you need?" He said, "Listen, I need permission to turn on the sound system." I said, "What, are you crazy?" He said, "No, we've got to do garbage detail and clean up in front of the stage. We've got to wake everybody up and got to get cleaned up." I said, "Mel, they all just went to sleep." "No, I got to have permission." And he's carrying on that the garbage is important, it's got to get clean, and we'll get closed down by the sanitation people, and this whole long saga. So I said, "Well, wait here a minute."

And now very guiltily, I go to the back of the trailer and I poke Hanley. "Bill, Bill." He looks at me, "*Hunh?*" I said, "Mel Lawrence is outside. He wants to turn on the sound system so they can clean up in front of the stage. He needs your permission." Hanley says, "He has my permission." And he goes back to sleep.

Fete on Friday: Freedom, Pot, Skinny-dipping

Times Herald Record Middletown, N.Y. August 16, 1969

MEL LAWRENCE: I'd stayed up most of that night, but I had fallen asleep probably about four o'clock and had woken up just at dawn, when it's starting to get a little light. And it was quiet out there and I went outside—I was sleeping in my trailer—and looked down and I started to walk down and it looked like everybody was sleeping—people were horizontal, people in their spots. And I went to backstage and everybody was sleeping. They were sleeping in the trailers. It was like after a big party—cans all around, dirt, everything. And I could walk anywhere; very few people were up and about. There were people wandering, sort of like, "What happened? What was that?" And I knew that pretty soon people would start getting up and wondering what the hell was going on. And it was now getting to be about eight o'clock and like, it was summer, so around that time it was starting to get a little hot. And I wanted to—it's sort of like brushing your teeth in the morning or washing your face or something like that—to get a good start on this next day. I just took this on myself—I didn't ask for permission to do this—I just felt it, that something had to be done.

JUDI BERNSTEIN: Now, Mel can't turn on the sound system. And I haven't got anybody to turn on the sound system. Hanley's dead to the world and I can't get him up. But I have his permission—*wonderful*. So, I put on my raincoat and I go trekking out with Mel over to the other trailer, and I don't remember which of our guys was over there, sleeping. I kicked him a few times and I said, "Get this thing turned on." And so they turned on the sound system in the middle of the rain and you hear

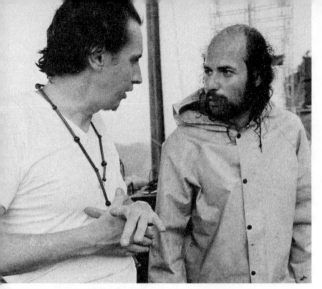

Bill Hanley (left),
Steve Cohen

Mel starting to make these announcements that everybody should get up, and they should start cleaning up. He was intent on getting it cleaned up. And the sound system never went off again.

MEL LAWRENCE: I went out there and the volume was on too loud, you know, and I wanted to be really cool. And I got out there, and I wasn't too nervous—but I mean, it was amazing to look out there and know that—and I wanted to be cool and say, "Good morning," but it came out "GOOOOD MOOORNNNINGG." It was like *loud*, and people jumped, you know. But then I yelled to the guy to lower it and he lowered it. And then I gave a really neat speech to the effect of, "Last night was really groovy, and today is going to be even better," and I ran down the lineup. And, "We have one of the biggest cities in the United States and we ought to be proud of ourselves. And everything's O.K. and we're on top of it. The rest of the world thinks that we're having trouble but we're not." And people were like—I could feel them sort of responding. "And we're going to do this and within fifteen minutes we're going to be distributing these bags to everybody." And we had gone over how we were going to clean up. We made the system in which we'd hand the bag on this side and it would get passed, all the way, and people would clean up their area and then pass it to the other side and then it would be picked up. And that worked perfect. The guys came, after I was all through talking to them, you know—"And it's going to be great, don't worry, and here's this and here's this," and that kind of thing. Then I went back and I woke up some guys and I said, "Let's get the trash bags out," you know. And they started giving them out—I mean lots of them; we had boxes and boxes and boxes. And then everybody sort of got together. I remember Morris got up and said, "We ought to have some music," you know, and put on an album and it was very mellow, you know. What could have been—if we didn't reach that and make that effort, maybe people would have felt a little anxious, you know, about whether the show was canceled or what's going on.

JOHN MORRIS: At the end of Friday night, I think we still had so many things to do that were stacked up. It was more like it was the first round. What can we do here? What can we shore up? Where are we? What's happening? What are we lacking? What are we doing? We worked all that night. We were on telephones trying to arrange supplies. We were trying to figure out if there was anything we could do about the traffic. Were we going to have to keep using the helicopters, how were we going to schedule the next day, how were we going to notify people. That's where Annie, my wife, and Lee Blumer in the office and Annie Sullivan, an English girl who worked for me also—they were arranging with managers and acts for the next day and to try to get stuff straight. We were trying to get food in. Where we had broken pipes and lines, Langhart and his crews were out doing it, repairing what they could.

222

Joel and John—or Joel or Michael—were probably still up negotiating with Mister Filippini to rent his land that fifty thousand people were already camped on. It was sort of like, *Keep going, just keep going, keep it together.*

Miriam Yasgur: After the first day, we realized that maybe it was going to work and that things were not turning into the riot I anticipated. And then we got a little bit more comfortable with it. I don't think we got any sleep at all. We just would go up and wash up and come back to the office because we were manning phones, we were doing everything we could. Max was helicoptered over there to see what was happening. He couldn't get through the crowds. And there was a veterinarian who had his own helicopter that he used to make calls in the western end of the county or in Pennsylvania, and they paid him to leave the helicopter near our office so that in case of emergency they could get people out. And when things were finally going smoothly, Max said to me, "Would you like to see what it looks like?" And I never have trusted little planes—I've logged tens of thousands of miles in big planes all over the world, but getting into a little plane was always something of a block for me. And I thought, "I'll never see it otherwise." So I said all right and I got into this little two-man helicopter with no doors and he flew over the festival field to show it to me and it was a sight to remember.

Frank Fava: One of the funny incidents I remember is my altercation with Bill Graham on Saturday morning. He came over and I guess somebody directed him to me to get a helicopter out. And he said, "Hi, I'm Bill Graham and I gotta get a helicopter out of here." And I said, "Hi, I know who you are. I used to scream at you in the aisles of the Fillmore East when you used to come out and tell us what a great thing you were doing, and we used to tell you that we needed free concerts." Anyway, I said, "I can't get you a helicopter out now. I got all these people ahead of you." He said, "But I'm Bill Graham and I gotta get out of here." And I said, "I'm sorry, you got to wait your turn and if you

223

Bill Graham

keep it up, you'll never get out of here." So he kept insisting who he was and that he had to get out of there and he was going to report me to the authorities, and I think I said to him, "Right now, I'm the authority here. You want a helicopter? You get in line. You keep it up, you don't get out." And he started ranting about, "I'll see to it that you never work in this business again," blah, blah, blah, blah, you know, and I basically just walked away from him. That's the kind of madness that was going on there.

BILL BELMONT: Graham showed up one afternoon, kibitzed, and then I think he left. I didn't see him around a lot. He stayed kind of at a distance.

One of the big underlying currents of Woodstock was, "We gotta prove to Bill that we can do it ourselves." Graham closed Fillmore East for that week and everybody working at Fillmore East came up and some of them volunteered and some of them actually worked on the show and some of them agreed to help. But Graham never forgave John Morris—ever—for having ignored him. And Graham kind of sent Barry Imhoff—Barry had a club; well, he was involved with Whiskey-a-Go-Go and a club called The Generation in New York, and Imhoff wound up in San Francisco working for Graham as an agent. And Imhoff showed up, ostensibly to grandmother Santana and the Grateful Dead, but in reality he was Graham's spy. Every day he would call on the phone he had in his briefcase; he would call Graham and report.

Graham never thought it would happen. He had considered it to be a disaster. He wouldn't talk about it. I think Graham really detested Michael Lang, couldn't abide by Artie Kornfeld. I can imagine him pulling a face at the names of the other two guys, Roberts and Rosenman. Because they were just guys. They had money and they'd showed up and—kind of like Wozniak doing the Us Festival: "Gee, if I pay all these people and I put a show on, I can go backstage at my own show!" That was the attitude. Graham never got over the fact that he didn't do Woodstock.

JOHN MORRIS: Saturday, Albert Grossman showed up wearing a white guru outfit followed by a whole bunch of people, and his hair pulled back into a gray ponytail. Albert and I were not close. We knew each other, we'd had dinner a bunch of times and a couple of times we had been on opposite sides of some agreement or disagreement about an act. And Albert came up to me, took my head in his hands, kissed me full on the mouth and said, "It's beautiful John. It's so beautiful." And God rest his soul. Albert died two years ago on a plane flying to London, having, I'm sure, just finished the Indian meal and thinking about the restaurants he was going to eat in in London, which is something I really understand. That was probably the next to the last time I ever saw him. I was surprised. It was like a blessing from the guru—Bob Dylan's manager and this wonderfully super, super, super bright man. Albert was so intelligent. Hard as could be. And it was a great compliment.

Albert Grossman

JOEL ROSENMAN: Saturday, I woke up with the hives. I'd never had hives and I thought I had caught some kind of creature from the mattresses in this fleabag that we were staying in. But, in fact, it was just nerves. We deserved nerves at that point. Everything that we thought might be difficult about running this event proved to be so. The only thing that really wasn't difficult was that at no time did I think under all this that we were actually going to snap and go nuts or something. It never felt like that. I never lost it. I never thought I was about to lose it. I thought it was very, very hard. I'm sure that underneath, it was worse than that, and that's where the hives came from. I woke up on Saturday morning, scratching like a madman, and went out.

JOHN ROBERTS: Saturday morning we got served with our first lawsuit, in the White Lake building, bright and early. Some process service got us with our first lawsuit, for blocking the entrance to Monticello Raceway the night before.

LEON GREENBERG: I was president of the Monticello Raceway, which is right at the intersection of Route 17 and Route 17B. I had read something in a local newspaper called the Middletown *Record* that they anticipated there was going to be a concert and the magnitude of it was an unknown quantity, but we didn't have the slightest idea what the hell it was all about. And I had a sensitivity about how

it might affect my business because of ingress and egress. Route 17B was the only entrance you could utilize to get onto the track, off 17 coming east, or you could come in from the reverse side. And as it got closer and closer, I recall vividly that I recognized this thing was going to be of great magnitude. And when it finally struck, it literally shut me out—put me out of business for three or four days.

It got completely out of control, particularly when I used to walk out of my office and see a bunch of characters sitting in a circle smoking pot. It was the first time I'd ever seen marijuana being used. There were a lot of straight kids, too, but the group that I noticed, because they

225

Leon Greenburg

stood out, was real bizarre. These kids were dressed in a bizarre fashion and had no respect for any other's property. They just would walk onto your property as if they owned it.

I ended up starting a lawsuit, but I couldn't measure the damages because by the time the thing cleaned up, when I finally did open up, there were so many people around that, if anything, I profited from the thing. And the publicity value was enormous. It became the hub of an entire national situation. So I withdrew my lawsuit. We couldn't prove damages because we weren't damaged. We could have certainly proved that they were wrong. We could have certainly proved that they didn't have any management and lacked planning and security. And we would have won that aspect of it. But then the law provides you got to establish damages and the truth of the matter is I made money. So I withdrew it.

JOHN ROBERTS: I looked at the lawsuit and I laughed. Again, the one thing that was not emotionally impacting either Joel or me that weekend was the money issue. All in all, I guess, a lot of it came down to money. When Mister Filippini was standing there saying, "What are you going to do about the people on that piece of my land that you didn't rent from me? I wanna know what you plan to give me for it"— that was a money discussion, I suppose. But it didn't feel like money. It felt like, "Well, gee, Mister Filippini"—or Mister Jones or Farmer Brown—"I hope you don't do any harm to these people. You understand that getting them off that land may be very difficult now and we'll take care of it later." And it was really just cooling them out. But when a guy sues you for two hundred fifty thousand dollars—I remember thinking that they were very impatient, you know. Here was Friday night, we had done this horrible damage, didn't they even want to sort of sit down and think about it for a while and figure out whether it was really worth the expense of drawing up a summons and complaint? I think that was about my only thought.

The press starting hounding us like crazy. They located the telephone building in White Lake and it seemed like there was a constant barrage of press people there. I have never been irritated, before or since, by it, but I can imagine, having been through it once, what it must feel like to be in the eye of that kind of a storm. Because you really don't want to talk to those people. You want to get back to your phone conversation. You don't want to answer a question like, "How does it feel to be mayor of the third-largest city in New York?" That was a frequent one. I mean, what do you say to that question without sounding really fatuous? But that's where we had set up for them to file a lot of their reports.

JOEL ROSENMAN: My first reaction to the press was the one I always have, which is, "I don't wish to be bothered with it; I don't see the use of it." It always comes home to me later that it's very useful. My second reaction is to be flip. When they asked me how I felt being the mayor of the third-largest city in New York, I would say something like, "I'm thinking of raising the taxes." And finally it got through to me the opportunity we had to let our own group of people know what the outside world was thinking about them. It became important to us to

say the right things to the press. Important for what we used to call crowd control, which really was a euphemism for what was going on, control being a totally inappropriate word for that. So what we did was do reverse information dissemination. We took what was being said to the outside world and piped it back to the crowd. I thought that, therefore, we were responsible for the beginning of that chain and should say only what we felt was a) true and b) helpful to the press. And I think we did both. And I think that after a while—with the possible exception of the New York *Times*—most of the reporting was pretty responsible. As it progressed through the weekend, it became clear to everybody that this was an "up" event.

JOHN MORRIS: It became obvious that we had worldwide coverage. We knew that we were in front of the world. We knew that. So we also knew that it was an extra added sense of responsibility: You had to do it right because everybody was watching. And also, of course, there was the anger and upset with the way it was being reported, because a lot of it was being misreported. I mean, there was some favorable stuff, but a lot of it was totally inaccurate and biased. Rightly or wrongly, I've always had a belief in the American press. And I've found myself in a lot of trouble a lot of times by saying something off the record or trusting a reporter when I shouldn't have. But I still believe it. I think it saved this country so many times. I've had a lot of situations where it's worked and this was one of them.

The Band's Robbie Robertson (left), Levon Helm

I was also manipulating some of them. I gave access to people who I knew or who I felt would write what was really happening. And I would talk to them and tell them what was going on, being totally straight with them about it. On Saturday, the Jets played the Giants in New Haven and when I was going back and forth to the stage they would keep me informed of what the score was; I was a big Giants fan. And there were those kind of things. Certain guys I let use my office. Half of my trailer ended up going to Richard Reeves and a bunch of other people like that who were from the New York *Times* and were involved in writing for it, some of whom had some real serious problems in reporting because their words were being changed by editors and turned around entirely. Al Paraccini, who now writes for the L.A. *Times,* was then the UPI stringer. He came to me with tears in his eyes and showed me his copy that he had sent and what was printed. They were a hundred eighty degrees opposite.

JOHN ROBERTS: The *Times* had, I think, a generally favorable reporter and report of the festival, but the overall impression they had was that—well, the headline of the editorial called it a "Nightmare in the Catskills." They ran this editorial on Monday morning and they felt that

what had happened out there was youth getting out of control and disorganized festival producers.

JOEL ROSENMAN: I think the phrase was "a paean to the depravity of youth" and "the lowest state to which youth had fallen." They talked about drugs and "God, this rotten music" and it was quite an ill-tempered editorial and represented a segment of the *Times* that, I guess, had control over the meeting about that editorial.

MIRIAM YASGUR: We had one interesting experience with the newspapers. The New York *Times* had published a very negative story the first day about the festival. The daughter of one of the principals of the *Times* at that time—whether he was an editor or somewhat in a similar position, I can't recall—flew into the small field in Bethel to come up to attend the festival, not as a working reporter. Apparently, she met the reporter who had written the negative article at the airport or somewhere between the airport and the field and she questioned him about it, and she went onto the field and she observed for herself how well mannered everybody was and how people were trying to help each other and what a feeling of brotherhood was in that place. And she realized that this reporter was making up a story, that it was better to say things were bad, that makes the headlines, and that he hadn't even been to some of the places she'd been to. He had stayed out on the fringes of the crowd or at the airport and made up his stories and filed them from word of mouth with other reporters.

She took exception to that and she walked into our office and she said, "May I use your phone? I can't get through on the other phones." And we said, "We have to keep our lines open. We're not letting anyone from the festival use these phones because they might be needed for emergency," plus we were doing business. So she spoke to Max and she gave him a quick capsule of what she wanted to do. She said, "I have to speak to somebody on the paper about this." So he said, "All right. Use the phone in my office." She called up and she spoke to her father and she told

★★★ **FINAL** | **SUNDAY 🔲 NEWS** | 20¢

NEW YORK'S PICTURE NEWSPAPER ®

Vol. 49, No. 16   Copr. 1969 News Syndicate Co. Inc.   New York, N.Y. 10017, Sunday, August 17, 1969   WEATHER: Cloudy, warm and humid.

HIPPIES MIRED IN SEA OF MUD

They Don't Melt . . . Only slightly daunted by mud and other drawbacks, rocksters press on to the Woodstock folk-rock festival at White Lake, N.Y. Despite unplanned discomforts—and threat of medical emergency—more than 400,000 held their ground on the Catskill farm in hope of catching some sounds.   —*Story p. 3; other pics. centerfold*

him what this reporter was doing and that he had not captured any of the essence of the festival, and she gave him her version of what it was like, and her opinion of Max. The following day, they published a retraction—a completely different story—and they did a "man of the hour" or something about Max in the paper, which was a real reversal of what they had been doing.

JOEL ROSENMAN: Then there was that memorable headline, "Hippies Mired in Sea of Mud."

JOHN ROBERTS: It was the New York *Daily News* headline. Well, that was just a headline, but they *were* mired in a sea of mud.

229

AL ROMM: As editor of the Middletown *Times Herald Record,* we had been covering the festival weeks before it started. At festival time, we decided to plan as if access would be almost impossible, so we made arrangements—my publisher fortunately approved—to hire a trailer, a camper, to stock it for three or four days as though there were going to be half a dozen reporters around. We got our own teletype in the trailer, we had our own telephone, we had a set of radios—walkie-talkies—and we hired an off-duty cop with a motorcycle to run pictures for us—pictures that we would take on site—down to Middletown to be processed. The trailer was in, or close to, what was called the press section. I think you'd have to say it was north of the amphitheater site, but close by. The press section that they ultimately set up was this van that was partly knocked over by the rain. It was later taken over as one of the extra emergency medical sites, when they found it necessary to set up more than they had planned.

Thursday night, after our paper was put to bed, my wife Ethel and I thought it would be a good idea to just go up and see our trailer in action and to make sure that everything was just right, and then our plan was to go back. But we had trouble getting up. We had to go up Swan Lake and cut back, and by the time we got there—we saw all the cars pretty well jammed up—we realized that it would be impossible to even contemplate leaving once we were there. So we stayed until early Sunday morning.

A fellow named Fred Germaine was our main man in charge of the coverage and there were about eight others that were assigned to come up for part or all of the time for pictures, stories, whatever. But about half of them never showed up—couldn't make it—and three or four others came because they wanted to be part of the scene—it was their day off or whatever—and we shanghaied them for service, which they were willing to do. Ethel was a writer and a good reporter herself. I stayed, by virtue of my office, editor, and sort of ran the operation mostly from right there at our command post, and Fred Germaine and others became part of the reporting team. We regrouped and did the best we could, which was better than, as far as I'm concerned, anybody else did or could do.

CHARLIE CRIST: I was the Monticello bureau chief for the *Times Herald Record* and I had I think three other fellows working under me, so we sort of split up the chores and then we got out on the road. I would say the paper did a pretty fair job. We put out—this was before we were printing a Sunday edition—we put out a special edition that Sunday and we had covered it well. We had teletypes out there at the scene and teletypes in the office connected right directly to the office in Middletown. I think we did a good job. I couldn't see where there were too many flaws in the coverage; we had good pictures. We had a motorcycle guy who was running back and forth carrying messages and carrying film and all the rest of it, because that was the only way you could get through.

AL ROMM: When I saw the lack of preparation and what was happening—the sale of drugs uncontrolled, heavy-duty drugs, and the problems that arose—as far as I was concerned, it was a disaster. I went to a couple of places that were high on the amphitheater finally about three or four o'clock one morning, probably Saturday morning, just to get the feeling for what was going on. It was raining but it was all right. I couldn't believe it, I had to see it with my own eyes—and I did—where the drugs were being sold, peddled in the wooded area. And the people approached us to buy drugs. Not just marijuana, there was methadone or whatever the hell it was they were hawking. And they even had prices posted on trees.

Another part of the area was where a lot of people slept and the Hog Farm was in that part of the territory. I visited them, spent a little time with the doctor, Goldmacher, and he was a very useful source. I visited him a couple of times, asked him the extent of the emergency he saw—he was trying to cope with it—and estimates on drug usage and his own views on that. To get to those places you had to pass by thousands and thousands of people. Some of them were just normal people and some of them were clearly under the influence of drugs. I saw a beleaguered state trooper at one corner inside the compound and a couple of kids walked up to him and blew smoke, presumably marijuana smoke, in his face and

Johnny Winter

he just made a sigh; he couldn't do anything.

We tried to keep track of what was happening, the alleged births and the alleged deaths. There were supposedly a handful of births that took place. We couldn't find proof of it in the aftermath. It was just a rumor. Whether there really was a birth, we don't know. ABC tried to track that, I think on the tenth or maybe fifteenth anniversary. They wanted to get somebody who was born there and talk to the kid. They went to the hospitals, which I would have thought would be a good thing, but they ran into a snag. There was no way that they could get, the way hospitals keep their records, the births of that date, on an emergency basis or whatever it was. And the fact isn't known that if there was a birth, the woman and child would have ended up in the hospital in any way, shape, or fashion.

There were many stories that went unreported. I heard some weird stories from our own people, after the moment had passed, of things they had seen that they thought were too macabre, outrageous, unbelievable, to report. I don't even know if they're true. One of them was supposedly a sex scene accompanied by drums and music over a half hour or hour period of time. It was a show or some ritual or something. I asked the reporter why didn't he tell the staff? He was a young fellow and maybe he was protective of the scene, maybe he was still too shocked by it, or didn't consider it representative or whatever. I would have probably found a way to use it as one little piece of the kaleidoscopic action.

● ● ● ●

MICHAEL LANG: I remember Iron Butterfly called. I think it was Saturday. And they were at the airport in New York. They were really the one act that I realized was a mistake to book. Because they were, it seemed like, more interested in creating problems than in playing their music. It became their thing at a show to bring the crowd over the fences or to incite them onto the stage. It was more like a heavy metal act, if you will.

JOHN MORRIS: There are only two people that I can think of that didn't show up. One of them was Jeff Beck; he was canceled in advance. And the other was Iron Butterfly, whose management sent a telegram that said, "You will send helicopter to LaGuardia. Pick us up, bring us back. We will go immediately on stage, in front of everybody else, and then we will be given a helicopter and flown back." And I called up Western Union and asked Western Union if they could figure out a way to say a word that I can't say by telegram and a woman came up with a word and we sent that back. We never heard another word from them. That was the end of that. They were the only no-show.

Janis Joplin

MICHAEL LANG: Saturday, the act that stands out in my mind was Janis Joplin. And I didn't think that the performance was that wonderful, frankly. I didn't like the band much. I thought it was a strange group for her to be with.

MYRA FRIEDMAN: I was working for Albert Grossman, who was Janis' manager. I showed up at the Holiday Inn, because that's where all the bands were staying. It was absolutely zany and colorful and exciting and charged and nutty and funny. It was like Old Home Week, with all these rock bands from all over the place. There was a dining room and of course the bar. You can be assured that's where I found Janis.

The lobby was jammed with rock musicians, the whole place. And everybody was all over everybody and running and table hopping. It was very exciting and people were sending messages through the P.A. system. And the poor people behind the desk at the Holiday Inn were just going crazy because they didn't really know whether these were legitimate. They didn't know. You'd hear it every other minute: "JOE COCKER, PLEASE COME TO THE BAR." And then "MICK JAGGER, JOHN LENNON CALLING FOR MICK JAGGER." And "CASS ELLIOT, WOULD YOU GET HERE. CASS ELLIOT, TIM HARDIN WANTS TO TALK TO YOU." And "JANIS, JANIS TO THE FRONT DESK." And everybody was cracking up. They were putting these people on. It was all good-natured but it must have been pretty hard for these people. They were really conservative people up there and here were these lunatics running around in crazy colors and loaded down with instruments and speakers and all this stuff coming into their hotel. It was like a busy beehive of crazies.

BILL BELMONT: There was this big floating crap game, big poker game, going on at the Holiday Inn. There were a bunch of people playing poker on the floor; it was a permanent floating poker game that went on and on and on. And a number of people that I have talked to spent their whole time doing that and drinking. Finally they all decided that it wasn't any fun out there so they came out to the festival site.

RICHIE HAVENS: The hotel was like a big backstage scene. I relate it really to the Newport Folk Festival backstage scene. Everybody knows everybody, everybody who doesn't know everybody is being introduced to everybody, and it's a wonderful family atmosphere. And sometimes you are in awe of people who you like yourself. I mean, all of that was going on. The hotel room doors were all open and we just hung out. A lot of people were down in the restaurant, a lot of people in the hallways, and it was basically people coming in all the time, a million hellos and introductions, and just the festive occasion of being backstage with a couple of hundred people. The hotel was backstage—the whole thing—and it was wonderful in that sense because it was a room.

MYRA FRIEDMAN: I believe that Janis and Country Joe were together in the dining room or the bar, or they turned the dining room into a bar. People were very blotto, high. I don't mean dope high, I'm not so sure about that. Not that first day. We ate a lot and it was real noisy and bustling.

JOHN MORRIS: Janis had just been in the Virgin Islands, where I had a house. And she'd come back and had had a great time down there. She was walking towards the stage at Woodstock and she had a bottle in each hand and had just gotten totally ripped. And I hadn't seen her. She walked up to me and said, "I loved staying in your house." And I said, "Well, how was it?" She said, "Oh, like anywhere else. I fucked a lot of strangers." And I thought, "Uh-oh. We're in trouble." I mean, I knew her well enough to know if she said a sentence like that and the way she said it and what she was doing, she was past it. We weren't going to get a great one. And it was an awful performance.

HENRY DILTZ: She was tortured and crying in the microphone. I don't know really how to describe her. I mean, she really screamed in agony in those songs. She really meant it. You could see that in the way she contorted her face and her body and everything.

MYRA FRIEDMAN: Her performance was disappointing. And she was very upset about that because, I believe, she either followed Sly or preceded Sly. That was one of the big moments there, was Sly Stone. I think that she was boxed in between Sly and Ten Years After. And she really

wasn't as great as she usually was. I'm not saying it was a complete disaster, I'm saying that it wasn't of the par. And then also that was her second band, which wasn't really right for her anyway. It was not Big Brother and it wasn't Full Tilt Boogie. It was what we used to call the Cosmic Blues Band.

When she walked offstage, I was backstage and somebody from *Life* wanted to talk to her, and I caught her coming back off and she was just very, very down. I said, "Do you feel up to talking to her?" Janis said, "I'm not fucking talking to anybody." She went into a tent and, I am sure, shot up instantly. So it was sad. And her behavior that weekend was indicative of her depression and addiction and booze. The other thing was that Janis was not real thrilled by the size of that crowd at all. She said, "I can't relate to a quarter of a million people." She either wanted to think that—that she couldn't relate to a quarter of a million people—or she was just so pissed off and down from the whole thing that she said it.

HENRY DILTZ: On Saturday, The Who was absolutely fantastic. Just Roger Daltrey up

there with his cape flying around, the fringe of his cape flapping in the wind and he'd twirl that microphone around. He really had that down where he'd twirl it around and just miss the floor and it would come arcing through the air and he'd grab it just in time to get him to "Talking 'bout my generation." And Townshend, leaping in the air, doing splits in midair, landing on the deck.

MICHAEL LANG: The Who was the high point of the day for me. And I was sitting with Abbie Hoffman onstage watching The Who. A bunch of people were onstage for that when he got whacked on the back of the head by Townshend.

The Who's
Peter Townshend

JOHN MORRIS: Abbie I knew as the contra, the enemy, when I was running the Fillmore—the Yippie, the clown prince of the revolution. But Abbie turned the minute the festival started. Abbie stopped being the revolutionary, he stopped all the contra stuff. Abbie went to work in the trips tent. And Abbie worked his tail off. He held kids, he talked to people, he worked with them. He just became a medical assistant and the whole thing. And he really just kept doing these wonderfully supposedly out-of-character things. What he did was show what his real character is, what he was, and that he did care and that he was involved and that he understood.

And Saturday I thanked him publicly on the mike and it flipped him out. He'd also taken a little something, too. And he got real upset with me. He said, "You're going to blow my whole thing. You go up there on the stage and you tell those people that I'm a nice guy and I'm helping, you know, all the rest of the shit. You're going to destroy me." And he sort of went off and I think he did some more drugs or whatever it was. Then, he decided in the middle of The Who set that he had to tell the world about John Sinclair being held prisoner in Wisconsin or Michigan or wherever he was, and free him. He came up from behind Townshend and Townshend didn't know who the hell he was, and Townshend laid him one upside the head with a guitar and Abbie went off the front of the stage and just kept going till he got to New York City.

MICHAEL LANG: Abbie was a little out of it. At one point in the day, he came to me and said, "Somebody's got a knife. We've got to get him." He and I were running around below the stage looking for this—I think—fictitious character. I think he was just tripping. I said, "Abbie, there's nobody here with a knife."

We talked for a while and I think he had taken a little too much acid. I said, "Why don't you come up and watch The Who?" I sat him down at the side of the stage and we were sitting there. He kept saying, "I gotta go say something about John Sinclair, I gotta go say something about John Sinclair." I said, "It's not really the time. Nobody really wants to hear that right now. There's an act on stage and it's just not the time for this." I guess we were about twenty minutes into the set and he couldn't take it any more. He just could not contain himself and he leaped up and ran to the microphone and started talking about John Sinclair. He got maybe a sentence out—they were in the middle of it— and Pete Townshend turned around and whacked him. And I guess he was stunned. Anyway, he jumped off the front of the stage onto the camera platform and then into the crowd and ran off and that was the last time I'd seen him. I heard that he turned up in a hospital in Monticello later that night, saying that he was me and that he was taking over the hospital.

ABBIE HOFFMAN: That was a big crackdown year, 1969. Nixon was already into Operation Intercept and everything, and there was a big war and one of the twelve major wars on drugs in this century was happening then. There was a symbol of the Youth International Party, John Sinclair, because he was a leader of the White Panther Party— they were Yippie affiliates in Ann Arbor—and he was given ten years in jail for either passing a marijuana cigarette in a circle to a narc, or selling him two—I'm not exactly sure about that. Anyway, the sentence was way outrageous. It was obvious they were going after him because he was a political leader as well. So, "Free John Sinclair" was, for the counterculture, the same as "Free Huey Newton" was for the black-power movement.

I told Michael and Artie, "We have to do something about legalizing marijuana, making a case that it isn't fair for people who are smoking marijuana to be put away. Because you've got five hundred thousand people here, ninety percent of whom are smoking, right off the bat. And we have the power of the people." There it was being demonstrated: No one's being arrested at Woodstock. No way. So I wanted the boys—the promoters—to kind of help out in terms of making a contribution through a bail fund. I'm not sure whether NORML—the National Organization for the Reform of Marijuana Laws—had been developed yet, but that thinking was in my mind. Let's set up some kind of fund, so we can bail people out, so we can get

Fete Drug Arrests: 235. Weather Prediction: Mud

Times Herald Record Middletown, N.Y. August 16, 1969

236

publicity. That this isn't the biggest crime in America. And they were quite receptive to this.

At first they weren't. They said what all promoters do: "Look, everybody's in free. We're taking a bath." And I said, "I know you're taking a bath, but I see all the cameras here—I mean, you've got forty-five cameras around here." The biggest guards were concentrated on one van—it's not where the money was, it's where the cans of film were. That's how they were going to recoup their losses, was through the film. So I saw all that. "But why don't we tithe ourselves like the churches do? We tithe ten percent to a fund." "Great idea." Artie was ready to give away the house. So they agreed.

So we're sitting around the stage. A huge stage—wow!—I don't think there's ever been a bigger stage in the world. Kind of Indian fashion—our legs crossed—and being in the movie, having a good time. It was the most relaxed state I'd been in in days. And I said, "Well, when are you going to announce this?" And they said, "We're thinking of having a press conference when it's over." And I said, "*Over!* No! You don't understand. I like you guys, but you've got to announce it now. There's five hundred thousand people. The world should hear it now. Just tell them." "Well, we don't want to interrupt the music," and all of this. And they're hemming and hawing.

The group before The Who—I don't remember who it was—they had shut down. And there were gaps. And in these gaps, there were a lot of announcements being made—a whole system of communicating through the microphone. Mostly it was Chip Monck's voice: "Mary,

meet Adam at the green tent." And "Don't drink the water from the stream over beyond the big boulder; that's bad." Or "The red tabs of acid are not so good." The announcements were done in a calming, reassuring voice, but with a lot of important information given out.

So I got up and said, "If you're not going to announce it, I'm going to announce it." And I walked up to the microphone and I started giving a quick rap, which I'm good at. If you've given political raps at musical concerts, you know you've got to be quick; you've got to be visual. You've got to ask one thing and get the hell out of there as quick as you can. So I said something to the effect of "Four hundred thousand of our brothers and sisters are in jail for doing no more than we're doing on this hill. It's only fair that we help out. We are the Woodstock Nation. We are one." Something like that. And the mike got cut off. They cut the mike, which was an insult. Because this announcement was just as important as all the other announcements they were making.

It could have been between The Who doing a song, then readjusting their instruments. It could have been before The Who came on, or during their set. But they weren't playing. I didn't run up and grab the mike out of Peter Townshend's hand, that's for sure. There was a pause, and I got up to make my announcement. So they cut off the mike and I exploded. I said, "What the fuck did they do that for?" and I kicked the mike. And as I turned around to walk back, I remember, Townshend was turning around and we bumped—that was it, we just bumped.

And Lang was saying, "That was uncool." They were saying, "Booooo. That was bad vibes." And I'm saying, "That's exactly what should have been said. You should have been the ones that said it. Fuck you! I'm with them." I don't think Townshend was a major player here. They were just in their heads about playing their song. And I ran to the front of the stage—which was about ten, fifteen feet—and I leaped. *Meshugena.* Good thing it rained; it was kind of muddy. And I landed and climbed over the next fence and just walked up into the mobs of people. And people would slap me and say, "You said it right. You told it, brother."

HENRY DILTZ: I remember standing on the stage. I think The Who were about to go on. It was one of those times when the stage was quite crowded. I'd be on one side of the stage looking across at Chip Monck and all these faces of people out on the fringes of the stage, which was just this big open platform. And Abbie Hoffman suddenly ran out and grabbed the microphone and said, "Remember John Sinclair and the guys in prison for smoking pot," or something like that. And he was haranguing the crowd and he wasn't supposed to be doing that. He grabbed the mike and suddenly Peter Townshend was standing there with his guitar and I saw him raise it up, kind of holding it over his shoulder, and walk up behind Abbie Hoffman and just go *boink* right in the back of the neck. It was almost like a bayonet thrust. He had it shoulder height with the body of the guitar next to his head and his hand outstretched holding the pegs of the guitar. And he just thrust it, you know—one quick little jab right in the back of Abbie Hoffman— who fell down, I remember. It looked like a fatal blow. He was really pissed at this guy taking over the microphone when they were about to go on. And I thought, "Whoa!" It was like an electrifying moment that kind of just passed.

ABBIE HOFFMAN: If this is such a big incident, where's the goddamned picture? There were at least twenty thousand, thirty thousand cameras taking pictures. The people were as stage-oriented as everybody else in the media. So you had thousands of reporters—legitimate reporters—twenty, thirty thousand amateur reporters, you had movie cameras going continuously. Where the hell is the goddamned famous picture?

HENRY DILTZ: How come I didn't take a picture? I was transfixed watching this. I guess my instincts as a photojournalist gave out. I was more of a guy hanging out just digging this stuff. I remember seeing that all happen. It was electrifying. I was very close, maybe twenty feet, something like that. It was almost like a ringing in my ears. I remember it as quite an intense moment and I remember being very shocked by this. And then things just kept on going and the show went on. The Who went on and nothing happened and no one said a word and it just passed. The Who went on and played this great show.

MICHAEL LANG: The Jefferson Airplane was Saturday night's headliner—actually Sunday morning's.

HENRY DILTZ: The Airplane were playing as the dawn came up, as the sky started turning light, pale color. That was very beautiful. I was up behind the stage, up kind of on the rafters looking down at the stage and the audience and taking pictures of that. I know I can't really wax philosophic about it. It just was wonderful hearing the sounds and it was a great band—playing "Somebody to Love," you know. That was quite an enthralling time.

PAUL KANTNER: That was the true medieval times, because we were supposed to go on at ten-thirty at night and we'd been up and down about four or five times on acid that night, getting ready to go on, and then everything was delayed for whatever reasons. So, we didn't get on until like seven o'clock the next morning and everybody was pretty much burned out. About half of the people in front of the stage were

Jefferson Airplane

Backstage: Jefferson Airplane, Country Joe McDonald, Bill Graham, and friends

alert, semi-alert. And we weren't that alert ourselves. I mean, we were probably there at eleven o'clock in the morning just for the celebration and to walk out among the camp, sort of disguised. We really didn't have to bother with that. Nobody was much into that sort of Beatlesque kind of stuff in those days, so you could walk pretty much undisturbed— "Hey, how ya doin', Paul"—and just check out all the camps, what was going on on the stages. Medieval, very medieval. Perhaps early Renaissance, not full-blown Renaissance—muddy Renaissance.

There was one point during the afternoon where I was really fucked up on acid—not fucked up, but having a good time. They were worried about the stage sinking into the mud. They wanted to clear everybody back off the stage. And most everybody went except me, who was just glued to the floor sitting next to a big mound of Roquefort cheese, which was all we had to eat at the moment because there was no food; it was primitive on a level of stagecraft. "No, I'm not moving, because I'm the person with the cheese," while everybody else was moving on. I forget who was playing, it was somebody I wanted to see. I think it was Janis. So I just hung on. Sometimes you just can't move.

I can barely remember our performance now because, like I say, it was early in the morning and it was probably pretty ragged, I would think, by that time. Although it was spirited. Well, the cameraman fell asleep because he'd been up twice as long as we had and, setting up in the morning, and filming all day and all night. By the time we got on he was sort of dead asleep. We had Nicky Hopkins with us, which was delightful—great piano player—and we just went out and played as best we could what we normally play.

The crowd was into it, surprisingly, once they were awake. There were a lot of people just sleeping-bagged out who had gone out actually even before us, during The Who. The fires were starting to go out, and people were crashing and burning.

• • • •

WES POMEROY: Max Yasgur's wife was remarkably good. I thought she was a very attractive woman and pleasant woman and clearly cared for Max a great deal. In fact, it was about the second night of the concert I guess, she called me up where I had gone for three or four hours sleep—we had a house we rented right on the lake; my then-wife and my two younger daughters were there, plus anyone else who wanted to crash. And she just gave me hell because Max was having one of his attacks and she was really worried and angry and said that if Max died it would be my fault. And I thought that there was nothing I could do about it, and I never saw her again. I haven't seen her since. But I talked to somebody who had talked to her and she said that she was really sorry she said that. And I think she probably was.

MIRIAM YASGUR: I was getting nervous. I was getting scared. I thought, "Well, we're going to have all kinds of problems." You cannot take an area like that and put that many people in it without creating problems, I decided, and I called Wes Pomeroy and said, "You know, this is going to be worse than what they said it was going to be and you better make sure you have enough help out here and so forth, because if we have any trouble it's going to be on your head." I really was very, very upset about it, and poor Wes, you know, he was doing the best he could and I made him feel worse. But I really frankly was not concerned with anybody but Max at the time. I thought if this goes bad, he's the one that's going to pay for it. Wes didn't deserve that, surely, but he was the only one I could tell. I really owe him an apology. He did the best he could but anybody that crossed Max I would rise up against, I guess, rightly or wrongly.

• • • •

JOEL ROSENMAN: Originally, the performances were scheduled to go from seven o'clock till around midnight. And then, the theory was that

everybody would be tired and toodle off to the campground for a restful night, then resume doing something groovy the next morning till seven in the evening, when the performance would begin again.

We quickly recognized that this was a stupid idea. Nobody was going to leave the performance area at twelve or one o'clock in the morning after having been revved up to the pins by the last rock act. And we found ourselves with a need for talent to play from midnight through dawn, and no talent. We had only hired enough to play for the first five hours. So we decided we would ask every act to play a second set. That way we could double up the time; it seemed like an obvious solution. And most of the acts were all too happy to oblige, but a couple of them were concerned. One or two of them had heard enough about this being a free festival and a few others had heard that the Woodstock promoters were going to lose their shirts—and we were. Business managers being what they are—which is, you know, they are, essentially, charged with the responsibility of making sure that their clients don't get stiffed—they demanded cash.

This all came to a head Saturday night—sometime around midnight or thereafter—and it was impossible to get cash for them. I think that at that point the Grateful Dead and The Who spring to mind as acts who were just not going to play unless they were paid in cash.

We pleaded with the Grateful Dead's manager. In fact, we decided that we were going to one-up them. We decided that if they were going to be so pigheaded, we were going to have them go down in history as the two acts that didn't play at Woodstock. The most

famous festival of all times. And by this time you could almost tell it was going to be that. So I called up John Morris at the stage and I said, "John, the Grateful Dead and The Who are giving us a lot of gas about getting paid cash. We don't have cash. Let's take them off the talent roster. What would happen if you told the crowd The Who and the Grateful Dead are not going to play?" And John said, "They will tear us apart. They will riot, they'll go crazy." And I hung up and I said to the manager of the Grateful Dead, "No problem. I'll have your cash here in a few minutes."

And then I called up Charlie Prince who was our faithful banker at the White Lake branch of the Sullivan County National Bank, the man who had probably clucked sorrowfully over many an odd payment that we had been making over the previous four or five weeks. I got Charlie—he must have been about halfway through his night's sleep, in deep beta or alpha or whatever you are in. I woke him and I said, "Charlie, this is Joel over at the command center." And he said, "Joel, what time is it?" And I said, "It's as late as you think it is, Charlie, but we really have a problem here and only you can help us. Charlie, I need

Canned Heat's
Bob "The Bear" Hite

twenty-five thousand dollars in cash." And he said, "I don't have that kind of money." And I said, "Charlie, I know you don't have that kind of money. You're our banker; you can get it from the bank." And he said, "That sort of thing goes into the vault on Friday. And that sort of thing comes out of the vault Monday morning and nobody gets in. It's on a time lock. That is what bank vaults are."

Our whole lives flashed in front of us and we thought, "Gee, just this clever solution, having the acts play double sets, turns out to be the undoing of the entire fabric of the festival." And I said, "Charlie, what can you do? Anything? Think! Think!" And Charlie didn't say anything. Then after a minute or two, he said, "Wait a second. Usually, I take all the teller's checks, the cashier's checks, out of the drawers and lock them in the vault because they are as good as cash. I don't remember, I don't have a precise recollection of doing that for one of the drawers. It is a total longshot." I said, "Charlie, we have no alternative. You have to be right." He said, "It doesn't matter. I couldn't get to the bank anyway. I've seen what the roads are like." I said, "Charlie, don't worry about that. Just get outside in your backyard and I'll have a helicopter pick you up."

I could hear his wife saying, as he was hanging up, "Charlie, what's going on? What are you—" *Click.* And we got a helicopter out to his backyard. He didn't even get dressed—he was still in his pajamas; he had his bathrobe on. He had the keys to the front door of the bank. The helicopter picked him up in his backyard, airlifted him to the White Lake branch. He went in.

He was such a nice guy that he called me from the bank when he got into the bank and let me know that he had gotten in. I mean, just so considerate. What a nice guy he was, because we were all dying over at the White Lake office, at the phone building. He said, "I'm going to put the phone down now, Joel, and I'm going to go over and check the tellers' desks." And we sat there in the White Lake phone office while he went through, and you could hear him rustling around. And all of a sudden we hear this cheer from Charlie. He was normally a pretty mild guy.

He comes thundering back, picks up the phone and says, "I've got 'em! I've got 'em!" And I yelled to the assembled group in the phone building, "He's got 'em! He's got 'em!" They all cheered. Because, I guess everybody believed the threat that John Morris had interpreted from the Grateful Dead and The Who not playing their sets. So, they got their money. We airlifted the checks back to White Lake and we wrote them out. And, in fact, thereafter, we were able to get cash or cashier's checks or whatever back to a number of people who had suddenly the feeling or believed the rumor or correctly read our financial condition and determined they weren't going to get paid. In fact, everyone did get paid.

• • • •

CHIP MONCK: I was getting letters and notes and epistles and things written on everything from shirt cardboard to shingles to pieces of equipment that were no longer being used—scratched into it, "Help, I need my whatever. I'm standing underneath Sign Number Forty-eight." There was this constant flood of little bits and pieces of paper. The difficult thing, of course, is when one released the piece of paper as a finished note, having been read to the audience, whether important or not, it would likely float back into the audience's domain. They would capture it and use the other side. So, often the announcement might be read two or three times, and the new announcement coming up on the back of the old one might be discarded; you might forget to turn it over to see if somebody had reused that piece of paper. So the communication was a little difficult to handle. There was obviously a limited supply of clean paper, was there not?

Everybody had to have their medicine. It was very important that Joe meet Sally underneath Tree Number Four. Of course, there was no number on it so we were trying to describe the shape of the tree while looking at it: "If you were standing here, it is approximately fifteen degrees to my left, which is, of course, to your right, but it's going to be"—a hundred eighty minus fifteen is—"one hundred and sixty-five degrees to your right, as you spin around—no, no, no, clockwise." So trying to point out that tree under which Joe is standing, waiting for the aspirin from Doreen, was a bitch. Because the point of aim was it all depends on whose shoes on which or in which you are standing— or in what mud you are standing, unable to turn around that hundred and sixty-five degrees that it required.

Chip Monck

TOM LAW: A number of times, Wavy would ask me to lead everyone in yoga from the stage. I would come over and fill in for fifteen or twenty minutes. And I would just talk about, "Here's another way to get high. No drugs. Try this." I was just having everybody sit up straight. You don't have to be in a lotus pose, but basically sit up with your crossed legs in front of you and take these very deep breaths and then exhale them completely and squeeze all the air out. And I was having them raising their hands up when they were taking breaths or exhaling. And inhaling. Just doing things together. What I saw was phenomenal because I would say sixty to seventy percent of the audience was doing it, so what I saw was just this sea of hands raising in unison. In our society, that's very unusual. In China, it's not unusual. But in America, that was a very, very unusual sight because we are all individuals and we don't do those kinds of things. To see it all happening in unison, it was amazing at the time because it was spontaneous. It works. It always has worked; it will keep working forever. And you don't need drugs to do that kind of stuff.

JOHN MORRIS: It's amazing we managed to control it as well as we did. It's one of those things that if you were ever to do it again you should do it a different way. But we were the only source of communications through that sound system. So what happened was people would bring messages to backstage. They would give them to somebody who'd give them to somebody else and we did as many of them as we could in between breaks and the rest of it. We wouldn't like to take it all over because then you sounded like a public-information thing and that was not what you were there to do. We did sort of filter them out. I remember that after a while there were a couple of people who would take the messages and look at them and sort them out so that by the time I got them, one or two people had looked at them and got a judgment. And then I'd do the ones that I could. And the information

booth became a center—up in what I call the first-base line—and we just said to people, "We can't do all these announcements and everything and if you're looking for somebody you gotta do this, that, or the other. Go up there."

HENRY DILTZ: By Saturday, I guess, the New York *Times* was appearing with this aerial shot of this whole thing, which was like a big shock because none of us had seen that. And our first look at the gigantic proportions of this was to see the cover and that picture on the New York *Times*. In one of the production trailers someone had one. "Wow! Look at this! It's on the front page! What? All the roads are tied up for miles and traffic is stopped! They estimate four hundred thousand

245

people here! Unbelievable!" And at that point the proportion of this huge thing sunk in.

JOHN MORRIS: I had a very strong sense of history being at the microphone. And a weirdness, at least on my part. I knew what was going on. I knew where we were, as far as what we had to do at that point. Maybe that comes from an Irish-Catholic upbringing, maybe it comes from having been a Boy Scout, maybe it comes from having traveled all over the world, maybe it comes from not being somebody who was doing drugs. I have no idea what it comes from. But it was— I was very conscious of it.

There were two thoughts. There was one that I threw away, which had to do with the old peace sign with the "V." You could put up a third finger and make it "W" for Woodstock. People could always go around forever and do that to each other. But that was just too corny for even me. So that was never done. I have wondered often if I had done it would people still be going around doing the "W," the three-fingered "W." The other thing was the idea which came from an Indian thing of taking a piece of earth—I mean, I still collect a rock or a piece of wood or something wherever I am, bring them back to my girlfriend. I've brought them from Australia and all over the world, just a little piece of something. And there was a consideration—and I discussed it with Chris and a couple of other people—the idea of having everybody take a little piece of the dirt with them. And then we figured, "God knows what's in that dirt and who needs to start a plague?"

JOEL ROSENMAN: I remember discussing a topic that was always under discussion: "How do we keep all these kids happy?" Because the opposite of happy for us was unthinkable. And at one point I

remember somebody said—and you hear some of the news reports and you started thinking—"The reports said the world expects this to explode." I remember thinking to myself, "This is perfect. Let's tell them what the world thinks is going to happen. Because there's nothing kids like better than to disappoint what the world thinks they're going to do." And so we started feeding them headlines and news reports and whatever, and telling them what the world expected—how badly the world expected that they were going to behave—and they just were magnificent. I don't think that it took that to make them magnificent, but it didn't hurt. They loved that.

JOHN ROBERTS: It looked to the outside world like a very scary thing. Here was this ten square miles where no traffic moved, all the arteries were clogged, the kids were essentially in control, and it was lawless. There was nothing but the law of the—whatever the common will was, really. No one can enforce it. No one can get there to stop people from doing whatever mischief they wanted to do. If a band of kids wanted to go and ransack a house, the police couldn't get through to stop them or find them. They would all disappear into the crowd. From the outside, that must have looked very dangerous and we got offers from the state or the National Guard.

Greenberg Terms Festival 'Disaster'

*Times Herald Record
Middletown, N.Y.
August 16, 1969*

Did we want the National Guard? And we sat down and we thought about that. We said, "Well, what would that look like? To have a ring of National Guardsmen with rifles, you know, outside the festival area." And we thought that it would probably set the wrong tone. That seems sort of obvious now, but at the time, we were faced with considering, "Well, *will* these people do mischief? I mean, what if they don't like the music? What if it rains and someone doesn't show up? What if one of the groups refuses to go on for some reason or other?" There were a thousand and one "ifs." What if the Food for Love people start serving "funny" hamburgers? Or someone puts acid in the water? There are all these things. How do we control this beast that is out here? Which is perfectly amiable right now—and turned out, of course, to be wonderfully amiable. But that's all hindsight.

We sat down and talked about it with Wes and John Fabbri, Joel and myself, and probably a couple of other people, and it was our best guess that things were going along pretty smoothly and everyone was having a pretty nice time. And some of the reports from the stage were that it was a very peaceful, happy, enthusiastic gathering. The reports from the local people who had come by were "These are the nicest kids, you know. They always say "thank you" and "please." So, the indications were that this was a benign phenomenon. We based our decisions on that judgment and we were right.

JOHN MORRIS: Well, it was declared an emergency, a disaster area. It started out with Rockefeller's people, with the governor's people freaking out at what was going on and wanting to send in the National Guard and remove everyone. Not a very intelligent idea. I took a few hours to talk to them on the phone back and forth. Mel did some too.

I don't remember who it was that we talked to. They were saying that this is an illegal gathering. They were using exactly the same logic that they used in Attica later, after Woodstock: This was a confronta-

247

tion, it was a danger to the community, it was a danger to public health, it was a danger to any damn thing they could think of. They wanted to get rid of it. And they were stupid enough to believe they could mobilize the National Guard and move these kids out.

And I had to talk on the phone quite calmly and say, "Look, guys, I don't know how many people are out there but I can see five hundred acres of them. Count how many people you can put in five hundred acres. The roads are jammed up from what the state police tell me. We've got a circle area around here and we can't get things in and out. I've ordered helicopters to get people in medivac back and forth and bring acts in so I can keep them happy. There's one way to do this, that's to play it through. We need help." And in the end, there was an assistant to the governor who got it. And he said, "Well, what can we do?" I said, "What you can do is you can send me some medical teams. You can send me a field hospital. If I need food, you can send me food. What you can do is let's start thinking about what you can do." So they did. They had to go through the thing of declaring it a disaster. They might have done it already. I knew that they were going to send us some help. I didn't know what it was going to be. But what I really needed was field tents and a field hospital.

WES POMEROY: I called the head of the state police and said, "We have a lot of problems here. We may need medical supplies, water, food— we need your help." The only way we were going to get it was for them to declare it a disaster area. I knew about that from with my job as special assistant to that kind of thing. And as a police officer too. That's the only way we could get that stuff. You can't get National Guard help unless you declare it a disaster situation, like a flood or anything else. And the guard was all mobilized. The governor had already called out the National Guard on maneuvers nearby, because, they were still afraid of violence, which was outrageous. It would have been a perfect setup. But they wouldn't do it. I suppose for P.R. it wouldn't have been a good thing, but I wanted some help. I don't recall the National Guard helped us out. They flew over and from the stage the audience was being reassured, "These are ours, they are not the enemy's." But I don't remember they did a goddamn thing for us.

CHARLIE CRIST: The state police set up a command post and I was a little bit responsible for getting that for them. I belonged to a large hunting club between White Lake and Elder, and we had a big house there— what we called a clubhouse—with bunk rooms and the whole bit, a kitchen and everything. And my association with the state police had been great over the years because I had been a reporter from about 1933, in and out of there and the army and so on. But anyway, talking to the major, he wondered where they could set up where it would be convenient for a helicopter to land and for them to have a command post so that they could get out, even though the roads were clogged. I said, "Well, hell, you can use our hunting club. That's as easy as any place for you and you're fairly close, even if you have to walk or take a bicycle." So they did. They set themselves up an emergency heliport.

WES POMEROY: We did get an Army helicopter helping us, which

GROOVY WAY →
←

GENTLE PATH
HIGH WAY

shouldn't have been. Sheriff Ratner knew some people over at West Point and they had one of their Army helicopters over there and they even dropped us supplies a couple of times.

LOUIS RATNER: I had a feeling about two days before it. I made plans for when I started to feel the fact that they didn't know how many tickets they sold, I contacted our congressman, Marty McKneally, and I contacted the governor. At that time, it was the acting governor, Lieutenant Governor Wilson. And I made preparations because I felt something. I don't know what it was. It's like you get a certain feeling there, that something isn't right.

In the sheriff's association in the State of New York, we had a deal set up whereby we had mutual aid. I notified, I would say, twenty or thirty of the sheriffs that I was going to be looking for help. This was like two or three days before and getting down to the wire. By the time people got here, we had help on the way so the timing was good. And the only way we could get helicopters would be for them to come from the governor to our congressman in the area, or the United States senator to get them. So we had that all set up. So we got permission to get Army helicopters flown by Stewart Air Force pilots. And we already had them that morning. When that thing broke, I had the helicopters on the way.

JOHN MORRIS: I was standing onstage and it is one of the timing pleasures of that whole thing. I could see these—I guess they were Hueys or Chinooks—coming in. And they were coming in from behind the audience. There were three or four of them in a row. And I looked up and I saw them and I thought, "You gotta sell this. You gotta make this work right." And I waited—it was in between acts, thank God, nobody was playing. And you could hear the helicopters and the people started to look. It was like a wave. You could see people start to look up. They were used to the helicopters going in and out behind us. But this was from a different direction. And all I said was, "Ladies and gentlemen, the United States Army —" and you could feel it and you could hear it, the tension—"Medical Corps." And the crowd broke into a cheer that was just fantastic. And about then you could see the red crosses on the side.

• • • •

JOHN ROBERTS: We took a lot of phone calls from worried parents. A lot. Hundreds and hundreds, maybe even into the thousands. We had about a dozen people manning the phones in the White Lake office there. And a phone call would come in and we would, if it was like "Mary Jo, call home," we would get that announcement onto the stage. Relay it to there. Just worried parents wondering what was happening up there. You know, were people dying in droves? Were there riots? It certainly seemed like pandemonium to those outside. But it was actually quite orderly within the telephone building.

MYRA FRIEDMAN: I didn't really know I was going to Woodstock until the last minute, so I thought, "Gee, I really ought to let my mother know because what if she calls and I'm not here and she calls again —." We didn't have answering machines then. My mother lives out in St. Louis and she was a widow and you want to tell your mother where you are—or at least I did. So, I had called and it was a very hurried conversation. I said, "Look, I'm leaving, I'm going out of town for the weekend." She said, "Where are you going?" I said, "I'm going to this big rock festival, Mother, and I'll call you on Monday when I get back."

So, I think Saturday was when they were declaring it a disaster area and I knew that it had to be just terrible in terms of the news—helicopters flying in bringing in food, God knows what, you're dying, you know. So all of a sudden from the blue I think, "Oh my God, my mother!" And I go into a trailer in the back and I called my mother. And she was, indeed, absolutely hysterical. She was frightened out of her wits. She was crying and she said, "Well, they say it's a disaster." I said, "No, no, no. It's really not." And she was just carrying on and I said, "Mother, I got to get off the phone now. I'm knee-deep in mud." And there was a lot of mud out there. She said, "You're knee-deep in mud?" I said, "No, no, no. I'm really O.K." And she kept saying, "Well, where

are you?" And I guess that it was Bethel, White Lake, what the hell is this? She wouldn't know where. She couldn't get a focus on it. My mother, by the way, was a highly intelligent person and she wasn't a hysteric either. But the broadcasts were really scary. So I wanted to give her a focus. So I said, "Listen, Mother, I'm just down the road from Grossinger's." And there's this silence and she calms down and says, "Oh. Well, why don't you go *there* for the weekend?" This is like Jewish mother stuff. You see, my mother, on a trip to the East some years before, had spent a weekend with a sister of hers at Grossinger's. And this is where you went to meet a fellow then. But it was so funny that as soon as I said, "I'm just down the road from Grossinger's," it was so reassuring to her.

JOEL ROSENMAN: I talked to my parents. I called them. It is something that they remember to this day. Sometimes they don't remember a lot of things about me—mostly things they want to forget. You'd think they'd want to forget this too, in some ways, but they remember that in the middle of it all, I phoned them to tell them everything was fine. I didn't have the wit to use Myra's line, which would have been great. But I did want to assure them that, whatever they had read about it—and they were glued to the newspapers and the TV accounts of this thing— that from the inside it was going along quite beautifully. And that although it was difficult, everybody was managing fine, and I, personally, was fine. For years afterwards, they referred to that phone call because there was a ten-year period when I didn't call them at all. And now, in the middle of this, I picked up the phone and called them. They thought that was very considerate. In fact, I think I keenly felt the need to talk to them at that point, so I picked up the phone and called them for that reason, among others. It was nice to hear their voices.

• C H A P T E R   F O U R T E E N •

"It was a time to prove your philosophy, not to talk about it."
—*Tom Law*

DONALD GOLDMACHER: The first time I heard about the festival was sometime in the spring of 1969 when the promoters approached our organization, the Medical Committee for Human Rights, with the notion of us providing medical presence at the festival. That was the major activity of the group. We were present at civil rights rallies, antiwar demonstrations, and everything else, really providing a lot of medical coverage and first aid. We were the New York City chapter of the organization, and I was the chairperson.

We designated two of our members to negotiate with these folks. I don't even know who it was that they were dealing with, but we had gotten assurances—verbally at least and I think written—about what we wanted them to provide in terms of supplies and equipment, that essentially we were looking at fully equipped outpatient clinics and emergency capability to handle stuff on site and be ready to evacuate people should that become necessary. And they were assuring us all along, "Sure, no problem, no problem." And, of course, the site, as I recall, kept getting switched around. They didn't know quite where it was going to be, nobody wanted them, and the real joker in the deck was they didn't tell us how many people were showing up. I think the original projection was they were going to have a hundred thousand people, or something like that, and that we felt was manageable. We were recruiting our members—doctors, nurses, and other health personnel—to come up for that weekend, and hopefully it would be a peaceful weekend. We'd have three or four units around the perimeter to be available.

We were anticipating that since it was going to run several days, you could see a lot of different stuff in basically an instantly created city of a hundred thousand people—everything from accidents and injuries to people getting sick with whatever. We anticipated bad drug trips because that was '69 and people were using LSD and mescaline a lot. And then, you know, people were going to come up with preexisting medical conditions that they'd at least like to be able to talk to a doctor about. And then the issue of adequate food and water supplies was of concern to us as well—was there going to be adequate provision of that—because when there's clean water and adequate food, you've covered a lot of ground already from the public health perspective. The rest is manageable. Also, we asked that there be backup capability to get people out of there and get them to a hospital if need be.

I drove up with two friends, two other people in the organization, and we got to about within five or six miles of the site and then just saw this humongous traffic and said, "Well, this is it, folks." There was some kind of storefront where the promoters had some people who were handling logistics or whatever and we went in there and we said, "We're medical people, we're supposed to get in there but we don't see any way to get in there." So they said, "Why don't you turn around, drive back to the airport; it must have been Monticello airport. So we drove back there and they had a helicopter there; the helicopter, I guess, was flying in VIPs and entertainers. And so they flew us in.

I think we had about half a dozen people up there already beginning on Wednesday or something like that, and there were some tents set up, but there was nothing in them. There were no medical supplies. All of the stuff that we had insisted had to be there in terms of medications, equipment—nothing was there. It was a bad joke—maybe they had a couple of pieces of gauze and aspirin or something like that. We said, "Hey, wait a minute. We need all of these kinds of medications"—everything from antibiotics, if need be, to anti-convulsant medications, to being able to clean and sew up small lacerations, to at least temporarily immobilize an extremity if there was a potential fracture and get them out of there to a hospital emergency room and be X-rayed and then treated for the fracture. And it just wasn't there.

One of the people who was there was one of the people who had done the negotiating with them. She was livid. I mean she was just enraged, appropriately so. She said, "They don't have anything, nothing here we asked for." I said, "Well, I guess we're going to have to do something about it, huh?" She said, "Yeah, listen, we've seen everything here. We're seeing hepatitis, we've seen people about to give birth, you know, people with acute asthmatic reactions." So, I sat down and talked with our people already there and sort of got a full briefing on what they'd already seen and what they needed, which was already like a hospital emergency room setup.

I stopped by Bill Abruzzi's little clinic on my way in, and I said, "What have you got here?" He said, "Not much." And I said, "And you're the hired doc?" He had no grasp of what the heck was going on. He was from Wappingers Falls or something, near Poughkeepsie, and he'd never done this before, he'd never been at a rock concert—you know, staffing and doing medical presence at a big event where thousands and thousands of people were. So he thought he was going to be the local family doctor doing whatever. But this was really emergency medicine, not clinic medicine or private practice medicine.

I think it started to rain Friday evening, to which I said, "Oh, this is going to really be terrific." So we got ahold of Stan Goldstein—I'm pretty sure it was Stan that I met with—and one of the other functionaries or whatever, and I said, "Look, you guys have created a major situation here. We were very explicit with you about what we needed in anticipation of about a hundred thousand people. You have four hundred thousand people here, or you're going to hit that number shortly, and you have not provided us with the supplies and equipment that we need to handle this situation. We have the makings of a medical disaster here. You charter a plane out of La Guardia tomorrow morning and we will get on the phones tonight and call everybody we can call in New York City—and you can also put out appeals on the radio or whatever for volunteer nurses and docs. We want to fly a group up tomorrow as quickly as possible. And we want you to start ordering the following supplies. If you don't have it here by tomorrow at twelve o'clock, I'm calling the governor and having him declare it a disaster area and bring in the National Guard."

254

And we were prepared to do that. I was terrified because, first of all, the whole arena was so big, it was like I didn't know what was going on over there or over there. It was just hundreds of acres, and different scenes were happening all over the place. And I was not prepared to see people die or needlessly get hurt or get sick, because obviously they wouldn't have potable water or whatever. I said, "You've got to deal with this and you better deal with it quick because I am not happy about this. In fact, I'm enraged and my colleagues here are furious at what you have not done."

Penny Stallings: I was on the phone most of the time trying to locate stuff primarily to deal with the sick people, although most of the injuries were not serious at all. However, there were a lot of them. And that was really my job through the festival—to try and keep the hospital facility going. And then by the second night, the second facility, too. I had a big dramatic fight with Peter Goodrich who was to be in charge of feeding the crew—well, no one could eat, there was no structure, everybody did what they could. I don't remember eating once during that weekend. And so we converted the place that was going to be the staff dining room—which was another tepee—into a hospital. And he was livid. I just did it anyway, which I thought was the nerviest thing I'd ever done in my life, because he was an older man and I stood up to him and went right ahead and did it. And I don't know who had authorized me to do that, if anybody. I don't remember what possessed me to decide I could do that, but that was pretty much it.

Donald Goldmacher: By the next afternoon, essentially a field hospital had been set up. It was not just our people but a lot of folks, and I don't even know where all of them poured in from. From probably surrounding areas as well as New York. And there were docs and nurses who had just come up to party, you know, and had suddenly found themselves recruited.

Miriam Yasgur: My daughter, who was killed in an accident several years after Max died, was a registered nurse, and she and her husband came up from New York, thinking to go to the festival. They couldn't get through, so they left the car and walked a few miles. At that point, 255

they needed help in the emergency tent, which they had set up near the festival grounds. They were using helicopters to take young people out to the hospital, most of the injuries—they were barefoot—and they would step on wire or glass, or they would be injured because of the crowds, and they would take them out. So she went into the hospital tent and worked there and then went home. I never saw her.

• • • •

GORDON WINARICK: I was president of the Monticello Hospital. Presently, the hospital is merged in one large one, but at that time there was a hospital in Monticello, there was a hospital in Liberty, and there was another hospital in Callacoon. We decided that if the Woodstock festival was coming into this area it would impact on these hospitals and we should start to have some conversations. So, as president of the Monticello board, I went to the doctors and asked, "What do you fellows know about this particular situation?" They said, "We don't know much." But there was another event happening—I think it was in Jersey, about a couple of months earlier—so the doctors took on the responsibility of finding out what the impact of that large a gathering was and how they dealt with it. It was not that they were unfamiliar with the fact that there would be drugs and other kind of ailments.

So we inquired what the Woodstock event itself was doing for medical care. And they had a doctor, Bill Abruzzi, and he said, "Don't worry. We got it all under control." Fine. So I said to the doctors, "You better talk to them because when he runs out of his control, whatever is out of his control he's going to dump on us and we'd better be forewarned." And that's just what happened. So they were really part of his medical team on the site.

Originally, they intended to take care of their injured people in their own tents, and it was intended that the roads would be opened and they'd be able to move ambulances back and forth and everything would be nice and normal. It would just have been a huge gathering and nothing catastrophic, but you know what happened. The thing got so large that the roads became jammed. The roads became jammed because they could only park on the side and nobody had opened up the fields so they could take them over. And the crowds kept pouring in. They parked their cars and they kept pouring in by foot, and they walked miles and miles. Then, you heard the stories: that they ran out of food, they ran out of water, then health care became an issue, people were hurt, overdosed, like that.

They were able to bring out cots and blankets, and then there was a call for help. So basically the community came together. We were

256

listening to the radio, listening to the press, that here we have this large group of people—two hundred fifty thousand or more gathered here—and they're in need of help. The word got out: Did they need food? Did they need water? Are there people sick? Drug situations? And then we recognized as a hospital we were going to have to deal with it. And then we knew we were going to evacuate them by helicopter.

We had meetings by phone. The administration of the hospital said, "O.K., bring them to the Monticello hospital." So we did it out of human kindness, bringing them to the hospital. But we couldn't land a helicopter on top of the building. So when they started to want to bring helicopters, we had to say, "Stop, you can't do that, you'll shake the building to its very roots and you'll destroy the building." We decided to let them land in the parking lot. So the first one we put in the parking lot. We took the first passenger out, and they said, "There's going be more of them." And then there were bigger things, so we had to go to an evacuation procedure for which, from the conversations I recall, we brought a lot of forces together. It just kind of evolved. Where's there a big landing field? Near the school. The school's clear, it's up on a hill, got a big ball field. It's got a facility in the school. The gym can be set up as the emergency service.

CHARLIE CRIST: Saturday morning, when these kids were doped up real good and boozed up, they started to need emergency help so there was a chopper flying those kids in here to Monticello. They landed in the street just right across, maybe three hundred yards from my house, right out here on what they call Richardson Avenue. That was the first place that they landed. The ambulance corps here then transported them from there up to the school—the Rutherford School—which was probably a mile and a half from where they were landing in the road. Well, eventually, through the police and the firemen and so on, we

worked out an emergency landing spot right by the school. Of course, this was pretty dangerous; there was quite a lot of wires. Volunteers of all kinds came. There were three doctors that came in and volunteered their time, and set up, as I say, this emergency station. And some of these kids were out cold. It was impossible to figure out what the hell was wrong with them other than the fact that the doctors said, "What the hell. It's just dope." They were on drugs, and that's all you could do about it.

GORDON WINARICK: So the helicopters started to come in. By this time, you had guys who were pilots who were out of Vietnam, and this was a piece of cake to them; they knew just what to do and how to do it. And they flew in and landed, and they started to take people out. Of course, we had to make decisions about where to take them. We were the first place; they took them from a landing spot at the festival site to one of the middle schools up on the hill, and there they were triaged by the physicians. They were moved. Depending upon the degree of ailment, they either went into the gymnasium, which was set up like a drug rehab situation; if they were hurt, they went to a hospital—either to Monticello Hospital, to Liberty Hospital, or Kingston Hospital. They had the whole ambulance corps, state police, local police—everything came together. It was an outpouring. Everybody did what was right. I don't even think there was any one commander who was doing the ordering. It was just an evolvement. People felt the need and what they were trained to do they did.

The doctors, on their own, made up this list of who was going to go out to the festival. They each went and spent a couple of hours. They kept going in and out. Some of them, the old-timers, knew the roads—how to get past the routine traffic—and they got out there. Many of them devoted a lot of hours to service. A lot of them had no experience with drugs. Prior to the event they had some seminars on drugs and how to handle them, what to expect from the medical point of view. Some of the doctors on the board made it their business to find out what was happening, what to anticipate, and they told their colleagues.

GLADYS CRIST: The doctors in town took turns on emergency room call-up at the Monticello Hospital. Some of the people went to Hamilton Animal Hospital, which was open at the time. Some of the people were brought into the doctors' offices where I was a nurse. Most of them with cut feet. They were barefoot out there in that mud and stuff and we had a lot of cut feet, bruises, and things like that.

All I can say is that I never saw such feet in my life. People had been going barefoot for I don't know how long and I know this one girl—the doctor, he couldn't get over it—she had calluses on her feet like a shoe has crepe rubber soles. And he asked her if she thought she would ever get a pair of decent ladies shoes on and she said no, she didn't care. She didn't have any shoes. He fixed up the cuts on her feet the best he could. No socks to put on and no shoes. Away she went.

GORDON WINARICK: We had to have all the medication. An interesting sideline, by the way. The medical tent was set up. They needed more medicine than they anticipated, and we gave everything out on open account, and medicine was moving up and down the roads with state police—everybody was cooperating. The cooperation was phenomenal, if a call went out to another hospital—they needed penicillin or this kind of drug—they kept it moving up. We gave everything from the hospital to the festival on open account, and by the end of two years, we got paid, every nickel. But we just did it. You know, we had a decision, "What are we going to do? They're taking thousands and thousands of dollars' worth of drugs." I said, "What can you do? You can't not." So we did it. It was really an inspiring situation when you saw all those people moving out.

• • • •

TOM LAW: The first thing that happened the morning of the festival was that this kid died in my arms. I got a call on the walkie-talkie, "Some kid's been run over by the honey wagon." Some local farmer had just hopped in and hooked his tractor to the honey wagon—where they put all the shit from the Port-O-Sans or whatever other company was there—and rolled over this kid instead of looking to see that he was sleeping underneath the honey wagon. But this young, rather frail, probably sixteen- or seventeen-year-old boy from the Bronx had his last few breaths in my arms while I tried to hold his head and tell him everything was going to be O.K. They took the kid away in an ambulance, but he was already dead. Stupid, totally unnecessary mistake. It was a local farmer who had hooked his tractor up to the thing and just pulled it right over the kid because he hadn't looked and seen some kid sleeping underneath his wheels. It was a real heavy trip.

STANLEY GOLDSTEIN: That was a bloody shame. A tragedy. I wasn't shocked. I was dismayed. I certainly expected that we would face more than one critical situation. There was a very strong probability that someone would die during that event. And that as the size of the crowd grew greater and greater and reached the kind of numbers that it did, that it was inevitable that there were going to be some kinds of serious problems develop. And the thing was, with that particular thing, it was so unnecessary. It was just one of those things. There was nothing anyone could do about it. It was just, "Oh, fuck; oh, shit." It was really an "oh, shit" reaction.

CAROL GREEN: I remember waking up and being told that this kid had been killed, and I never thought that there would be any death. I mean, there were three or four births, and that was fine with me. After having had a kid now, lo these many years later, the idea of going out there in your ninth month is just serious kamikaze stuff. But I was just bereft that someone should die there, and I remember talking to other people from the festival during the day going, "What happened? How could this happen?" and hearing that this was cool. I mean it wasn't cool that somebody died, but the law of averages—we were in good shape, only one person thus far had died. But no one knew who he was. This person was as yet unidentified, the kid in the sleeping bag, and my brother was out there somewhere. So I went on a mission to see if he was all right, and did find some people that thought that he was O.K., but I didn't really find him. So for the rest of the festival, that was kind of over my shoulder.

• • • •

MICHAEL LANG: Abbie Hoffman played a critical role. He was very helpful. He worked a lot with the medical people for a long time and helped with a lot of acid casualties until I think he finally wound up taking too much acid himself and he sort of started to wig out a bit. He probably was very helpful in turning around a lot of energy that could have detracted in some way. I mean, there was such a strong vibe and there was such a positive feeling that it was hard for anything to set off a spark. There were not a lot of those sparks and they were cooled very quickly, because nobody was into it. When you looked around and saw what was going on, it was ridiculous to try and get too negative. But I think he helped in channeling a lot of energies in a positive way after he saw what was going on.

BONNIE JEAN ROMNEY: I remember Abbie in two incidents. One is organizing all the medical teams, where it was just chaos and they had flown in a bunch of people in helicopters and were all just running around. People who had been lifted out of a hospital somewhere and suddenly were in the middle of us hippies. And he sat them all down and said, "O.K., we have a situation here. How many people have experience with this? Go there. This is the Hog Farm. They know about this. Don't be fools, use them." And he organized that whole scene. And at the same time he organized publishing a newspaper so we all could know where to get food, where to get water, how to deal with the shit—I mean physical excrement—that was all being created. And big applause for him. He had an opportunity to get on his soapbox and turn the whole thing into a sort of a political media event, which I think might be some people's impressions of the sort of things he would do. And he very definitely went to work putting his considerable talents and energies into making the physical world work for all of us who were there. And that's one of my strongest memories of Woodstock. I wanted to be sure to say that.

ABBIE HOFFMAN: I immediately knew Friday night that we were going to be in some serious trouble up there. At the crack of dawn Saturday, I was all over the promoters: "I need more access to helicopters." I was with a couple doctors from the Medical Committee for Human Rights. They had worked in the South at the civil rights movement and they were all anti-war. Their center was on the Lower East Side and I said, "We need more doctors. We need more medical supplies. There's going to be many more people up here, with the mud and everything. There's barbed wire all over the place. We're just not prepared to handle any of this." Mostly I was getting polite shove-offs.

Emergency Grips Rock Festival Town

*Sunday Star
Washington, D.C.
August 17, 1969*

I distinctly remember going over to the press tent and cutting it down and taking the tent away and making a hospital—I think it was the second of about five canvas hospitals that we actually did set up. We set up a main hospital area as you faced the stage off to the right. There were huge tent areas and there were fences and we'd have a red cross sign. There was one tent that was drugs-related and the Hog Farm was running that. And there was this other tent with medical doctors, nurses, volunteers and there was no doubt in anyone's mind that I was running that.

It was one of my best organizing moments—you can see I'm not a modest person—but it was. I remember very clearly saying, "You're Doctor Bill, you're Nurse Anne, you're Quartermaster Sue"—you know, giving them names so that people would remember, organizing in terms of a hierarchy so you could know where to go to get things. Printing up the leaflets in terms of medical—many of those I had written in less than two minutes and they were distributed to tens of thousands of people about where to get help, what to do if you were cut, where to get first-aid-kit stuff. So, you know, that's where I was. And I was commandeering helicopters, throwing out—I remember one scene, actually throwing out bottles of champagne that were being flown in for the singers and telling the helicopter guy—he had been a captain in Vietnam—what to do.

I mean, I'm a famous person and I can walk backstage and see the performers. And many of the performers are completely unconscious as to what is going on out there. I mean, they had only been flown in from a fancy suite in a hotel to a launching pad. And they'd go into a place where they had pomegranates, grapes, champagne, foie de gras, etc. It looks like a Southern debutante party in Charleston. And their talk is so trivial and there are guards all around and you can't get at them, and then they're led by their bodyguards onto the stage and they do their number and they're back at the hotel.

So I started throwing out the damn champagne cases and saying, "Look, we need stretchers, we need plasma. What the hell is this?" And

261

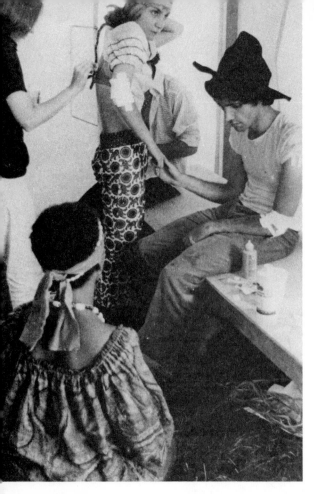

I would go to the organizers and say, "Look, I'm going to tell the goddamned story unless we get helicopters out there." That's the way I negotiate. "I'm going to tell that there are goddamned people needing blood transfusions and you're shipping up grapes and foie de gras and champagne for the goddamned singers. You want this goddamned music played to dead people or what?" You know, I can express myself very well in these kinds of situations. And they understood it and they helped us out. I'm not trying to portray myself as someone who's storming the Bastille, with a saber in each hand, crying, "Give it all free to the people." I'm just trying to prevent disaster from occurring. I'm trying to save lives, I'm trying to not let Rockefeller have his day. Because he's lambasting the casual sex, the drugs—he later passed the harshest drug laws of any state in history. And, of course, he later died in the arms of a woman a third his age, who no one in the family, including his wife Happy, had met until the quiet settlement. That kind of hypocrisy we're blasting all the time.

We had a helicopter shuttle, and on the helicopter would come doctors, cots, plasma, and there would be somebody that says, "Where's Abbie?" And they'd come over with Abbie and they'd say, "Well, here's a list of things we need," or "Here's what we got," or "Here are the volunteers we got." And we used radio station WBAI. We would send down messages: "Anybody that has cots, that has plasma, that has food, bring it over to such and such a drop-off point," and we would bring it up.

There were banks of pay phones and we would have one pay phone where we would have our organizers the only ones in line. It would be used for us. Eventually, after some hours on Saturday, the festival owners gave us walkie-talkies, gave us access to a helicopter, and we were glad. After all, this was now being called a nightmare in the New York *Times*, a state of emergency on the part of the governor.

It was kind of interesting because the people who were flying the helicopters were, of course, National Guard. And they were ready to go to Vietnam, you know; they were military types. And here we were the antithesis, we were the Woodstock Army. But, you know, when it came to things like saving lives and getting out good information about not drinking certain water, you know, all of a sudden the casual sex and the nudity and the drug smokers and the fact that we were against the war didn't matter. So, in a sense, we were all Americans and I can't remember a single moment of friction, even though there was—what can I say? We were in a state of civil war in the country.

When they announced Rockefeller's edict that it was a disaster, I can remember thousands of people just defiantly standing up and—you know, they didn't say, "We will survive," like the Grateful Dead did, but that's what they were saying with their beat, "We are here. We are having a good time. We are Woodstock. This is great. Keep playing." It was a great goddamned party.

· · · ·

TOM LAW: At the Monterey festival I had put up a tepee and used it as a trip center. If people really got too wild, we'd bring them in there and set them down and shove some incense under their nose, and let them sit in front of a fire, and talk to other people who were stoned. That was a method that the Hog Farm developed for working with people that were too wild or too tripped-out on drugs. And it always worked. What it came down to at Woodstock was, as soon as you could get someone's attention, you turn them on to helping someone else out and all of a sudden they became responsible. Five minutes earlier, they'd be peeing in their pants or giggling ecstatically or screaming or something: You get them centered somehow and then tell them that this guy needs them more than their problem and pretty soon he's working with that guy and all their problems turn into mush and they start helping each other out. That was the feeling that we came there to set up. That was security. We were hired to be the security. Security came from inside and the philosophy was to create security within the festival by telling people that they are people, that they're not governed by police.

There were very few bad drugs. There was a lot of LSD and a lot of crazy flip-outs, but they all got calmed down. They all got helped instead of hurt. I mean, LSD is so powerful and it opens you up so much that you need to have a setting that is supportive. And believe it or not, that was a very supportive setting because the mood was set by the environment and the people that put it on, their relationship to each other and how they were going to handle it. We had meetings before about how we would handle it and we talked and I always gave my two-cents' worth as to how people should be relating to each other and what not to do and what to do and the whole philosophy of helping each other out. It was a simple thing that permeated the entire festival.

CHIP MONCK: I was trying to figure a way of explaining—and I probably should have said, "Bring it all here because I want it"—but I was trying to explain about the green acid, that it wasn't specifically good. It was lacking something or it was laced with something else or it had been made in a hurry, and I wanted people to watch out for it. The panic that you can cause by explaining to someone that what they had just taken and they're in the middle of some sort of trip, whatever, is probable poison, can make an unpleasant situation perhaps even more disastrous. So the idea was really to try and say, "If you run across it, I would just suggest bury it under your heel. Those of you that have taken it, have a lovely time." And, of course, you try and ride the gutter between those that have taken it having a nice time and those that have it in their hand who want to take it; how do you stop them from taking it without freaking those who have? So I guess it just ended up, "Well, you know, it's not specifically a good trip but it's your trip, so be my guest." And in its sort of stumblebum fashion, it became rather funny, because I really didn't say anything. It wasn't a warning and it wasn't a suggestion, it was just that "the green acid isn't really specifically—oh, Christ what do I say now?—er . . ." I don't think it's ever going to be lauded as something that's important in public speaking.

WAVY GRAVY: So Chip makes his announcement: "If you have taken the green acid you have just been poisoned. Strychnine. Strychnine." And at Woodstock there were at least fifty different shades of green acid and only one of them had strychnine in it. So all of these people would run up to me. I was standing there at the freak-out tent. And they'd say, "I took some and here's the rest of my green acid." Until I had so much that I was almost falling over. And the Hog Farmers would take it from me because they were convinced it magnetized them to people that were having bum trips. They kept eating it and going off and bringing people back that were having problems.

TOM LAW: The announcement was a real bad idea. I don't think there were any bad drugs. I think there was just too much of it or something like that. I think some folks got caught up in that. That was not an intelligent thing to say to four hundred thousand people. Because then everybody gets paranoid. If there were a few people that had some bad drugs, they were being taken care of by their friends or by somebody else anyway. And if people in the audience couldn't take care of someone's trip, we had set up a couple of hospitals—a main hospital and smaller stations—and we had these areas that we could bring people to. Constantly, there would be just people out of the audience, volunteers or Hog Farmers or somebody, leading people out and taking them over there and cooling them out.

BONNIE JEAN ROMNEY: We weren't scared of drugs. We had all used drugs. We had all used psychedelics, probably several times, probably all of us. And we weren't scared of getting in there with someone. It

was a new thing then and most people who were from the medical world considered these people as dangerous or frightening, or they had no clue to know how to handle it. And I think our wish originally was to keep these people from being sort of preyed upon and brutalized by the insensitive medical community.

WAVY GRAVY: I remember when the first guy came in. I was wearing that cowboy hat that used to belong to Tom Mix and it had a yarmulke inside it that Lenny Bruce gave me, so I could say, "Howdy, *goyim.*" And at the time it had a hole in it that had been eaten by some guy— I don't know, some meth head or something—and I had taken a rubber pig and stuck it through the hole and I had no teeth; it was before my rainbow bridge. And I was supposed to tell these doctors what to do about crazy people.

Festival Chiefs Tell Rocky It's an Emergency

*Sunday Star-Ledger
Newark, N.J.
August 17, 1969*

So there were these five doctors in white coats and shirts and ties and me. And this guy comes in screaming, "Miami Beach, 1944! Joyce! Joyce!" And this three-hundred-pound Australian doctor lays down on top of this guy and says, "Body contact. You need body contact." And the guy is screaming and moaning and going, "Miami Beach, 1944!" And this psychiatrist leans in and says, "Just think of your third eye, man." And the guy is going "Joyce! Joyce!"

So I figured it was time for me to make my move. I said, "Excuse me, I am going to make my move." And they all backed away. "What's this hippie going to do anyway?" And the guy says, "Miami Beach, 1944!" And I said, "What's your name, man?" He says, "Joyce!" I said, "What's your name man?" He says, "1944." I said, "WHAT'S YOUR NAME, MAN?" He says, "Bob!" I said, "Your name is Bob!" And you could just see the Lost Hotels float out of his eyes. I said, "Your name is Bob. Your name is Bob. Your name is Bob." And he is getting it and he's getting it and he's getting it. And when he's got it I say, "Guess what?" He says, "What?" I said, "You took a little acid and it's going to wear off." He says, "Thank God." They don't want to know about third eyes. They just want to know they're going to come down.

And then—which is what made Woodstock unique—when he was near normal and ready to go back and rock 'n' roll, we said, "Hold it. You see that sister coming through the door with her toes in her nose? That was you three hours ago. Now you're the doctor. Take over." And then they'd take turns.

LISA LAW: Your job was to help the next guy who was in the same condition you were in. And that also helped you get to the end of your trip, by helping that next guy. So instead of having all those Thorazined-out people who can't finish their trips—because on Thorazine, you can't finish your trip; you are cut off and it's not helpful to you—you are allowed to finish your trip. And it's rare when you can't come down off a bad trip and go into a good trip with help. I mean, it's a rare person that freaks totally. Basically, you freak because you are not getting help, you're not getting guided; you've found yourself in a situation you're not prepared for.

BONNIE JEAN ROMNEY: The medical community surprised us. As we began handling these people in ways that they considered successful,

265

they began respecting us and working together with us and so the time would actually come when we would say, "This person needs to be given a drug to bring them down." That's very rare because we were dead against it: "Don't give them Thorazine, don't give them this, help them through, treat them this way." They began respecting us and working cooperatively with us with people on bad trips. And we did the same with them. You know, on the street we might have been scared of each other if we passed at a street corner somewhere, but we began to see the value of the people there who were there medically trying to help, and vice versa. It got very nice. And altogether, we created a harmonious, decent place to take care of medical emergencies.

There were a lot of people taking drugs way beyond their capacity to process the information. It became the thing to do. Everybody was taking it. And I don't think these medicines are for everybody. I mean, I am very grateful in my own life for having been given the gift of psychedelics and what it has taught me. I'm really grateful for it. And it's made my life a much greater one than it would have been. But I do not recommend them across the board. I don't recommend them to anyone. It's really a personal decision and I think that it sort of got into a thing where everybody takes acid. And there was a lot of fallout from that. A lot of good experiences and many bad ones.

I remember this one guy who I was with for hours and hours who had driven a car or a motorcycle on which his sweetheart had been killed. And so he took a bunch of LSD and of course was just reliving that crash over and over and over and over and over again, and I thought, "Boy, this is not a good way to use this medicine." I still remember him clearly. There was a lot of that.

Tom Law

Tom Law: I was called in the middle of—this must have been the second day—I got a call that there was some guy hanging from the wires of the bridge going over to the stage, who was nuts. He was way overamped. He must have had some speed and acid and whatever. And I went after him. This bridge was maybe fifteen feet above the road. And this guy was out hanging on these lights that were lighting up the bridge, screaming, "I am something." He was wild. He was completely wild. And I jumped up there and joined him and I peeled him off—I thought he was going to electrocute himself. And I told this guy below me to back the van up underneath us. And the only way I could get this guy out of there was to physically peel him off of these wires. It was all the communications and shit running to the stage and back and a bunch of lights jerry-rigged with wires and stuff, lights going to light the whole area up over to where the performers had their cordoned-off area, where they would get ready to perform. This guy was just up there going completely nuts. And I peeled him off and fell backwards with him in my arms—about an eight-foot drop on top of this van. We must have dented the top of the van a couple of feet. But I got him out of there and then someone took him up to the trip tent.

But I threw my back all out and I went up to the doctors—it was right by the hospital, which was right next to that area—and I went up to this doctor I had been working with before, bringing kids in and dealing with them and stuff. I grew up knowing a lot about chiropractic and when I went around the world I would always get adjusted and pulled and pushed and moved in every country I ever went to so I could learn stuff. So I'm pretty well versed in all that. And I said to this young doctor, "Listen, I just had this event happen and my neck is all fucked up and I want you to grab it and yank it?" He said, "Oh, I couldn't do that." I said, "Listen, just do it, O.K.? Don't worry about it—just do it." And he did exactly what I wanted him to do and sure enough he just yanked my neck out of my—it was like stuck into my—I really screwed myself up badly. And then I had him do a lumbar roll on me. I just told him what to do and this guy just—I wish I knew who he was because he was great. He just took my directions, straightened me right out, and I jumped up and went back into the festival, back to work.

It was one of the great beauties of it, that people were taking care of each other and they'd pay their dues first and then they'd pay their other dues. And it got to be a really quite beautiful scene, just people looking out for each other. And then I got Bobby Neuwirth and Rick Danko and Johnny Sebastian and a whole bunch of people to come down and do a little concert in the tent.

BONNIE JEAN ROMNEY: We were working so hard I just cannot describe. I cannot overemphasize how hard we were working. There was almost no possibility of sleep. I didn't sleep at all. I would lay down for a few minutes in the tent and maybe sleep thirty minutes and then wake up and go at it again. And so we sort of came to be this ongoing turning of massive effort to create a beautiful scene. Interacting with so many people to make it all work. And at one point when John Sebastian started to sing in the freak-out tent, through my exhaustion and tiredness, it was like an angel had visited me. I remember I just began to weep with the beauty of it. I really felt like I had been visited by an angel and I just stopped and I cried. And he sang so beautifully, and so lovingly. And the people who were writhing around and who were in pain, psychic pain, were just soothed. I was refreshed and it was just like a gift from an angel. That was the moment I remember most. I've never told him that. But it really was a transporting moment in a whole two weeks of transporting moments. That's the one I remember most.

STANLEY GOLDSTEIN: I remember seeing, just watching a guy in the crowd freak out as I was walking back down through the area—just jumping and walking through that crowd. I don't know how I saw him from what must have been a thousand yards away. I was walking through the crowd down to the very foot of the stage, where this guy was just jumping. He wouldn't notice me—he was obviously in a bad way—until I started jumping with him. And so we jumped through the crowd as though we were on pogo sticks and cut through the crowd another three, four hundred yards. Jumping the whole way with this nut case on my hands and dancing him over to one of the freak-out tents and going in and spending an hour with him.

There were a lot of people who took a lot of drugs under very strenuous circumstances. And a lot of people were incapable of dealing with that. To my knowledge, no one has ever analyzed or kept any stock of drugs from Woodstock to determine the quality and whether the assumed vast number of freakouts were because of the poor quality of drugs or a combination of other things. And it's assumed as well that there was a vast number of freak-outs, which I don't really think there were. There were no more than six or eight of the supposed freak-out tents, which were relatively small tents scattered throughout the site, and there weren't dozens and dozens of people in these places. There were a few people at a time. Now, if everyone can see twenty people freak out and they've never ever seen anyone freak out before, because there are no walls— it's not behind doors or anything—then you've seen twenty times more freak-outs then you've ever seen in your life, and that seems like a lot.

But the freak-out tents were cool oases of a sort, in which people were reassured by folks that knew the experience and understood it. In general it was a natural kind of reaction and, while these things were things to be concerned about, they were reflections of real-life concerns. But this horrible sensation was going to go away. All it needed was a little time and it was going to go away. This was an area that, if nothing else, took you away from these multitudes and some people feel very diminished in those circumstances.

Wavy Gravy: I remember doing one thing. This guy had swallowed a benzedrine factory and it would take three people in shifts for a couple of days to talk him down. I said, "No, just shoot him up with some injectable Valium." We were avoiding Thorazine because we knew that did not lead to good aftereffects, side effects, that kind of stuff, and can really hurt somebody psychically and physically I think. We used injectable Valium and every time we told the doctors to do it they would. If we wanted to talk them down we talked them down. But only if it was doable. There were lots of people that wanted to talk everyone down and didn't want to give them any of those chemicals. But I looked at it like if you want to spend a day on somebody, great, but we've got a scene to deal with.

Donald Goldmacher: The first or second night I was there, this young man came in very paranoid. Very paranoid. "They" were after him— *everybody* was after him—and somebody had brought him in. And I sort of had to spend half the night with him talking him down. He clearly was on amphetamines and had become quite paranoid and delusional on the drug. He had a knife and he was going to use it if anybody got near him. So we sort of talked him down a little bit and said, "Everybody is safe in here. I want to tell you that. I'm the doctor here and it will be safe in here, and if you need to hold onto the knife it's O.K. for now. But in a while when you're feeling a little more relaxed, I'm going to ask you again to give me the knife so I can feel comfortable." And eventually we got the knife from him and he actually got some sleep finally. I didn't, but he did.

• • • •

JOSEPH COAKLEY: My cousin Jim and I went over to the pink and white tent and decided to volunteer our services in whatever capacity we might be needed. I happened to have a Red Cross card. We were actually motivated a little bit by hunger. There was someone there that was in charge and we just basically said, "Hey, we're here to help, what can we do?" They put us on this truck and, you know, we spent some time hanging around the festival compound.

I remember going over there and talking to this guy and he had this big wide-brimmed hat on and I remember there was something about his teeth—maybe one of his teeth were chipped. The thing I remember most about him—and this turns out to be Wavy Gravy—was he introduced himself and he says, "Hello, I'm Hugh." But the guy was talking like an inch away from my face and it wasn't because there wasn't any space to talk. I think that's just, at the time, maybe how he talked to people, I don't know. But I remember initially it made me uncomfortable and I just kind of challenged, probably, some of my own inhibitions or whatnot. But being there in the hospital compound, what eventually happened was we ended up riding on the back of a U-Haul pickup truck that the festival promoters apparently had rented. We had two cots, we had some guy that was about thirteen years old in the cab with a walkie-talkie, and somebody else that had no idea how to drive a stick shift. Every time we came to a stop or close to a stop, we lurched to a stop. He hit a guy on a motorcycle at one point, not going very fast. At another point he smashed into this guy's relatively new GTO and all these people were shocked, looking at—you know, "My God, look what this guy has done." And the guy in classic New York accent says, "Charge it to Woodstock." And my cousin and I were in the back making ambulance sounds and trying to get people to believe that we were, in fact, involved with a medical type of function, which, you know, driving a U-Haul pickup truck, it's an issue of credibility.

I remember some of the people we brought in, we picked up, were real strange. This lady had passed out somewhere on the other side of the festival and we went and

NO SOAPING SHITTING PISSING SWIMMING ETC. IN THE DRINKING WATER (OR YOU MITE COME DOWN WITH THE →SHITS← TRY FURTHER

picked her up. She appeared to be breathing but appeared to be unconscious or something; she wasn't awake, and we brought her back to the hospital compound and she woke up and apparently, so she says, she passed out because she had to go to the bathroom so bad. Well, she regained consciousness as soon as she got back to this tent area. I remember another guy that had this thing on the side of his cheek the size of a baseball—an abscess, I think—and this guy had been taking whatever people were giving him. He said he had taken fifteen or twenty different pills since Friday night. He seemed really pretty coherent for what he possibly had been taking, but he was definitely having problems and looking for some help.

Tom Law: I think some of the most interesting moments to me were just the types of places that people would go with their minds when they were tripping out and losing it and how easy it was to just throw your arm around them and take them for a walk and say, "What do you need to do this for?" or whatever. I don't know what you said; at those times everything was on automatic. We were so tuned in to what we were trying to do that everyone just performed like masters. Everybody that I knew, and a lot of other people. They just got the idea of having to help other people out. And pretty soon, I bet that just transferred itself to most of the people at the festival, so that most people got the idea that they were trying to help each other out. There was some banter and rhetoric from the stage about it, but it really happened. It didn't really emanate off the stage. It emanated just kind of—it communicated out through the people because that's what they saw happening to them. I felt like I was on acid but I didn't have a drop or a bit of it. Just the energy was so—I couldn't believe it. And that's getting very little sleep and up early and at it and falling out late at night and just constantly running. I was always involved in the problem areas. Whenever there was a problem I would go there and try to deal with it. One thing after another. And then, some moments, we would go and jump into the lake and take a swim and have some fun. But that was like ten minutes and then back to it.

The doctors, believe it or not, were taking orders from us as to how to deal with these psychedelic flip-outs. And they respected what we did because our methods worked. Their methods were to give them Thorazine, which turns them into some sort of animated vegetable state, or deanimated vegetable. And we wouldn't allow it. We said "Forget it, man. Don't do that." And we got our philosophy into the doctors' heads and they started treating people like we were treating people. Somehow it was like we were the professionals; we knew how to deal with these kids because they were our generation and we had been through enough to know what they were going through. So we became the professionals. And everybody else took orders from us. And the orders were just simply, "Don't do anything stupid. Help people out. Minister to them rather than do your trip on them."

Henry Diltz: I made the circuit a number of times—going through the woods and looking in at the Hog Farm and all these different things. At one point, I went up through the acid casualties tent, where there were all kinds of people writhing around on stretchers. The Hog Farm people were talking to them, saying "Hey, man, just let go, and dig it," and trying to be loving to them. That was a wonderful scene, seeing Wavy Gravy and some of these old hands at it, talking to these young kids and saying, "Look, just dig it and relax. Dig the beauty of things." I didn't squat down there and take it all in, but I remember walking through and seeing all this going on. I remember at one point going up there by that tent and seeing a guy standing on his head doing a perfect yoga headstand with his feet straight up in the air, another couple of girls walking by and a guy on a motorcycle coming by, and suddenly it looked like a circus, you know. It looked like Fellini, a totally Fellini scene. And I was probably getting a contact high from all the acid that was around there.

ABBIE HOFFMAN: It looked like five thousand people on bad acid trips coming down the road doing the St. Vitus' Day dance, half-naked, stoned, and they all came in to the trip tents. They got in the farm. And Wavy, he was quick and good. He just said, "Jump on them all, everybody." They have a term for it—I don't know, some kind of happiness hill. And everyone was just in these human piles and the ones that were freaking out and the ones that were giggling were just like mixed up like a whole can of worms. And I'll tell you, it worked. I tell you it was damn good and it worked and no one got hurt and everyone got out of it in one piece. But just seeing that mound of hundreds of people piling in and him being so good and setting a kind of tone that was jovial and "We're having a good time" was exactly right because the wrong vibes, as we used to call it, could have sent that thing into a violent riot like that. Woodstock could have turned into the tragedy that Rockefeller had envisioned so easily. I mean, it could have been five hundred to a thousand dead just from panicking, from bad information or, you know, "Someone's got a knife, run!" And you know, you could have seen thirty thousand people start to stampede up a hill, I mean very bad. Especially in the nighttime.

WAVY GRAVY: There was no question about the fact that—this is going to sound straight out of Shirley MacLaine—but there were energies that as long as we kind of complied with whatever the universe wanted to see go on, that would lift us and move us to amazing levels of proficiency. But the minute we thought that it was us and we were doing it, we would just fall on our ass in the mud. It was very spiritual that way. But I think that we had learned to surrender to that kind of energy and just enjoy the ride. Let's face it: Woodstock was created for wallets. It was designed to make bucks. And then the universe took over and did a little dance. And the fact that some of that dance—I mean, they need human beings to actualize that through. And you could just feel these little tendrils of invisible energies kind of like— I felt at times like a marionette almost. Your arm goes up and, "Did *I* lift my arm? Was that happening from my head?" No. So it was that we were being divinely used somehow. That's spooky.

LISA LAW: Wavy, I will give credit. His philosophy and the philosophy that goes along with the Hog Farm—Babbs and Evan and Foster, all those people—is a certain type of philosophy that is what's going to

Hospitals at Capacity; Area Doctors Alerted

*Times Herald Record
Middletown, N.Y.
August 18, 1969*

271

save anybody in a catastrophe. If you ever hang around Wavy and his people—especially Wavy—he knows how to talk to all ages and calm people down and make people feel like part of the family. And if he hadn't had that philosophy, you wouldn't have seen what went down. So that whole philosophy of "take the path of least resistance" is Wavy's philosophy. That saved Woodstock.

ABBIE HOFFMAN: It was like *M*A*S*H*, when you think about it. We had medically primitive equipment and many, many more people than we could deal with. And the way which people responded, how they volunteered, how they became so professional at this so quickly, was absolutely wonderful, wonderful. It confirmed everything that I felt about people having the capabilities of becoming community, that they didn't always have to look out for number one.

That was, for me, the event. That's what made the event, the sense of community that had just spontaneously erupted and had been felt, and it was something that people had been prepared for for years because they had been reading the underground press. They're listening to the words and the music, they're fighting against a war, they know that there is a "we" and an "us" out there. There was a concept of that, of a "we." There was a concept that when you were at Woodstock, the world was watching and you wanted not just to show them that you were O.K. You wanted to show them that there was some model here, some ideas that could be used to save the planet. Five hundred thousand people, four hundred thousand. It was pretty big. And so there were no murders, there were a couple deaths. There were maybe three or four births, but if you had looked at a city that size for that weekend, the death rate, the stabbing rate, the crime rate, essentially was immensely bigger.

BONNIE JEAN ROMNEY: There was a lot of compassionate, loving behavior going on, brother- and sister-wise. Wavy says, "There is always a little bit of heaven in a disaster area." It elevated the whole place. My vision of Woodstock is that we had a chance to either be in a disaster area or uplevel the whole game. And we chose to uplevel the whole game.

When I think about Woodstock, I think about this great flowing mass of people who all just sort of lifted off the ground together and then looked around and said, "I don't believe this, but isn't it wonderful?" And then it lasted a little while and then things became ordinary and police came in and cars got hauled out and we all went home. But it was really something. It was not nothing. There was a transformation of human beings that took place that was cosmic or spiritual or whatever word one would use for a higher level of interacting with people. There was an awful lot of that going on. And the music was a backdrop. The music was like if I was doing something here in my room and playing music in the background. It would make it just nicer.

Tom Law: On the first day, there was a bunch of political groups there and they all came there to try to make their statements, but they realized—I think they realized with our help, too, because we tried to explain to them—that this wasn't the time for that. It was a time to prove your philosophy, not to talk about it. And if people were resisting the war and wanted peace, well then, act peacefully. And they did.

• CHAPTER FIFTEEN •

"Hmmm, something other than the usual is going on here."
—David Crosby

Aquarian Exposition: Messy, Not Violent

Times Herald Record
Middletown, N.Y.
August 18, 1969

JOHN MORRIS: Saturday was quite possibly the best night because in a way we sort of came up to speed when the sun went down. It's sort of like we were back producing a show. I guess we got to a point where we felt more comfortable. We were in the middle of this disaster situation but we were still on top of it. We were getting the acts in. And maybe we were proving to the press and the outside world that we could do what we were doing. The feeling had pervaded back and forth between the stage and the audience that we were doing something, that this was special, that there was some kind of magic here. I would say that probably gave us the second wind. And the show was good that night. It was a bit easier. And if I remember correctly— you gotta remember too that after twenty years, a lot of it is a blur— I think probably I got some sleep during Saturday.

And then it was Sunday and we were into the home stretch. And that really is what it felt like. It was a cheerfulness. The sun started to come out, which was a lot better. And then all of a sudden it turned into "Uh-oh, they're going to bake out there." It turned into a storm, turned into slogging our way through the night—again, some phenomenal performances—into Monday morning, and it's over. Boy, it's easy to say it. It wasn't so easy to do it.

A guy named Mole read the funnies and the paper on Sunday morning. I had remembered when I was a kid, Mayor La Guardia used to read the funnies—on the radio, there being no television. And my dad was one of La Guardia's aides, among all the other things that he did. Mole was an usher from the Fillmore who was one of the crew who came up. And he looked a lot like a mole in those days. I don't remember his real name. He sat on stage on Sunday morning and read the funnies to everybody. And he sat with the New York papers. He read the headlines about Woodstock to everybody and he did the comics. This was after Wavy announced, "What we have in mind is breakfast in bed for four hundred thousand. It's going to be good food and we're going to get it to you. There's a little bit of heaven in a disaster area."

WAVY GRAVY: When I announced breakfast in bed, we were introducing hippies to granola, really for the first time. But we didn't make it exactly right. I think the oats weren't toasted enough, but still, what we tried to do was go around with Dixie cups full of granola and so that wasn't just some rant that I was running. We were actually going for it.

JOHN MORRIS: The sun came out and we were headed for home. We were trying to get fire hoses out to spray the audience before that storm happened because they were starting to bake on Sunday morning. It was really hot going into the afternoon. It was boiling hot and we were trying to get fire hoses somehow that we could shoot up into the crowd to create a mist and get them wet. We were worried about heat prostration.

And we thought it was going to be O.K. We were casual enough to read the newspapers. I knew that John Roberts was what he said he was, and I was amazed at his strength. I hadn't realized that he hadn't actually made it to the festival. He wanted to come in on Sunday and see it. And we talked about it. I said, "Try, but doing what you're doing there is more important than your coming here. I mean, you got every right to come; this is your party. You're paying for this party. But we need you there." And I know we had a lot of conversations back and forth about that kind of thing, with him encouraging me and me encouraging him. My respect for him was just—I think it helped a lot. And that's not to put Joel down. But it's also to give John a credit that he really, really deserves. It's amazing. It was amazing. And I think on Sunday we probably had a home stretch conversation—you know, "We're going to survive this." I knew all of that stuff because I think we sort of felt we could make it. We could get there. And if it was humanly possible, we relaxed a bit. The sun did come out.

Wavy Gravy

I think the energy ebbed and flowed. The energy between the stage—communicating with that many people over that period of time—it certainly kept me going. Because there was reaction and there was responsibility that was—I understood in my head what I could and couldn't do; I thought I did. And they understood. And you could make it go back and forth.

LEE BLUMER: Sunday, Bert Cohen finally showed up with the program books. I remember the truck coming in. He was physically there but the programs were in a truck stuck in traffic for four days. The programs were on their way, I guess, from Philadelphia in traffic. They thought they were going to sell the program books and they had to give them away. And I remember the truck showing up. It was one of those funny moments that you wish you had a camera at that time. I remember the truck and the Port-O-San guy got there around the same time.

MICHAEL LANG: By Sunday, it became almost a way of life. I mean, suddenly, it was such a strong experience and such an intense experience that it was like that had become your life and your home and your reality. And by Sunday you were almost sort of used to it. You were expecting to see the things you were seeing. I guess your mind adapts to anything after a while. And it was so intense, having lived that for a month.

And Sunday the music was really exciting. It was a high-intensity day and went through the night. It was a long day because we had a

AQUARIAN EXPOSITION

From the
festival program

lot of stops. There were big periods of time when we couldn't do music because of the rain. There was a lot of rain on Sunday.

As soon as the rain started, it became funky and progressively more so, I guess. But Sunday wasn't dramatically different from Saturday in that respect. At least not from my perspective. The stage was basically in the same kind of shape it was in the day before. The crews were all getting a little bit worn. But everybody was able to hold out until the end. I guess Sunday evening people started to leave and that started to alleviate a little of the pressure. Not a lot of it, though.

It just seemed like everything and everyone was coping. At least that's my recollection now; I may have eliminated a lot of the horrors. But it seemed like everybody was coping pretty well. I remember going to the free stage and the campgrounds and the free kitchen and seeing Wavy and those people, and everyone seemed to be holding it together nicely. There were problems with the medical tent, I guess. But it just seemed that in all those situations, everybody coped pretty well.

I remember being constantly surprised that John and Joel didn't show up. I was kind of expecting to see them. I know that they were a little nervous being there. At least, that was the feeling I had. And I'm sure they had their hands full, you know, and having talked to them since, I know that they had a lot to do. I don't remember ever talking to them over the weekend.

Joe Cocker, I think, was the first act that came on Sunday. And he played for an extra forty-five minutes to stall for us.

JOE COCKER: If I can stretch my memory, we were finishing a tour. I had a band called the Grease Band. We were billed as Joe Cocker and the Grease Band most places. We did the Atlanta racetrack that year, and a few really exciting gigs with Hendrix and different players, and Janis Joplin. So we were all getting pretty tired; we'd been out there for about three or four months. We knew something was going on in upstate New York, even though we'd been in Atlanta, which had seventeen thousand people and, at that, we'd never played for such huge crowds. So that night, I remember, none of us slept much. We were all wondering what it was all going to be about.

I remember we flew in the next morning by helicopter and I got the royal treatment. They gave me the bubble kind of helicopter, and the band were all in this military thing. Everyone had just taken LSD so you can imagine. That's one of the things that always sticks in my mind: I was the only guy in the band that didn't drop acid that day and it was like something I think I regretted to some degree, although God knows I might have been too scared to go on there.

It was quite incredible. That's what it was. The helicopter pilot told me, "Joe, wait till you see this," like I'm not going to believe that big a crowd. I know that when I talked to the rest of the band members that a couple of them got sick and threw up outside their helicopter going over the crowd. That can't have been nice for someone under. It was quite a sight. I remember because as we dropped, we ran straight to the stage and we were pretty much on instantly, so there was no time to wonder about or get really awestruck about it.

But my big impression was the stage. I'd seen some well-put-together stages, but that was like a carpenter's dream or something. You felt when you walked up there that you were on something that could stay there forever, that stage. It was a sound piece of workmanship.

We got out there and I think we only did like an hour set, and so I felt we were struggling because I kept looking among the crowds and you'd see everyone was—it was more like a family deal: chatting among themselves and passing sandwiches and all that. I just didn't feel that for this mass of people that I was getting through, until we got towards the end of the set and we did "Let's Go Get

Joe Cocker

Stoned," which sort of got all of them up because most of them were. Got everybody a little interested. When we got into "With a Little Help from My Friends"—as I said, I was feeling pretty badly that day after four months of touring—I just felt as we got towards the end of the tune that, even though it was only for a brief moment, that we'd caught the massive consciousness. I was desperately trying to get through, and it was like I suddenly felt as we got towards the end of that song that— it's not something that you can explain, but it felt that I'd got them to accept what we were doing. It's hard to explain. But it was like a powerful feeling for me.

And then it was shattered when somebody yelled to me. "Joe, look over your shoulder!" I looked and saw massive clouds coming in. I just thought, "Oh dear, had we done this?"

LEE BLUMER: About twelve o'clock I walked out of the office and I found a cloud. It was midday. And I didn't find it, it was there. It was like this big, charcoal gray cloud. And I went back in and I said, "Do you want to see something?" and they all came out and it was like moving towards us. There had been no rain forecast that day and the cloud moved and we called over to the site and they said, "Ooooh." At that point, they hadn't buried all the wires so that there were exposed wires from the stage, the lights, the sound system, and whatnot. And there was immediate concern because this rain was coming quickly and there were a hundred thousand people sitting in this electricity. Then the wind started coming up and the rain was really coming and everybody got really pumped up and they had to do something really

fast and it was like, "Oh my God, oh my God, oh my God," and it started to rain and they still hadn't done anything.

JOHN MORRIS: It was Dante's Inferno. It was all hell breaking loose. It was everything you could ever have possibly wrong at one situation at one given moment. It was there. It was Sunday afternoon. The wind started to pick up. Cocker was knocking them dead. The weather report was not good. You could see the storm rolling in. So it started to build up. It actually qualified as a tornado. We're talking fifty-, sixty-mile-an-hour winds. And the roof, of course, this great structure—the stage canvas was whipping like crazy.

The spotlight towers were guyed but there were not safety chains on the follow spots. And the follow-spot operators weren't going to sit up there and hold the damn things. And the towers were starting to sway. The follow spots, they were Super Troopers, so they weighed two hundred fifty, three hundred pounds. And there were people crowded all around the towers and people climbing up on the towers to see the music better—it just gave you more weight on the top. So you had this pendulum thing that was just insanely dangerous. And you also had nothing in the world you could do about it except try to talk them off the towers. To say, "Look, it's dangerous, come on down." And you can't overdo it. You can't say, "Look, if that thing falls down and kills people it will kill hundreds of people," because then the people underneath are going to panic. One whole thing about being on the mike and being there the entire time was you have to gauge in your mind—and it's true in any kind of crowd situation—not to panic them or spook them, not to talk down to them, not to treat them as "them." To try to make an identification with them and to try to get people to understand.

TOM LAW: The storm just hit like a major country storm. It was not a tornado, but it had that kind of feel to it. And everything shut down and everyone scrambled to cover equipment. There was a billion volts of equipment. You wouldn't believe the humongous amounts of electrical energy on the stage and in those towers. So it was really kind of a "Steady as she goes, Captain. The ship is listing."

JOHN MORRIS: We cleared the stage of electrical equipment. It was raining like crazy, the sound system was on, the mike was shorting into

278

my hand, and it was like *zap, zap, zap.* I had just been told that Baez was having a miscarriage; that my wife Annie, who had a bad ankle from a skiing accident, had fallen down and rebroken the ankle; that my dog Caduggan had disappeared and taken off; and that there was a guy in the audience with a gun. This was all the information that was in my brain at that moment. I knew that I had to try to get people off these towers, and that I also had to try and keep everybody calm and cool, and that I had to get everybody just to ride it out and it would be O.K.

There I was, on the stage with the rain and the whole thing, the mike in the hand, all of this stuff going on. And all of a sudden, down on one knee is this silly guy with a black cowboy hat with a camera aimed up at me. We were the only two on that whole stage. It was Michael Wadleigh. And I never felt so alone in my life.

I also felt in my mind, "You can put this microphone down now and you can go back to your trailer and you can ride this storm out and no one will ever be able to blame you. No one will ever know that you stopped, that you let down, that you were scared." And that's about the time I realized Michael was there. It's as close to a nervous breakdown as I've ever come in my life. And it was as close to wanting to hide or get away or get out of a situation. Of course, I realized the obvious trite thing, which was, "*I'd* know." And I think Wadleigh and I have a very special bond because of that, because he knew it through the lens. He knew what was going on. I think that point has had an awful lot to do for me with the intervening twenty years. The damn problem is that once you tell yourself you have to be tenacious and stand there, you're stuck with it for the rest of your life.

And Annie did not break her ankle, the dog was not lost, Joan Baez was fine. And the guy in the audience with the gun, nobody ever found.

WES POMEROY: I think the most critical decision I made in terms of safety was when we had the lightning storm and thundershower. We were deciding whether to keep going or not keep going. It was raining like hell and there was lightning. The kids were staying in the rain; there was no place else to go anyway. As I recall, it had been hot before that, hadn't it? And the rain felt good in the beginning. But it was lightning and a lot of close lightning, and I was real concerned about whether we ought to keep the thing going—the sound and the lights—because someone might be struck by lightning. And it was my advice to take a chance and go with it.

HENRY DILTZ: I remember all these people were out there getting soaked and kind of loving it. And then some of the crew came onstage with some beers and they were standing there throwing the beer out at the audi-

ence and the guys were catching this beer. Of course, we could only see the first couple of hundred people, faces you could recognize over the day. There was some black guy that was sitting on something. There were some crazy faces out there. Pretty girls. And you'd recognize some of these people—mostly guys with their shirts off and stuff, fists in the air. So here were all these people, you know, catching this beer in the rain. And from up on stage, it was funny watching these guys lob these cans out into this sea of faces.

MIRIAM YASGUR: I just kept thinking, "How on earth are they managing over there?" We were deeply distressed about it. But I was not there and I had no knowledge of what was happening at the field. We just kept right on doing the best we could. At that point, I was getting phone calls from the family, from the city—from all over the country—telling us that they'd been watching this on television and, "Oh, my gosh, what's happening to you!" and so forth. And that was the first I knew that it was on television.

JOHN MORRIS: One of the things that got washed out in the rain was a jam session that I had arranged. Johnny Densmore, who came, even though the Doors weren't there, was going to play a jam with the Grateful Dead and with guys from the Fish and everyone else. And then Barry Melton goes out on stage yelling "No rain, no rain!" with Joe. And then there was Santana with the Coke cans, the kids beating cans on

each other keeping up that kind of energy thing. They filled time, which we were very conscious of. But they were energy sources. It was like they kept rising up to give you the strength to get on to the next thing. But we couldn't put it on. It would have been one of the great jams of all time.

MEL LAWRENCE: I missed the big storm. My girlfriend Rona and I decided to take off and grab a couple of hours of sleep in one of those rooms in the hotel. We grabbed a helicopter, which was like a shuttle helicopter, and there was a courtesy car at the helicopter pad, and it took us to the hotel. And we checked into the room and made love and slept. And then all of a sudden the phone rang and I looked out and it was black, the sky was black. And I knew, like, "Whoa. Something is happening out here." When I came back it was all over except the mud. And I started to see people really groove with the mud. After a while the mud was all part of it, you know, people were playing games with mud. Mud slides, guys like running, running, running—*whoooosh*, sliding on mud. But then it got caked, you know, as it started drying out. It was a problem in cleanup.

RONA ELLIOT: I remember seeing the steam rise off of everyone thinking, "These people are sitting in the mud. This is incredible." You know, just sitting there listening to rock 'n' roll, sitting in the mud, steam rising off their bodies. You couldn't have paid me to be sitting there in the mud. It just would not have been my thing.

LEE BLUMER: It was really one of the Woodstock miracles that no one really got hurt during this storm. This was like a huge summer rain that only happens when you least expect it or want it. There were raindrops as big as golf balls coming out of the sky and it's drenching everything. People were trying to make the rain go away, but it was raining and we were stuck there. We couldn't get back to the site. We were in the building and we were listening back and forth and we were calling back and forth. And all I remember is that everybody was really hysterical.

But the rain obviously only added to the mystique of Woodstock. It just made everybody have to work harder to not freak out and stay together. It was like a common thing to overcome the mud. Now the discomfort was something that added to this whole experience. It was no longer just like laying down in an idyllic pasture and watching the stars. It was like, find a place in the mud to sit. So in an odd way, I think it did contribute. It toughened people up a little bit.

HAROLD PANTEL: The rain caused some scary electrical problems because a lot of the wires were buried under the ground—a foot and a half under the ground—and the amount of foot traffic that was on it just dug them up. They rose up out of the ground. Like you keep plopping on top of it, thousands of people, and the ground was soft to start with, so they came up. And a couple of people, not from the work that we did, but they had run some microphone lines out that

281

gave us some slight shocks. Nobody was hurt at any time, but that got them moving to a degree. People were sitting all over the place, but there were certain areas where you can see where the wires were and nobody was sitting in that area there. These were the lines that went out to the towers for the P.A. system. Some of those wires had come up and we had one line shut off until the people were taken off the area. They reburied the wires and put plywood over the top of it. So that protected that. How the heck we survived, I don't know. But everything was intact. It all held.

CHRIS LANGHART: There were a lot of guitar amp kind of arrangements up there on stage. Spider boxes, with multiple plugs for musical instrument gear. Musical instrument gear at that time, and still is to some extent, very high impedance. Guitars have a lot of swing in the audio range, more so than a microphone. And so the input circuits for guitars are pretty tolerant of wild overloads. They go down from microvolts all the way up to a couple or three volts. And as a result, a guitar amp has the tendency to hum. One of the standard ways of beating that problem was to put a capacitor from the line cord to the chassis of the amplifier. And if you rain all over the stage and water gets everywhere and all these amps are sitting around and their line cords are plugged in this way and that, there gets to be enough leakage current even from 110 volts to make the scaffolding tingle if you're well grounded. The scaffolding was grounded but scaffolding isn't really— it's sort of resistantly connected with little spindles that go between the sections that are sort of rusty. Even though the scaffolding was built solidly from a mechanical standpoint, it's still got rusty places and it

doesn't conduct very well. So if you put a big ground clamp on one place and you have a big hot lead hooked on somewhere else by accident involving all these guitar amps, there's going to be a gray end of distributed voltage from the place where it's hot to the place where it's grounded. So it didn't seem to have much logic to it the way it behaved and I think that's what led them to turning off the lights at the time that they did during the portion of the movie where there's no lighting. I'm not sure that

that was actually necessary, because most of the lighting that was scheduled to be put on the stage never did get put on the stage because the roof structure never got finished and so was not available to hold it up. So it ended up being almost entirely lit with follow spots. But luckily, there were many, many of them and they did a good job. It solved the problem.

So I don't think it was a problem that was extreme. Nobody is going to get electrocuted badly enough in a situation like that. Everybody was being careful and there were a lot of rolls of plastic around. It certainly wasn't what you do if you could avoid it, but there wasn't much avoiding it.

Lee Blumer: On Sunday, I got a call from a Polish guy from the New York *Daily News* who wanted to talk to me about deaths and who died and what was terrible. And at that time I had somehow been elevated. I saw the crowd, and it was a really good feeling. It was really like something had happened. The fact that the rain was over and everything—we had come through this enormous thing. Everybody was much more ebullient and the significance of it started to sink in. So the next thing, I get this call from the *Daily News* and they wanted to know who died. And I was just appalled. I remember feeling, "All the press ever wants to know is who died."

John Morris: And then the rain was over. It was gone, and Cocker only played a short set, probably the most effective of his entire life. Then it was, "Let's do it. Let's go ahead and let's finish it. Let's get it done."

• • • •

Mel Lawrence: Sunday afternoon, I remember I thought that Max Yasgur should go up and say something, and I asked Michael. I said to Michael, you know, "Let's get Max up there." I wouldn't go and say to Max, "O.K., you're going up." I went, "Wouldn't it be good . . . ." He said, "What am I going to say?" but he's already walking to the stage. He wanted to do it. He didn't know what he was going to say but he was already going up there. And he said the perfect thing: "I think you have proven something to the world—that a half a million kids can get together and have three days of fun and music and have nothing *but* fun and music. And I God-bless you for it." So that's the kind of guy he was. Max was beaming, man.

Miriam Yasgur: He went over to see what was happening and I think they prodded him to go up—I don't recall whether he asked to say

Max Yasgur

thank you to the crowd or they asked him to. But he came back and said, "You really can't believe what it looks like from up there," and "They're so nice that I just had to thank them." I never saw that until I saw the movie.

I don't think it was really important. It's just that he wanted to express his thanks. Whether he was up on stage or not was not the issue with him. He wanted to let them know that he appreciated the way they were acting.

Lisa Law: It was an acid trip in itself, even if you weren't on acid. That's what you feel on LSD: the oneness of mankind. And when you can have that experience without taking LSD, you have faith in humanity. And that's what Yasgur said. You can have as many people together and have three days of nothing but love and music and peace. He was knocked out. I was knocked out.

• • • •

Surrealistic Sights Compete With Rock Singers

Times Herald Record
Middletown, N.Y.
August 18, 1969

Henry Diltz: Crosby, Stills, and Nash was great. When they went on, they caught me unawares because they were probably my best friends there at the festival and I was way back of the crowd, way back up on the hill overlooking the thing. The sound was so great up there. It was like you were right onstage. Even better because the field sloped up so the speakers were right straight at you at that point. And it was incredible sound. I remember all the famous lines—"We're scared shitless," and all this—that Stephen Stills said. And then starting their set. I had to make my way down through that whole crowd while they were onstage. I got there towards the end of their set. I took as many pictures as I quickly could. I got there in their last song. I think I got a roll of pictures.

David Crosby: We were just starting our first tour as Crosby, Stills, Nash, and Young. We had played the previous night in the Chicago Auditorium theater, two shows. That was our first show anywhere—ever—with Joni Mitchell opening. Joni wanted to come but was supposed to do "The Dick Cavett Show" the next night or the night after. And by the time we were ready to go here, her manager told her, "Hey, look, you can't go. You might not be able to get back out."

We hired a plane somewhere, probably Long Island, and flew out to where the helicopters were picking people up and taking them out to the site. I don't know where that was. I don't remember much about it. At the time I was high as a kite. We got in the helicopter and flew out to it and by this time I was realizing that it was way more than anybody had realized was going to happen.

We flew in. I think Nash told me that his helicopter lost its tail rudder and auto-rotated down the last twenty feet and scared him to death. I got in easy as pie and slogged through the mud. If there is an overriding impression of Woodstock, it's mud. There was a ton of mud everywhere, all the time. And after that it was a blur. I can remember flashes. I remember a tent. I remember that Christine, my girlfriend, was very unhappy that she had dressed up pretty to come because we were in a field of deep mud and a tent. At one point, I think I went to a motel. They got me to a motel. I'm not sure how they did that because the roads were impassable in all directions all the time.

Part of my haziness about it is due to the fact that this was when I first encountered a kind of pot that I've since come to call Pullover Pot. It was Colombian Gold, little tiny budlets of gold Colombian pot; it still had that fresh-turned dirt furrow smell. But if you smoked it— I remember smoking it for the first time in Florida, and I was driving someplace and I smoked it and I pulled over and listened to the radio for a while because I couldn't remember where I was going. And some friends of mine, a guy named Rocky and another guy named Big John, had brought a bunch of this stuff up and they were just giving it to their

Graham Nash (left),
David Crosby

favorite people. And so I was in a ripe old state wandering around there. A lot of people were on psychedelics. I didn't take psychedelics to play; I couldn't. If you take it and try to play, the guitar gets three feet thick and the strings turn to rubber and it just doesn't work.

I remember images. I remember we didn't just stay backstage. I snuck out and I wandered around; nobody really knew who anybody was. I remember being out at dusk and seeing this state trooper carrying a little girl who had just cut her foot. A pretty little girl. She had stepped on a piece of glass in the mud and he was carrying her back to his car. He carried her back, put her in the seat, got something wrapped around her foot and it was soaked with blood. And I watched about the nearest twenty or thirty hippies push this police car out of the mud. And I thought to myself, "Hmmm, something other than the usual is going on here."

Because there was no animosity. There was a feeling going on with everybody at that point. We felt very encouraged by seeing each other. Everybody was thrilled that there were so many of us. We thought, "Hey, we're going to change everything. We're going to stop the war tomorrow." Well, it didn't work out that way. But at that point we were all thrilled with the idea that our values were triumphant someplace in the world. That, at least for this one small space of time in this one little town in New York, the hippie ethic was the ruling way to do. And it felt great. I can't say that it would have solved all the world's problems if it had spread and taken over everywhere. I don't even know if it would work. But I know that for that weekend for that town in New York, it was great. It felt great. It felt wonderful. There

285

wasn't any of the classic "I don't want to get involved." If somebody had a problem, you tried to help them. If you had a sandwich and somebody was hungry, you'd tear it in half. That was how everybody was doing it right then.

I remember being terrified playing. Stephen said it when we were onstage, but we *were* scared. It wasn't that we were scared of playing in front of that many people because frankly you didn't know it was that many people. It was nighttime when we played, so we could only see the first forty or fifty rows of people. But also, your mind just doesn't count that high. Your mind goes, "One, two, three, many." Imagine for yourself half a million dots. How many is it, what space does it take? We were scared because everybody we thought was cool in the world that played music was standing around behind us in a row, all in a huge semi-circle behind the amps. Everybody. Everybody that we respected in the world was right there—the Dead, Airplane, Hendrix, Sly, Country Joe, and just a ton of people, you know, a ton. We were not intimidated but we knew we were on the line because we were the new boy in town. Everybody else knew how everybody else sounded. The first blush had been worn off of Hendrix lighting his guitar on fire and The Who kicking their drums apart. They had already seen that. I think a lot of it was just that we were so different from everybody else. It was the year of the guitar player. Everybody wanted to be Clapton and Hendrix. And we came along singing three-part harmony and it was just great timing.

Merchants Praise Hippies' Behavior

*Times Herald Record
Middletown, N.Y.
August 18, 1969*

But nobody had seen us get up and try to sing harmony together. This was *it*. This was *the* first time. The only time we'd done it, like I said, was the night before in Chicago. So they all came. Everybody came out of every crack and crevice and cranny and tent and mud hole in the area and they were all standing there on stage. Everybody that had a right to be on that stage under any circumstances at all was on it at the time. If it was going to collapse, that's when it would have collapsed. And, of course, we were nervous.

And we were good, thank God. It went down very well. Oh, they loved it, everybody loved it. How could you not love it? "Suite: Judy Blue Eyes"—what's not to like? They loved it because they're musicians and they knew that this was something new and something good so they all loved it. And the people who were my real close friends—Paul Kantner and Grace Slick, Garcia, and a lot of people—they were all thrilled. They said, "Wow! You tore it up!" It worked.

Since then, because we were in the movie and because everybody knows who we are, I've been asked what Woodstock was like probably more than any other question except, "How did you guys meet?" So I've gotten very tired of talking about it. In general, somebody asked me what was Woodstock like I tell them muddy. But it was, if you want to know, it was a thrill.

• CHAPTER SIXTEEN •

"You can lose your money many times but you can only lose your good name once."
—John Roberts

RONA ELLIOT: There were moments where the event overwhelmed anything the music could say. The morning of the end of the show, and I was up in the operations trailer, I can remember hearing this unbelievable guitar lick. It was like four-thirty in the morning, and I came out to a deserted sea of mud with maybe ten or twenty or thirty thousand people left—a sea of mud which had been turned over because of the rain and smelled from the manure that had been fertilized in the alfalfa. And I mean turned-over mud: you put your foot in it and you went down six inches, eight inches, you know, with the smell of manure wafting up at you at four-thirty in the Catskills. And it was Jimi Hendrix playing "The Star-Spangled Banner." It is burned into my memory. I mean, it was a remarkable experience.

HENRY DILTZ: A lot of the crowd had left. And I was onstage for the first part of the show and I was shooting sort of right next to him, profile. I was looking right across the lip of the stage as he was playing and he had a strange assortment of guys with bandanas. One guy had a bandana over his eyes as he was playing. I thought, "These guys must be weird." They looked like some kind of an Arab nomad or something. I was fascinated by seeing this group of gypsies in these bandanas. Then I went out in the front of the stage and looked up as he played "The Star-Spangled Banner," with all the sound effects and everything. Everything was so still, everything just stopped.

WAVY GRAVY: I couldn't believe it. I said, "God, somebody is taping?" It's funny. At the end of my children's camp, on the last day, the kids are all asleep and we'll just crank that up full blast and lift them about three feet up. I remember when Crosby first played Jimi Hendrix to me. I was walking down Eighth Street in New York and David Crosby comes up with Al Kooper and they stick these headphones on me and they play this thing and say, "What do you think?" I said, "My God, it sounds like a musical version of World War Three."

CHIP MONCK: Hendrix's "Star-Spangled Banner" was exquisite, I was always amazed at that group because there were so few of them, which was always a great pleasure, from a lighting point of view. I was always amazed at Mitch Mitchell and the rest of them, that they were so complete as far as sound goes with so few people, and it was a delight, an absolute delight to hear. It was wonderful because it was also over. It was absolutely brilliant. I thought "The Star-Spangled Banner" was one of his best pieces. I think it was a perfect capper.

TOM LAW: When he did the national anthem on Sunday morning, that was a quintessential piece of art because he hooked us up with

Jimi Hendrix

Vietnam, with the devastation and the sin and the brutality and the insanity of that end of the world. So the festival became a symbol of intelligence and humanity and cooperation and love and affection. It wasn't screwing. I'm sure a lot of people got it off and had their moments, but that's not it. It was just an awesome feeling of all being there together, helping to get through it together, treating each other right—and by God, getting through it—listening to a lot of great music and really experiencing something that was probably a phenomenal change in a lot of people's lives. It really spun them around.

JOHN MORRIS: I heard "The Star-Spangled Banner" from my trailer. It was the first time I actually had a chance to lie down and it was Monday morning. And I had actually put Hendrix on the stage, gone back to the trailer and said, "That's it, baby. I'm going to lay down." And I can tell you that the rented trailer had a plastic cover on the mattress and I was just sweating like crazy. Of course, I was totally exhausted. But I woke up on this mattress, face down on this mattress, out like a light. There was sweat draining down me and what woke me up was hearing "The Star-Spangled Banner." It went right through the exhaustion and woke me up and I lifted up and I looked out and the sun was up and I could see Jimi playing and I could hear it. I thought, "Oh my God, it's over."

CAROL GREEN: We had finally decided to leave and we rolled our bus— we realized our bus had no gasoline in it—and we rolled our bus down the hill to the stage where there was a gas tank, and I'm standing there listening to Jimi Hendrix play and it was glorious. It was sad, though, because there was so much that had gone on—people had died, people had been born, the land was decimated.

HENRY DILTZ: There was a sort of a stillness and it really looked like those old photos you see of old Civil War battlefields, where you see a dead horse and these mounds of things that have been left. And there was Jimi Hendrix up there playing "The Star-Spangled Banner." It was just a moment that was wonderful. It was still ringing in my head as I walked through the place an hour later. I mean, it was like a very strange, eerie close to the whole thing, you know. Because it was suddenly all over and that was kind of a strange haunting ending to it. I just remember those two images together: him playing that song and everything being very still while he played that—a solo thing, just his guitar ringing out in the still morning air in this field; and the field was this sea of mud.

288   I remember after Hendrix played, looking down from the stage,

which was a couple of stories high. I took a picture, as a matter of fact, looking down at Jimi Hendrix in his purple cape, walking away, looking straight down, and this sort of crowd of little people around him. One guy with his hand on his shoulder and a couple of girls, another guy, just a little entourage of people kind of in front and on the sides and all around him as the man walked away.

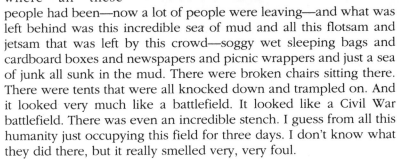

The whole field where all these people had been—now a lot of people were leaving—and what was left behind was this incredible sea of mud and all this flotsam and jetsam that was left by this crowd—soggy wet sleeping bags and cardboard boxes and newspapers and picnic wrappers and just a sea of junk all sunk in the mud. There were broken chairs sitting there. There were tents that were all knocked down and trampled on. And it looked very much like a battlefield. It looked like a Civil War battlefield. There was even an incredible stench. I guess from all this humanity just occupying this field for three days. I don't know what they did there, but it really smelled very, very foul.

ALAN GREEN: I remember Hendrix playing "The Star-Spangled Banner" and looking around and thinking these were the best three days of my life. And I thought, "Well, that's sort of corny," but I knew that I was certain that ten, fifteen, twenty years later, I was going to still believe that and I think I still do, oddly enough. In some ways, I look back and think of it as a substitute of—you know, "What did you do in the war, Daddy?" although my nieces, for example, are not impressed. When I try and talk about Woodstock—they're in college now—they talk about the stupid hippies and how they hate hippies. But I remember clutching this program and putting it in my sleeping bag and thinking, "I'm holding onto this thing." And the tickets, although I was a little embarrassed I bought tickets when I heard it was a free concert and I thought, "Well, I'm the only jerk who bought tickets." But I was certain that this thing I would always remember as a highlight of my life. I'm sure that when I'm eighty years old, I'm still going to look back on it as one of the highlights of my life.

• • • •

JOHN ROBERTS: We left about midnight Sunday night, I think. In one of my conversations with Jack Gillam, who was the bank officer at

National Bank of North America, he impressed upon me that it was imperative that we be at the bank at nine o'clock on Monday morning to meet with the bank, the bank's bankruptcy lawyers, the president of the bank, and any other interested parties, so that we could put the best possible light on what had happened up there and let them know what we were planning to do. Because the bank was very worried, not only about the checks coming in and covering those checks, but about their reputation. It would be very reassuring to them if we could be at the bank the moment it opened, the moment they opened for business.

So Joel and I undertook to get there at nine o'clock the next morning. We figured if we left around midnight we would be back in New York by three or three-thirty. We could get a couple of hours sleep and be there at the bank the next morning, looking presentable. We were there on the dot.

JOEL ROSENMAN: It was like an inquisition round table. They were a very righteous bunch. We had the top brass at the bank and they were upset. And understandably. The event had gotten out of control. Anybody at that table probably read the Monday morning editorial in the *Times* and they could see the name of the bank sooner or later coming into the news articles. They were clearly concerned about the overdraft, which was not your garden-variety overdraft. It was a huge overdraft at this point.

There was one instance that really sticks in my mind. It was a beautiful moment. These bankers had everything on their side. And we had done them wrong. And I think bankers like to be in that position. I guess everybody likes to be in that position sooner or later, although they made us squirm. We had done everything wrong that you can do. We busted a business venture, we'd written a lot of checks that we couldn't cover, we had done something that the *Times* had reviled. And now we were sitting there in front of them and they had us, because we had personally guaranteed all of these overdrafts and the original loan. And at one point, one of them had our file folder and he was waving it and talking to us like an irate dad. At a certain point for punctuation and emphasis he slammed the file down on the table and it fell open and there were our guarantees—and they were unsigned. Just because of a clerical whatever, the entire process had been initiated and brought through to this horrible conclusion without their ever having dotted that "i" and crossed the "t" of getting us to sign the personal guarantee forms. And so essentially, we were not on the hook, as they had all imagined. We could have been scot-free.

And the entire demeanor of that table changed in a flash. Everybody became very solicitous, very concerned—how horrible it must have been for us. And was there anything that they could do at the bank, because they stand behind their customers the way their customers stand behind them. And I remember that within a moment or two John and I looked at each other and there was never a doubt that we would sign them after the fact because we did feel obligated to them. It was just one of those great moments.

John Roberts: Sort of a funny irony. We had gone from a weekend of being the money cats, the capitalists—hip capitalists at best—to being ranked out at the bank the next morning for suddenly being irresponsible hippies throwing this drug fest, not caring about money, spending willy-nilly on dropping flowers on this crowd after they found out there was going to be no gate. "Well, who was going to *pay* for the flowers?" That sort of thing. And we spent a good part of Monday morning trying to figure out exactly how much money we owed, how much debt we had. Because we could add up all the checks we had written and we could make some guesses about what we were going to have to pay to clean the place up and pay the staff for another week or so. We had no idea about the legal bills or the accounting bills or all that kind of thing. We didn't know what was still up in the ticket outlets. And we didn't know what the attorney general was going to make us give back, if anything, to people who had bought tickets and then it became a free festival. So we didn't know where we were.

We huddled with my brother Billy and thought that the right thing to do, the thing that would be really consistent with Woodstock and what we wanted for ourselves in our life, was not to go bankrupt if we possibly could avoid it. And that there was enough money in my trust fund, for one thing, to cover the worst possible scenario, we thought. So at some point in that room—there with the bankers and the bankruptcy people—my brother said, "Well, I've spoken to my brother John and his partner Joel and they have assured me that under no circumstances will Woodstock Ventures declare bankruptcy, and that they intend to honor every last debt and they intend to sign the guarantees. Right now if you like." And that atmosphere went from hostile to supportive to euphoric in the space of about a microsecond. The bankruptcy lawyers got up and said, "I guess you don't need us anymore," and they vanished. And it was the last of any bankruptcy people. And then fortune really smiled on us because it turned out there was about eight hundred thousand or a million dollars lying around in the ticket outlets—that we had sold some tickets the last weekend. Warner Brothers paid us a lot of money for the movie later on and in the fullness of time it all worked itself out and everyone got paid; the bank got paid.

Joel Rosenman: It was wonderful that it did. I personally felt while we were at the bank that morning that—because I felt that way about bankruptcy too, the way John and Billy did—that it just wasn't something you did. These days, of course, it's quite common and not at all a stigma. But in those days, you could pretty much, if you declared bankruptcy, you could pretty much write "The End" to any career in business or finance, or so I thought. And I felt personally that what was stretching ahead of me was a lifetime of paying John back for my half of whatever Billy and he were going to cover with the bank, and I was so relieved when we discovered that we had sold more tickets than we thought and that there was a lot of uncollected money and that Warners was willing to step up and take a chance. Not much of a chance as it turned out, but we were grateful for all of that. I was very relieved.

**Woodstock:
A
Peaceful
Logistic
Impossibility**

*Post
Washington, D.C.
August 18, 1969*

JOHN ROBERTS: I think I said this one memorable line to Al Aronowitz, the music writer for the New York *Post.* He interviewed me after the festival and wanted to know why we had done the things we had done, if we were supposed to be the money men. It was clear we weren't the music men. But if we were supposed to be the business cats, why we had not declared bankruptcy, why we kept writing checks, why we had done all that stuff. And I said, "I had heard from my father that you can lose your money many times but you can only lose your good name once."

MIRIAM YASGUR: John could have walked away at that point, left the whole festival and just left our place to be destroyed and people to be injured or whatever. He did not. He did everything he could to make sure that everyone got paid. He did everything he could to make sure that things would go on smoothly. And after the festival was over, he didn't have to, but Max and he discussed this and Max said, "Look, John, I could sue you. You broke the contract. It's ten thousand people a day, and you broke the contract so I have a lawsuit. But I feel you acted very honorably and I do not want to involve myself in lawsuits. Let's work something out here. Leave my place nice and compensate me for the damage and let's remain friends." And they did negotiate a deal and that's what happened. And John called us every once in a while and when Max died in 1973, he contacted me. He was a real gentleman about the whole thing. I can't speak highly enough of him.

• • • •

CHRIS LANGHART: It was very smart that Sunday the music went all night and carried on and let it happen in the morning so that the motion of everybody happened under daylight and it could be dealt with. You know that they endured through quite a long concert. They weren't exactly hopping around when it was done. They had got poured on, it was muddy, everything was pretty bedraggled. But they were still in good spirits and they just trudged off with the memory. Slowly, over time, it cleared right out and in a day and something it was gone. And we had to try to figure out how to clear it up and clear it out and decide what we were going to pack up and save and what we were going to put away and what we had to do to return Max's property to something like it was. And so we organized getting the office trailers and began collecting all the piping that was over lands and straightening out the

wellheads and trying to get things tidied up. People and other crews came by and collected endless dead, wet blankets and took them all off to I-don't-know-where, and these people came and scavenged all the cars up.

When the moment of truth came and we were near the end, my crew was like one hundred twenty-five, because it had been built up to that extent. As we wound down and had to take the thing apart, we still had a couple weeks of labor. I kept the better ones and we carried on from there. And I ended up paying those people out of my pocket because the office was in a state of disarray after it was over. I mean, those were the people who had helped you through the Battle of the Bulge; you weren't not going to pay them to clean it up. So everybody just kind of had that sort of trust. Later on, John and Joel called me up to New York and they made good on it. I don't know what with. It wasn't that much—a couple or three grand. I never had any word from them that they would pay it, but everybody had done everything up to that point, so why wouldn't they carry on from there?

That's one of the great differences in this era. When people think about doing these jobs today, their first consideration is not "What are we trying to do?" or "What is the spirit of it?" or "What is the goal?" The question is, "How is the money going to work? Can we arrange a business plan? What is going to happen when this happens? What is going to happen when that happens?" And I don't think if it had been approached with that uppermost concern for money at the front that it would have been pulled off with the degree of cooperation it was.

PENNY STALLINGS: There was probably six inches of mud and trash and it was smoking. Smoke was coming up from the ground, almost like the smoking auras of five hundred thousand people. And I've never seen anything, I've never had that experience before, but it was smoke.

And you are talking about half a million people pushed together. When they left suddenly, because I'm sure most of them had to be back—maybe they had their father's car—when they all left, that ground was smoking and it wasn't fog; it was body heat or something.

• • • •

MIRIAM YASGUR: It wasn't only the field. The sides of the roads all the way from one community to another, the side roads, where everybody had camped and gone through. Where were they going to put the trash? There were no containers to put it in. There was no place. It's true, too many people drop trash even if there is a container, but with all these people, one on top of the other, where were they going to put the trash? So, you couldn't fault them completely and there was really a mess—the biggest mess in history probably—and John cleaned up our place and the church, and the community cleaned up the sides of the road. But I don't know that they had to complain about it because there wasn't anything left in the local stores to buy and people had never sold so much before or since, and they certainly made enough money in the community in order to clean up the roads.

The storekeeper in White Lake was so disturbed by this. He was so angry about this whole thing. He couldn't stop raving about it. But if you went in there to buy, not a loaf, but a slice, of bread, he didn't have it. I had never seen shelves as bare as his. There was nothing left in that store to buy, and he certainly didn't lose out by it financially. But his principles were violated. And I just became so angry with his attitude that I closed our mailboxes there and put a box on the road to have our mail delivered. And they would give me a big "Hello" whenever I would see them anywhere, but I would walk away. I don't want to even talk to people who are so two-sided. They were willing to accept money from these people and they sold all the gasoline and all the food. They could have put up signs in the front and said, "Don't come up on my property," and kept all their provisions. They didn't give them away; they sold them and nobody abused them. Nobody stole from them and then they complained afterwards. I don't think that was nice.

LOUIS RATNER: The last thing we worked on was to draw a schematic map of how they could be dispersed. I don't know how many hundred thousand of them were made up and given out on the site to show them, that if they were going out west toward Pennsylvania, for example, how to get out to the other end of the county and out to Pennsylvania. Or if they were going upstate, to go up Route 97. So then you don't have everybody coming down one road. And they disappeared just like they came, in the silence of the night. The next day, it was just like a tornado came in and had blown away.

STANLEY GOLDSTEIN: Many people who were left there had no place to go and no means to get there. Many of them were still dazed days afterward, and folks were still sharing what they had, so there were hundreds still camped in the area. We eventually contracted trucks and ran them back to the city by the truckloads. I stayed up there. I came

Chaotic Aquarius Yields to Peace

Times Herald Record Middletown, N.Y. August 19, 1969

294

out and went back and came out and went back and then I stayed up there for weeks afterwards supervising the cleanup, and a contractor was hired. There were a lot of insurance claims, a lot of unhappy neighbors. So we had to sit there and take claims and collect people's wallets and send them back in packages and try to safeguard their valuables. It was just a slow process, and there was money in escrow to clean the place up, and no one could quite get it together contractually to release the funds, to make the deal, to do it right.

MEL LAWRENCE: There was the job of how we were going to clean up all this shit. We wanted to save all the things that could be washed and given to the Salvation Army. So I got these Boy Scouts to come in. They had many things to do. I mean, they had to pick up all the trash and then they had to separate the trash. At first, bulldozers went and put everything into mounds. They made these big mounds of clothes and sleeping bags. And then we had it trucked, dirty, to the city, where it was dispersed to the Salvation Army and Goodwill and all of this. Then we also had our crew, guys who would stay. I forget how many there were. And people would call up and say, "My fence was broken down by those festival-goers," and we'd have to go and fix the fence. I think Ron Liis was one of the guys who stayed, and a couple of other really great guys; I wish I could remember their names. We got a phone call one time from a church that said that people had really dirtied up the inside of this old barn of a church. And we went in there and it was all these newspapers from like the 1930s, you know. I mean, it had nothing to do with the festival. We were cleaning up the whole county as it turned out, and we'd still be cleaning if we didn't decide to just stop it. People would still be calling up and blaming everything on that festival, you know.

STANLEY GOLDSTEIN: We had our last real staff meeting on the porch of I-don't-remember-where. But I remember Mel and Wes and some of the others and myself talking about cleaning it up. What are we going to do to clean it up? And everyone wanted to get out of there. And most folks doing so. It was a very, very depressed meeting in a way. I think

295

a lot of it was simply exhaustion. People had been working at this for months and months and months against incredible odds, and then we had the weather and none of us, for that period of time, ate decently. For all I've talked about the food service, I may have eaten a couple of spoonfuls of granola on the run and gone over to the kitchen to sample and see what we were doing, but I don't think I ate— maybe I ate some of those famous hard-boiled eggs. I don't recall. But I know that at the end of that, I was fucking hungry. I was tired and I was hungry. And so were all the other guys.

For Wes it had been just a horrible experience in so many ways. His brotherhood had turned their back on him, and not only had they gone mad, broken their word, and not lived up to their code, but the cops that we did hire, all these guys that showed up with all these Mickey Mouse names, really took advantage of the situation. Not all of them—I certainly don't want to imply that it was even most of them necessarily. But there were enough. We had purchased a lot of motorcycles and radios and other things that had all disappeared. The cops stole it all.

And Mel was burned out. He couldn't talk any longer. Everyone was just burned. And trying to sit down and have a meeting or conference of any kind about what to do, particularly at this point—and there not being the availability of any of the supposed leaders, the folks that signed the checks, or commit the organization to doing anything—made it very uncomfortable and probably the least productive in a lot of ways. One that had us really snorting at one another, very civilized, but snorting nevertheless, about what we were going to do and how we were going to go about doing it for the next period of time. And, of course, for most of us, there was no more period of time.

The Hog Farm stayed and worked all day, cleaning up, cleaning up. I had gone back and decided not to stay at the campgrounds that night and checked into a motel. I was sick, for a day. After I checked into the motel that night to get a decent night's sleep, I woke up in the morning really quite ill, shaking and shivering and so forth. I had the runs, probably occasioned by having eaten something, and I drove down to Middletown, New York, and saw a physician in the area. He medicated me and sent me back and I went back to camp, to my tent, on Thursday night.

The Hog Farm, as I recall, then had some negotiations because there were some differences of opinion. The Hog Farm was leaving and there was quite a bit of material there and I wanted to give it to them to take back with them: portable field generators and the cooking pots and the portable burners and the various kitchen implements. Again, the Hog Farm did not make a lot of money on the gig. When it came time for them to go, there were differences of opinion within the organization itself about whether or not the Hog Farm had been stealing; there was a very small group that thought the Hog Farm had been a band of thieves. That was primarily from the stage contingent. And part of it was because in normal rock 'n' roll fashion, of course, the stage crew was trying to maintain the stage in some kind of order and maintain their own kind of discipline, and the Hog Farm arm band was an all-areas pass that went outside of anyone's experience of stage security. And as more and more Hog Farm arm bands became available to more and more people—folks tend to gravitate to stages—there was some conflict there. I'm blowing this somewhat out of proportion because it's the only area that we're addressing. And so there were some ruffled feathers in the stage area.

I spoke to John Roberts on the telephone and said that I thought the Hog Farm had done more than anyone had ever conceived that they would do and that of all the people there who were employees, they had received the least compensation for doing an extraordinary task and doing it extraordinarily well. And that the least we could do was—and I don't think I ever got to finish saying whatever it was I was going to say in that line. John said, "Give them anything they want. Let them take it all."

And then we all went into the Port-O-Sans and dropped our drawers and on a signal, opened the doors, and Kenny Babbs, as the final shot of his Woodstock movie—and I don't know that anyone has

297

ever seen it—panned this line of fifty, sixty, eighty, ninety johns, all with their doors open with everyone standing up with their dorks hanging out. And then the Hog Farm got on the buses and went to the airport to fly home.

And then I stayed on, taking insurance claims and supervising some cleanup crews and getting the bodies back to New York, and closing up some of the facilities and trying to get my petty cash paid, trying to find the rental cars—they were all on my credit card—and trying not to lose my credit.

JOHN MORRIS: Stanley is one of the people about whom one would have to say when it came down—when it was out of proportion and it was reality and it was in our face—Stanley was one of the people who stood up and was counted. And did it. There were a couple of people who really weren't, which is best left alone. But they're in the backs of everybody's memory.

Yasgur, With Few Regrets, Hails Aquarian

Times Herald Record
Middletown, N.Y.
August 19, 1969

MEL LAWRENCE: I remember staying there I think two weeks or something and I remember a couple of meetings over here at the offices on 57th Street, the Woodstock offices. You know something? I can't for the life of me even remember what I did or where I went after that. See, I remember what I did after Monterey, I remember what I did after Miami, but I don't have any recollection about Woodstock. I don't remember like taking up my bags and my car and where I went.

LEE BLUMER: Penny and I stayed for the following week. By Monday morning around ten o'clock, it was like it almost never happened, except there was a *lot* of garbage. I mean a lot of garbage. But it was like the land had been decayed, like the surface of the moon almost. It was like crevices and craters, places where bodies had been. I guess I drove with Wes at one point. We drove around surveying what the damage was and realizing that all that escrow money was going to be eaten. And it was very hard to really figure out what to do. The enormity of cleaning it was there. We kept a number of staff, not all of them. And after this whole anticipation, all this work, the breaking it down—making it go away—was very, very hard to do. There was nothing to motivate it. There was nothing. There was nobody. There was no Michael shining on a horse. He'd gone back. Most everybody had.

One of my jobs was to find the cars. We had leased thirty cars that summer and I couldn't find any of them. None of them. Thirty cars all missing? I think everybody got a car. A souvenir from Woodstock.

PENNY STALLINGS: I was really into my self-righteous mode. If you remember, it was a very self-righteous time. Everybody had their own versions of what they were self-righteous about but in that case I really felt that we had endangered every single person there. I didn't see it as an idyllic, wonderful event. That came to me later, really after the movie. Up until that point I really disapproved wildly of all the guys that were involved and the way they'd handled things.

That was the point at which the Hog Farm people were taking everything that wasn't nailed down. And I really felt that the big guys were—I had not been exactly angry at them, but I was appalled by how close we'd come to a major disaster. For a while, I thought these guys are the lowest. And they weren't. Really, it swept them away too. They had no idea. You had to know if you put that many acts there the entire world was going to try and get to it and the planet would shift on its axis as a result. And anybody who understood what was happening at the time should have known that and either planned accordingly or said, "I'm out of here. I don't want any responsibility for this."

We thought more people had died. Monday morning we were told that there were more bodies out amongst the debris. I was horrified because the kid who was run over was covered with mud and in his sleeping bag, and we were informed that there were more out there, and during the cleanup we would be finding them, that bodies had been spotted. My hair stood on end from that, and I felt responsible to some extent, too, but I very quickly blamed all the big guys instead of myself. And so I was really indignant as only I can be.

John Roberts: I remember that vividly. We were in the offices of the National Bank of North America, Monday morning, where we had been summoned by the bank to give an accounting of this phenomenon. And Jim Mitchell called from the site and said that he had heard— he didn't say he had heard, it turned out he had heard, he didn't know this for a fact—he said, "They are going through mounds of garbage and finding dead bodies." And I felt crushed. I felt utterly crushed by that piece of information and filled with guilt.

Joel Rosenman: It was disgusting. What he actually said was, he said to me, "They are going through the woods and finding bodies." He said this in this deranged voice, like a person who had been on the search parties. So I thought he had firsthand experience; that's why I repeated it to John that way. But it turned out to be an exaggeration. Somebody who was probably high saw a form and they reported it; then later on it turned out to be just a heap of canvas or a sleeping bag that somebody had left behind. But everybody was so stretched thin the morning after the festival; these stories tended to spring up.

• • • •

Wavy Gravy: We were out of there. We left immediately, probably the next day. As soon as it was over, I remember seeing the desolation and the stuff that was left in the mud and being real upset that we weren't going to stay and clean up. But the airplane was chartered. So what came on the airplane had to get back on the airplane. We had some people that stayed behind a good long time and worked to reseed and we tried to get all the sleeping bags dry cleaned and given to homeless people, but we couldn't pull that one off. That was a terrible waste.

The plane ride back was amazing. First of all, my friend Robert Frank got on. And he had a couple hundred hits of green acid. He passes it out and starts filming. At one particular point in the flight, he made me read some strange Greek thing. I was laying on the floor of the aircraft reading from *Mr. Natural Takes a Vacation* over the plane's public address system.

The stewardesses turned over the airplane to us. They locked

Officials Clamor for Aquarian Expo Probe

*Times Herald Record
Middletown, N.Y.
August 19, 1969*

299

themselves in first class or something, as I remember. And the deal was we had to give them the plane back when we got to Albuquerque. Fine. We could live with that. And I remember people putting on stewardess suits and cooking omelets. It was very bizarre. And everything was going on. I mean, it was a very, very high-altitude situation. And like I said, I'm laying on the floor reading over the plane P.A. and this hippie comes up to me and says, "Hey, man, the pilot wants a sitar player in the cockpit because he's bored." And it was then that I thought that somebody actually dosed the pilot. And ran—*ran!*—to the cockpit and got about four inches from the guy, and was looking at his eyes to see if they were pinned. Talk about talking something down—we were at thirty thousand feet. And so I asked the guy what I thought the total question was: "Can I steer?" The guy lifts up his hands off the steering wheel and says, "Sure, son. Fly anywhere you want as long as you fly American." And my brain just shorted out.

BILLY SOZA: The trip back was this amazing flight. There was guys that had never taken any pot, had never even heard of acid, and the Hog Farmers being the way that they were then, they handed out little Kool-Aid glasses and everybody really thought it was Kool-Aid. And it wasn't Kool-Aid; it was laced with LSD. So there's guys who were from Taos who never left the pueblo, looking out the window and calling me over saying, "I didn't know they could show movies outside the window." I said, "Well, they're not. That's you. That's just you seeing that." A couple of guys we had to baby-sit because they didn't really tell us what we were drinking—the guys were thirsty and they were just drinking little shots of Kool-Aid saying, "Give me some more." They had no idea that it was laced with LSD.

And the stewardesses were changing clothes with the Hog Farmer girls and they were acting as stewardesses and the stewardesses were acting as the Hog Farmer women. The pilot put it on automatic pilot. The plane was flying by itself—literally. There was nobody sitting up there in front. The plane was just going on automatic pilot. There were banjos, kids everywhere, diapers everywhere, animals—they had some animals that went along, little dogs and stuff. There was a parrot, I believe, a big green parrot that was flying around the damned plane. And I don't think that they even knew it was on there. There was probably a lot of government regulations that we just blew because nobody anticipated this was going to happen.

WAVY GRAVY: We got back to Llano, New Mexico, and because of the media from Woodstock, Llano looked like a DP camp with a view, you know. It was insane. All these hippies from all over the United States came to live with us forever with all this stuff and we only had a twelve-acre spread. It was silly. So we'd take the spare-change people and aim them back towards the Haight or the East Village. And people that seemed sincere we tried to find communal situations for them, but it wasn't us, babe.

BONNIE JEAN ROMNEY: We were very, very, very poor. And for a long time, we incorporated as many of these people as we could and we had sort of an encampment in our little farm. But finally, because of

300

the sheer smallness of our farm, most of these people went away. A lot of people ended up settling in New Mexico, having come that far. We still have our little farm in New Mexico. Ultimately, we went on the road again. We continued to live on the road for another five or six years after Woodstock. And ultimately, we settled down, many of us here in California; some of us still live in New Mexico. Our family lives together as a communal family and owns things in common. Woodstock was just one of many shared adventures, although a major one.

WAVY GRAVY: The only thing I remember is that after we landed in Albuquerque, we were unloading. We had all these tools that we scored from the tool thing and bags of granola. We distributed granola to all the communes in New Mexico and everybody ate oats—endless oats—for a year, I think, as a result of Woodstock. That was our booty: bags of oatmeal. Thanks a lot, Warner Brothers.

• • • •

MIRIAM YASGUR: The people started to leave and there were a lot of them that had hiked in and they started standing on the road with little signs which might say DETROIT, MICHIGAN, or PARIS, FRANCE, or IDLEWILD AIRPORT. I thought it was very funny. I went out and I looked at this and I laughed. And it worked. Somebody going to Chicago would pick up another guy that was standing with a sign—CHICAGO. Somebody going to New York would pick up the girl who had to make a flight going to France. We had one boy, I will never forget, who was wearing boots and a big hat and he came from somewhere in Texas and he kept coming back to the dairy and wandering around. I don't know how much of the music he heard but he was having a wonderful time, and when it was time to leave he stood out there with a sign— TEXAS—and somebody gave him a ride. I don't know how far down, but he was headed out toward Texas.

The kids wrote so many little thank-you notes. We found thank-you notes on the doors and on the trees. They were left in stores and near homes where other people had helped them and, in fact, the owner of the Monticello diner for many years had framed some of these and had

them on the wall in the diner where the young people had given him thank-you notes for feeding them—you know, bringing food out to them and so forth. The thank-you notes were a lot of fun afterwards; we were finding them all over. Almost every one had the peace symbol drawn on them.

And then we started getting letters and the letters were beautiful. There were so many letters. Some publisher wanted to do a book just of the letters and then before we could really do anything about it, Max died. I didn't want to go on with it. And the letters, many of them, contained peace beads and trinkets, which we gave to young people. I didn't save them.

• • • •

JOHN ROBERTS: Sunday night, we gave a lift when we were in the car going back to New York. The roads had cleared a little bit by then, enough for us to go, and we gave a lift to about four girls. This was an immodest little moment, I suppose, and they said, "You guys were involved in this!" And I said, "Yeah, I was a producer." And they were squealing and carrying on. It was really the one ego-gratifying moment of the entire weekend.

CHAPTER SEVENTEEN

"I wish this were India so that they would have released the fourteen-hour version."
—*Jeanne Field*

JOEL ROSENMAN: Somewhere early on in the festival production phase, most of Artie Kornfeld's duties and areas of responsibility were taken over by other people and Artie's job was to get the film deal. We weren't sure, but we had always hoped we could get a lucrative film deal, maybe even an advance from a major distributor. I don't know what his negotiations were like with any number of different majors, but he must have spoken to all of them at one point or another because he had contacts to do that. But no film deal materialized. I don't think we even got close to one.

In the shuffle, especially in the last three or four weeks, fine details like gates and ticket takers and so forth and movie deals weren't able to push their way to the front of the line the way food or water or portable toilets or transporting the acts or quieting the fears of the local community pushed to the front of the line. In a sense, we all had the funny feeling that having delegated getting a movie deal to Artie probably meant no movie deal, and I was surprised when we actually had a movie deal when the smoke cleared.

ARTIE KORNFELD: The movie was always my baby and they decided that I was crazy and I could never get it together. So they went and they hired agents and they went to William Morris; Joel and John wanted to have all these big agents. And nobody could get a deal.

STANLEY GOLDSTEIN: I had been in touch with Howard Smith of the *Village Voice*. Howard wrote a column called "Scenes" for the *Voice* that was a weekly compendium of what was happening, what was hip and where things were going on. Everything from the fact that there were marijuana delivery services available to that there was an art exhibit here or someone was going to bare their breasts there—and so on and so forth. But Howard was very much in touch with the underground scene. Howard had an interest in film and got me together with the folks who at that time were Cannon Films; Dennis Somebody and somebody else and somebody else. Cannon had just been very, very successful with a film called *Joe* that just poured enormous amounts of money in and it was a hot company at that time and Cannon offered to pay half a million dollars for the rights to participate in Woodstock. They would finance the film in its entirety, and Woodstock Ventures would be coproducers and fifty-fifty profit participants with Cannon in the film. A deal like that, to the best of my knowledge—a deal so good for the producers of an event—has never been offered to anyone else ever at any time. Artie rejected it out of hand because he was going to do better. He had all these things going on, and he was going to do better. And as we well know, he never did any better.

Michael Margettes
(left), Malcolm Hart

ARTIE KORNFELD: Michael Lang had the foresight to have Malcolm and English Mike shoot some prefestival film. Michael had arranged to have cameras up there filming him on his horse and some of the preproduction works. There would be something on record of the preproduction. That footage was in the movie and the guys who shot it never got the credit, and that was Malcolm Hart and Michael Margettes—English Mike and Malcolm Hart. I don't think they ever really did get credit for doing it.

TOM LAW: Michael Margettes was a friend of mine. He's the guy that shot the first part of the movie. He had one leg. One leg had been run over by a bus when he was a kid in England. But he was a fine cinematographer. He's dead now. He shot a lot of that first footage that got used. At one point, we put up a tepee right off the left-hand side of the audience in this little pocket in the woods and a bunch of Indians were trying to put the tepee up and couldn't so they called me in to put it up because I had put up a lot of tepees. And I put the thing up in about fifteen or twenty minutes. Michael was always playing tricks on me because I was this pure yogi and not into drugs or anything at the time and he was a real druggie, so he had a case of cold beer there and after we put the tepee up he shot this shot of me grabbing a cold one. And I'm from Hollywood, right, so I just hammed it up for him and sloshed this big beer down. There's a shot of that in the movie. Just before they get into music, there's a shot.

• • • •

JEANNE FIELD: The first time I heard about Woodstock it was just about the music festival. My boyfriend at the time was Larry Johnson, who was Michael Wadleigh's assistant. I said, "Larry, let's go to this music festival. This sounds great." And so we went to Wadleigh and said, "Wadleigh, don't you wanna go to this music festival? We'll take your VW van and we'll camp out." And he said, "Yeah, let's get tickets." So I bought four tickets for Michael and his wife and Larry and me. And never used them, obviously. I still have those tickets.

JOHN BINDER: Michael and I had a company called Paradigm Films and Bob Maurice was part of that company. He ran the distribution that we were setting up for documentary films. Jeannie Field was working with him. We used people like Marty Scorsese; he worked as an editor for us when he could or when he was available. David Myers, a cameraman from San Francisco, sometimes shot films that we worked on. We were pretty much doing documentary verité stuff with one sound man and one cameraman or two cameramen and one sound man. We shot for public television or what have you. There were several little companies like that in New York. And the same people circulated around town—you know, they were basically cameraman/ sound man teams.

We had done film segments for one of the television shows— Merv Griffin or somebody—and we would go out and do some film shooting and it would be edited as a small piece in the television show. Merv, I think, produced some music specials and so there was James Brown and others, and there was an Aretha Franklin show that Michael filmed with a couple of other cameramen.

We had bought a new KEM, the first KEM—a modern horizontal editing table of a certain kind—that had been brought into America. We bought it and you could hook three pieces of film together, as everybody now does, but it was rather new in those days and there weren't too many of that kind of machine around. And we got used to seeing two and three images of film at the same time because of this new equipment we had bought. So, Wadleigh got the idea of getting us matching projectors with sync motors. We had a screening room with a big white wall that was not the screening wall but the other wall. He got three synchronous projectors and starting showing this extraordinary footage of Aretha Franklin that he had filmed some- where. And it became a kind of popular demonstration. People began to come to the office to look at it.

Meanwhile, Michael had begun to think about doing a rock 'n' roll revival film. He had this urge to do music and he thought this multiple-image thing was the way to do it. As I recall, the Maysles brothers came over to the office one day to see the footage with some other filmmakers and they said, "We're talking to some guys about this Woodstock festival," and as far as I know, Michael knew no more about it than I or anybody else did. They said, "We'd like to shoot the documentary stuff, but I love what you do, so why don't you take charge of the stage, the music filming?" And it started there. At some point, the Maysles brothers couldn't make the deal or whatever, and Michael inherited this film.

I think it was only three weeks before the festival when all this started. As a unit, everybody in our company had just finished shooting the new-car releases for Chevrolet. And so Wadleigh was finishing those, Thelma Schoonmaker was editing them, and I think Marty Scorsese was editing—I'm not sure who was on the job—but I recall Michael telling me that there was some cache of like twenty-four thousand dollars in the bank. That was all the company had. We had just dissolved Paradigm; we had been owned by another company and we had all just resigned and the company was disintegrated. But there was this income of cash from this one unfinished job and they had to finish that and Michael had this money in the bank, undisbursed.

Then they went and tried to sell that idea to other people and Warner Brothers got involved. Michael, with an agent—and perhaps with Bob Maurice; I don't remember—had a series of meetings with various people. And they ended up at Warner Brothers with Wein-

Michael Wadleigh

traub, who was associated with Warners somehow. They were interested, but they never committed. Warner Brothers kept threatening to make a deal with them, but time was wasting and they don't move that fast, so they never did make the deal. Michael took—as I recall, the figure was twenty-four, but it might have been fourteen thousand dollars. They used credit at every place in town, because in those days, you went out and borrowed—got a camera or three or four—and did a job and paid them later. We got all the equipment in New York on credit. All of it, as far as I know. So fourteen thousand dollars bought the first load of film; Eastman doesn't give you film free. And that is how the Woodstock film was made.

JOHN ROBERTS: Michael Wadleigh and Bob Maurice were the guys Artie had fastened upon and Bob put together some money and basically started filming on his own, but before he did that—I guess Artie had said, "See if he could get some money out of my partners." So Bob Maurice called me. It was a Sunday, one or two weeks before the festival. It was terrible, but I decided I didn't want to be where I could be reached at my home; too many people knew the number. So I went to my father's apartment, knowing he was in New Jersey. It was an August Sunday in New York and he had an apartment in town, and I figured I'd hide out there for the afternoon and get things worked out quietly. But I couldn't stand it so I left my number on the service. "If it's really important—I mean really, *really* important—I can be reached at . . ." and I gave the number.

And sure enough, who calls but Bob Maurice. "I know it's Sunday. I don't mean to disturb you, John," he says, "but this is really important. For seventy-five thousand dollars, you can own the movie that we're going to make of Woodstock. We need the money to get going and we'd like to get up and start filming right away." So I said, "Bob, it's very tempting, but I've just been writing checks for the last four weeks for everything, and I'm real low on money, and I don't think documentary movies will make a lot of money for anybody. So"—and I was thinking I was being real clever and real canny—"I'm going to turn this one down. Thank you for the opportunity." So we didn't end up owning the Woodstock movie, which did eighty-three million dollars or whatever worldwide. We owned a little bit of it, because it was our festival.

ARTIE KORNFELD: Two days before the festival, I got in my limousine and went over to where Warners was, which was in the Pan Am Building then. Freddie Weintraub, who owned the Bitter End, was there, and Ted Ashley, who was the agent for the Cowsills, who I had, was now head of Warner Brothers pictures. I just went to them with Paul Marshall. We sat there with pencil and paper and wrote out our movie deal. Fifty percent split, Warners and Woodstock Ventures, after negative costs. Then we had to bring Wadleigh in to make a deal with him to do the direction. And that was the movie deal. It was for a hundred grand for film footage. It was only signed by Ted Ashley and me. I just said to Ted Ashley, "Why don't you dice with a hundred grand?" I said, "If there's a riot and everybody dies, you'll have one of the biggest-selling movies of all time. If it goes the way we hope it will go, you'll have a wonderfully beautiful movie and it will make us all a lot of money, because the festival is not going to make money. It's going to be free." I told him that.

And that was the Woodstock movie. That's how it happened. And then I got in the limousine and went upstate. The limousine broke down and my wife and I wound up hitchhiking up to the festival. We hitched a ride with a commune and we had to walk. We went there the way everybody else did, Linda and I. I'm sort of glad that's how it happened.

JOHN MORRIS: We'd done the deal for the film on the stage in the middle of the afternoon Friday. The festival was on, it was going. Wadleigh and Bob Maurice were out on a limb. They had their eighteen cameramen and the stock and the this and the that. And there was no movie deal. The Maysles brothers hadn't done it, the Cannon deal had fallen through. And there was Freddie Weintraub, who used to run the Bitter End or whatever it was in New York, with his contract to sign to go ahead and to do the thing. And I stood there with Michael while he signed the contract. I think for twenty-five thousand dollars, including the recording rights. It was insane. It was nuts. But they did it; otherwise it wouldn't exist.

JOHN ROBERTS: Unfortunately, Artie had done a somewhat sloppy job and the deal we made with Warners—under that deal we were required to get all kinds of releases and permissions that we simply had not gotten from the artists. So what we had when the weekend was over was all this incredible footage in the can—at least we hoped it was in the can—and Warner Brothers jumping out of their skin with excitement that this had gone from a rock festival to a news event and they couldn't believe their good fortune in having gotten this movie. And then they discovered that they didn't have all the releases they needed from the artists, and there was a lot of homework to be done here. But it turned out, of course, that they didn't care at this point. They wanted to take the whole thing over somehow because this was suddenly big business and we were able to work it out. We were in violation and in breach of our representations to Warners.

So we renegotiated with them. It turned out that Wadleigh and his crew had shot this incredible footage and Warners wanted it desperately and we needed the money, so about six or nine months after the festival—

February, I guess, of 1970—we concluded a deal to sell the bulk of our interest in the movie to Warners and Warners took over all the responsibility for securing the releases with the artists. The movie came out that spring, won an Academy Award, made millions of dollars for Warners and a fair bit of money for us. So that was a happy ending.

• • • •

JOHN BINDER: I got in the car and drove up from Long Island somehow up to Bethel, was stopped by this real dumb farm boy, about six-feet-four state trooper, who had been told to "Stop these hippies." I hardly consider myself a hippie at the time and so the guy abused me a little bit verbally. And finally he said, "What do you think you're doing up here?" And I said, "We're going to make this film." And the word "film" or "movie" suddenly began to melt the guy. He opened the trunk of the car looking for drugs and all this, and Michael and the rest of us were somewhat straight. We really were such hard-working people that we were not hipsters at the time, maybe never were; never became so, either. But anyway, this guy was looking for drugs in my car, opened the trunk, and there was a carton of something in the back and it had some kind of red ink or paint and this big farm-boy cop looked at it and said, "What's that, *blood?*" And he wasn't kidding. So that was the introduction to coming to Woodstock.

DAVID MYERS: I had been a freelance photographer/cameraman for years and in the early sixties, I used to do a lot of N.E.T. specials. They do these good documentaries—one hour, two hour—good budgets. I did a lot of them. And in the course of shooting those I met Wadleigh and Larry Johnson and John Binder. And they were another crew and on some projects there would be two crews. We did a big special on

smoking. I remember, that's where I met them—in San Diego. We worked as a two-camera crew. And we got friendly and we'd meet that way occasionally.

I knew that Wadleigh was shooting in Wyoming on a mountain-climbing film. I happened to be home at the time and I got a call from Wadleigh. And he said that this thing was going to happen and that John Binder, his partner at the time, actually found out about Woodstock. And he talked Michael into it as I understand it—or at least gave him the idea and they decided it was worth a try. So he called people that he knew, good cameramen, and said, "Let's go do it. I can't guarantee any money. If we sell it we'll get paid. If we don't, we'll have a trip." And I said, "O.K." And I went back and met them at White Lake. I met them there like a week before the event and we stayed overnight in a little motel about ten miles away. And in the morning we got up and went to the site. We expected to be back by mid-afternoon or something. And I never got back the whole time. So it was like ten days at the site and I had taken one toothbrush and I had one of these metalized sheets, you know—a space blanket, I think. Otherwise, I was just in a T-shirt.

We got there and I started shooting right away, their preparation. The stage was going up and people were actually starting to come in even then. And so I just started shooting documentary footage and we eventually got six or eight cameramen in and we all got together for about five minutes out behind the stage. The first thing Wadleigh said was, "Well, Dave, you know what to do. I'll see you later." And I said "O.K." and I just walked off. I wasn't even in on the rest of the meeting, whatever meeting they had.

So I did what I felt like doing. I spent the entire time just cruising the whole ten square miles, whatever it was, and shooting documentary. I had a wonderful time. It was really remarkable. I love to interview people and that's what I did. I shot doc. It was incredible. It wasn't just a mass gathering like a crowd in downtown Seoul or something. It was like villages and enclaves and all kinds of people—people like the Hog Farm that were very together, and then there were all kinds of little hippie communes and there were just individuals. It was fascinating.

JOHN BINDER: The two British cameramen, merrily on their way, fortunately were there that whole week and recorded all this construction stuff themselves. I remember feeling overwhelmed when this crowd started to come and I got a little nervous and anxious about the whole thing and about having responsibility for bringing film people up there and all this stuff that turned out to be rather naive because, obviously, you couldn't have responsibility for what was going on there in any overall sense.

But this guy Michael Margettes took me aside, having been up there all week and being much more of a hippie, I think, or in that culture more than I was. He said, "Look, the whole point of this place is that nobody is responsible for anybody else. I think that is what we are all doing here. So don't be silly." I said, "Yeah, but I've got sixty"—or I think we ended up with eighty—"we've got a whole bunch of people up here. What am I going to tell them they are supposed to do?

I mean in the sense of, how do we communicate with what is obviously going to be a gridlock?" And he said, "It doesn't matter because the reason I dropped out of serious filming in England was that I wanted to be spontaneous, and I think the only rule should be: Turn your camera on when you see something you like and turn it off when it no longer interests you." I took that, and that calmed me down personally and I snapped out of my two-hour anxiety or whatever I was having there. Then what I did when Michael asked me to sort of integrate the new cameramen who would show up at various times, I would tell them where we were, what was missing, what they might want to do. I just gave them that speech back. I said, "Just push the button when you see something that is interesting and turn it off when it stops being interesting. But come back and tell the rest of us what you have done so we don't duplicate it too much."

JEANNE FIELD: I had never made a film before. I had been in distribution and advertising for a couple of years, first with Janus Films and then with some other companies. I ended up being a camera assistant for Dick Pierce, who now is a director, and just hung out with him for three days, probably four days, I think, all during the festival. Followed him around, carried his lenses, was his backrest when he couldn't stand anymore, carried his cables, like that. Took some sound during the rainstorm. I mean, basically, you fit in wherever you fit in because it was so rigorous. I was pretty young at the time and so didn't need a lot of sleep. And when we did sleep, we slept under the grip truck, which was parked behind the fence.

DAVID MYERS: Most of our crew slept under the forty-foot trailer that we had but there wasn't any room so I got under—there was like a motor home backstage that was Jimi Hendrix's hangout. And I got under there and I had my space blanket and I had my toothbrush and it would often rain at night. I would stick my toothbrush out and there would be water running down the side of the motor home. I'd stick my toothbrush out and brush my teeth. And listen to Hendrix jiving about seven girls at once at three in the morning upstairs. And that's the way we lived.

JEANNE FIELD: My other job became just talking to this cameraman and this sound man and saying, "What did you get?" and making sure there wasn't too much duplicated. And then I would say, "Well, why don't you go in that direction." Because once you got up to where the Hog Farmers were, or down to the lake, you might not get back for hours. So we just made sure we covered things. And it was that uncentralized a thing. It was also why the guys who came up to assess the thing from Warner Brothers didn't think we would possibly get a film out of this. Because they thought everything had to be directed. In fact, nothing was directed.

JOHN BINDER: When the Woodstock phenomenon became apparent— that we were stuck in there and people had to sleep under the trucks in the mud with their gear—it was only those independent kinds of people who didn't feel at all insecure. They would get up and run four or five rolls of film in one place and make their own little stories. That

310

is what made Woodstock footage better than any footage I've ever seen of these kinds of things. Because the people themselves knew what they were doing on their own.

Marty Scorsese was the music expert and Michael Wadleigh and I, people like us, were pretty much film people and had been busy working for the last several years doing documentaries. Michael Wadleigh was a music fan and all that, but Marty was really pretty much of an expert. There was Eric Blackstead, who was producer of music. They really knew music. And they would say, "Oh, this is the one we want to get," because you couldn't roll through the whole festival with eight cameras. It was a matter of people being able to make selections autonomously without direction.

JEANNE FIELD: Bob Maurice, who was the producer of the movie, became the producer, actually, because John Binder and Michael Wadleigh were breaking up their partnership. Michael kind of was without a producer—he was basically the director on this—and so Bob Maurice worked his way into being the producer. Although he had never produced a film before, he was a smart guy and was big and would talk anybody down. So he got the job. He was smart enough to get Dale Bell in there fairly quickly. He functioned as the associate producer/production manager.

DAVID MYERS: I give Dale Bell a lot of credit. He kept film stock coming in, just flying in by dribs and drabs here and there, on credit. And we were shooting on the old Eastman reversal film, which was quite slow; it was like 25 ASA. So most of the night concert, they were pushing them like two stops. It was hairy, technically.

JOHN BINDER: Dave Myers shot a lot of the really good documentary stuff. Ed Lynch, I remember going out with him when we started it, shot most of the rural stuff of sleeping—whatever that area was called—you know, Bethel and the cattle and the farms and the dew and all that. Well, that was a whole day that Ed and I and somebody else got outside the periphery of the festival and couldn't get back in anyway, so we just went around and shot. I mean, Ed did the actual camera work, but we just went around and shot the barns and all those scenes because we figured there had to be a starting-up scene. I had been there as people arrived before the festival started and knew the way they kind of dribbled in at the beginning. And so we kind of sensed that would probably be the beginning of the show. The other guy, Al Wertheimer, was a cameraman along with David Myers, who I thought shot some of the most amazing of the documentary sequences interviewing people who were participating in the festival.

DAVID MYERS: The shot from the movie that got the most publicity was

311

the Port-O-San man. But that didn't happen by chance. I had been looking for one of these guys for three days. I didn't catch up with him until the last day. I didn't know who they were but I knew I wanted to interview one of them. And I caught up with this guy and he was a very businesslike sort of fatherly figure and just bustling around there and cleaning things up. And I just started talking to him and he just started rapping away right back without any embarrassment or hesitation. And it was quite touching because, as he said, he had one son that was there at Woodstock and the other son was fighting in Vietnam. And he was glad to do something for the kids there. He was a very nice man.

DAVID CROSBY: My favorite two moments out of all of Woodstock were in the movie, oddly enough. They weren't moments that I personally experienced. They were my favorite two people that were at Woodstock. One of them was Max Yasgur and what he said. And the other was my favorite person in the whole thing: the Port-O-San man. Remember the Port-O-San man? The guy who was sucking out the heads with the truck and talking about his son in Vietnam and another one out in the crowd and he was just trying to help out. He was my favorite guy. He was a nice guy. He was a really nice man. If I ever meet that guy, I'd shake his hand and be real proud to know him.

DAVID MYERS: It was just unfortunate that his wife talked him into suing. Actually, he came to the film's opening in New York and he was delighted, all smiles. And then the way I heard the story, he and his wife lived in a subdivision in New Jersey and apparently his wife had told the neighbors that her husband was a sanitary engineer, implying a higher status than the guy who cleans the toilets. And when the film opened in New York and it all came out, she was very upset. And they had two trials, actually. One was without a jury, a trial in Newark, and it was thrown out. And then his lawyer talked him into appealing to the Supreme Court and the Supreme Court heard the case but they didn't pass on it. They sent it back to a district federal court for jury trial. And the jury threw it out.

I was also involved in another lawsuit about Woodstock. It was also toward the end and it would rain, it would be hot and muggy, then a thunderstorm would come over, and then the sun would come out again. This was just repeated. And toward the end, the people were so soaked and hot they just sort of dropped their clothes. People were walking around naked with nothing but a blanket on their shoulders or something. And I was working all alone at that point. I had gone back to change my film magazine and I had a forty-foot trailer truck that was our equipment place. And the rear end was open. I was in there changing magazines and I saw this couple and they looked— something sort of in sync. And I thought, "They're going to make love."

So I slapped the camera on—there was a tripod sitting there— and started shooting them. They were just walking around hand in hand with hundreds of people walking by between me and them—it was like the Red Sea, you know. And they're walking off into this tall grass and they start to get a little far away and I look around for another lens and there happens to be a 25-mm-to-250-mm, a very long lens,

just sitting there. And I just left my camera running and took my lens off and slapped this thing on and tracked them over and never turned it off. And they lay down in the grass and made love. You could see his ass occasionally. Little gestures and humpings. Then they got up again. He had been wearing a hat with a certain kind of brim. And he got up again and he took his hat and turned it around a hundred and eighty degrees. That was the gesture. Then they walked off and then I ran out of film at that point. It was eleven minutes. This guy, it turned out, was a hairdresser in Montreal and he was supposed to be gay; his clientele expected him to play the gay role. And he sued for a million dollars because he claimed this was ruining his business to show him as a heterosexual. And besides, they didn't do it because the girl didn't take her pill that day. Anyway, I couldn't go to that trial. I was going to Samoa, I think. I had like a five-way conversation with a bunch of lawyers and gave a deposition and they knocked that one out, too.

JOHN BINDER: We had amassed an awful lot of equipment and other guys had brought their own cameras, etc., and when the festival was declared a disaster, the insurance was canceled. When you take equipment out of the rental house on your credit, you sign an insurance form and pay a few bucks and when you get your bill you get that insurance bill. If you were to lose that camera or break it, the insurance picks it up. Well, the governor nicely declared—which I think the insurance companies asked for—an emergency. Maybe that was to get the National Guard or somebody to bring some food or whatever they had to bring in. But what it also did to us was cancel our insurance. And so Michael Wadleigh was personally responsible for hundreds of thousands of dollars' worth of equipment. Well, the night that happened, I was walking around backstage. We had a whole bunch of people loading film magazines underneath the stage, a pitful of these. Anybody that was free went over and loaded film magazines for a while just to keep passing them up to the guys filming on the stage. At night, of course, you couldn't shoot documentary film of the gathering; you were shooting just the stage stuff.

I was coming back to check on something behind the stage and I saw Abbie Hoffman in a little circle of about five or six guys. And they were all whispering like an Eastern European Communist cell, you know. They were all whispering about some kind of a conspiracy. It was dark and so I just joined the group and listened. And they were plotting to liberate all this film equipment from Warner Brothers' truck. So they were pretty excited about it and some of them were street kids from the Lower East Side, and they were not the kind to probably be totally logical about. So I went and got a couple of guys. Fred Underhill was another guy on the film crew and a guy named Charles Grossbeck, who was a mountain-climbing expedition leader who was pretty tough, and a plainclothes security guy that we had hired to help watch the equipment. And we went over and waited until these young guys including Abbie Hoffman all jumped in our truck and picked up the most valuable telephoto lenses and stuff and were going to make off with it and then we confronted them and stopped them. And it was very funny to me because Abbie Hoffman was really pretty funny in those days and very bold, of course, and he had a guy with him who was kind of a tough-looking kid and he was a real asshole.

So we tried to talk this over and they said, "No, we're going to steal the equipment from Warner Brothers." I tried to explain the realities of this: it wasn't Warner Brothers' equipment. And this one guy—Abbie was just kind of having fun, I think, more than anything. But the other guy was kind of rough about it, and he and I got a little bit out of sorts. And I was going to hit the guy and Abbie saw it coming and he stepped in front of me and shook a finger in my face and said, "Are you going to be the first guy at Woodstock to throw a punch?" So I didn't know what to do about that. He then calmed the whole thing down, and also the cop and Grossbeck were not going to let these guys out the door anyway without a fight. So, they dropped everything and Abbie Hoffman walked. And then I realized as he walked out the door and walked off into the dark that he had stolen my flashlight.

ABBIE HOFFMAN: The biggest guards were concentrated on one van. It's not where the money was, it's where the cans of film were. That's how they were going to recoup their losses, was through the film. So, I saw all that, and, of course, my aides would point this out all the time; they were political people. They would be very interested when a lot of cops go somewhere. I would point this out to Michael Lang, that the red van was very important. We all agreed it should be protected.

JOHN BINDER: I had a musical moment when it was almost over, which involved Jimi Hendrix, which I thought was for me one of the most powerful moments in music I ever experienced. We had been up by that time many nights, and some of the cameramen had gone for extraordinary lengths of time filming. And I remember going up and working with Wadleigh because I think maybe I had gotten some sleep and come back to the stage. I just remember standing behind Michael when he was filming Hendrix and I think there were only about three cameramen that filmed that piece. Maybe they only used one or two cameras of footage. But what I recall was that people were restless; some were leaving. People were restless, people were leaving, other people were drowsy. Jimi Hendrix and the Band of Gypsies, I guess was the group, were futzing around in a way and they obviously couldn't get in a groove at all. And Jimi would stop it all the time. And it must have gone on for a long time, an hour or more. And the people started to shout for some of the old stuff that he used to do. And he obviously had gotten at that time into his most extreme stuff to date, and he was still obviously hearing it, trying to find it as he played. I had never seen Jimi Hendrix except on footage from that early festival at Monterey. And I thought, "Boy, what an amazing artist that can just hold this crowd off." And every time they got too loud he would go over to the microphone and say something about, "Well, why don't you all go home if you don't want to listen to this. I'm just trying to find something here." And he would speak to that effect. And then at a certain point he stepped on that pedal that he had on the floor and turned around and hit the first couple of notes of "The Star-Spangled Banner."

That was the whole festival for me. That still shakes me up. It was just great. And to be that close to it—I mean, I was six feet away from him as Michael was filming him—that was really great. And it was like it was in reverse. The whole festival then made sense backwards. I think it sort of put that patriotic irony at the end of Woodstock and made it a very different event than it really would have been—defined it differently. Hendrix was saying, "This is the left-handed version of patriotism." And I thought that ended it. And it ended that era, I think, for me.

When everybody got back from Woodstock and the film was back from the lab, there was a horrendous job of synchronizing the footage. Because in those days, they never used what they call slates, or clapsticks, or that stuff. Everyone would just turn their cameras on and off, but they had these continuous rolls of sound to synchronize the picture to. And that became this Herculean effort. I suppose we started with forty editors, night and day, trying to synch up these many hours of film. And when it was finally synched up, it became—I mean, the great version of *Woodstock* was, "Were you there for five days to see all this footage?"—or however many days it was. I remember just dipping in and out of it myself. And, again, there were the same synchronized projectors that Michael had before all this started. So they put all these on the wall. And it looked like a version of what you finally saw in the film, eventually printed on one strip of film. They had just these images lined up—three on the top and three on the bottom; they'd painted the wall with this beaded material that you make screens out of, so they had this gigantic wide-screen version of all the footage of Woodstock. And the people who were then going to edit the film had a hard job to sit there and pick it out.

I remember seeing Crosby, Stills, and Nash come in there to watch their footage. And it was really exciting because they were really extraordinarily energetic and full of optimism. I don't think they had ever seen themselves, by any means, represented this way. And I remember their excitement was extraordinary. I remember sitting around with a bunch of people in another office associated with that production, where there was some other editing going on. And there was a circle of people sitting around—we were kind of telling stories— and we were all, for some reason, looking downward, looking at the floor. And I remember seeing these little red-and-blue boots come in

with the silver stars on them, and it was Joe Cocker. But you recognized him by his boots. So then Joe would go in with the other guys and Michael would show him his footage. And those were really nice moments. I saw some of those.

JEANNE FIELD: I remember the fourteen-hour version, which really was great. It was the one time where they said, "O.K., this is the rough cut." And we sat for fourteen hours. And I think they brought in Fred Weintraub and Arthur Baron—the Warner Brothers representatives—for that. That really was the movie. I wish this were India so that they would have released the fourteen-hour version.

In December, we all came out to L.A. Warner Brothers rented us three houses and we all lived communally. Warner Brothers would not allow a KEM to be brought onto their lot. The editors' local was dead-set against this new technology. And that was fine with everybody, because we didn't want to be on the lot anyhow. Again, it was that independent urge. So we had the *Woodstock* offices at Yucca and Vine, up on the second floor. And we finally did have to interface with Warner Brothers, which became very interesting.

JOHN BINDER: It was Warner Brothers sound department that did the rain sequence. I'm disparaging Warner Brothers for being so different. But it was interesting. The documentary people from the Woodstock side didn't understand. When we talked about sound, we talked about one microphone. But when it came to sweetening a film to make it sound like a feature film, the Woodstock people came up a little short. As I understand it, Larry Johnson had to play Ping-Pong with these guys to kind of break through the distance. Then they got charmed by that. And they came to have the confidence to come back into this bunch of radical-looking people and bring in their traditional experience. And that rainstorm, for instance, wouldn't sound like that if documentary people made it. That was one of the examples of Warner Brothers people, who had the experience to build up those sounds. Those sound effects weren't all recorded at Woodstock.

JEANNE FIELD: It was the *Gone With the Wind* wind. The wind in *Woodstock* was the *Gone With the Wind* wind. To give you an idea of the generation gap that we've got here, George Groves, who was head of the sound department at Warner Brothers, had mixed *The Jazz Singer*. Al Green, his assistant, became head of sound at Warner Brothers. And honest to God, they did love Larry and Michael and Thelma. It was hard put for a couple of weeks there, until we got going on it. But I think they truly came to love working on this film. We had

316

more fun in the mixing rooms there than they'd had in years.

• • • •

ARTIE KORNFELD: I sort of resent the fact that Wadleigh went up and got the Academy Award, because he didn't produce it. He had nothing to do with it until the day of the festival. He just shot someone else's event. And I guess there was resentment. I could never put my name on someone else's song, and I felt he sort of put his name on a song he didn't write. If he would have said "Arranged by Michael Wadleigh," or "Conducted by," then it would have made sense. I feel the four of us produced the movie—Joel, John, Michael Lang, and me. Without a doubt. We did produce it, we did create, we built the set. We raised the money for all the actors, because Joel and John paid for that. And the cameramen took the credit. And I always resented the fact that at the very end in a blurred frame they say, "The Woodstock festival was produced by" and they list the four of us and you can't even see it in the last frame.

JOHN BINDER: I always thought Michael took too much credit. I mean, I thought his five-foot credit on the screen was an insult to a lot of people who worked really hard on the film. As it wasn't directed—as I said, it was a segmented thing where people worked on their own with their own ingenuity and were just experienced enough to coordinate what they were doing with each other, and you got a coherent film out of it—in that sense, I think Michael took too much credit. But I will say something else. I don't think that there was another person around that would have kept the film together. They had horrendous fights with Warner Brothers. Now that we've been out here in the film business for many years, we understand that this is sort of normal behavior for these guys; this is how they do business. But none of us understood that. And I didn't have the nerve to put that film together. Michael did, and Bob Maurice did. I know Michael had a very hard time thinking, "Oh my God, I'm somehow responsible for all this." But he hung in there. And it was his ego. He had an absolutely unbridled ego about some things. And I just don't think that anybody else in that group of eighty people would have had the nerve to be the center of that film. Michael's mistake was he took too much credit for it, as if he had somehow controlled it and directed it. And I don't think that's correct.

I remember when the film was finished and the publicity came out, there was a larger swelling of criticism from the extreme left side of things about, "Well, here goes Warner Brothers, a major corporation, ripping off our movement and the one big glorious moment of our counterculture." And it's true that Warner Brothers naturally reaped the benefit, because that's the business they're in, collecting money from people who watch movies. But I don't think those people really did understand how much that movie was made by every person who went up there because of the fact that it's provable that nobody could direct the moment-to-moment work on that film. The film really did mirror the festival: it was a bunch of individuals who knew how to cooperate. And a very good film came out of it. And there was no such

317

possibility of that kind of a film being made in a centrally directed place, like Warner Brothers' Hollywood.

ABBIE HOFFMAN: I was invited to the premiere of the movie. And of course, when I was asked, I got off one of my favorite American lines: "The book is better than the movie." But I immediately noticed that there was kind of a conscientious effort to take out the politics. I don't mean just scenes of the hospital tents and who was doing it and all that, or that I'm not in it. I mean leaflets and, you know, the more political discussions were removed. And I called up the producer, Weintraub from Warner Brothers. I said, "You know there's a lot that's missing and everything—all the politics that happened. We were trying to stop the war in Vietnam, you know. Just a few little things here and there." And he said, "Abbie, why don't you go up to Berkeley and then take a knife and cut the screen. We'll get a lot of publicity out of that." I said, "Yeah, you're a funny guy, you know?" Because I knew he knew that he had me. I couldn't use my particular talents for attracting attention. It would just make the movie better. So he didn't hang up. He just said, "Hey, we can use you. We'll fly you out."

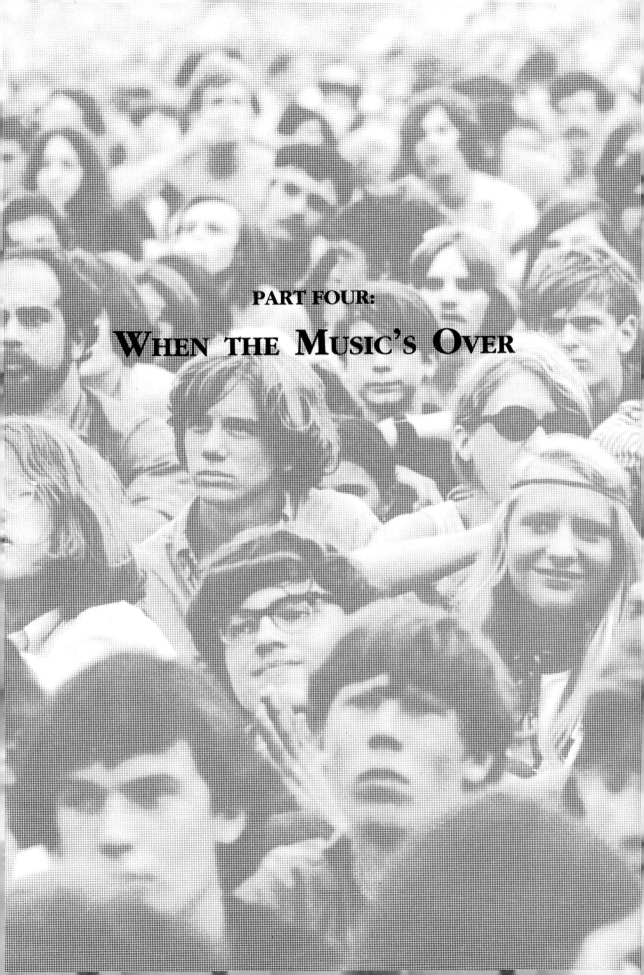

PART FOUR:

WHEN THE MUSIC'S OVER

"It was a hell of a lot better than going out and jerking the teats on a cow, I can tell you that."
—Charlie Crist

ARTIE KORNFELD: If you've never taken any psychedelics and someone gives you a diet pill and it winds up being psilocybin and you are in a position where you are basically responsible for half a million lives, you're seeing the troopers opening up fire, seeing the stage collapse and the bridge behind it, blood. As one of the big trippers from the Hog Farm said, "You absorb the negative vibes." We certainly did and we had to be Thorazined down, Linda and I. And I was walking up hearing Hendrix in the background playing "The Star-Spangled Banner" when Michael said—Michael seemed to always keep giving me the shit jobs—"You go in and talk to the bankers. I'll stay up here."

So, there I was, coming off this trip, waking up from my first Thorazine experience, put on a helicopter and getting off at Wall Street. And walking—full of mud—from the heliport up towards the bank and all these people in suits coming at me. Then going into this banker's office—John and Joel were already there—and the guy had a tank of piranhas, I remember, on his desk and kept feeding them raw meat. Michael said, "I'll stay up here and clean up. You go take care of the money people." Michael had a way of doing that.

MICHAEL LANG: I left Monday afternoon. Artie and John and Joel and Artie Ripp and Albert Grossman and somebody else and somebody else were on Wall Street at the bank in a meeting. I don't know how they all got there, actually. Anyway, they called to have me come down and join them.

This was kind of a dramatic moment for me because one of the helicopter pilots gave me a lift down to Wall Street, and I remember taking off in the helicopter and for the first time getting to see the festival from the sky. I hadn't had the opportunity to take that trip, which I should have done; I'm sure it was pretty amazing with the people there. But it was pretty amazing without the people there. There were people cleaning up and dragging garbage together and there was this huge peace sign made out of garbage; as they were gathering it they were making it.

Flying out of there was I guess the first time I really realized it was over. I must have been a little stunned by that. And it was kind of a culture shock coming into Wall Street. From the front of the stage to the heliport at Wall Street. And I remember there was this intense meeting going on in the bank about all of a sudden everybody buying everybody out. And I don't remember quite why Albert Grossman was there; I think Artie Ripp had brought him in. We were discussing the film. I guess we were discussing the film and Artie Ripp was going to help bring people in—investors or something—to help us out of this problem. The problem being at the time that the gates never existed, so there was a loss, or potential loss, of revenue.

It was odd. We hadn't seen John and Joel all weekend—at least I hadn't. Artie Kornfeld had disappeared sometime on Sunday; I hadn't seen him and now there he was. So suddenly we had Artie Ripp, who was a friend of Artie's and who I had met—but suddenly having these people in and everybody sort of dealing with this thing that just occurred—literally just occurred. It was a very odd feeling. It was a rude awakening, shall we say. And there was all of a sudden all kinds of paranoia—who was trying to do what to who.

Anyway, I left. I remember not much got accomplished in that meeting other than the discussion of trying to figure out what we owed and who we owed it to. And I went back up because we still had cleanup to do—cleanup had just started. So I went back up to get that going. And I remember I stopped off at this motel, which was in the town of White Lake, and at one of the ticket outlets, and picked up about thirty thousand dollars in ticket money. It had suddenly dawned on me that somebody might not have picked it up. So I picked that up and I went upstate for a couple of days. Then I went to see John and Joel at their apartment on the East Side. And it became, "What are we going to do and whose side are you on? Are you going to stick with Artie?" Suddenly, it became sides. The whole character of everything changed dramatically. I guess because we were young and nobody knew how to really handle it. The financial aspect of things as well as the physical aspect of things was so overwhelming that nobody knew how to really handle it. Nobody had a perspective on it.

ARTIE KORNFELD: Michael and I were not looking at it as a financial disaster. I thought it was a big success because I knew the movie was going to make millions—a hundred million. I knew it. I didn't even care at that point because we did it. Of course, I didn't have a million, four hundred thousand dollars in debt, either.

JOHN ROBERTS: Artie Ripp was an executive with Kama Sutra Records, I think, who'd had a religious experience at Woodstock. He spoke in a very deep gravelly voice. It was he and Artie and Michael and Albert Grossman and a couple of other people I didn't know, but from the music end. It occurred to them pretty swiftly that a phenomenon had occurred here and that what we owned might be valuable. And that they could form a little group, the four of them—there may have been a couple of others involved, too—and manage that asset. And that they would do a better job of managing that asset than Joel and I and Michael and Artie, or Joel and I by ourselves. So they came to see us with a proposition that day.

Bad timing. We were spent, in every conceivable way, and battered emotionally, and concerned about a lot of stuff. And the one thing that we weren't concerned about, maybe naively, was how to maximize this thing that we had done. We wanted to put it to rights, somehow, make sure that everything was cleaned up and if there was anything hurt that it was taken care of, all the cleanup stuff. You know, collect the money from the ticket outlets that was still there, deal with the attorney general, start handling the lawsuits, and all the rest of the stuff. And they approached us with this concept. They were very patronizing as I recall: "You're kids. You don't know the music

Another Festival?

Times Herald Record
Middletown, N.Y.
August 20, 1969

322

business. We're the doctors and Woodstock is a sick patient. We can nurse it back to health." I think that's the way Albert Grossman put it. And their proposition was that we give them the Woodstock rights, or whatever we owned, and they would work those rights and maximize the profits on it. And when the profits had succeeded in repaying us whatever money we had put in, that they would own those rights—lock, stock, and barrel. So, for us, it was at best a break-even proposition.

Joel and I were a little put out by that suggestion. First of all, we wanted to know why Michael and Artie had decoupled themselves from John and Joel and suddenly had thrown in with Albert and Artie Ripp. Second of all, we wanted to know why any sane person would want to do that. If these rights were truly valuable, we hardly needed Artie Ripp and Albert Grossman to maximize that value for us. Third of all, we wanted to know why there was no upside built into this. And fourth of all: "Go fuck yourselves." That was sort of the way we responded to them. Almost that rudely.

MICHAEL LANG: I remember Artie and I went to Warners to try and get them to give us an advance so we could resolve the problems that were starting to be generated among the four of us because of the financial situation we were in. Which was basically: John's family had guaranteed the money and it became a burden for them and, as I said, everybody was talking about buying everybody else out. And Artie Ripp and Albert were saying, "Well, if they have no faith in it, we'll find somebody to take them out. We'll give them X number of dollars." There were those kinds of conversations that started to come about. So Kornfeld and I went up to see Warner Brothers and said, "Listen, we're having these big problems with our partners. If you'll give us an advance we can relieve it." They wouldn't hear of it. There was no way. "Who knows what it was going to be worth and it's already costing us four hundred thousand to five hundred thousand." They really didn't want to get involved in it. Apparently, John and Joel's faction at this point had had some conversations. I think John's brother had some conversations with Warner Brothers. And I think they kind of felt they would be able to buy John and Joel out.

They couldn't buy *us* out. We would not have sold our rights to Warners. I think they even asked us and we said no. But I think they had the sense that they could deal that way with John and Joel. So they weren't interested in relieving our problems. It was in their interest to keep it problematic, as it seemed later. And anyway, it was obvious that the four of us were growing further and further apart. I had come into it with Artie so I was going to go out of it with Artie, whether or not I agreed basically on who was right and who was wrong. I don't think any of us were right or wrong. It was just circumstance.

ARTIE KORNFELD: Michael and I and Albert Grossman were raising money, because we knew the movie and the record rights were going to be valuable. And John and Joel had given us X number of days to raise the money and we were supposed to sign a paper. We had raised a million at that point and we needed a million four, and we didn't have the other four hundred thousand. I believe those were the figures; I'm

The Horde Gone But Not Odor

*Times Union
Albany, N.Y.
August 20, 1969*

not sure because I wasn't all there at the time mentally. In a little shock still.

The night we showed up to sign the papers where they were giving us ninety more days to raise the additional money and the rights to the movie—all they wanted was their million four and maybe a percentage of what we'd make—they said, "We're going back on our word and if you don't sell to us tonight then we're going to bankrupt the corporation and we're going to not pay Chip Monck and John Morris and Stan Goldstein and Mel Lawrence. We're not going to pay your people and your name is going to be ruined and you'll never be able to do anything together." And at that point, Michael and I were still friends and we had plans to open a record company and do other concerts. The four of us—there was no way we could get together. Because we didn't want Woodstock toilet paper and we felt that's what they wanted. And it probably wasn't. I guess nobody really took the time to hear what the other was saying. No one trusted anybody and probably we all could have gotten along real well and the movie would have probably been better and it would have been a better feeling all around. We wouldn't have had to live with the bitterness all these years.

I just remember the piranha and the absurdity. I mean, here was the greatest expression of a culture since maybe people got behind Christ to help change the world. And here were these people worried about dollars and cents, not even taking a couple of days to see what happened and evaluate it. And it was just amazing to me the hatred, because here was all this love I had just left and here was all this hatred. Not hatred—I guess that's what those people are trained to do. I guess it wasn't hatred, it was just all they knew how to do, be themselves. So I don't put them down for it; I just didn't understand it. Because I was spaced—I will admit that—and yet I was aware of what had happened.

I told them that it was a total success. And they said, "But it's a million, four hundred thousand in the hole." I said, "By the time the year is out it will be fifty million dollars in profit." I guess they never did quite believe it. They could not understand my description of what had happened and how we were going to get out of it.

JOHN ROBERTS: Michael and Artie decided that if that was the way we were going to be—pigheaded about it—that we could have Woodstock and they wanted to go on to the next thing, whatever that was. God knows they didn't want to be tied down with cleaning things up and handling lawsuits and the rest of that. Michael went off to the Isle of Wight festival and he was never around anymore and we had cross-signature provisions; we couldn't write a check without him. It was really messy. And he was on TV and on the radio and was being interviewed here and there and saying, "Well, we're coming back next year," and all kinds of irresponsible things. And the phones would ring, the Concerned Citizens of White Lake would say, "We'll sue your ass if you come back next year. You're never welcome in White Lake again." I said, "Well, we didn't say that. Michael said that. He's not speaking for us." It was ridiculous and got to be a big headache.

He had us over a barrel really, because we figured we couldn't

Farmers Mull Suit Against Aquarian

Times Herald Record Middletown, N.Y. August 21, 1969

324

go anywhere. He could stymie us. We couldn't correct the deal with Warners, we couldn't make a deal with RCA, we couldn't do any records, we couldn't do anything. We could barely clean the place up without Michael's cooperation. He was more of an unguided missile within the corporation than outside of it. So we gave him thirty-one thousand, seven hundred and fifty dollars, and we gave Artie thirty-one thousand, seven hundred and fifty dollars, for their stock. And they resigned and they agreed never to have anything to do with Woodstock again, never to use the name, the marks—to go away permanently. And they went away and that was really it. And then we just set out putting it right.

ARTIE KORNFELD: I always sort of resented the fact that Michael and I were forced out of our share by Joel and John. And we made the decision willingly—I mean, we willingly signed a piece of paper. They did say they would sell to us and they did go back on their word. And there was a conspiracy, we believe, between Warners and them at the time. Because Warners backed them. But it cracked me up that they actually sold to Warners just to get their money back and very little profit. And that's why Warners wanted Michael and I out, because we would have insisted Woodstock Ventures keep our fifty percent. And we wanted rights to edit.

JOHN ROBERTS: They were pretty resentful for a while. That following spring, they sued us for ten million dollars because they maintained we misrepresented the deals we had with Warners and that we had made millions and millions of dollars.

In 1980, we broke even. That's assuming, of course, that neither of us ever got paid a salary for doing it or interest on any money that we had put up or opportunity costs or any of the other things that, if you are a real grownup businessman, you're supposed to take into account. In terms of actual dollars laid out, the sale by Warners to NBC-TV of the movie resulted in enough money to us, ultimately—I think, forty, fifty thousand dollars—to put us over the top. So it took eleven years to get to an actual break-even point. There was sort of a rough justice in that, that it all worked out financially.

JOEL ROSENMAN: Michael and Artie somehow managed to get a very responsible, even famous, law firm in town to represent them. A senior partner named Ray Gregory called us in to examinations before trial on the theory that—as he had been told by Michael and Artie—John and I had made millions of dollars in a very short period of time wheeling and dealing the Woodstock rights. That, in fact, we had begun these lucrative negotiations even while we were playing dead with them and allowing them to be bought out for a mere thirty-one thousand dollars apiece. And this sort of scam could only be exposed in the courts. They demanded satisfaction to the tune of ten million dollars.

I think this was one of the shortest lawsuits that we ever had to fight, because we sat down and in the first examination before trial, Ray Gregory launched into his questions, designed to pinpoint exactly how many millions we had made so far and how many millions were to

Aquarian Sponsor Denies Rerun Plan

Times Herald Record
Middletown, N.Y.
August 22, 1969

325

come. And he got about to question number three, determined that we had lost a tremendous amount of money and were unlikely to see much in the future. And, in fact, it took more than a decade for some fictional break-even; we really haven't broken even on a realistic basis yet. And he looked at his clients. His clients looked at him. I don't even know if they understood what he had just discovered, but he understood it very well. They asked for a short adjournment. They came back and said, "We have no further questions."

JOHN ROBERTS: I recall offering them my tax returns, Woodstock Ventures tax returns, the certified ones by our accountants. "Please do some discovery on this and stop this nonsense."

Sullivan D.A. 'Quietly' Investigates Aquarian

*Times Herald Record
Middletown, N.Y.
August 22, 1969*

JOEL ROSENMAN: "Spend as many hours as you like," we said to this fellow, who had allowed himself to be retained on a contingency, not on an hourly fee basis. Michael and Artie were not going to pay him for this. *They* knew how truthful it was. Or should I say, how truthful it *wasn't*. But for us, it was a real slap in the face. We were so hurt that our partners—who, to us, had never seemed totally loyal, but still we were partners—were suing us. We had been through an incredible experience together. We were hurt when the festival was over that they had, to our mind, to some interpretations, actually extorted sixty-two thousand, five hundred dollars from us at a time when we were negative a million or two million dollars. I guess what they hoped was they could settle for something.

It's that sort of hard-boiled entertainment business hardball. It's entertainment business hardball, and that's the way you play it. And I guess we had a reputation for being softhearted or softheaded or both, and I guess maybe we were good targets. But it didn't work out for them that time.

ARTIE KORNFELD: I love all three of those guys. We did something that was very special. They are my family in a way. We gave birth to something. Not that we conceived it. I think God conceived it. But we gave birth to it. And so it wasn't until 1988, when I talked to John and he told me the deal they made with Warner Brothers, that I finally felt relieved because I realized that they did not make all these millions of dollars off our idea.

JOHN ROBERTS: We were in considerable trouble after Woodstock, financially. And you could draw a line between August 18, 1969, and everything that went before that, which was the day after the festival, and everything that came after that. And I can tell you there's a handful of people that know what happened after August 18 and thousands who know what happened before. The Penny Stallingses and the Mel Lawrences and the Stanley Goldsteins, and, God knows, the Michael Langs—their knowledge of Woodstock ends as of the final day of the festival, essentially. What went into cleaning it up, and the lawsuits, and the negotiations with Warner Brothers—none of these people know a thing about that. But as far as we're concerned, to a large extent we redeemed ourselves by working our way out of that and we preserved the aura of Woodstock by honoring all of the commitments.

326

You know, there was no trash left on Yasgur's. That didn't happen by accident; it happened because somebody made sure that happened and paid for it. And the deal with Warners was cleaned up. One of the things that happened over the ensuing months was that in order to meet our debts we had to sell the large portion of what we owned of that movie to Warners; they paid us a substantial amount of money for it. We kept a residual percentage, which still pays royalties today, and we used that money to pay off the bank. The bank had funded us a lot of money to cover the million-plus in debts that we had incurred over the course of that weekend. And then the hundreds of thousands in debts we incurred in cleaning it up after it was over and settling with Farmer Brown whose cows didn't give milk for three days, and fighting the owner of Monticello Raceway, who sued us because we blocked his entrance, and that sort of thing—none of which is particularly interesting to anyone, I guess, but ourselves, but all of which went on and had a lot to do with Woodstock.

JOEL ROSENMAN: We only settled one lawsuit, or two at the most, of the many, many we had. The rest either were dropped or we won them outright. One was this farmer's cows that didn't give milk. We settled that for seventy-three dollars. Just about a week before the statute of limitations ran out the town of White Lake filed a lawsuit: Disturbing the peace.

JOHN ROBERTS: They dropped it.

JOEL ROSENMAN: Among other reasons for dropping it was that it was so unattractive. By that time, Woodstock was gaining legend status and I think White Lake was as much enjoying it as they were licking their wounds. Their wounds weren't that bad. By that time, the grass had regrown on that field.

JOHN ROBERTS: I was up there a lot that fall, visiting with Max, visiting with the district attorney—not visiting with him, but seeing him. We became friendly actually. We had a lawyer up there named Richard Gross, who was quite involved settling disputes with the local landholders, most of whom were quite content after it was all over with. We never really heard from any of them in terms of having any problems that I recall. I would guess by mid-late September, you wouldn't even know that anything had happened there. It was amazing; you really wouldn't have known.

MIRIAM YASGUR: Some of my neighbors were very nasty. Many of them were not. After the festival they said, "You know, these people were very nice. We were inundated and we didn't like the garbage and so on, but we had very good experiences with these people. It went better than we thought, and most of them were very nice." As a matter of fact, they gave a testimonial dinner for Max a year later in Bethel. John Roberts came up and somebody had brought *Life* magazines with the pictures of the festival and everybody signed it for Max.

The community made the dinner. A committee decided that they wanted to express their appreciation to Max in order to show him that

White Lake: It's Not the Same Anymore

Herald-News
Passaic, N.J.
August 23, 1969

327

the entire community was not against him, because he felt very badly when people that he knew and had had good relationships with would either be nasty to him or would not talk to him after the festival. And he felt very strongly that he hadn't harmed his neighbors—hadn't meant to harm his neighbors certainly—and he had a strong sense of neighborliness and he felt very badly about this. It really affected him. And so some of his friends in the community, realizing this, spoke to other people in the community and they said, "Why don't we show Max that we appreciate the fact that we all did a lot of business, that nobody was really hurt by this, and that he intended to do a good thing. And let's thank him for it." So they did have this dinner and they were very nice.

JOEL ROSENMAN: They asked John and me to come up and give a testimonial. We were not the only speakers; there were others. So we did. We gave kind of a gentle roast of Max Yasgur. And it was fun to be up there on such a positive occasion and to be invited by these people who had almost been at the other end of a shotgun just a year earlier. It was fun. It was a nice evening. Max was so happy.

MIRIAM YASGUR: Some of the neighbors' wounds never healed. There was a terrible thing that happened that I will never forget and never forgive. I saw this woman about a year ago and she started to say hello to me—we hadn't seen each other for a long time—and I pretended I didn't know her. We were close friends with a particular couple. They knew of Max's physical condition. I believe they did not rent their land, but yet some of the people probably trespassed because they were close enough that people were along the roads and so on. And they felt very strongly about this whole thing. Knowing Max's condition, he was driving along the road one day near their farm and he was alone in the car and he started to feel pain, and he took a nitroglycerin. He stopped the car and he had little oxygen breathers and he started to take the oxygen and he leaned his head against the window and he heard a car coming and he thought, "Oh, good. It's either a neighbor or one of my men. Somebody's going to help me out here." And he opened his eyes and it was this man, who drove by in his truck, looked over, saw Max, knowing that he was not well, and kept right on driving. And that I have never forgiven. And when I have seen them I will not speak with them. They probably don't know why.

ARTHUR VASSMER: Well, the neighbors did not want Woodstock. Clarence Townsend—I shouldn't mention names, but what the heck, he's dead now—he was very bitter. In fact, you saw him in the movie when they asked him what he thought about this thing, Woodstock, and he said, "You know what I think? It's a shitty mess." And they didn't want it. They fought it tooth and nail, the Townsends and Gabriels and so forth—tooth and nail they fought. And yet they were the ones that benefited by it because they were right there. And I don't give a hootenanny—I can't prove it and I don't really give a damn—but they made money. Mister Roberts took care of them. They claimed their property was damaged and this and that. I think he treated them quite well, because it became such a big thing, and he realized it was going

The Woodstock Thing: Was the Music Paramount?

*Evening Star
Washington, D.C.
August 24, 1969*

328

to be big, and I think he took care of them, but I think they made some money. Boy, they were very bitter. I mean they were just bitter. I had one of them come in the store and said, "Well, you got your damn Woodstock. I hope you're happy now." I mean with a real bite. And this was a woman—I don't want to mention any more names—and really, you know, put me down. I didn't go against it. I didn't know what I was getting into any more than they did. The town supervisor, Mister Amatucci, he was taken out of office because of Woodstock. He was a good supervisor, too. And he only lost by about fifty votes, that's how popular he was. And George Neuhaus came in after that and, oh boy, there'd be nothing for Woodstock. They took everything down, took it away and forgot it.

ELIZABETH BROWN: Clarence Townsend was in the movie. He was fixing his truck because it didn't work. And he was cussing those kids every step of the way. And Mrs. Townsend was funny in the movie. She was holding the tools for Clarence, I think. They were madder than heck about it. They, I know, were very strict Catholics. They thought it was absolutely scandalous. To the day Clarence died, they never said a good thing about Woodstock. And of course George Neuhaus made political hay from it. It was an interesting twist there. There was a very competent, nice man named Dan Amatucci who was supervisor at the time. He happened to be a Democrat. The other four members of the board were Republicans, and whether he was for or against the project wouldn't have made any difference. The whole board voted for it. But he paid the price because those four Republican members of the board stayed, but George ran against this nice man Dan, on the Woodstock issue, and of course Dan got routed out of office by George.

The Great Rock Festival: Why Did It Happen?

*Long Island Press
Jamaica, N.Y.
August 24, 1969*

LEON GREENBERG: George made a career of it. He got himself elected on that issue. He incited a lot of people and he had a conservative element over there who just didn't believe that something like this could happen. And they didn't appreciate it. I think most of them were in a state of shock.

CHARLIE CRIST: Max belonged to Rotary Club. I was president of Rotary Club. He and I were good friends. We never lost any friendship over Woodstock. I don't know how many friends he did lose. But again, I'd like to say, that there wouldn't have been a soul in here, not one property owner, that had that kind of a piece of property that would not have done exactly the same as Max Yasgur did. Sure they would. And I'm a good friend of Herman Reinshagen's. And I think that he would have rented his property to them under the conditions that these promoters sold it to Max. The Concord Hotel would have done exactly the same thing, and they own a lot of open land, their golf courses and all the rest. Grossinger's, any of them that would have had the opportunity to make a few bucks. It was a hell of a lot better than going out and jerking the teats on a cow, I can tell you that.

HAROLD PANTEL: The same people for whom it would be controversial today, no matter what you wanted to do, are the same ones at that time. Some people like to see progress and some don't. If you walked past

329

their house they would resent it. After all, they've got theirs and you can't have any. And that's the way they are. Right to this particular day, those people are still obstructionists on different things that go on in the area. They want to put up a little factory, so vociferous individuals get together and they take care of that—knock it out, no matter what they try to do. And it's the same; I suppose it will be forever. Listen, some people are entitled to be a little angry because people trampled over their yards. They defecated wherever nature called, and they took a lot of liberties.

CHARLIE CRIST: I give a tremendous amount of credit to the local people. They opened their hearts and their houses and the diners, the churches, the church halls, the community centers—everything was opened up to these people. And they literally helped these people off of the street. Some of them were almost naked, young men and women both. And it was just really a disaster just completely waiting to happen. And how it didn't, nobody will ever really be able to tell because they were jammed in there like bees in a swarm. I don't know whether you've ever seen a swarm of bees hanging from a tree. Well, this is just about the way it was with these kids out there, laying around in this mud and rain. They were just shoulder to shoulder, sex going on in the open, drinking—and of course, the drugs. But the people that lived in the area were blocked in and realized that they had a serious problem and they didn't attempt to move. They just said, "To hell with it."

It gave Sullivan County a hell of a lot of publicity. You couldn't have bought the publicity that Sullivan County got over that thing. And they still are getting publicity as a result of Woodstock because now they're talking about a reunion and all the rest of it. I think that Sullivan County got nationwide and probably worldwide publicity as the result of it. And I have no way of proving it, but I still think that some of those kids that are now adults come back here occasionally just to drive around and see what it was that they went through and where it was that this all happened. Four or five years ago, we sat up here in the diner. Three of four of us were sitting up there talking as we do quite often. There were some people that came in there and they asked where this Woodstock site was. And we said, "Well, how come?" And they said they had been there and they just wanted to go back and take a look.

BARON WOLMAN: I went back the year afterward to photograph the site to see whether, you know, the grounds had reclaimed themselves, and there was still a little bit of a structure left. But there was a cornfield where the crowds had been. It was real interesting to stand at the same site and take a picture of the cornfields the way they were before Woodstock and after Woodstock. There was no sign except there was one kind of the framework, the log framework of one of the buildings. It wasn't the stage, it was the performers' pavilion. I don't know if it's still there.

One interesting thing happened to me. At Woodstock, I had photographed—I was just walking around because I was fascinated with the crowd and the people and the grounds and stuff, and there was a little girl dressed in a little white pinafore. She was so out of place

Family Puts Up $1 Million to Cover Woodstock Debts

*Evening Star
Washington, D.C.
August 25, 1969*

330

visually that I just started taking pictures of her. She was dancing around and stuff and I took all these pictures. Anyhow, to make a long story short, about four years ago this girl from the high school in Mill Valley came to work for me part-time. And she was going through the contact sheet and she said, "Hey, that's me." She found it herself. I said, "How do you know it's you?" She said, "Because I've seen pictures of me there." This is Lisa Law's daughter, she turns out to be. It was like here she had grown tits and everything like that. Real attractive and smart. And here she was this little bitty two-year-old at Woodstock. Boy, that really marked how the years had gone by.

• • • •

WES POMEROY: I few days before Woodstock, I called Paul Estaver, a good friend of mine, and said, "Come on up, Paul, you're going to enjoy this." Because Paul has quite a background. He was professor up in some little New England college and got one of the first federal grants to help kids at Hampton Beach; they had riots before, now he has the money to diffuse that. And that must have been 1966. Then came down to Washington, D.C., and they offered him a job in the Office of Law Enforcement Assistance, a small office that preceded LEAA.

Minister Sees God's Hand in Aquarian

Times Herald Record
Middletown, N.Y.
August 27, 1969

PAUL ESTAVER: By that time I was becoming more persona non grata in the Justice Department. These were the early Nixon years and I was identified with Ramsey Clark and a lot of other wild types of operations. My boss said to go as an observer and write us a report afterwards, so that's how I happened to go.

The thing that seemed important about it to me was that it was just such a unique experience where it demonstrated something that Wes and I had been trying to prove for several years: that if you give people their own resources, if they have a stake in what's happening, they won't tear it apart. And I have a feeling that the subsequent music festivals of this kind that were held elsewhere—until it finally just became so raucous that everybody just outlawed them—that there probably wasn't that kind of an attitude that worked with the participants, to let them be responsible for their own peacekeeping, but instead, probably they had various kinds of security or law enforcement agencies there.

I came back and wrote my report to the people who represented Nixon in the Justice Department and they hated it, because I incorrectly used the term "entrapment." I think some of the police were trying to catch some of these kids at drugs and I called that entrapment and it really wasn't. I mean, the police really did pull back—both the state and the county police—and I think Wes played a major role in its working.

WES POMEROY: A few years after Woodstock, I was in a small conference with Margaret Mead. It was a small conference and we had the chance to sit there and talk after dinner. On her own, no one had mentioned my involvement, we were talking about large youth gatherings and she said, "Woodstock was the best-planned and most significant gathering of young people in the history of the world." And, boy, I tell you. We really felt good about that. We were just like a couple of little kids who had been given candy. We didn't tell Margaret Mead—it was not that appropriate parading our ego around. But I am very proud of that.

• • • •

JOSEPH COAKLEY: I miss the spirit of that whole period of time. In a way, I was kind of naive but it was a very naive time and it was a lovely time. I mean, people were really trying to make the planet a better place to live and I think in a lot of ways that spirit still lives on in a lot of us, but it's just kind of melted into the big melting pot, so it's not so predominant. I remember when people had long hair and called each other "freaks" and you'd always stop if you saw someone hitchhiking on the freeway with long hair; you'd always stop and give a brother a ride. Today, I wouldn't pick anybody up; I'd be afraid to. I guess everything goes full circle.

RONA ELLIOTT: I think a lot of us, in ways that depend on how much you delve into your psychological self, were really in shock from Woodstock, some more than others. I think you can't participate in that kind of thing and see the fruits of your labor reach such an unexpected height without kind of going, "Hey, wait, what is this for me? Is it a music show? Is it something else?" I know that one of the big decisions that I came to in my life was I wasn't willing to work with people who I didn't consider responsible. Now, how do you come to that conclusion after working on a big rock 'n' roll show? You wouldn't think that would be the experience that I gleaned from that kind of an experience—that that would be the end result of it—and yet it was a real life-changing thing for me. And it wasn't because anything bad happened. It was the potential to what I saw. It was the way I wanted to participate in life, who I wanted to be participating with, the kind of standards I had. This is just my stuff, not right or wrong, but the way I evaluated this experience.

It was also unbelievable: You can count on people. On the other levels, the people out there were great. Those people that go to rock 'n' roll shows, you know, when the shit hits the fan you can count on them; they sat there and they were mellow. It was unbelievable. So your great, optimistic, idealized hopes for humanity that came to be known as the Woodstock Generation got realized.

WAVY GRAVY: Everybody dropped their egos, their petty trips, whatever their trips were. Suddenly it was all dropped and focused on life support. And that was truly exciting. I yearn to do it again. It became more and more difficult—well, Nixon to start with. That's why we did festivals for so long after Woodstock, so as to not make it impossible to have them, because they were breeding grounds for all kinds of things that I found extremely stimulating. And so we would end up running interference for really cretin pig-swine promoters that would put people in the middle of the Okefenokee, if they could make a buck at it. But then it became harder and harder and now you just can't get that many people together for that long—they can go for one day and even have sort of semi-camping. The Dead can pull that off. But for three days or for two days, forget it.

It was all of us that did something amazing. That's what Woodstock was. And I think that when everybody was sitting in this collective mud and Janis made that great announcement that, "If you have some food left, share it with your brother and sister—the person on your left and the person on your right," people would look and say, "Well, I got a little left," and they would do that. And they would get a deep print in their spiritual cement as to what sharing was all about and what helping each other out was all about. And it caused a great awakening of a lot of people of what everybody could do if we all just kind of made this gestalt that if we all hooked together and lit up, we could fly. We could fly just by flapping the wings of our hearts. And I think that we carry that with us through all our lives.

Tom Law: There was a tremendous amount of naïveté in our actions, but they were very pure. They were pure in that we were really interested in bringing people out of their shells and having fun. And even today I'll debate anyone on the issue of the sensibilities of the sixties. We were simply living off of what we could live off of and have as much fun as we could have because everything was so miserable in the other directions. And all of our peers were being destroyed over in Vietnam. And we took a different tack. We were politically active, but we were also socially active.

If you look at it without the perspective of what was happening in America at the time, you wouldn't know what the hell it was all about. That's why there's so much bullshit that goes down when people try to just lightly talk about Woodstock, the music festival. The music had very little to do with it. The music was great and it was there and kept everybody focused on that. But the event was so much bigger than the music. It was a phenomenon. It was absolutely a phenomenon. And it was also the most peaceful, civilized gathering that was probably happening on the planet at the time, other than some major religious festival in India, where twenty million people gathered together or something. They're focused enough to not be beating each other over the head. But I never saw one actual fight.

The thing I kept thinking when I look back on those times is, yes, you can say we were naive, but we were naive with a vengeance. What we were trying to avenge was the nastiness of what America had become in the Vietnam era. And I think that was the prevailing motivator: to do something different and to do something right. And it was also a very giving thing because no one was concerned with their own future and their own economics. Everybody was really pouring their time and energy into trying to heal this gaping wound, which, as you know, got worse and worse for the next three years. I think the bitterness ended with Watergate; it was like the last laugh, you know. We were vindicated—our fifteen years of resistance to Vietnam and to American society and materialism and greed and lust and anger. I think the hippie movement and the sixties was just the opposite of all that. And it wasn't easy because there was no economic base for it.

Abbie Hoffman: I think we were lucky. It could have been a disaster

Long Life Seen for Spirit of Woodstock Festival

*Globe
Boston, Mass.
September 1, 1969*

with ease. It was always on the edge. But it was that feeling of being on the edge, and also that sense of community—that we were going to hold the determination to make it work by people, not just promoters. It was something very, very hard to repeat, very, very hard to reenact, as all the attempts to redo Woodstock were inevitably failures of one sort or another. They never did attempt to recapture that moment. It's very sad now when I go to concerts, which I still do on occasion, and they're all in enclosed stadiums with very heavy controls—you know, guards that are very security conscious and well trained as to how to stem any problem. It's a long way from the press of the flesh and the expansiveness that was Woodstock. It's definitely sad. I have sad memories of it even though I had such a great time. It's sad because it isn't going on today, because it's part of the past, because it's not happening now, because youth makes revolution, youth makes social change. The question is not, "What happened to those of us who went to Woodstock?" It's "Where's the Woodstock for today's generation?" That's more important, because out of that sense of community, out of that vision, that Utopian vision, comes the energy to go out there and actually participate in the process so that social change occurs.

PENNY STALLINGS: I had to go back to Texas and tell everybody what I'd done; it was very important. It was the first trip I made back to Texas after being in New York for a year and a half or two years, and I went back with my fringe jacket on and short blond hair, so I was a very big contradiction right there. Lots of makeup, Twiggy hair, fringe jacket, and nobody bought it for a second. Nobody believed that I'd been there, let alone worked there. But I knew.

· · · ·

MIRIAM YASGUR: Once the people started to leave, they left very quickly. The place emptied out within two days. And when they were all gone, the worst of it was the anger that we felt from people that didn't like the trash. We were unhappy about it too but there was nothing we could do about it at the time. Other people in the community hailed us like movie stars because we had been involved in this thing. And it never went back completely to normal in that sense because many times where we went, we would be involved in answering questions about the festival and getting into discussions about it. But it was not the major part of our lives and within the year it died down considerably, although right until the end of Max's life kids were coming to visit and people were coming to the field and people who recognized him would stop and talk with us. We took it in stride; we were more interested in getting on with our lives, which we did.

We got calls from perhaps a half dozen or so people or letters from California and across the country who said, "My name is so similar to yours. Are we related?" And we discovered that, yes, we were. Apparently everybody with a name similar, whether it's "Yasgor" or "Yasgour" or even some of them start with a "Z" instead of a "Y"— they're all one family. And we kept correspondence with some of them; some came to visit. I've lost track since Max died.

Occasionally, a parent would call and say, "I'm having problems

Max Yasgur for President: That's the Way It Is, Baby

Times Herald Record
Middletown, N.Y.
September 24, 1969

with my youngster, who doesn't want to go to school"—or "He's getting into drugs," or whatever—"and I feel that since he looks at Max as a hero, perhaps if Max would talk to him it would help." Max would say, "Send him over." So we would end up with little groups of kids sitting on the chairs, on the floor, whatever, and they would sort of rap, they would express themselves. Max spoke slowly, stopped to think before he answered, and he would express his point of view and he would always offer to help if they needed help. And they would confide in him. Or they would say that, "I'm having this problem because my parents don't understand," and he would take the trouble to call the parent and discuss it with the parent if it was warranted. And he did this for the few years that he lived after the festival because he felt it was a worthwhile thing that he could do, that maybe the festival gave him this opportunity. I don't know that he had a sense of trying to atone for any damage the festival did, but he was always interested in young people. He just liked working with young people, and he felt this was an opportunity. And he enjoyed having them come over. He enjoyed listening to them.

APPENDIX

WHO'S WHO

BILL ABRUZZI was a physician practicing in Wappingers Falls, New York, who was hired by Woodstock Ventures to run medical operations. As a result of that festival, he gained notoriety as a "rock doc," ministering to other music festivals. He is no longer in practice and is reportedly living in or near Canada.

Bill Belmont

DANIEL J. AMATUCCI was a White Lake town supervisor who generally supported the festival.

KEN BABBS was part of Ken Kesey's Merry Pranksters and friend and fellow traveler of the Hog Farm. He is now a neighbor of Kesey's in Oregon.

JOAN BAEZ is a world-renowned folksinger and social activist, based in Menlo Park, California.

THE BAND, originating mostly out of Canada, rose to prominence in 1965, when Bob Dylan went electric and the group toured as his back-up band, later developing its own reputation as foremost among country-rockers.

Judi Bernstein

DALE BELL served as associate producer of the *Woodstock* film crew, and is credited with heroic efforts in getting film stock and related supplies to the festival site. He is now a film producer in Los Angeles.

BILL BELMONT was Country Joe McDonald's manager and served as artist coordinator at Woodstock. He now is international director of licensing and copyright for Fantasy Records in Berkeley, California, as well as a consultant in the music business.

PETER BEREN worked as a hamburger flipper for Food for Love, the food concessionaire at Woodstock. He is now marketing director for Sierra Club Books in San Francisco.

JUDI BERNSTEIN was business manager for Hanley Sound. She is now executive director of Hadassah in Boston and is married to Harold Cohen.

Lee Blumer

JOHN BINDER was partner with Michael Wadleigh in Paradigm Films. He worked as location coordinator for the *Woodstock* film crew. He is now a Hollywood screenwriter.

LEE MACKLER BLUMER was assistant to Wes Pomeroy, the director of security. She has since worked in publicity for ABC Records and RCA Records, and helped with the Amnesty International World Tour in 1988.

ELIZABETH BROWN was credit manager and head bookkeeper for a food wholesaler near White Lake. She is a former councilwoman from Bethel and is now an accountant for a CPA firm in the area.

339

PAUL BUTTERFIELD, a blues harpist, headed the eponymous Paul Butterfield Blues Band, which pioneered the white blues explosion of the sixties. Butterfield died in 1987.

JOSEPH COAKLEY came to Woodstock from his home in Cleveland. He is now project manager for a large homebuilder in northern California.

Joe Cocker

JOE COCKER, a vocalist whose successful career has been largely credited to his performance at Woodstock, has been called the finest rhythm-and-blues singer to come out of England. At the time of the festival, he was beginning his rise to prominence with his remake of the Beatle hit, "With a Little Help From My Friends."

BERT COHEN, through his Philadelphia-based company, Concert Hall Publications, designed the Woodstock Ventures' West 57th Street offices, coordinated advertising to the underground press, and produced the festival program booklet. He died in 1985 at age 49.

HAROLD COHEN worked for Hanley Sound. He is now manager of Needle in a Haystack audio stores in the Boston area and is married to Judi Bernstein.

Harold Cohen

STEVE COHEN was largely responsible for designing and building the Woodstock stage and for managing the stage during the festival. He now lives in San Francisco, where he is a cabinetmaker for Classical Constructs, which builds sets and props for the TV and film industry.

CONCERNED CITIZENS OF WALLKILL was a group of disgruntled local residents who fought successfully to keep the Woodstock festival out of their town.

CHARLIE CRIST was Monticello bureau chief for the Middletown *Times Herald Record*. He ilives with his wife Gladys in Monticello.

DAVID CROSBY was one-fourth of Crosby, Stills, Nash, and Young, a group that debuted a day before Woodstock. He is still touring nationally, often with Stephen Stills and Graham Nash.

Rona Elliot

RICK DANKO was a member of the musical group The Band.

HENRY DILTZ was the official photographer for Woodstock Ventures. He is a freelance photographer, living in Los Angeles.

JAY DREVERS acted as the head carpenter for many of the festival's facilities, including the stage.

FRED DUBETSKY is president of Port-O-San Corporation in Kearny, New Jersey, one of two suppliers of portable toilets to the festival.

SAMUEL W. EAGER, JR., is an attorney in Middletown, New York, who was retained by Woodstock Ventures.

Rona Elliot worked for Woodstock Ventures in community and public relations. She is now music correspondent for NBC's "Today" show.

Paul Estaver worked for the U.S. Justice Department's Law Enforcement Assistance Administration and came to Woodstock at the invitation of Wes Pomeroy. He is now director, reference and dissemination division, of the National Institute of Justice in Washington, D.C.

John Fabbri was an undersherrif in South San Francisco, California, who served as a security associate of Wes Pomeroy. He died in 1976.

Frank Fava

Frank Fava was part of the "black shirt" heavy security at Woodstock. He is now a certified life underwriter for Diversified Planning and Consultants, Inc., in New York City.

Jeanne Field worked for Paradigm Films and worked in a variety of capacities for the *Woodstock* film crew. She is now a Hollywood film producer.

William Filippini and his wife Clara were neighbors of Max Yasgur. Their land was overtaken by festival-goers. Mr. Filippini resented the Woodstock festival until the day he died.

Joe Fink

Joe Fink was a deputy inspector and precinct commander in the New York Police Department's Ninth Precinct on the Lower East Side. He served as a consultant to Wes Pomeroy in recruiting New York police to serve as security at Woodstock. He retired in 1971 and lives in Pompano Beach, Florida.

Food for Love was the official food concessionaire for the festival.

Michael Foreman worked for Concert Hall Publications and was chiefly responsible for producing the festival program booklet.

Myra Friedman was director of artist relations for artists' representative Albert Grossman and author of *Buried Alive: The Biography of Janis Joplin*. She is now a writer living in New York City.

Roy Gabriel was a neighbor of Max Yasgur. Against his wishes, his farm became a camping ground for thousands of festival attendees.

Don Ganoung was an aide to Wes Pomeroy, specializing in community relations. He died in 1973 at age 44.

Rick Gavras

Rick Gavras attended Woodstock from his home in Montreal. He now lives in Minneapolis, where he is studying to be a chemical dependency counselor.

Steve Gold attended Woodstock from his home in nearby South Fallsburg, New York. He is now president of Steve Gold Enterprises, an entertainment-industry firm in New York City.

341

Donald Goldmacher

DONALD GOLDMACHER, M.D., headed the New York City chapter of the Medical Committee for Human Rights, and served as a key medical coordinator at Woodstock. He now lives in El Cerrito, California, where he is a psychiatrist and heads the Media Center for Health Concerns.

STANLEY GOLDSTEIN served in a variety of capacities for Woodstock Ventures, including coordinating campgrounds and recruiting the Hog Farm. He now lives outside New York City, where he still serves in a variety of capacities.

PETER GOODRICH was in charge of food concessions and was responsible for the Food for Love operation. He died in 1974 at age 46.

BILL GRAHAM is one of the country's foremost rock concert promotors, beginning with his two legendary venues, the Fillmore Auditorium in San Francisco (later the Fillmore West), and the Fillmore East in New York City. He played a minor role in the Woodstock festival, although he reportedly still regrets that he wasn't the one to produce it.

THE GRATEFUL DEAD is one of rock's longest-running and most popular acts, and at the forefront of the San Francisco music scene of the 1960s. They have been widely quoted as saying, "We played terribly at Woodstock."

Stanley Goldstein

WAVY GRAVY, a.k.a. Hugh Romney, is a former stand-up comic who is founder of the Hog Farm, a decades-old commune based in New Mexico and Berkeley, California. He served in a wide range of capacities at Woodstock, including coordinating the freak-out tents and as part-time announcer. Gravy's efforts are now directed primarily toward the Seva Foundation, an organization he helped form to "help relieve suffering around the world with awareness, love, and skill."

ALAN GREEN attended Woodstock from his home in New Jersey. He now lives in Washington, D.C., where he is a journalist and editor of AlterNet, an alternative press news service.

Wavy Gravy

CAROL GREEN worked as a cook for Woodstock Ventures. She later was a TV producer for CBS in Los Angeles. She now lives in Miami, Florida, where, among other things, she does publicity for films in production.

LEON GREENBERG was president of Monticello Raceway until 1973. He is a lawyer near Liberty, New York.

TOM GRIMM was a former college roommate of Chris Langhart, and a former phone company employee, whom Langhart hired to oversee installation of telephone lines for the festival. He lives in Chicago.

GROSSINGER'S is one of the oldest and best-known resort hotels in the Catskill Mountains in upstate New York. During the festival, it served as the headquarters for many of the music acts. Among those who stayed there during the festival was Bill Graham, who as a kid had worked there as a busboy.

ALBERT GROSSMAN was widely recognized as the leading manager of rock and folk musicians in the 1960s and 1970s. Among his clients were several musicians who played at Woodstock, including Janis Joplin, The Band, Richie Havens, Paul Butterfield—and one hoped-for act that did not perform, Bob Dylan. He died in 1987 at age 59.

ARLO GUTHRIE is a popular folk-rock satirist and the son of the legendary folk singer Woody Guthrie. He lives near Stockbridge, Massachusetts.

BILL HANLEY is head of Hanley Sound, based in Boston, which did the sound for the Woodstock festival.

Alan Green

TIM HARDIN was a folksinger and songwriter whose hits include "If I Were a Carpenter." He died in 1980 at age 39.

RICHIE HAVENS is a longtime performer and songwriter who lives in New York City.

JIMI HENDRIX was a legendary guitarist and vocalist of the 1960s, who usually performed with his group, the Jimi Hendrix Experience. He died in 1970 at age 27.

ABBIE HOFFMAN is a well-known political activist and organizer and cofounder of the Youth International Party. He now lives near New Hope, Pennsylvania.

INCREDIBLE STRING BAND, a band out of Scotland, was at the forefront of the India-influenced Raga Rock movement of the late 1960s.

Bill Hanley

IRON BUTTERFLY, was one of the first heavy metal bands, perhaps best known for their 1968 hit, "In-A-Gadda-Da-Vida," which included what is probably the longest drum solo ever on record. The group was booked to perform at Woodstock, but never was able to make it from the airport to the festival site.

JEFFERSON AIRPLANE, featuring Grace Slick, Marty Balin, and Paul Kantner, spearheaded the San Francisco rock scene of the 1960s. In 1973, they updated their name and sound as the Jefferson Starship.

JEFFREY JOERGER was one of the proprietors of Food for Love. He is reportedly living in Florida.

LARRY JOHNSON was sound and music editor for the *Woodstock* film. He has been described as having "embodied the soul of Woodstock more than any other of the film crew people." He is still in the film business in Los Angeles.

Abbie Hoffman

JANIS JOPLIN was a legendary rock and blues singer, whose first group, Big Brother and the Holding Company, was a key part of the San Francisco rock scene. She performed at Woodstock with her band of the time, the Cosmic Blues Band. Joplin died in 1970 at age 27.

343

Artie Kornfeld

PAUL KANTNER was guitarist for the Jefferson Airplane, later the Jefferson Starship. He lives in San Francisco.

LEN KAUFMAN headed the elite "black shirt" security force at Woodstock. He died in the mid 1980s.

KEN KESEY, author of *One Flew Over the Cuckoo's Nest* and leader of the Merry Pranksters, did not make it to Woodstock, although most of the Pranksters did. He now lives in Oregon.

ARTIE KORNFELD was coproducer of Woodstock. He now is a record publicist living outside Los Angeles.

MICHAEL LANG was coproducer of Woodstock. He is now president of Better Music, Inc., an artists' management and representative company in New York City, which, among other things, manages Joe Cocker.

Michael Lang

CHRIS LANGHART was a technical director of Woodstock and designed many of the key operating systems for the festival site. He now lives near New Hope, Pennsylvania, where he continues to work on a variety of technical challenges in both the U.S. and Mexico.

LISA LAW was a friend of the Hog Farm, who helped design and coordinate the free kitchen and who photographed the festival extensively. She is now a freelance photographer based in Santa Fe, New Mexico, and is author of *Flashing on the Sixties*.

TOM LAW was a friend of the Hog Farm, who served in a variety of capacities at the festival, including leading yoga exercises from the stage. He is now a custom kitchen contractor in New York City.

MEL LAWRENCE was director of operations for Woodstock Ventures, responsible for all aspects of the site. He now lives in New York City, where he has produced a variety of events, including the 1988 film *Powaqqatsi.*

HOWARD R. LEARY was police commissioner of New York City from 1966 to 1970.

RON LIIS taught in the art department of the University of Miami with Bill Ward and was jointly responsible with Ward for coordinating the team of art students who was brought in to embellish the festival grounds. He lives in Sisters, Oregon.

MILES LOURIE was the New York lawyer who introduced Joel Rosenman and John Roberts to Michael Lang and Artie Kornfeld.

Chris Langhart

BOB MAURICE was producer of the movie, *Woodstock.*.

ALBERT AND DAVID MAYSLES, "the Maysles brothers," were leading documentary filmmakers at the cutting edge of cinema verité, whose credits included *Gimme Shelter.*

344

Country Joe McDonald performed solo, and with his group, the Fish, at Woodstock. He still plays, mostly solo, and is based in Berkeley, California.

Medical Committee for Human Rights was a politically oriented, health-care organization with a chapter on New York's Lower East Side.

Merry Pranksters was a group of friends based near San Francisco that was assembled by Ken Kesey, known for promoting theatrical cosmic jokes on the straight world. All except Kesey himself attended the Woodstock festival.

Mel Lawrence

Gene Meyer, a microbiologist, was hired by Chris Langhart to oversee the health aspects of the water and sewerage systems for the festival.

Howard Mills was owner of the Wallkill site originally intended for the Woodstock festival. He still lives nearby, although he refuses to discuss Woodstock-related events.

Jim Mitchell was the purchasing director for Woodstock Ventures, and was largely credited with producing equipment and supplies out of thin air when needed. He lives in San Francisco.

Joyce Mitchell was in charge of administration of the Woodstock Ventures offices.

E. H. Beresford "Chip" Monck was stage lighting and technical director for Woodstock, as well as one of the masters of ceremonies. He now works for United Production Services in Duarte, California, designing and producing stage facilities for events worldwide. He claims to be in the process of moving to Australia.

Chip Monck

Hector Morales was a booking agent who consulted with Michael Lang and others on acts for the festival.

John Morris was production coordinator for Woodstock, involved principally with booking many of the bands and coordinating the performances. He now lives in Santa Fe, New Mexico, where he has produced, promoted, and consulted for a wide range of events.

Jim Morrison was lead singer of the Doors. He died in 1971 at age 27.

David Myers was a documentary cameraman for the Woodstock film crew. He has since had a wide range of film credits, including *The Last Waltz, Gospel,* and *Mad Dogs and Englishmen.* He lives in Mill Valley, California.

John Morris

Bobby Neuwirth was a well-known Greenwich Village musician.

Harold Pantel is proprietor of Pantel Electric Company in South Fallsburg, New York, which provided most of the electrical services for the Woodstock festival.

345

Wes Pomeroy

WESLEY POMEROY was head of security for the Woodstock festival. He later became police chief of Berkeley, California, and worked for the Carter White House in the Office of Drug Abuse Policy and the Michigan Department of Mental Health. In 1984, he came out of retirement to head the Independent Review Panel in Miami, Florida, where he now lives.

QUILL was a Boston-based rock band hired by Woodstock Ventures to perform benefit concerts at social service organizations around the Wallkill community as a goodwill gesture.

LOUIS RATNER was sheriff of Sullivan County until 1971. He lives in Swan Lake, New York.

JOHN ROBERTS was coproducer of Woodstock Ventures. He is now partner, along with Joel Rosenman, in J. R. Capital, a venture capital firm based in New York City.

John Roberts

NELSON ROCKEFELLER was governor of New York during Woodstock.

AL ROMM was editor of the Middletown *Times Herald Record.* He is now vice president/news for Ottaway Newspapers, Inc., which owns the *Times Herald Record,* and is based in Campbell Hall, New York.

BONNIE JEAN ROMNEY, a.k.a. Jahanara, is a founder, along with her husband, Wavy Gravy (a.k.a. Hugh Romney), in the Hog Farm and served in a variety of capacities at Woodstock, including setting up the free kitchen and working in the freak-out tents.

JOEL ROSENMAN was coproducer of Woodstock Ventures. He is now partner, along with John Roberts, in J. R. Capital, a venture capital firm based in New York City.

SANTANA, led by Carlos Santana, is a popular Latin-oriented rock band from San Francisco that was just gaining national attention at the time of the Woodstock festival. Their appearance on the bill at Woodstock was due largely to the influence of Bill Graham and John Morris.

SWAMI SATCHADINANDA was among the Eastern gurus to set up shop in New York City during the 1960s, teaching the wonders of yoga. He made an unscheduled appearance onstage at Woodstock.

JACK SCALICI was an unemployed actor in New York City hired to lay pipe at the Woodstock festival site. He is now a working actor in Hollywood.

Joel Rosenman

MARTIN SCORSESE, now a leading film director (*Taxi Driver, The Last Temptation of Christ*), served as an editor on the *Woodstock* film.

JOHN SEBASTIAN, a singer, guitarist, and songwriter, formerly of the Lovin' Spoonful, performed solo at Woodstock, although he was not originally scheduled to play.

346

SHA NA NA, a fifties revivalist group, began at Columbia University in early 1969, played one of their earliest gigs at the Woodstock festival. Their subsequent success has been credited largely to their appearance in the *Woodstock* film.

RAVI SHANKAR, sitar player, performed at Woodstock. He was chiefly responsible for the Eastern influence in rock music in the 1960s.

Jack Scalici

JOHN SINCLAIR, a leader of the radical White Panther Party in Ann Arbor, Michigan, was sentenced to ten years in jail a few weeks before Woodstock, for possession of two marijuana cigarettes that he gave to two undercover police officers. Sinclair, through his radical newsletter, *The Sun,* had been an outspoken critic of police harassment of longhairs throughout Michigan. His case became a rallying point around the decriminalize-marijuana movement.

BILLY SOZA is a Apache and Cahuilla Indian who helped coordinate the Native American arts exhibit at Woodstock. He now lives in Santa Fe, New Mexico, where he works in a variety of technical and production-related jobs.

PENNY STALLINGS was an assistant to Mel Lawrence at Woodstock, coordinating a variety of activities, including, for a time, the checkbook. She is now a New York City-based writer, author of three books on popular culture, and is a regular essayist for the Public Broadcasting Service's "MacNeil/Lehrer NewsHour."

Penny Stallings

SYLVESTER (SLY STONE) STEWART was leader of Sly and the Family Stone, a jazz-soul-rock group, which just prior to Woodstock had a number-one hit, "Everyday People."

JOE TINKELMAN attempted to attend the Woodstock festival from his home in Poughkeepsie, New York. He now lives outside Washington, D.C., and is publisher of the *Potomac Almanac.*

CLARENCE TOWNSEND owned a dairy farm three miles from the festival site. He called Woodstock a "human cesspool," among other things.

PETER TOWNSHEND was a member of the rock band The Who.

UP AGAINST THE WALL MOTHERFUCKERS was a Lower East Side-based radical group whose views tended toward the Maoist left.

KEN VAN LOAN is proprietor of Ken's Garage in Kauneonga Lake, New York, about five miles from the festival site.

ARTHUR VASSMER is proprietor of Vassmer's General Store in Kauneonga Lake, New York.

Ken Van Loan

MICHAEL WADLEIGH is a film producer who is credited as director of the *Woodstock* film, although his direction in the film came largely after the festival itself, during the postproduction phase.

347

Bill Ward

BILL AND JEAN WARD coordinated, along with Ron Liis, a crew of art students from the University of Miami who helped to prepare the festival site. He is a professor of sculpture at the University of Miami. Jean Ward died in 1986.

DIANA WARSHAWSKY attended Woodstock from her home in San Francisco. She now lives in North Hollywood, California.

BERNIE WEINSTEIN is proprietor of Bernie's Holiday Restaurant in Rock Hill, New York.

JOSH WHITE was creator of the Joshua Light Show, the leading light show on the East Coast, which provided most of the light shows at the Fillmore East.

PETER WHITERABBIT was a member of the Hog Farm.

THE WHO, a British band with Peter Townshend, Keith Moon, John Entwistle, and Roger Daltrey, was one of the top rock acts of the late 1960s, renowned for their destructive stage theatrics. Four months before Woodstock, the group released *Tommy*, their acclaimed, groundbreaking rock opera.

MALCOLM WILSON was lieutenant governor of New York during Woodstock. In 1973 he became governor for a short time after the resignation of Nelson Rockefeller.

Miriam Yasgur

GORDON WINARICK is executive director of the Concord Resort Hotel in Kiamesha Lake, New York. At the time of Woodstock, he was also president of the Monticello Hospital and helped to coordinate some of the medical and food-relief efforts.

BARON WOLMAN was the chief photographer for *Rolling Stone.* He is now a freelance photographer living in Mill Valley, California.

MAX AND MIRIAM YASGUR were upstate New York farmers upon whose land the Woodstock festival was held. Max died of a heart attack in 1973 at age 53. Miriam has since remarried and lives in Florida.

Photo Credits

Chapter 12
page 204: Henry Diltz; page 207: Henry Diltz; page 208: J. Sculley, courtesy Peter Beren; page 210: Baron Wolman; page 212: Wide World Photos; page 214: Wide World Photos; pages 217-219: Baron Wolman; page 220: Henry Diltz

Chapter 13
page 222: Henry Diltz; pages 223-224: Baron Wolman; page 225: (Grossman) Baron Wolman; (Monticello) Joel Makower; page 226: Wide World Photos; page 227 (aerial) Wide World Photos; (The Band) Henry Diltz; page 228: J. Coakley; page 229: copyright 1969 New York News Inc. Reprinted with permission; page 230: Wide World Photos; pages 231-235: Henry Diltz; page 237: Wide World Photos; pages 239-240: Henry Diltz; page 241: Baron Wolman; pages 242-246: Henry Diltz; page 249: Baron Wolman; page 251: Joel Makower

Chapter 14
page 255: Wide World Photos; pages 256-257: Baron Wolman; page 259: Wide World Photos; page 262: Wide World Photos; page 264: Henry Diltz; page 266: Henry Diltz; page 269: Baron Wolman; page 272: Lisa Law

Chapter 15
page 275: Henry Diltz; page 276: Woodstock Ventures; page 277: Elliot Landy/The Image Works; page 278: Henry Diltz; pages 279-280: Baron Wolman; page 281: J. Coakley; pages 282-283: Elliot Landy/The Image Works; page 285: Henry Diltz

Chapter 16
page 288: Henry Diltz; page 289: Henry Diltz; page 290: Baron Wolman; page 293: Wide World Photos; page 295: Baron Wolman; page 296: courtesy ShortLine; page 297: Wide World Photos; page 301: Henry Diltz

Chapter 17
page 304: Henry Diltz; page 306: Wide World Photos; page 307: Baron Wolman; page 308: Henry Diltz; page 311: Henry Diltz; page 313: Baron Wolman; page 316: Henry Diltz

Chapter 18
page 335: Joel Makower

Who's Who
All photos by Joel Makower, except as follows: page 340: (Cocker) courtesy Better Music Inc.; (Elliot) courtesy Rona Elliot; page 343: (Hoffman) Steven Borns, courtesy Greater Talent Network; page 344: (Lang) Rick Gilbert, courtesy Better Music Inc.; page 345: (Lawrence) courtesy Mel Lawrence; page 347: (Scalici) courtesy Jack Scalici; (Stallings) courtesy Penny Stallings

Section title pages (5, 19, 75, 183, 319, 337, 349, and 353): J. Coakley

Acknowledgments

This book would simply not exist without the generosity of those who shared their memories, resources, and hospitality. The enthusiasm and warmth I encountered almost without exception as I conducted interviews around the country was gratifying and inspiring, to say the least. I am a richer person for it. To all of those who took the time to speak with me, my sincere thanks.

Several individuals' efforts went well beyond the call of duty, and they deserve special recognition and thanks. Stan Goldstein, a ready reference if ever there was one, was always available with a name or number or timely reference. So, too, Joel Rosenman and John Roberts, who subjected themselves to numerous interviews and phone calls, always with good humor, and who graciously provided brochures, posters, and other graphic material that are included in these pages. Michael Lang made available his resources, including newspaper clips and photographs. Rona Elliot, Lee Blumer, and Penny Stallings all provided support and encouragement, often steering me in the right direction, or away from the wrong one. Al Romm at Ottaway Newspapers was especially generous, making available his impressive scrapbook as well as creating a headline montage for use in this book.

Paul Bresnick, my editor at Doubleday, has provided a wealth of ideas and enthusiasm to this project, and this book is a credit to his inspirations. His colleagues and associates—notably, Mark Garofalo, Michael Carter, and Jacqueline Deval—have also been a joy to work with. The enthusiasm and efforts of Gail E. Ross—colleague, counsel, and friend—played a key role in helping to see this book to fruition.

Several people helped in the book's production: my transcriber, Felicia Tiller, who worked tirelessly and under tight deadlines; Linda Zaleskie, who helped to research the Woodstock story; Christine Gilder, and her fine-tipped blue pencil; designer Jann Alexander; and production director Sharon Rogers.

Others who provided valuable help along the way include Bill Adler, Jr., Bill Belmont, Peter Beren, Cynthia Bowman, Patti Breitman, Alan Carey at The Image Works, Joseph Coakley, Henry Diltz, Eugene Ferrara at the New York *Daily News*, Bill Fletcher, Bonnie Freer, Rick Gilbert and Tammy Grande at Better Music, Wavy Gravy, Alan Green, John J. Griffin and Tom Freeman at AP/Wide World, Jesse Hamlin at the San Francisco *Chronicle*, Richie Havens, Abbie Hoffman, John Javna, Margo Jones at the Sullivan County Office of Public Information, Larry Kelp at the Oakland *Tribune*, Lisa Law, Debbie Meister at Bill Siddons & Associates, John Morris, Larry Orenstein, Shayna P. Rosenberg, Michael J. Weiss, Gordon Winarick at the Concord Resort Hotel, Baron Wolman, and Miriam Yasgur.

And finally, my family: Ted and Frances Makower, whose inspiration and enthusiasm are always near; and most of all, Randy Rosenberg, whose love and support make my life complete.

—J.M.
Washington, D.C.
March 1989

INDEX

357